Hakumei & Mikochi 2
Tiny Little Life in the Woods

Takuto Kashiki

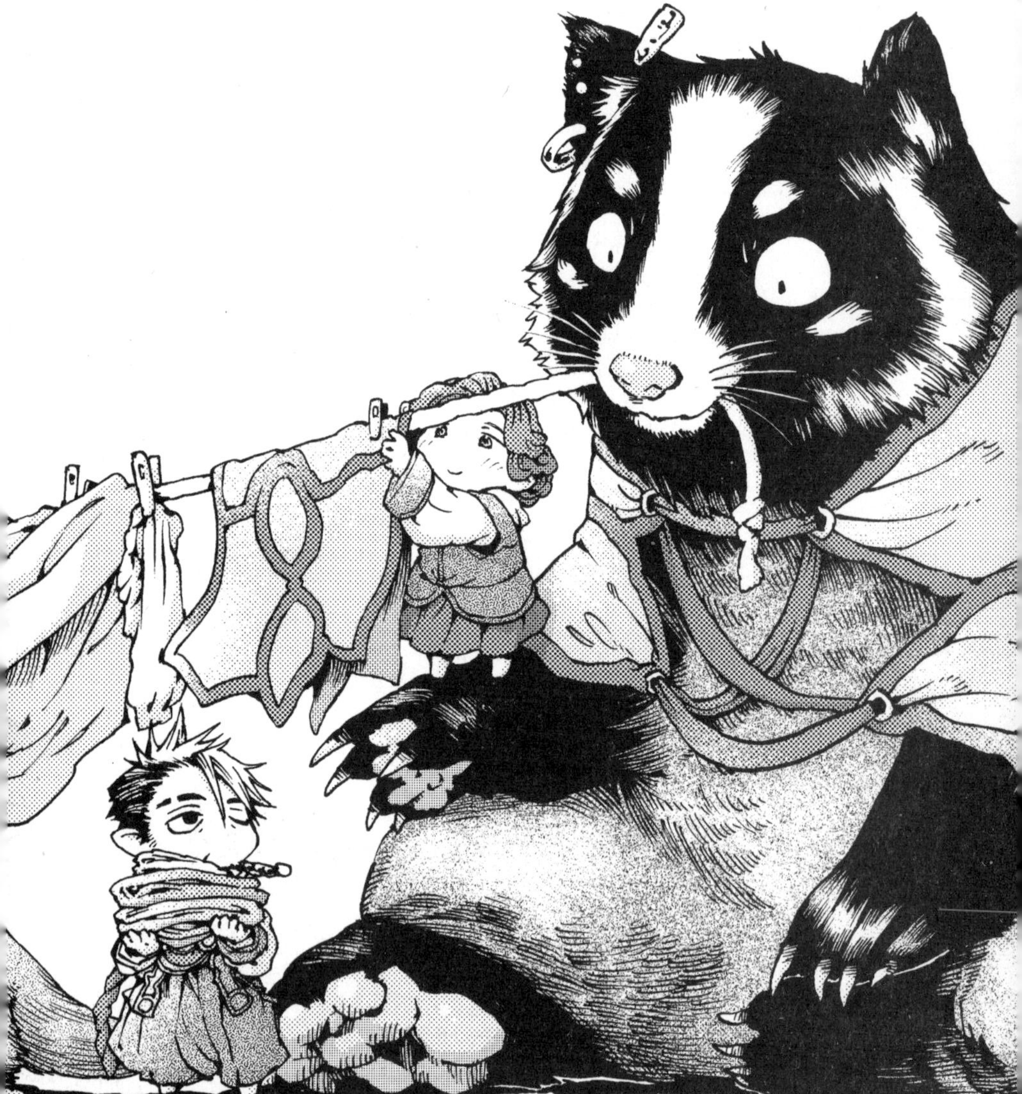

Contents

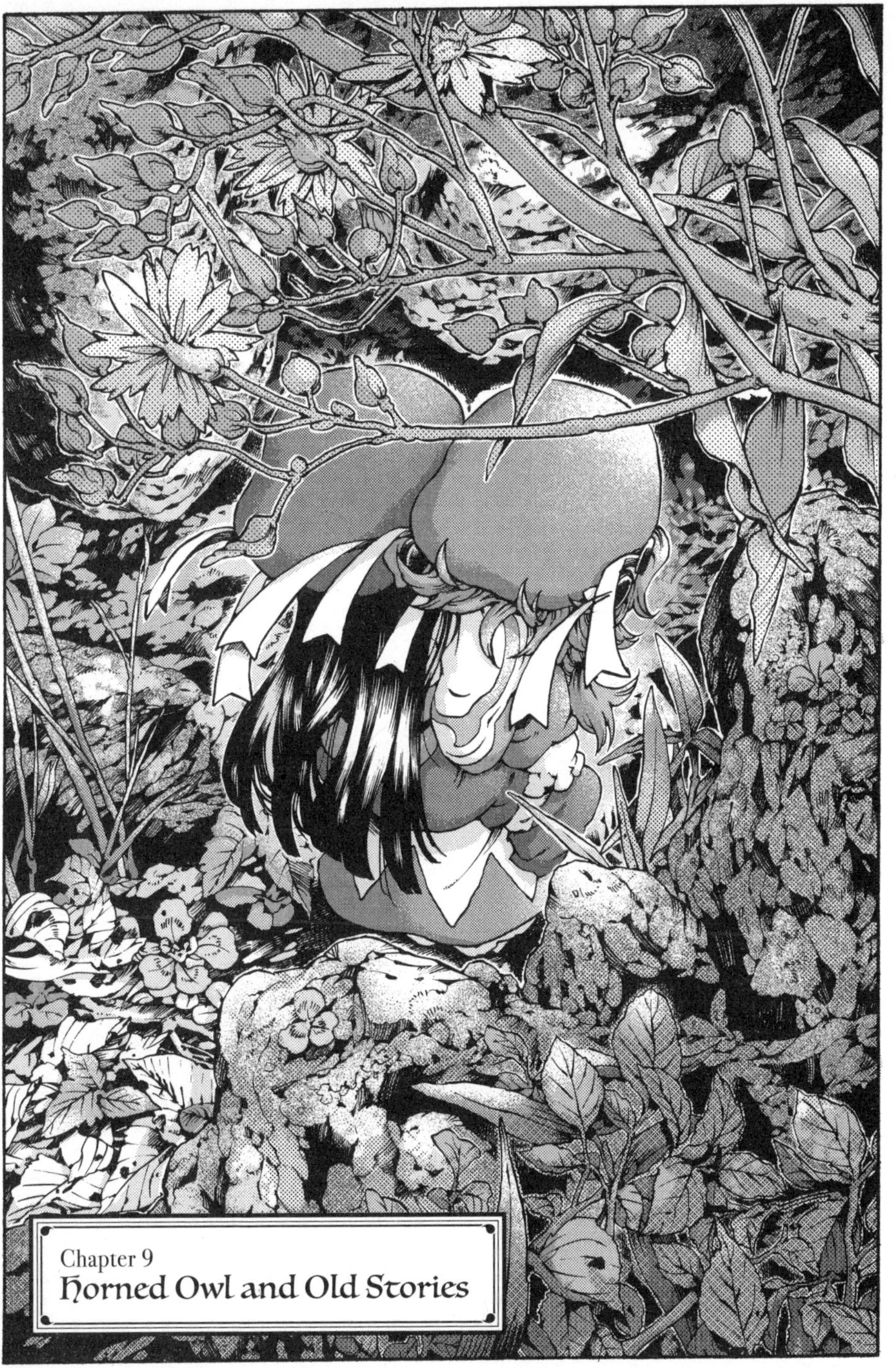

Chapter 9
Horned Owl and Old Stories

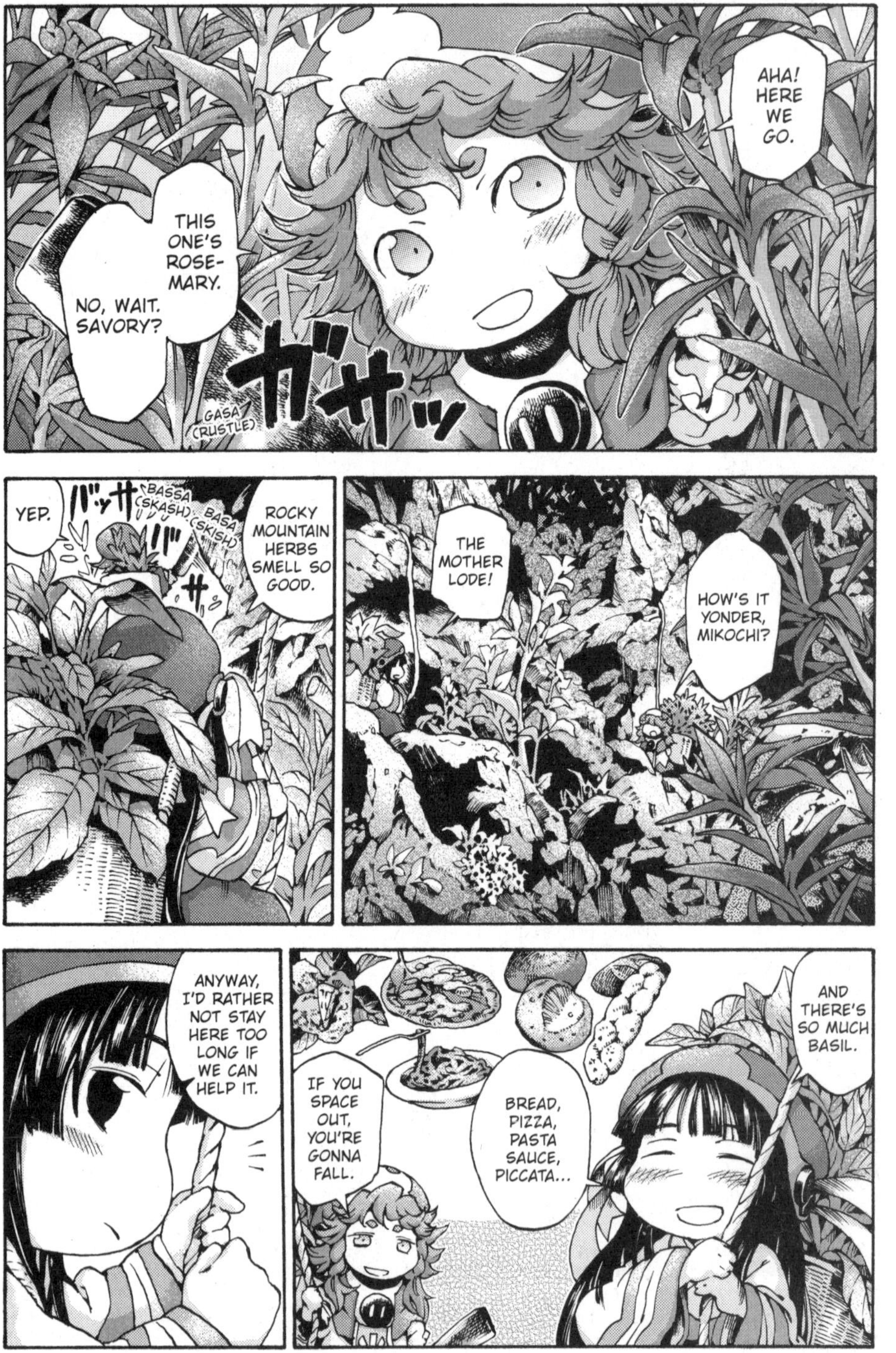
AHA! HERE WE GO.
THIS ONE'S ROSE-MARY.
NO, WAIT. SAVORY?
GASA (RUSTLE)
HOW'S IT YONDER, MIKOCHI?
THE MOTHER LODE!
ROCKY MOUNTAIN HERBS SMELL SO GOOD.
BASSA (SKASH)
BASA (SKISH)
YEP.
AND THERE'S SO MUCH BASIL.
BREAD, PIZZA, PASTA SAUCE, PICCATA...
IF YOU SPACE OUT, YOU'RE GONNA FALL.
ANYWAY, I'D RATHER NOT STAY HERE TOO LONG IF WE CAN HELP IT.

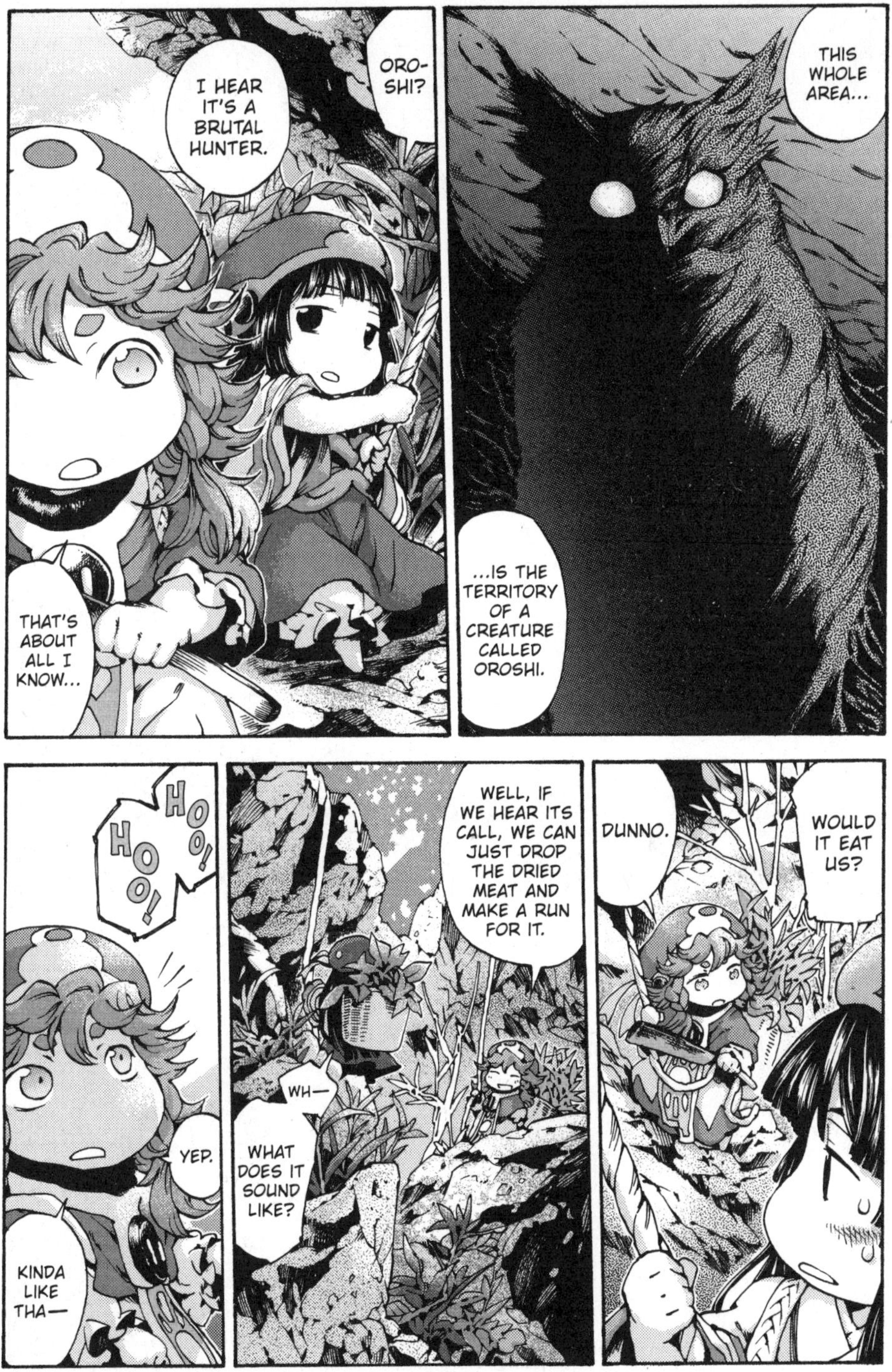
THIS WHOLE AREA...
...IS THE TERRITORY OF A CREATURE CALLED OROSHI.
OROSHI?
I HEAR IT'S A BRUTAL HUNTER.
THAT'S ABOUT ALL I KNOW...
WOULD IT EAT US?
DUNNO.
WELL, IF WE HEAR ITS CALL, WE CAN JUST DROP THE DRIED MEAT AND MAKE A RUN FOR IT.
WH—
WHAT DOES IT SOUND LIKE?
YEP.
KINDA LIKE THA—
HOO! HOO!

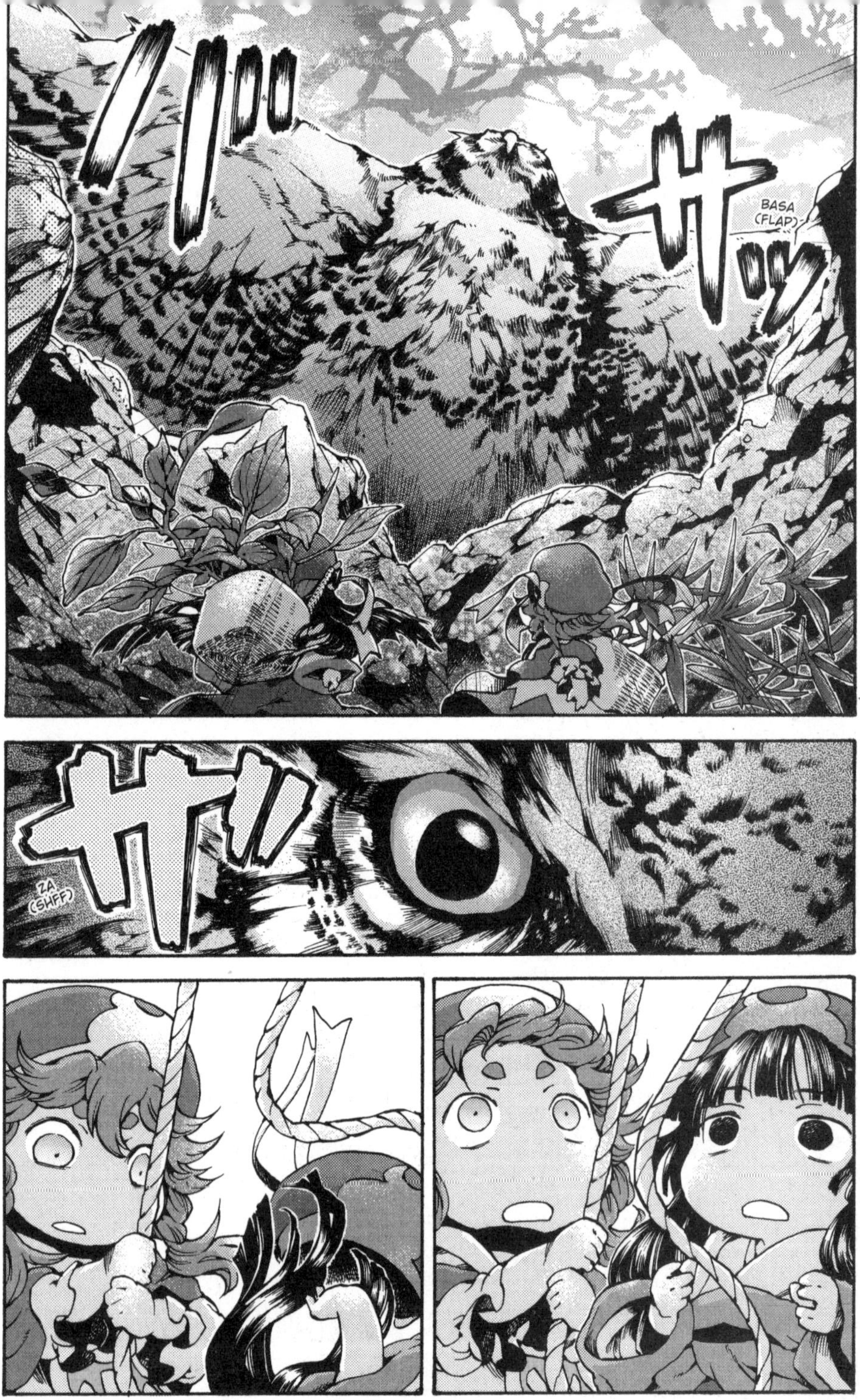
BASA
(FLAP)
ZA
(SHFF)

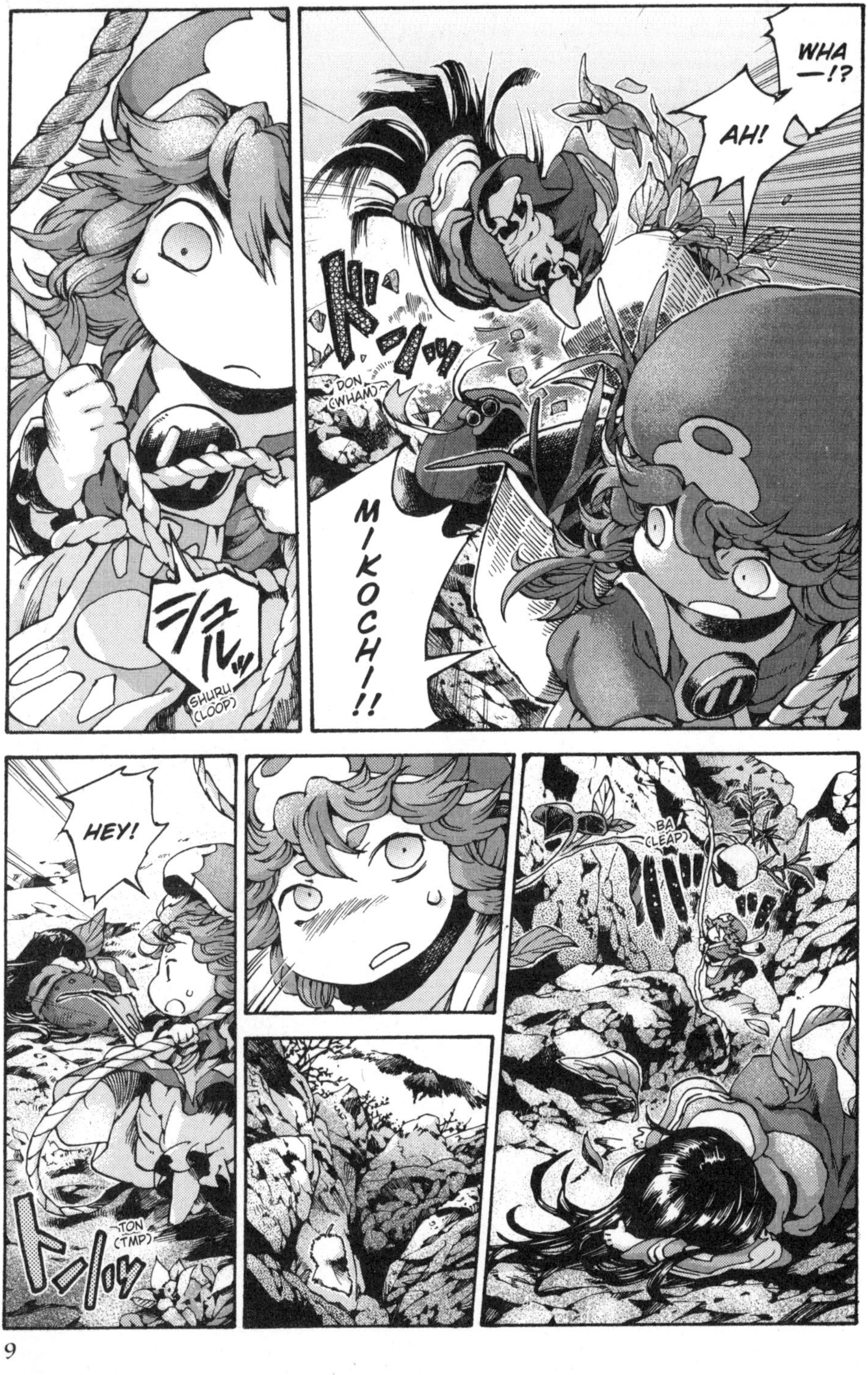
WHA—!?
AH!
ドーンッ
DON (WHAM)
MIKOCHI!!
シュルッ
SHURU (LOOP)
BA (LEAP)
HEY!
トンッ
TON (TMP)

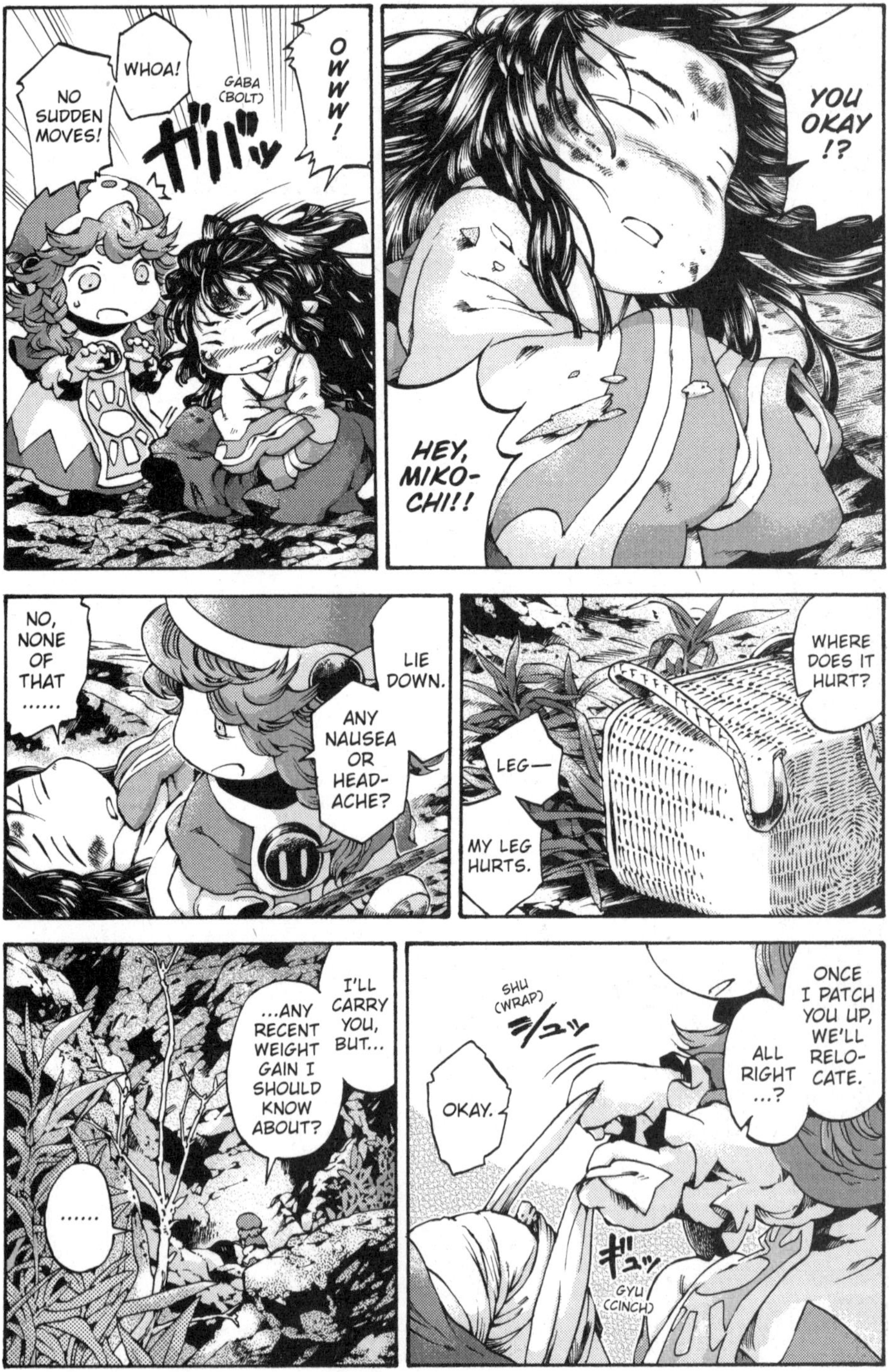
YOU OKAY!?
HEY, MIKO-CHI!!
OWWW!
GABA (BOLT)
ガバッ
WHOA!
NO SUDDEN MOVES!
WHERE DOES IT HURT?
LEG—
MY LEG HURTS.
LIE DOWN.
ANY NAUSEA OR HEADACHE?
NO, NONE OF THAT......
ONCE I PATCH YOU UP, WE'LL RELOCATE.
ALL RIGHT...?
SHU (WRAP)
シュッ
OKAY.
ギュッ
GYU (CINCH)
I'LL CARRY YOU, BUT...
...ANY RECENT WEIGHT GAIN I SHOULD KNOW ABOUT?
......

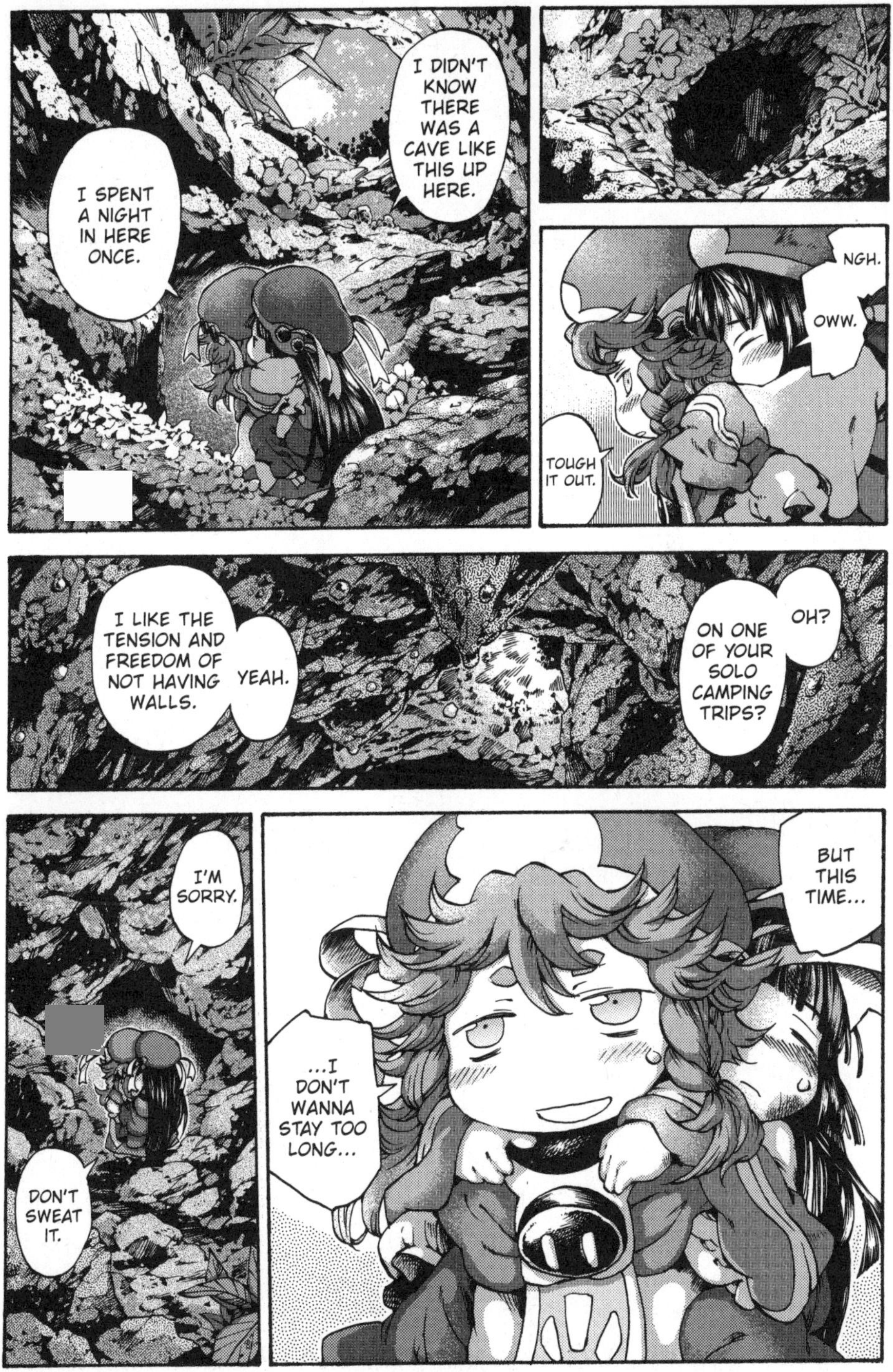
NGH.
OWW.
TOUGH IT OUT.
I DIDN'T KNOW THERE WAS A CAVE LIKE THIS UP HERE.
I SPENT A NIGHT IN HERE ONCE.
OH?
ON ONE OF YOUR SOLO CAMPING TRIPS?
YEAH.
I LIKE THE TENSION AND FREEDOM OF NOT HAVING WALLS.
BUT THIS TIME...
...I DON'T WANNA STAY TOO LONG...
I'M SORRY.
DON'T SWEAT IT.

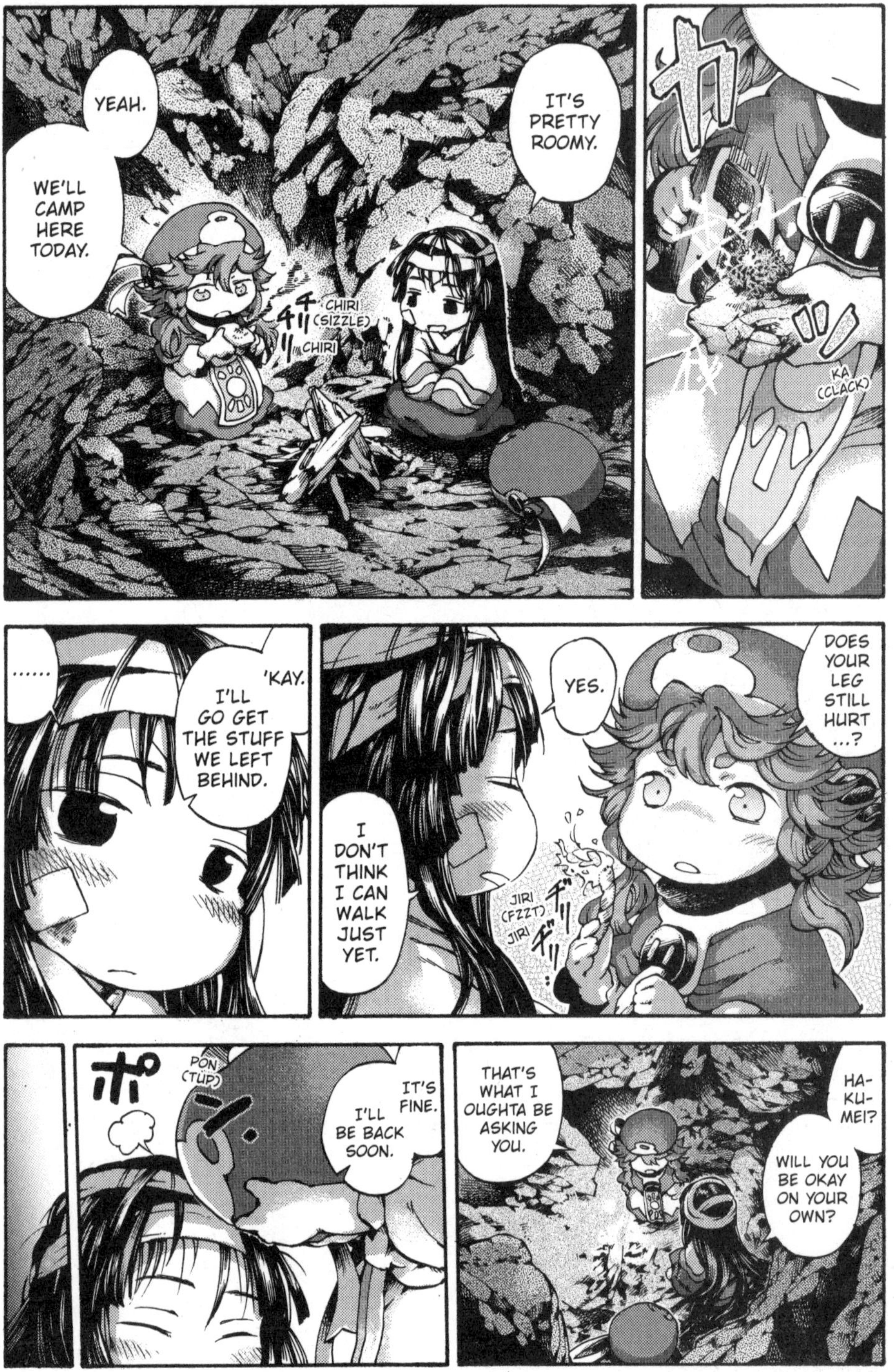
KA (CLACK)
IT'S PRETTY ROOMY.
YEAH.
WE'LL CAMP HERE TODAY.
CHIRI (SIZZLE) CHIRI
DOES YOUR LEG STILL HURT ...?
YES.
I DON'T THINK I CAN WALK JUST YET.
JIRI (FZZT) JIRI
'KAY.
I'LL GO GET THE STUFF WE LEFT BEHIND.
......
HA-KU-MEI?
WILL YOU BE OKAY ON YOUR OWN?
THAT'S WHAT I OUGHTA BE ASKING YOU.
IT'S FINE.
I'LL BE BACK SOON.
PON (TUP)

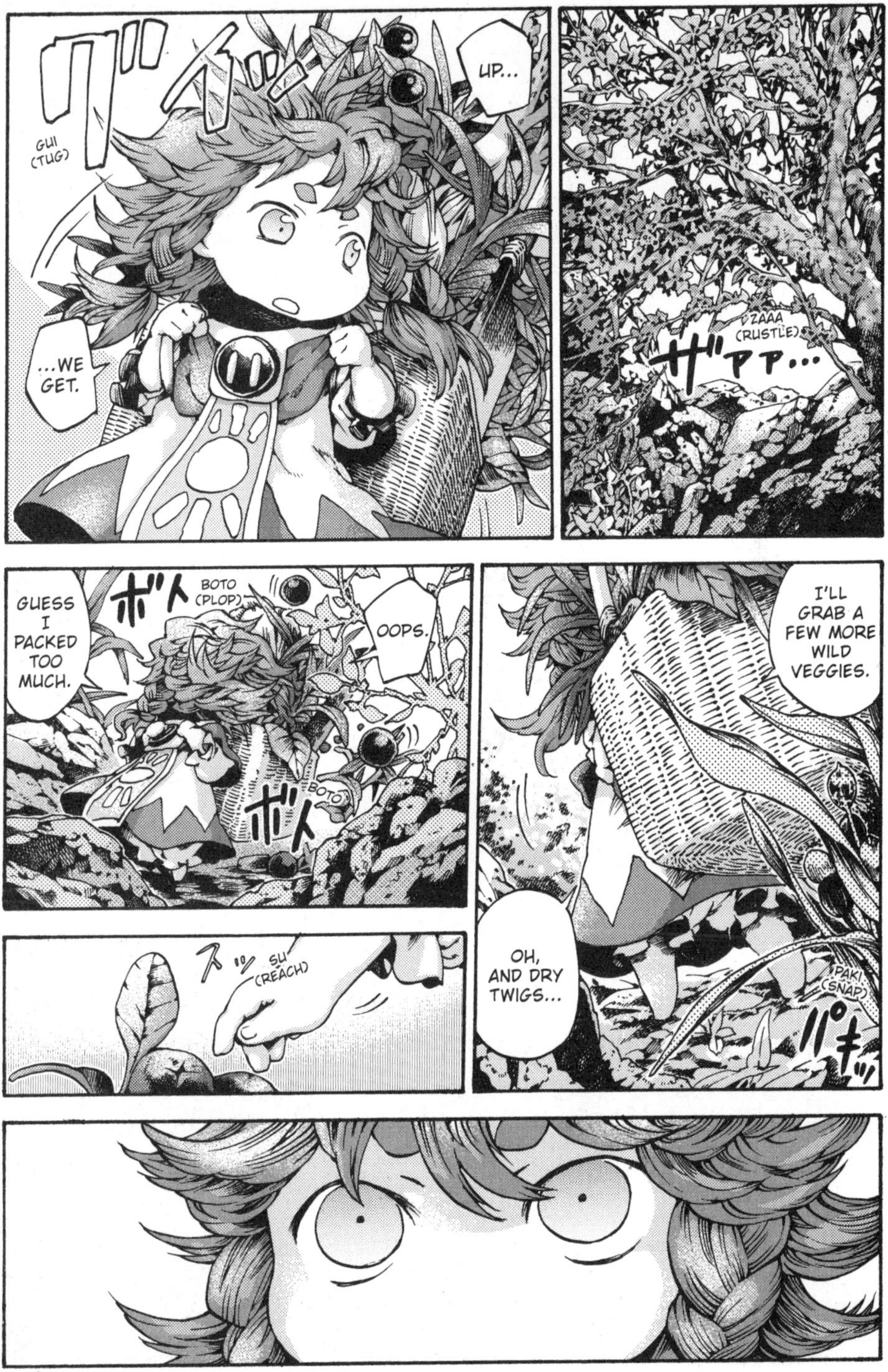
ZAAA (RUSTLE)
ザァァ...
UP...
グイッ
GUI (TUG)
...WE GET.
I'LL GRAB A FEW MORE WILD VEGGIES.
OH, AND DRY TWIGS...
PAKI (SNAP)
パキッ
OOPS.
BOTO (PLOP)
ボト
GUESS I PACKED TOO MUCH.
BOTO
ボト
スッ
SU (REACH)

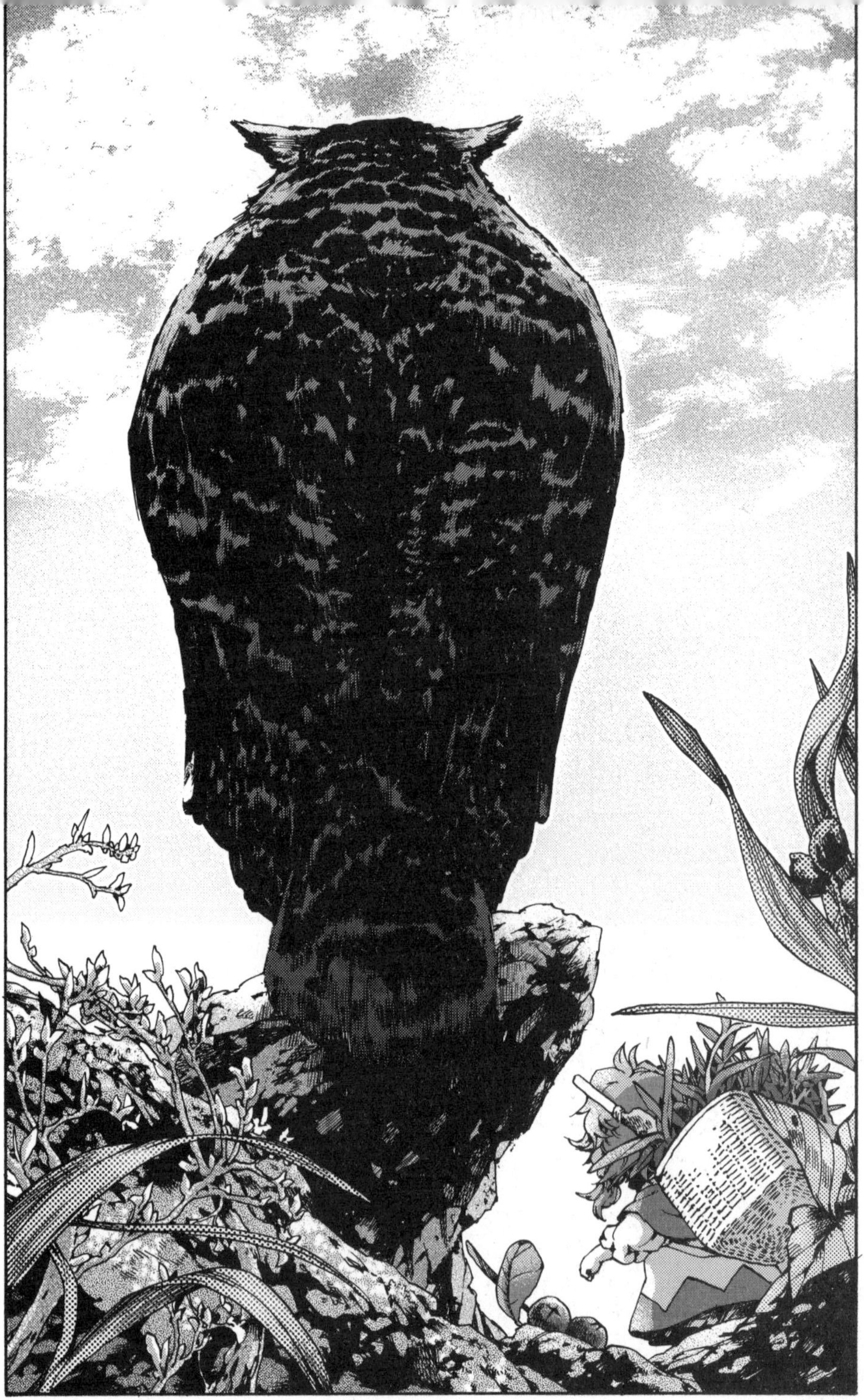

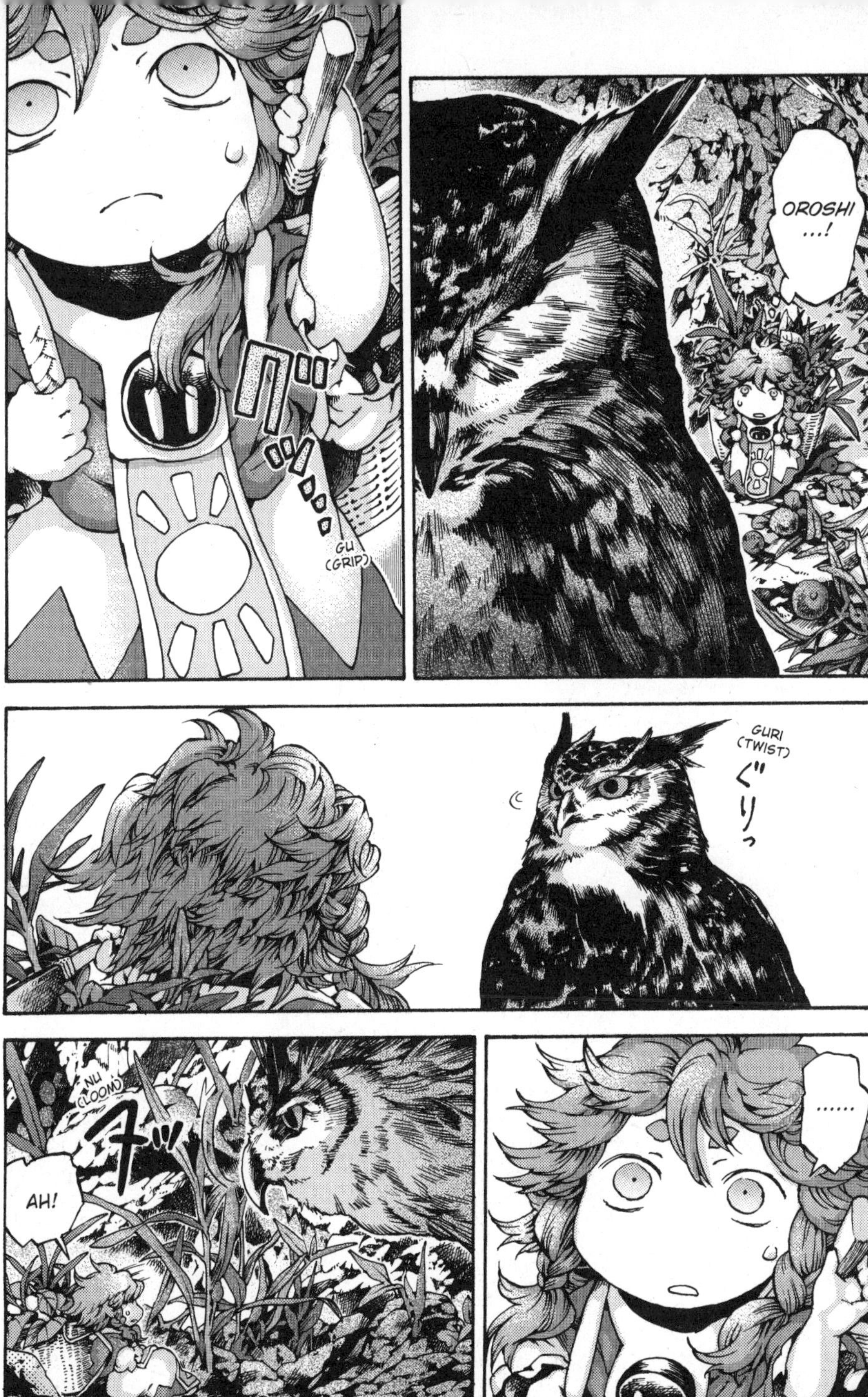

OROSHI ...!
GU (GRIP)
GURI (TWIST)
ぐりっ
......
NU (LOOM)
AH!

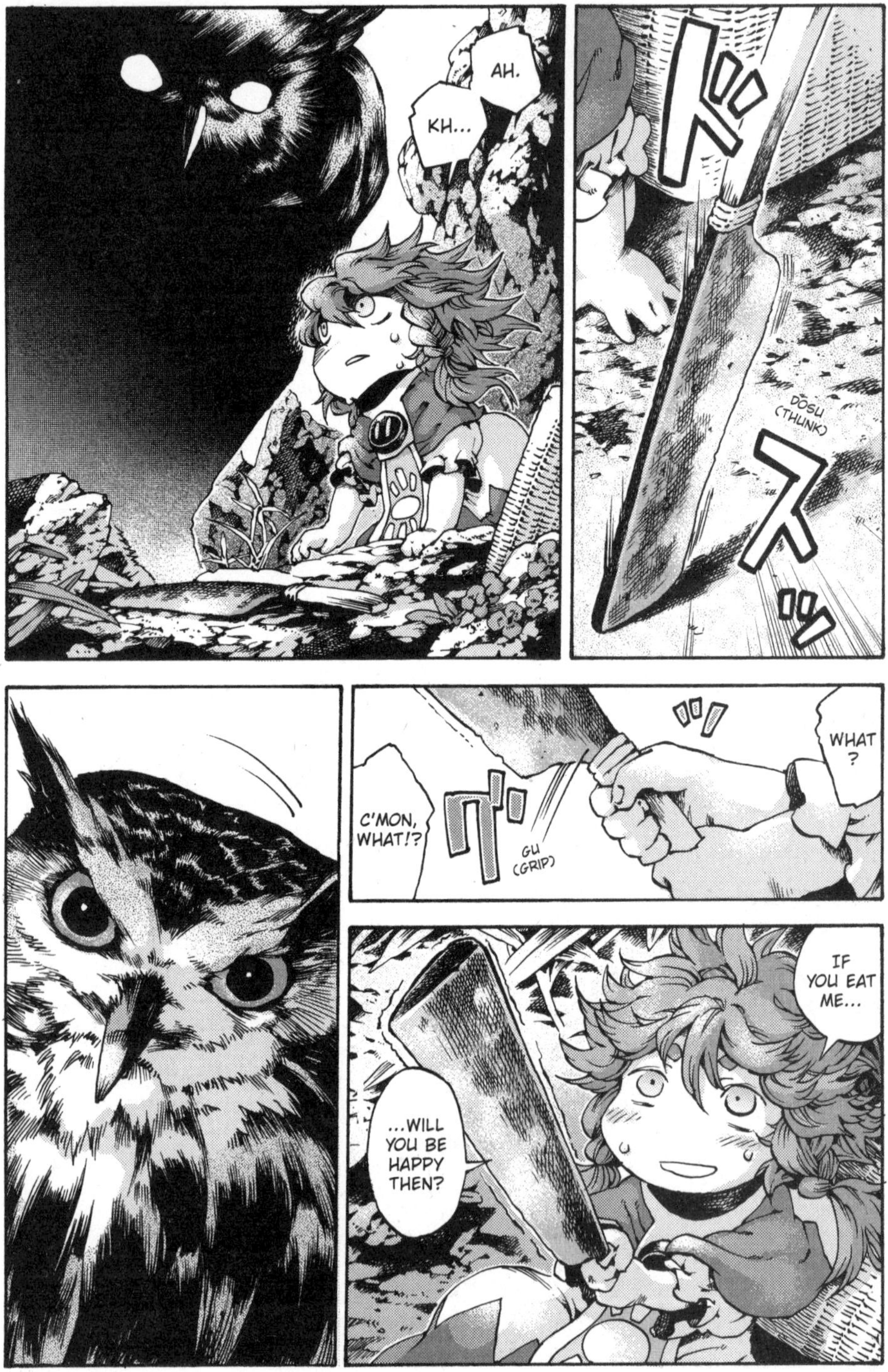
DOSU (THUNK)
AH.
KH...
WHAT?
C'MON, WHAT!?
GU (GRIP)
IF YOU EAT ME...
...WILL YOU BE HAPPY THEN?

THE
DRIED
MEAT
...

...IS
ALL
YOURS.

TAKE
IT.

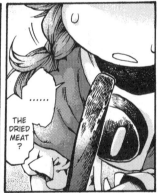

....

THE
DRIED
MEAT
?

ZAU
(SLAM)

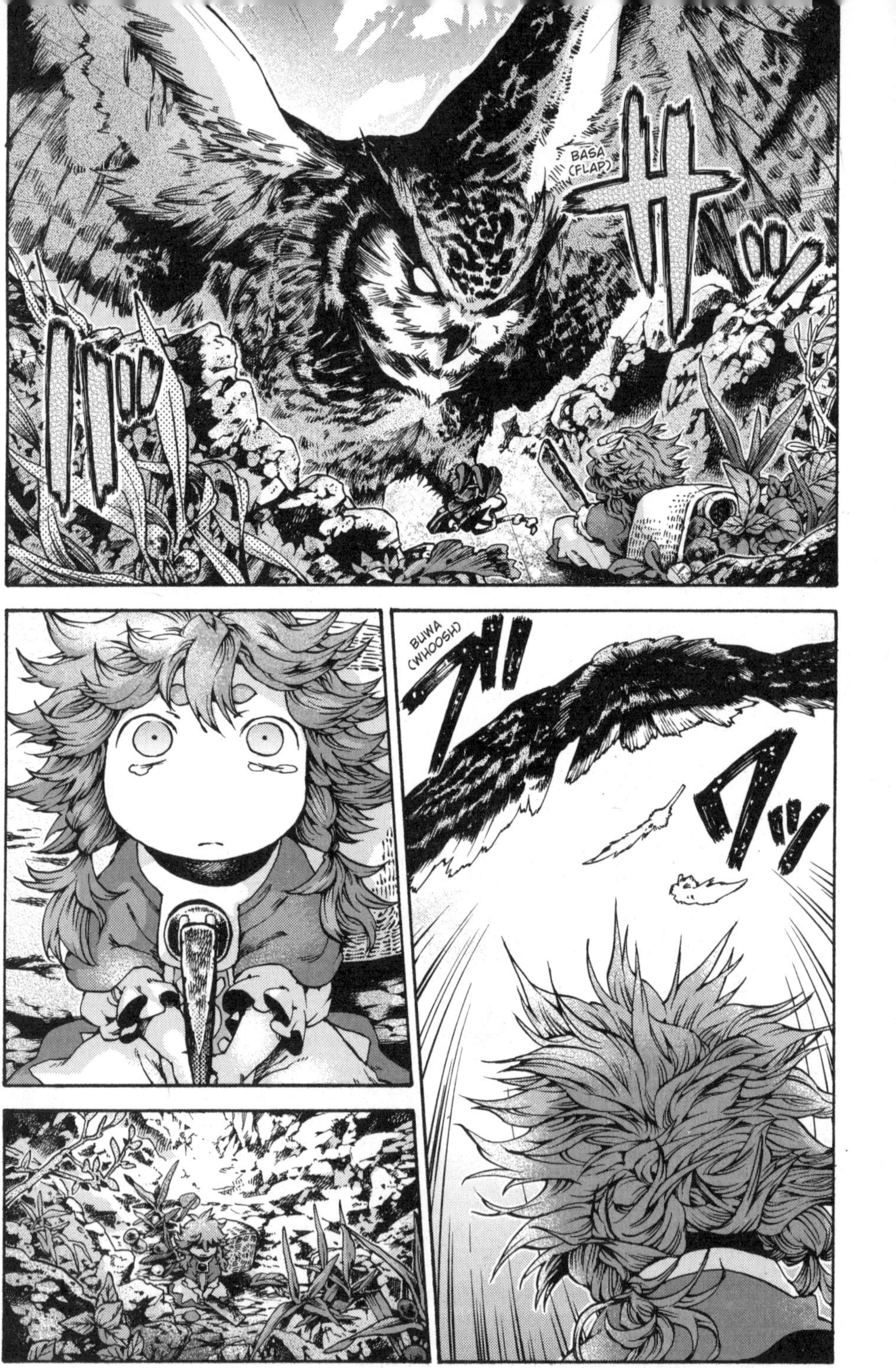
BASA (FLAP)
BUWA (WHOOSH)

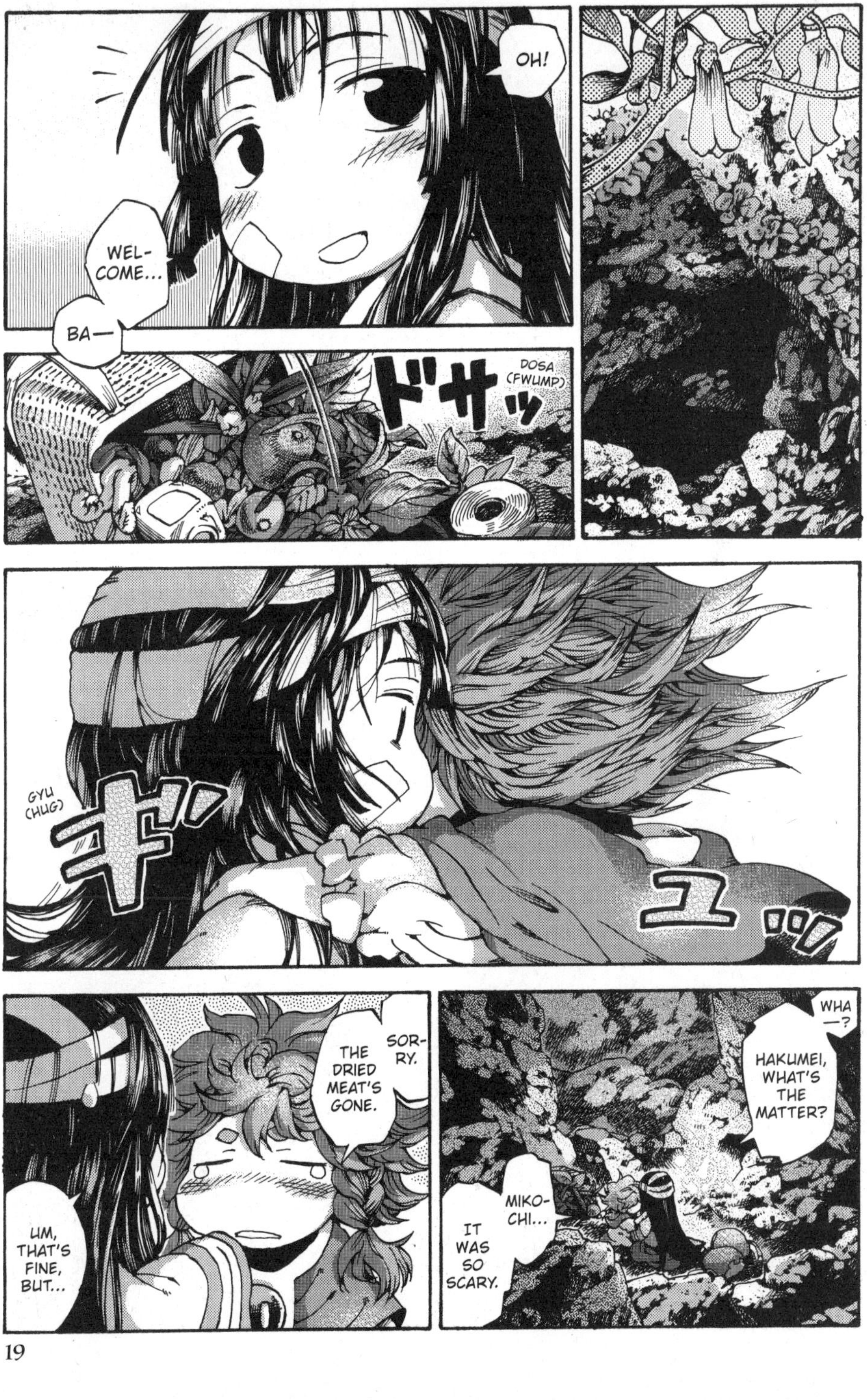
OH!
WEL-COME...
BA—
ドサッ
DOSA (FWUMP)
ギュッ
GYU (HUG)
WHA—?
HAKUMEI, WHAT'S THE MATTER?
MIKO-CHI...
IT WAS SO SCARY.
SOR-RY.
THE DRIED MEAT'S GONE.
UM, THAT'S FINE, BUT...

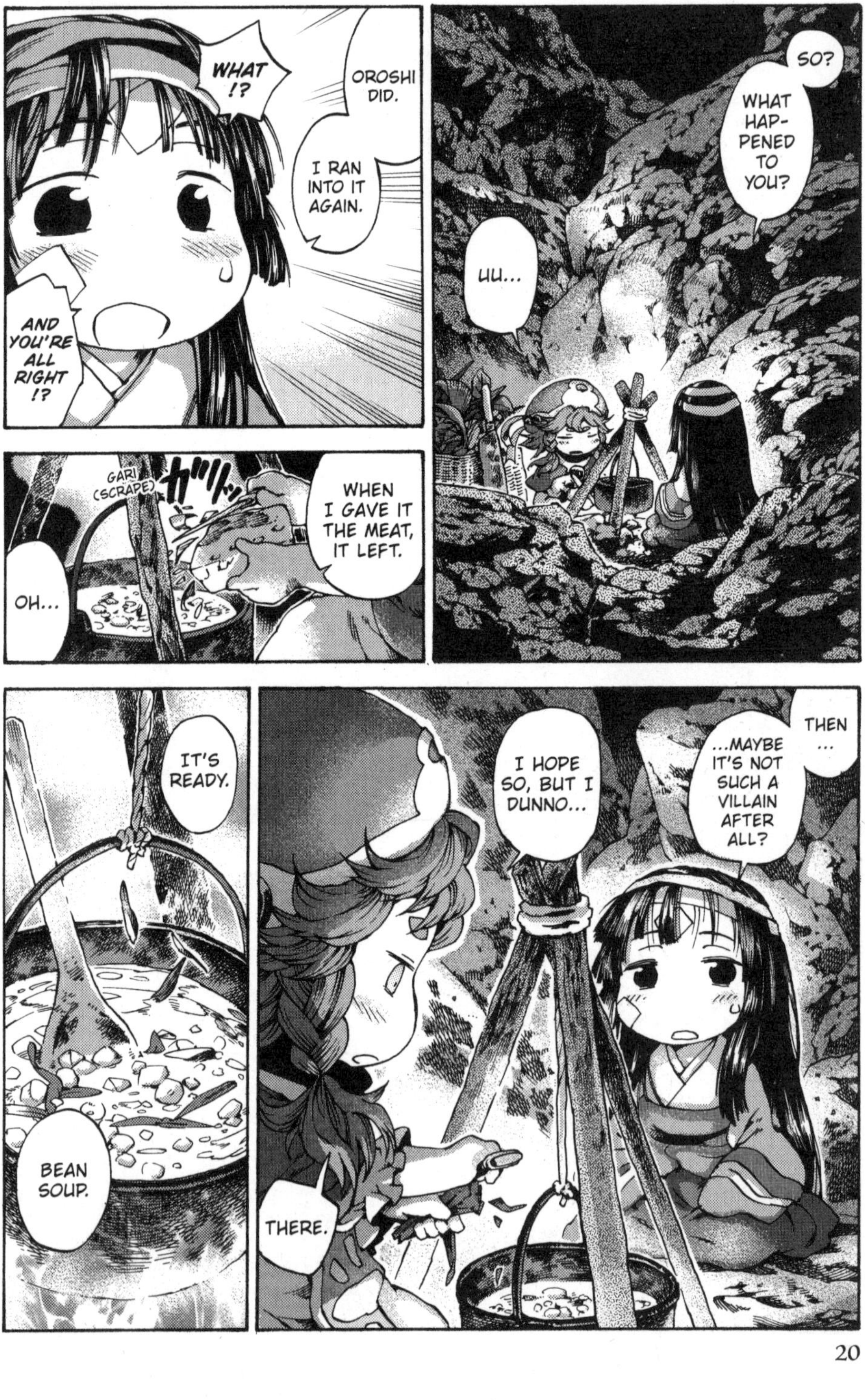
SO?
WHAT HAPPENED TO YOU?
UU...
OROSHI DID.
I RAN INTO IT AGAIN.
WHAT !?
AND YOU'RE ALL RIGHT !?
WHEN I GAVE IT THE MEAT, IT LEFT.
GARI (SCRAPE)
OH...
THEN...
...MAYBE IT'S NOT SUCH A VILLAIN AFTER ALL?
I HOPE SO, BUT I DUNNO...
THERE.
IT'S READY.
BEAN SOUP.

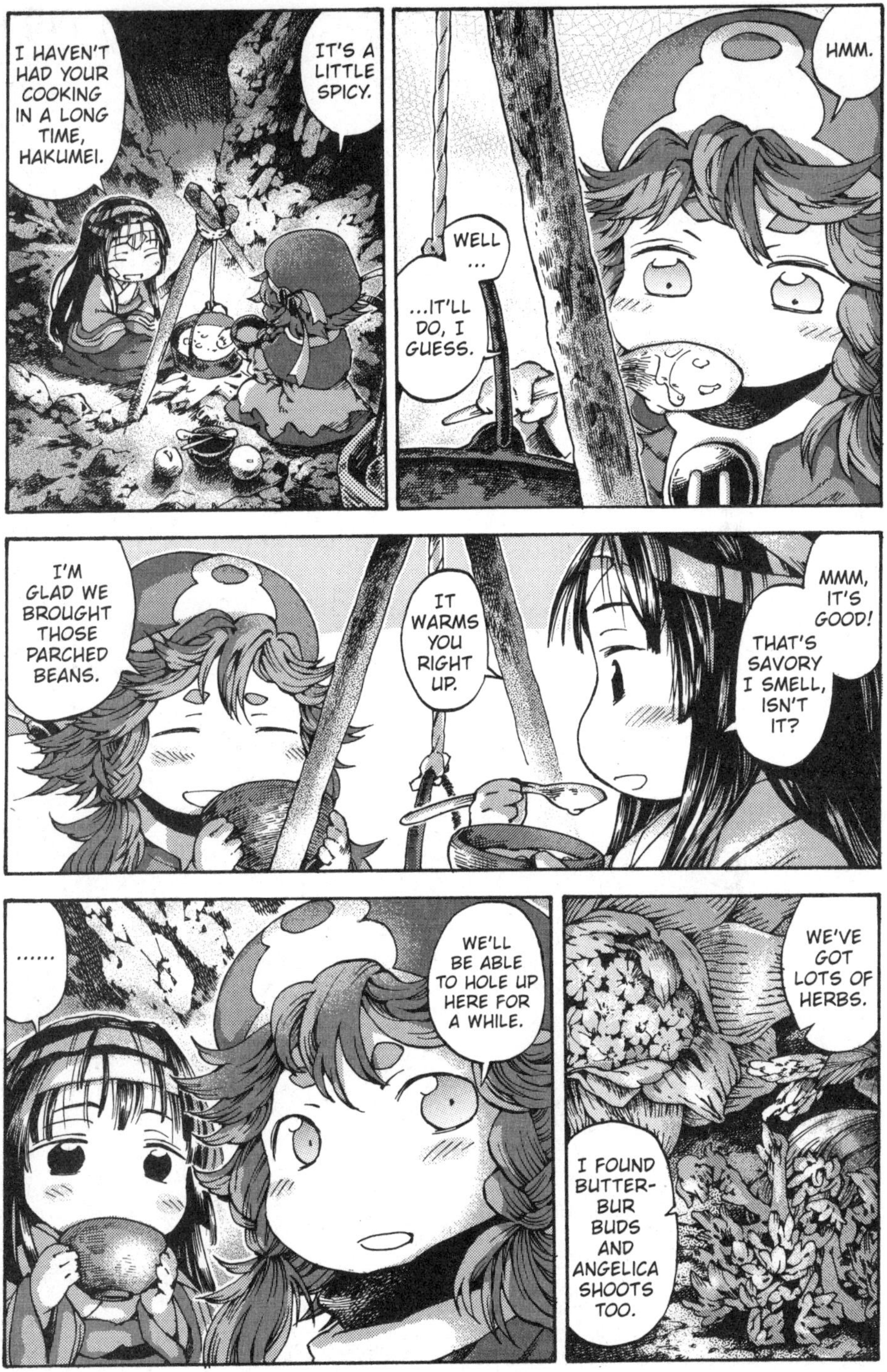
HMM.
WELL ...
...IT'LL DO, I GUESS.
IT'S A LITTLE SPICY.
I HAVEN'T HAD YOUR COOKING IN A LONG TIME, HAKUMEI.
MMM, IT'S GOOD!
THAT'S SAVORY I SMELL, ISN'T IT?
IT WARMS YOU RIGHT UP.
I'M GLAD WE BROUGHT THOSE PARCHED BEANS.
WE'VE GOT LOTS OF HERBS.
I FOUND BUTTER-BUR BUDS AND ANGELICA SHOOTS TOO.
WE'LL BE ABLE TO HOLE UP HERE FOR A WHILE.
......

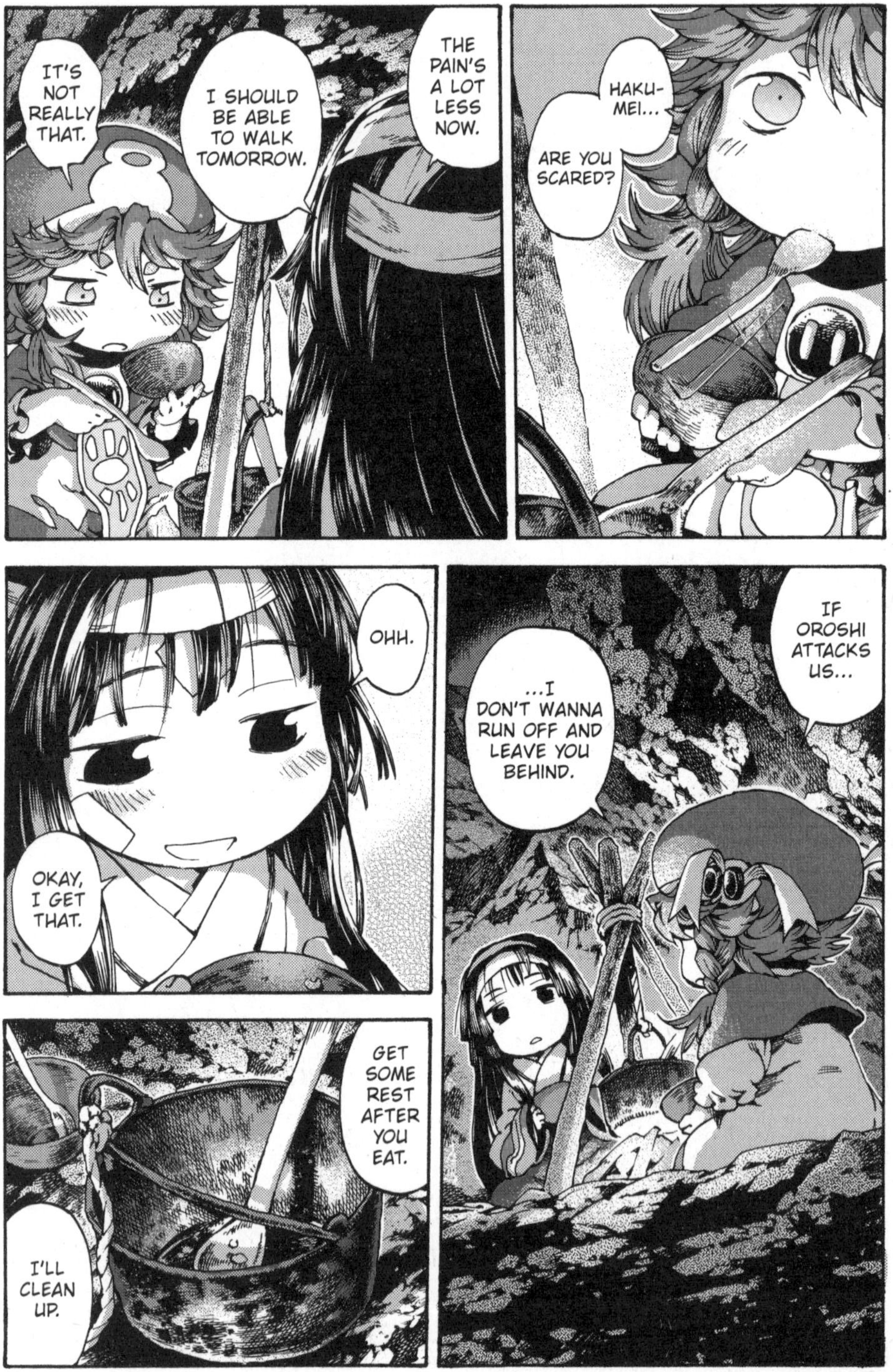
HAKU-MEI...
ARE YOU SCARED?
THE PAIN'S A LOT LESS NOW.
I SHOULD BE ABLE TO WALK TOMORROW.
IT'S NOT REALLY THAT.
IF OROSHI ATTACKS US...
...I DON'T WANNA RUN OFF AND LEAVE YOU BEHIND.
OHH.
OKAY, I GET THAT.
GET SOME REST AFTER YOU EAT.
I'LL CLEAN UP.

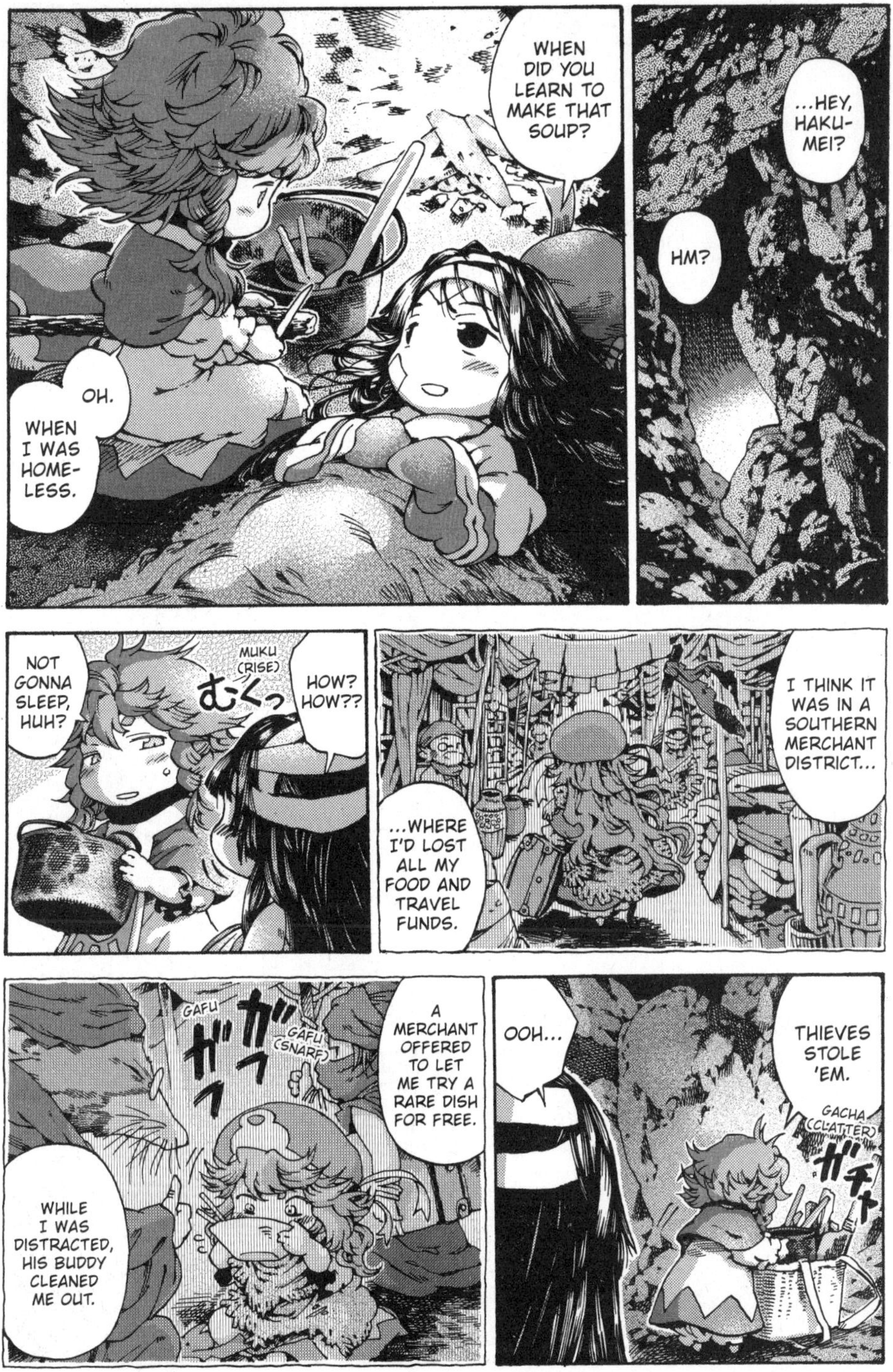
...HEY, HAKU-MEI?
HM?
WHEN DID YOU LEARN TO MAKE THAT SOUP?
OH.
WHEN I WAS HOME-LESS.
I THINK IT WAS IN A SOUTHERN MERCHANT DISTRICT...
...WHERE I'D LOST ALL MY FOOD AND TRAVEL FUNDS.
HOW? HOW??
MUKU (RISE)
むくっ
NOT GONNA SLEEP, HUH?
THIEVES STOLE 'EM.
GACHA (CLATTER)
ガチャ
OOH...
A MERCHANT OFFERED TO LET ME TRY A RARE DISH FOR FREE.
GAFU
ガフ
GAFU (SNARF)
ガフ
WHILE I WAS DISTRACTED, HIS BUDDY CLEANED ME OUT.

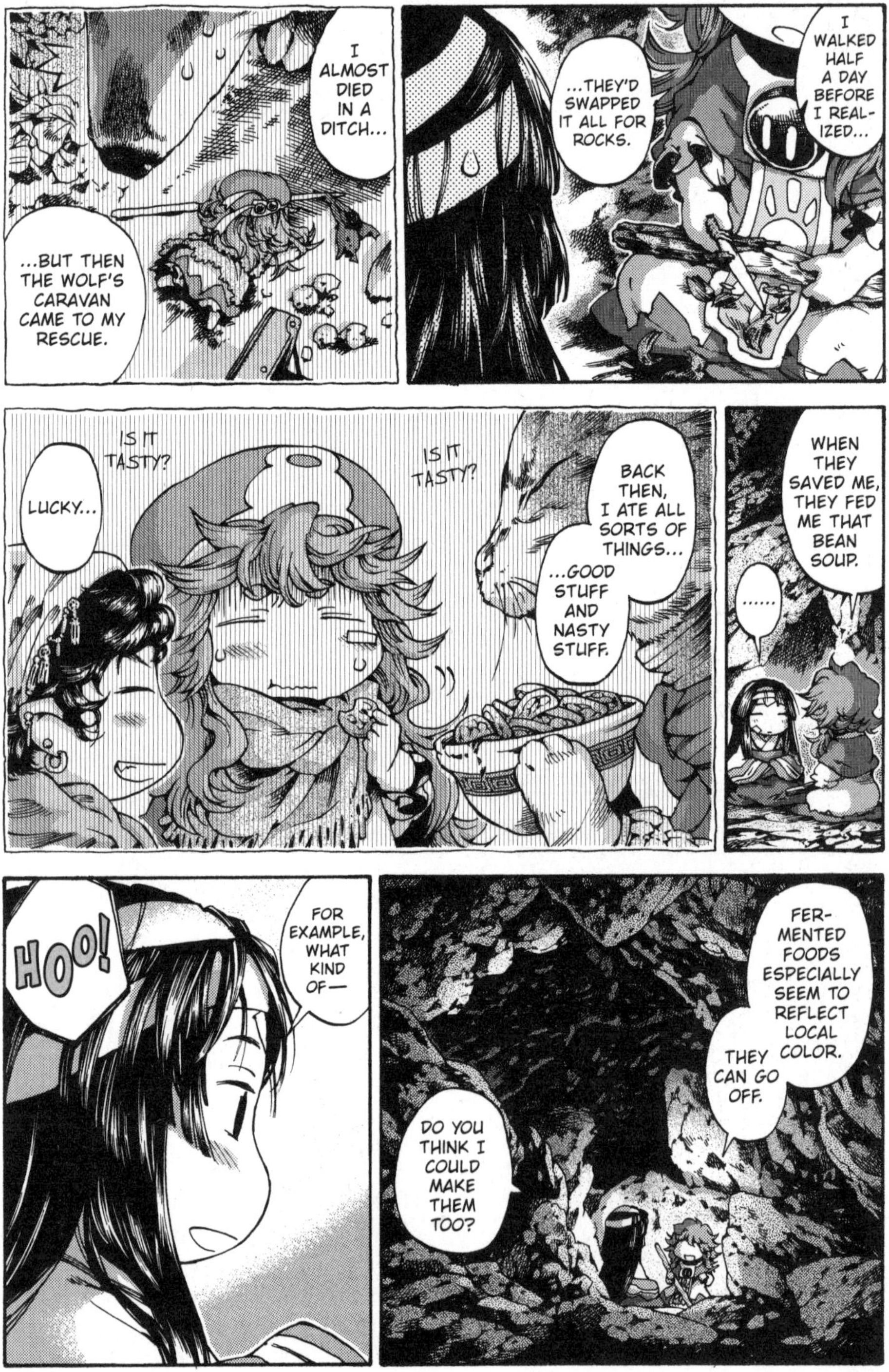
I WALKED HALF A DAY BEFORE I REAL-IZED...
...THEY'D SWAPPED IT ALL FOR ROCKS.
I ALMOST DIED IN A DITCH...
...BUT THEN THE WOLF'S CARAVAN CAME TO MY RESCUE.
WHEN THEY SAVED ME, THEY FED ME THAT BEAN SOUP.
......
BACK THEN, I ATE ALL SORTS OF THINGS...
...GOOD STUFF AND NASTY STUFF.
IS IT TASTY?
IS IT TASTY?
LUCKY...
FER-MENTED FOODS ESPECIALLY SEEM TO REFLECT LOCAL COLOR.
THEY CAN GO OFF.
DO YOU THINK I COULD MAKE THEM TOO?
HOO!
FOR EXAMPLE, WHAT KIND OF—

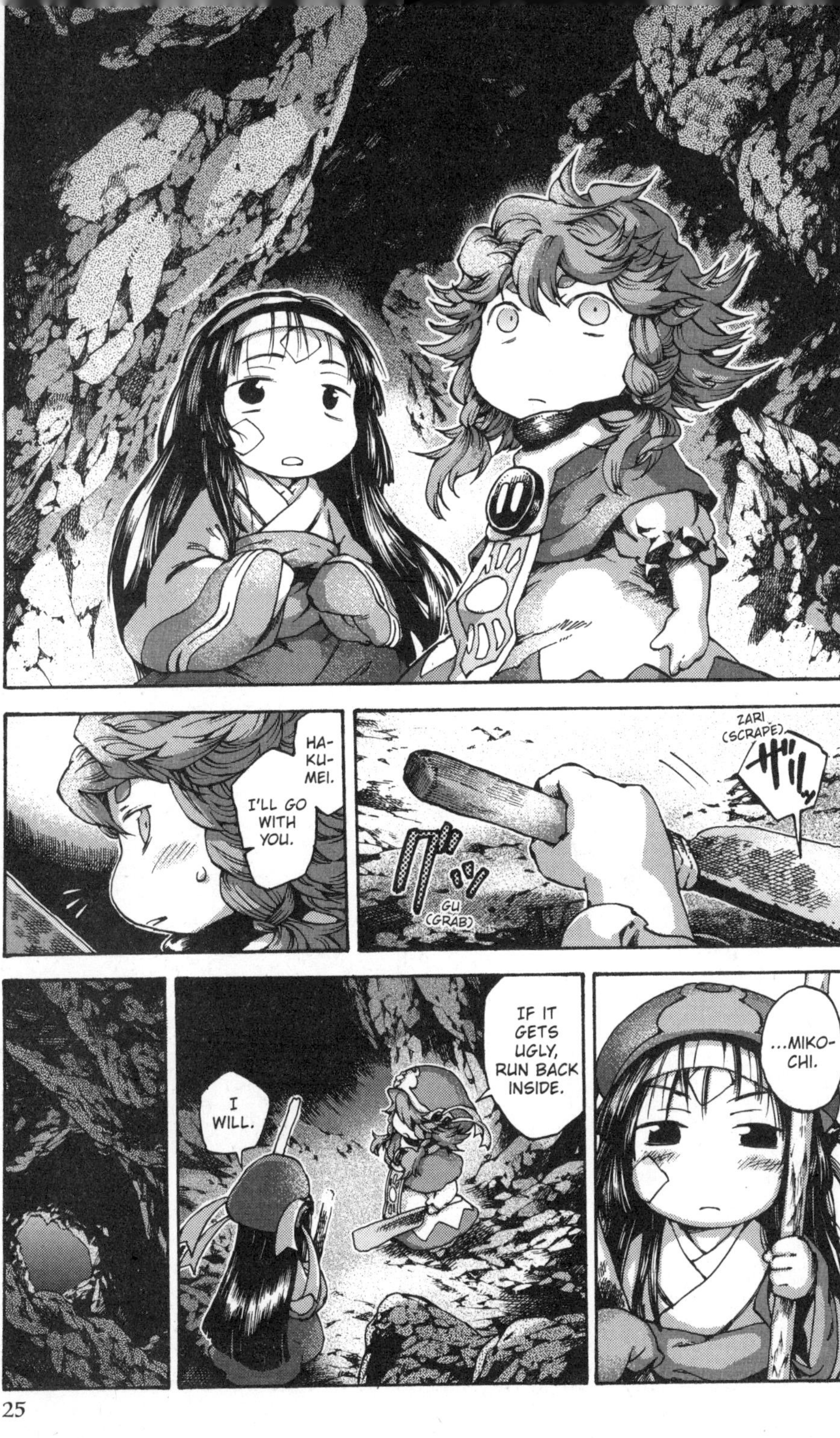
ZARI (SCRAPE)
GU (GRAB)
HAKUMEI.
I'LL GO WITH YOU.
...MIKOCHI.
IF IT GETS UGLY, RUN BACK INSIDE.
I WILL.

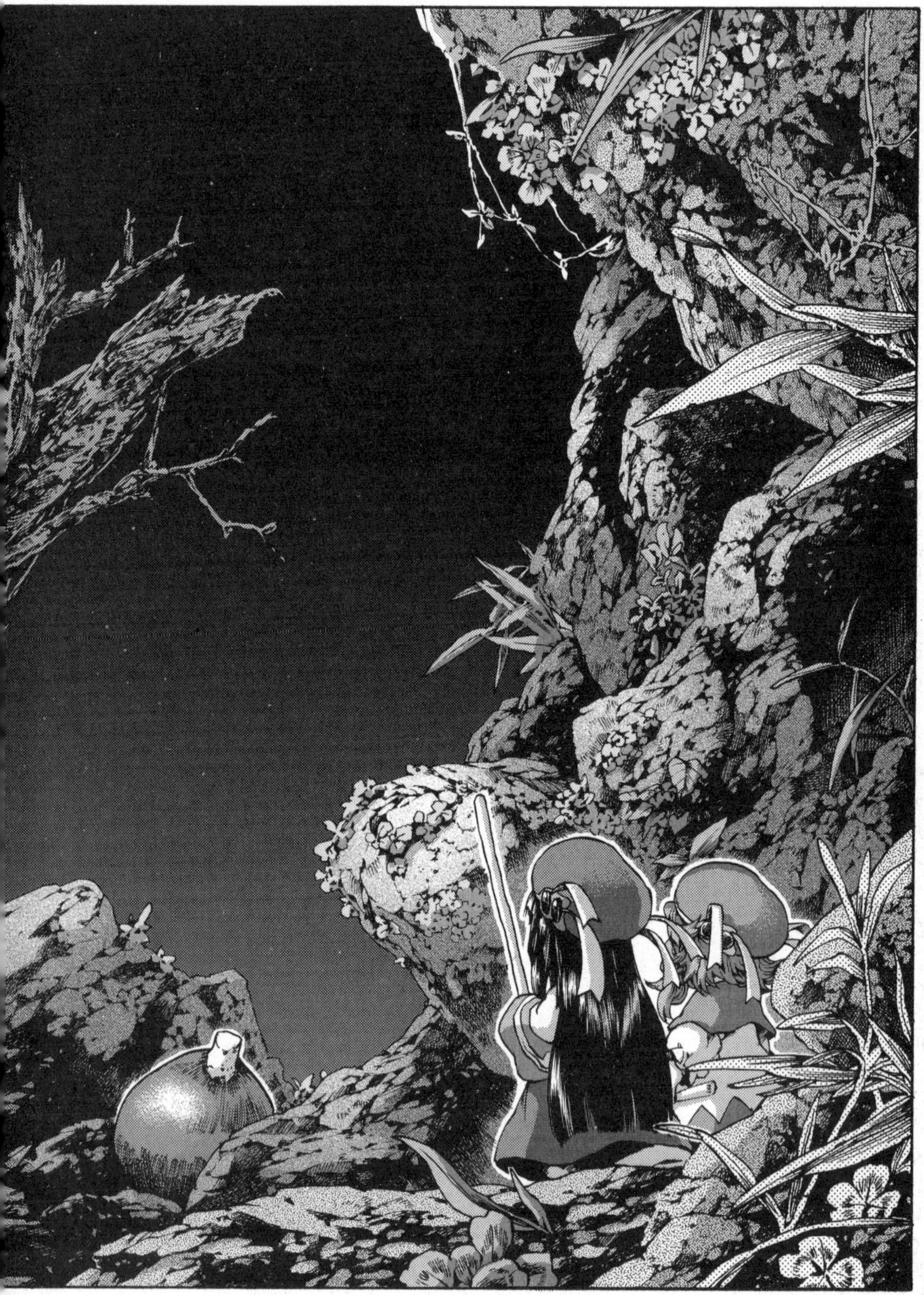

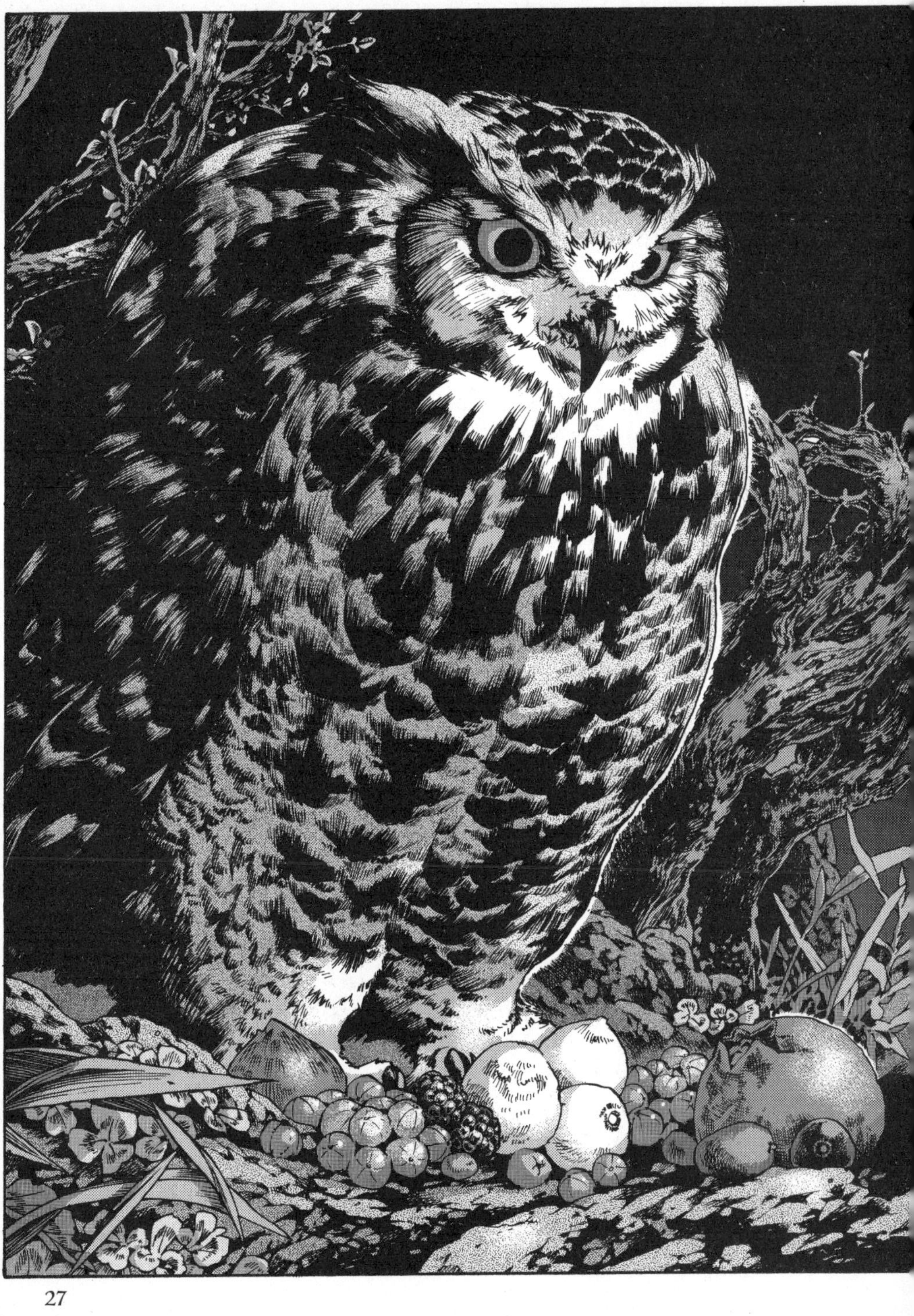

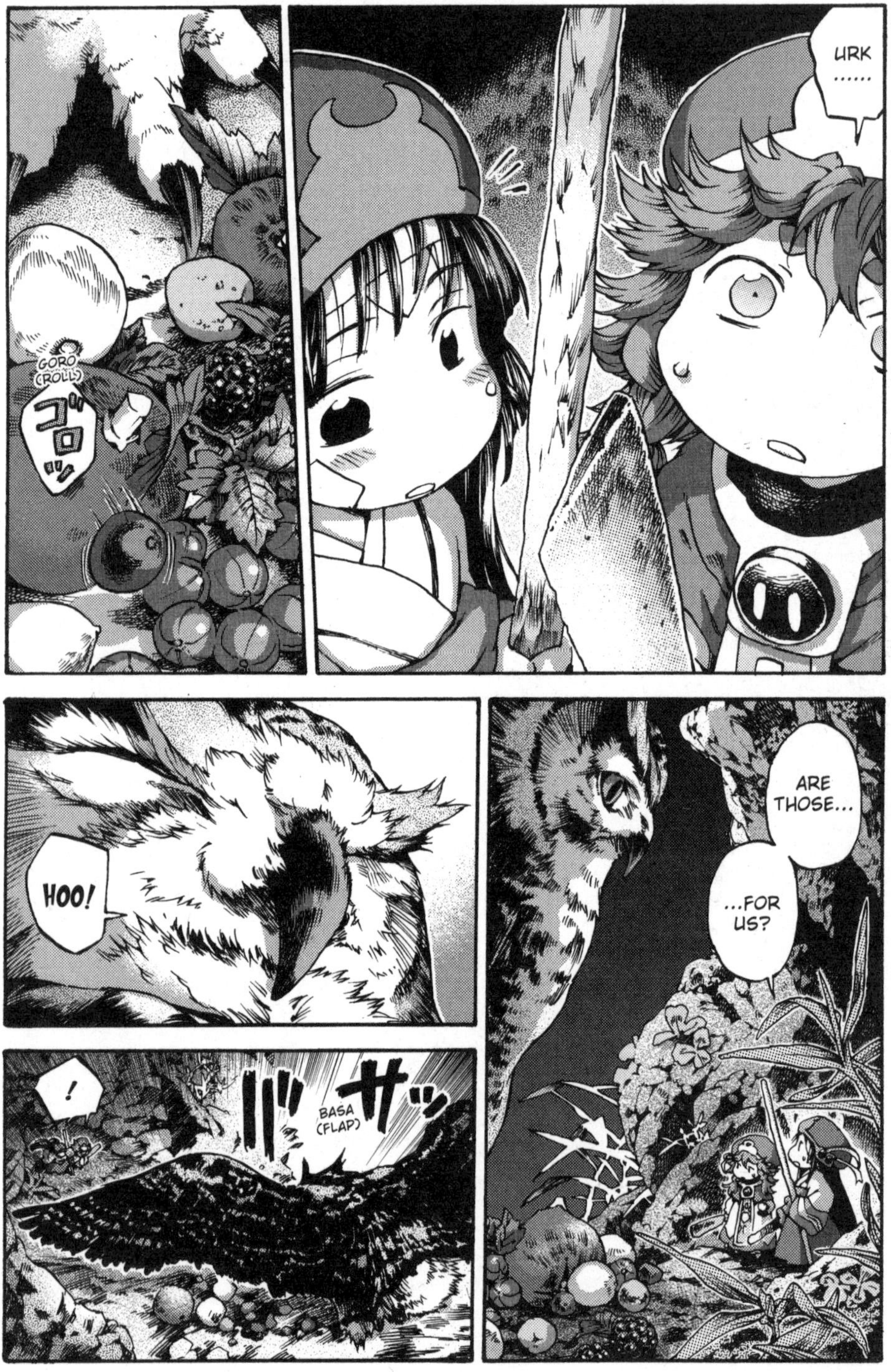
URK ......
GORO (ROLL)
ゴロ
ARE THOSE...
...FOR US?
HOO!
!
BASA (FLAP)
バサッ

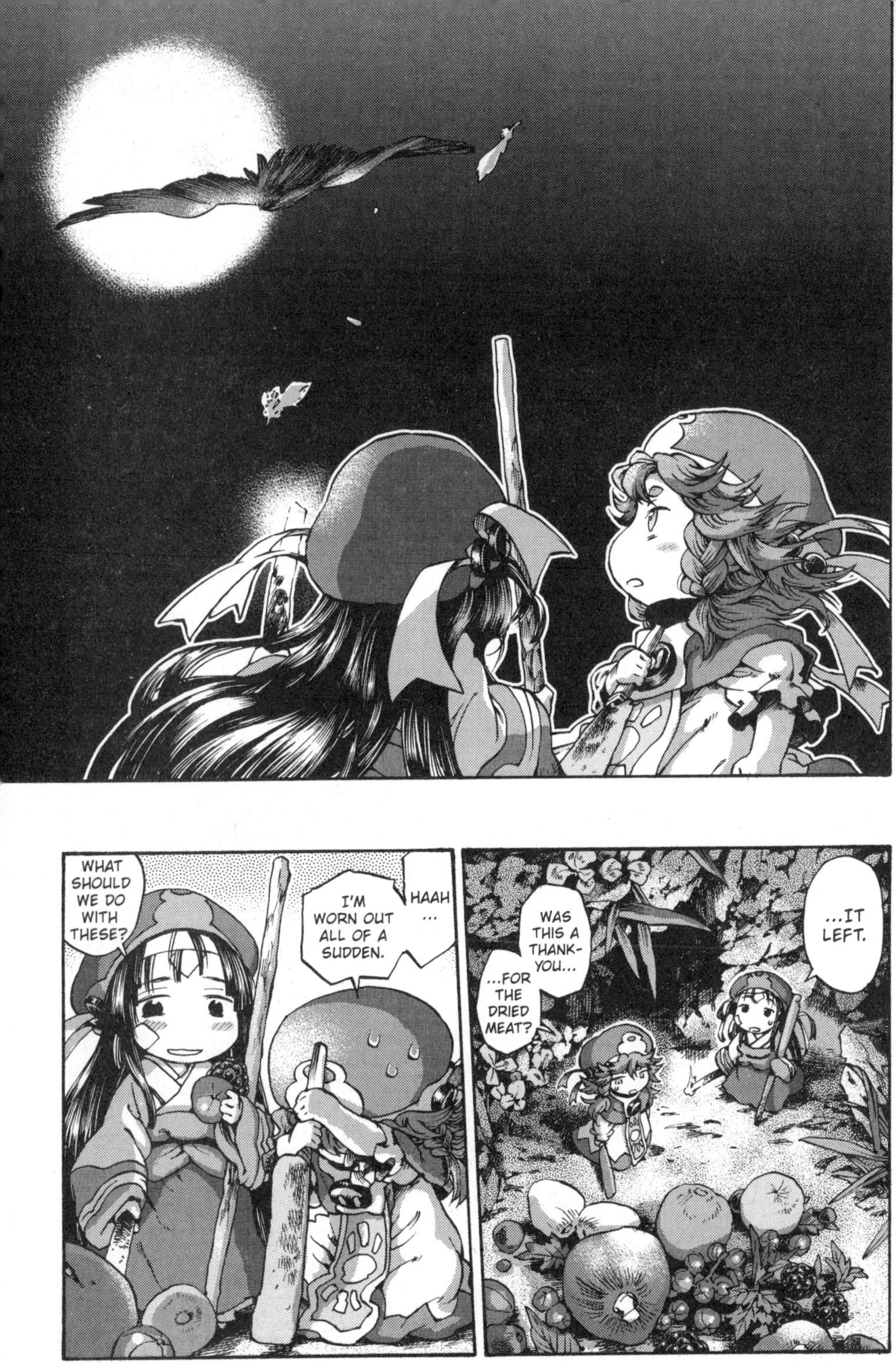
...IT LEFT.
WAS THIS A THANK-YOU...
...FOR THE DRIED MEAT?
HAAH ...
I'M WORN OUT ALL OF A SUDDEN.
WHAT SHOULD WE DO WITH THESE?

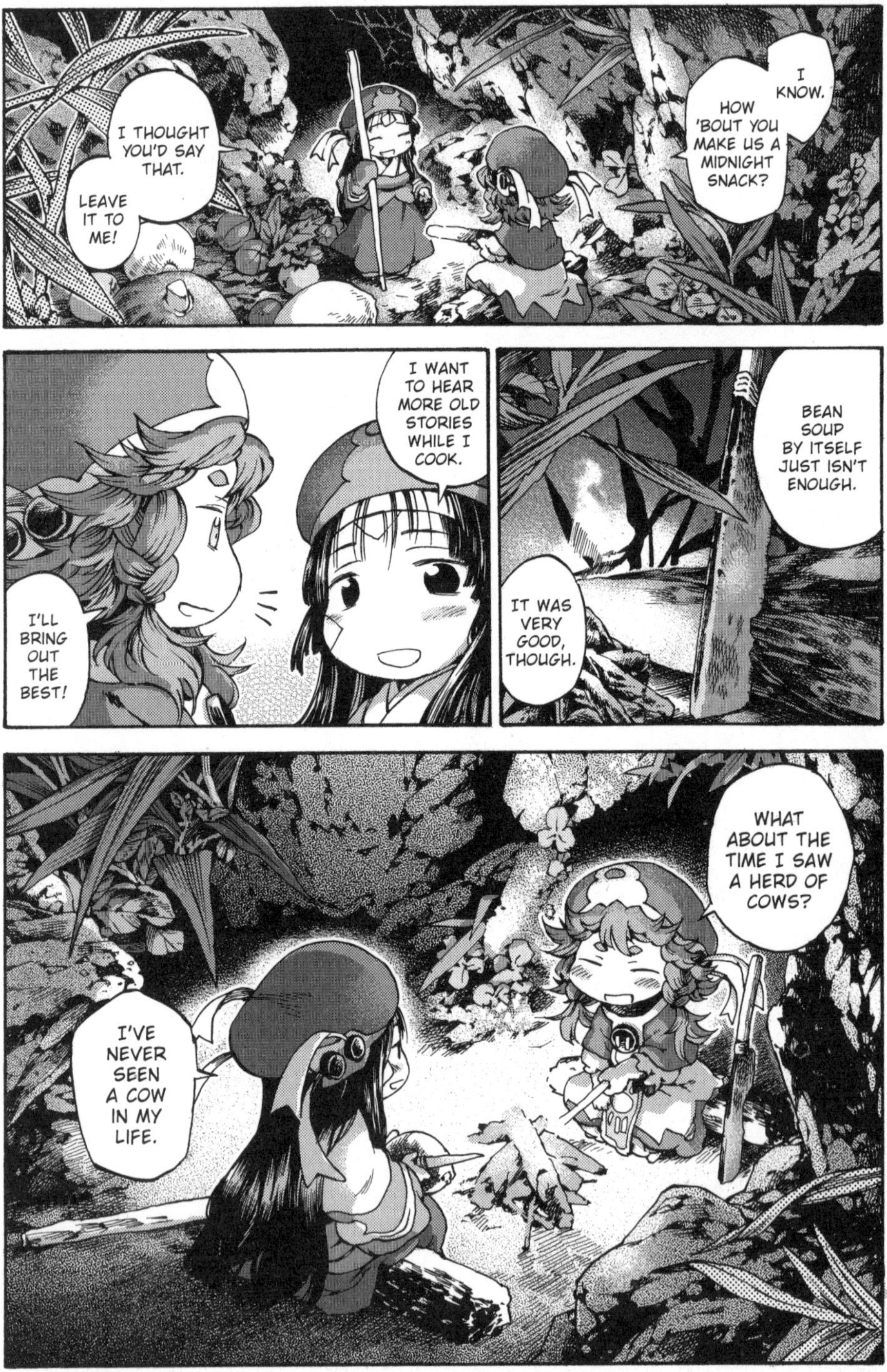
I KNOW. HOW 'BOUT YOU MAKE US A MIDNIGHT SNACK?
I THOUGHT YOU'D SAY THAT.
LEAVE IT TO ME!
BEAN SOUP BY ITSELF JUST ISN'T ENOUGH.
IT WAS VERY GOOD, THOUGH.
I WANT TO HEAR MORE OLD STORIES WHILE I COOK.
I'LL BRING OUT THE BEST!
WHAT ABOUT THE TIME I SAW A HERD OF COWS?
I'VE NEVER SEEN A COW IN MY LIFE.

A caravan formed by a commercial organization from the merchant city Yashiro. Its leader is Old Greentail, an elderly, one-eyed she-wolf who dyes the tip of her tail green. Word has it the group was assembled during the early days of large-scale trade between Yashiro and the ancient capital of Kiou with the intention of increasing exchange between the cities and keeping the peace on the roads.

That said, the only remaining caravan member from those days is Old Greentail, so the facts aren't clear.

When business dries up, the group stays in Yashiro as a security outfit. Old Greentail manages everything: cargo transport, travel arrangements, trade negotiations, and defense strategies. Due to her strengths in negotiations and battle, some people call her the "Smiling Amazon" and fear her.

The records say that, just once, the caravan traveled to the mountain town of Makinata, but the reasons for the trip remain a mystery.

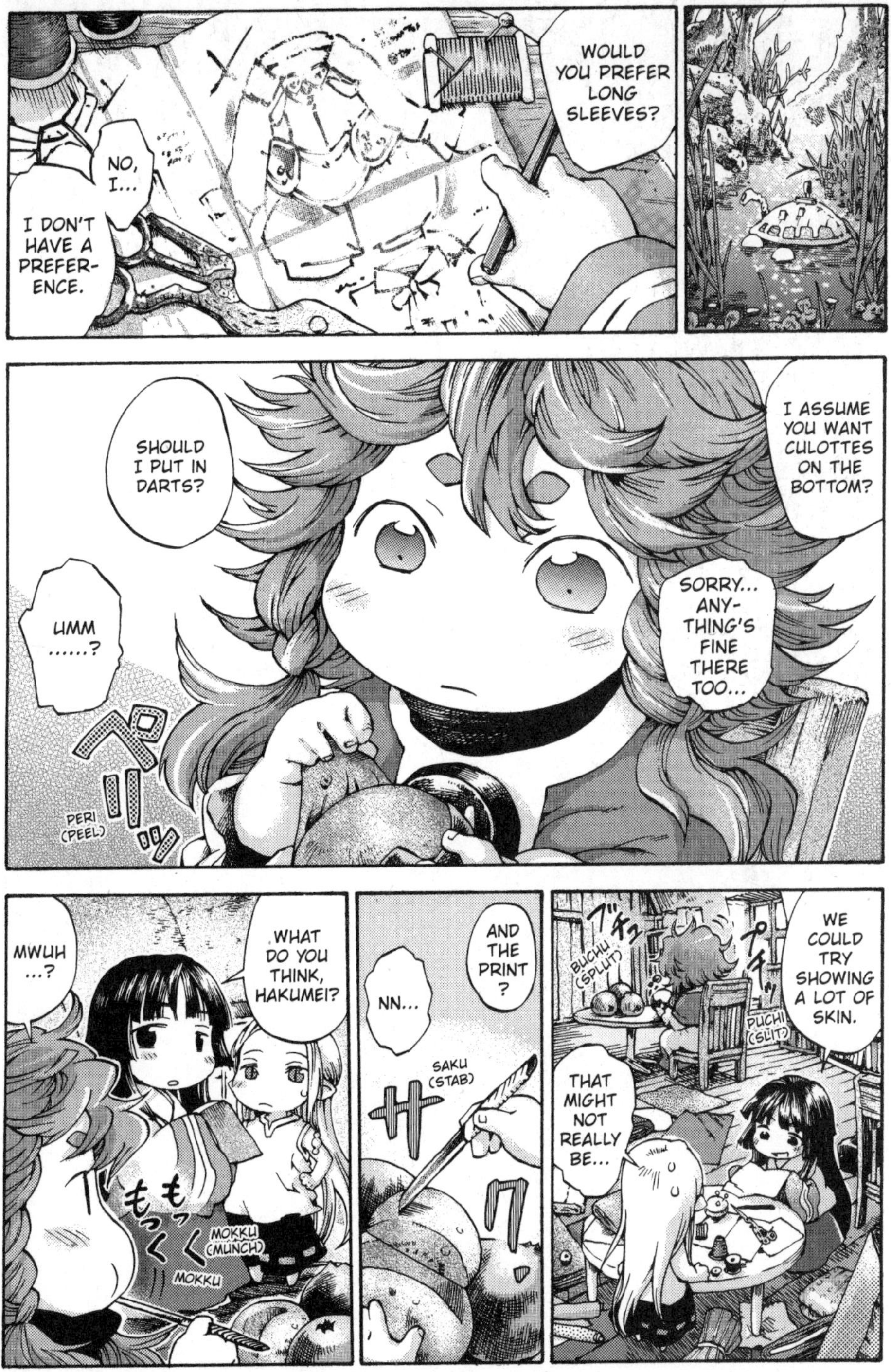
WOULD YOU PREFER LONG SLEEVES?
NO, I...
I DON'T HAVE A PREFERENCE.
I ASSUME YOU WANT CULOTTES ON THE BOTTOM?
SORRY... ANYTHING'S FINE THERE TOO...
SHOULD I PUT IN DARTS?
UMM ......?
PERI (PEEL)
WE COULD TRY SHOWING A LOT OF SKIN.
BUCHU (SPLUT)
PUCHI (SLIT)
THAT MIGHT NOT REALLY BE...
AND THE PRINT?
NN...
SAKU (STAB)
WHAT DO YOU THINK, HAKUMEI?
MWUH ...?
MOKKU (MUNCH)
MOKKU

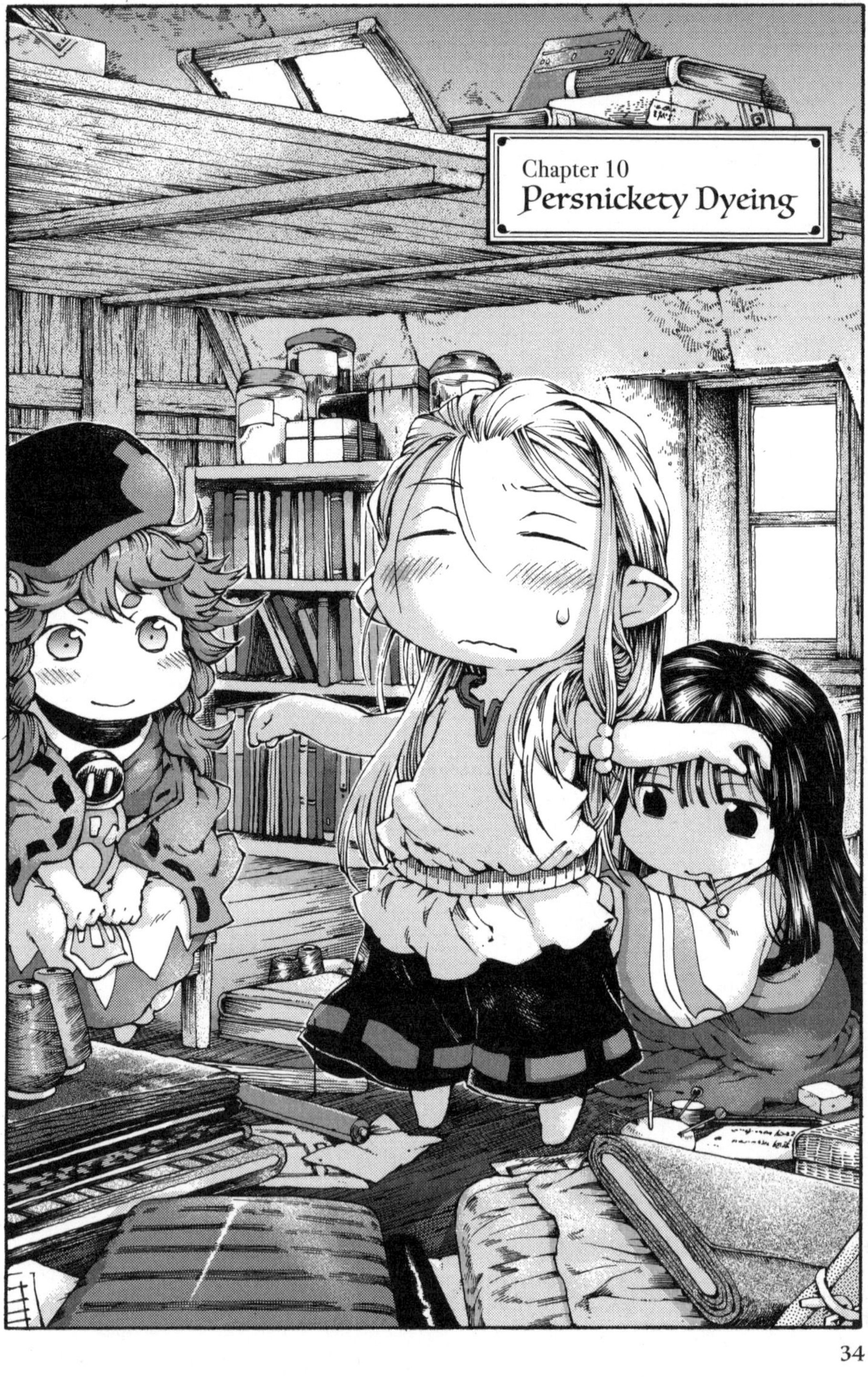
Chapter 10
Persnickety Dyeing

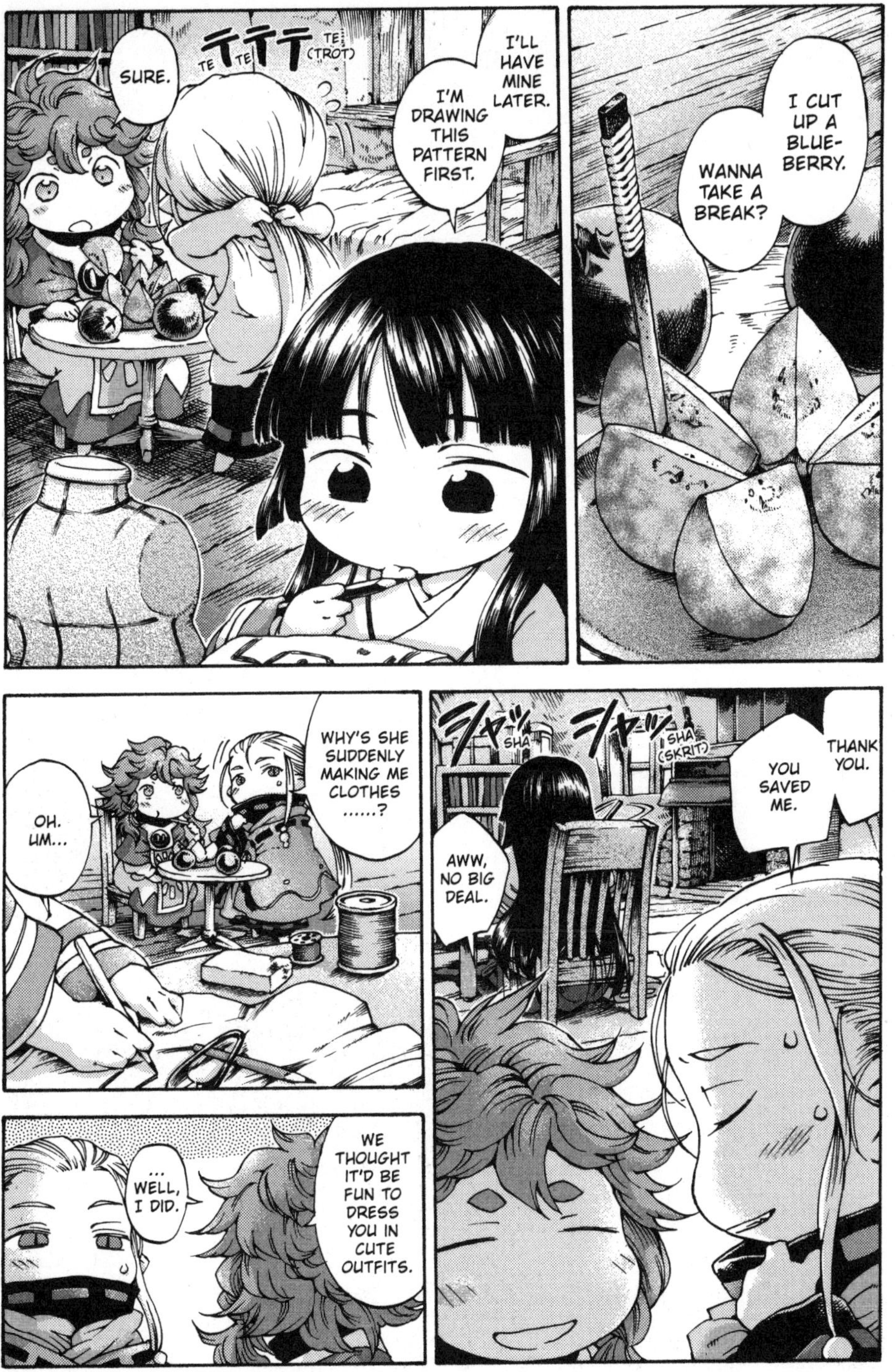
I CUT UP A BLUEBERRY.
WANNA TAKE A BREAK?
I'LL HAVE MINE LATER.
I'M DRAWING THIS PATTERN FIRST.
TE TE TE (TROT)
SURE.
SHA SHA (SKRIT)
THANK YOU.
YOU SAVED ME.
AWW, NO BIG DEAL.
WHY'S SHE SUDDENLY MAKING ME CLOTHES ......?
OH. UM...
WE THOUGHT IT'D BE FUN TO DRESS YOU IN CUTE OUTFITS.
... WELL, I DID.

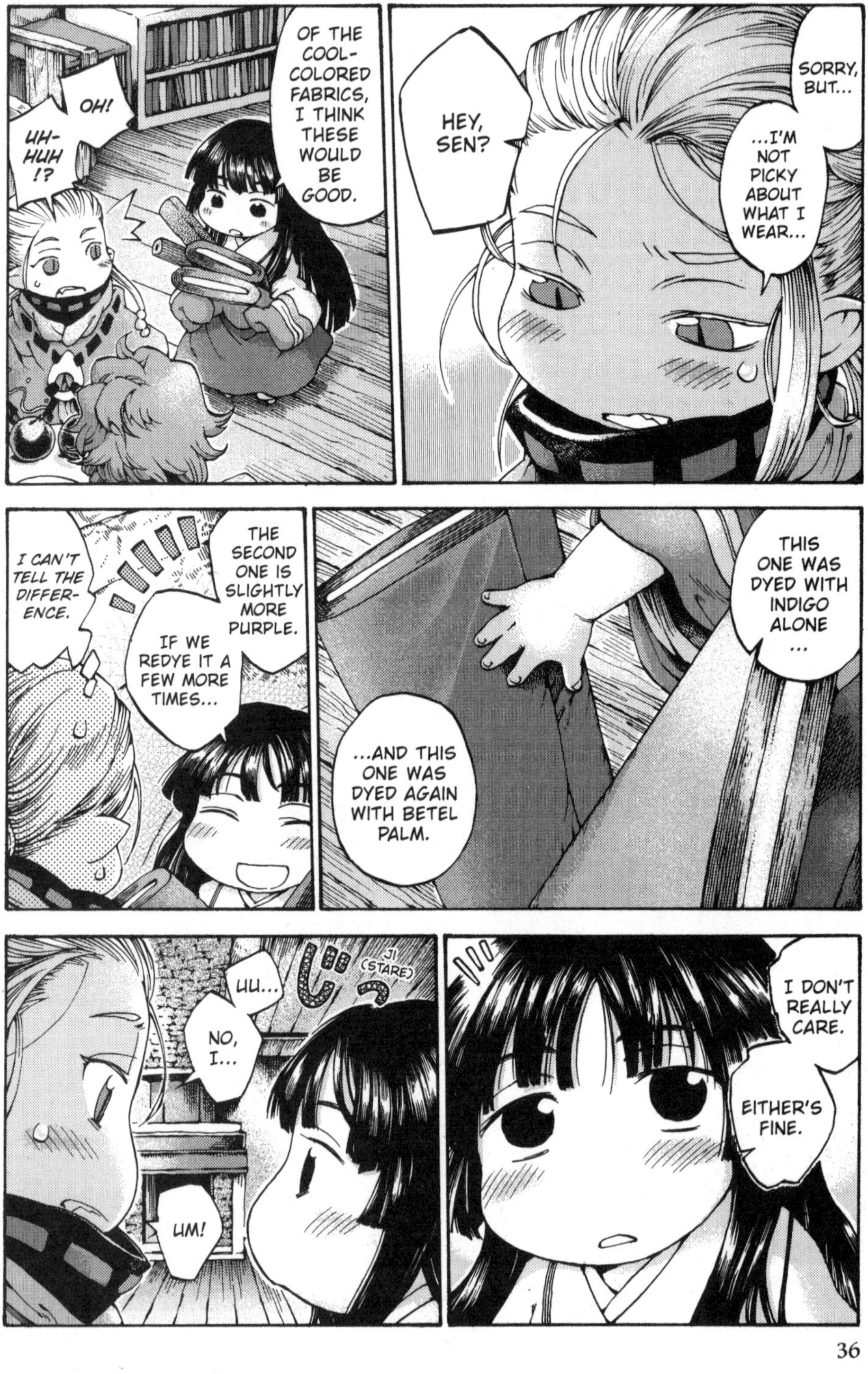
SORRY, BUT...
...I'M NOT PICKY ABOUT WHAT I WEAR...
HEY, SEN?
OF THE COOL-COLORED FABRICS, I THINK THESE WOULD BE GOOD.
OH!
UH-HUH!?
THIS ONE WAS DYED WITH INDIGO ALONE...
...AND THIS ONE WAS DYED AGAIN WITH BETEL PALM.
THE SECOND ONE IS SLIGHTLY MORE PURPLE.
I CAN'T TELL THE DIFFERENCE.
IF WE REDYE IT A FEW MORE TIMES...
I DON'T REALLY CARE.
EITHER'S FINE.
JI (STARE)
UU...
NO, I...
UM!

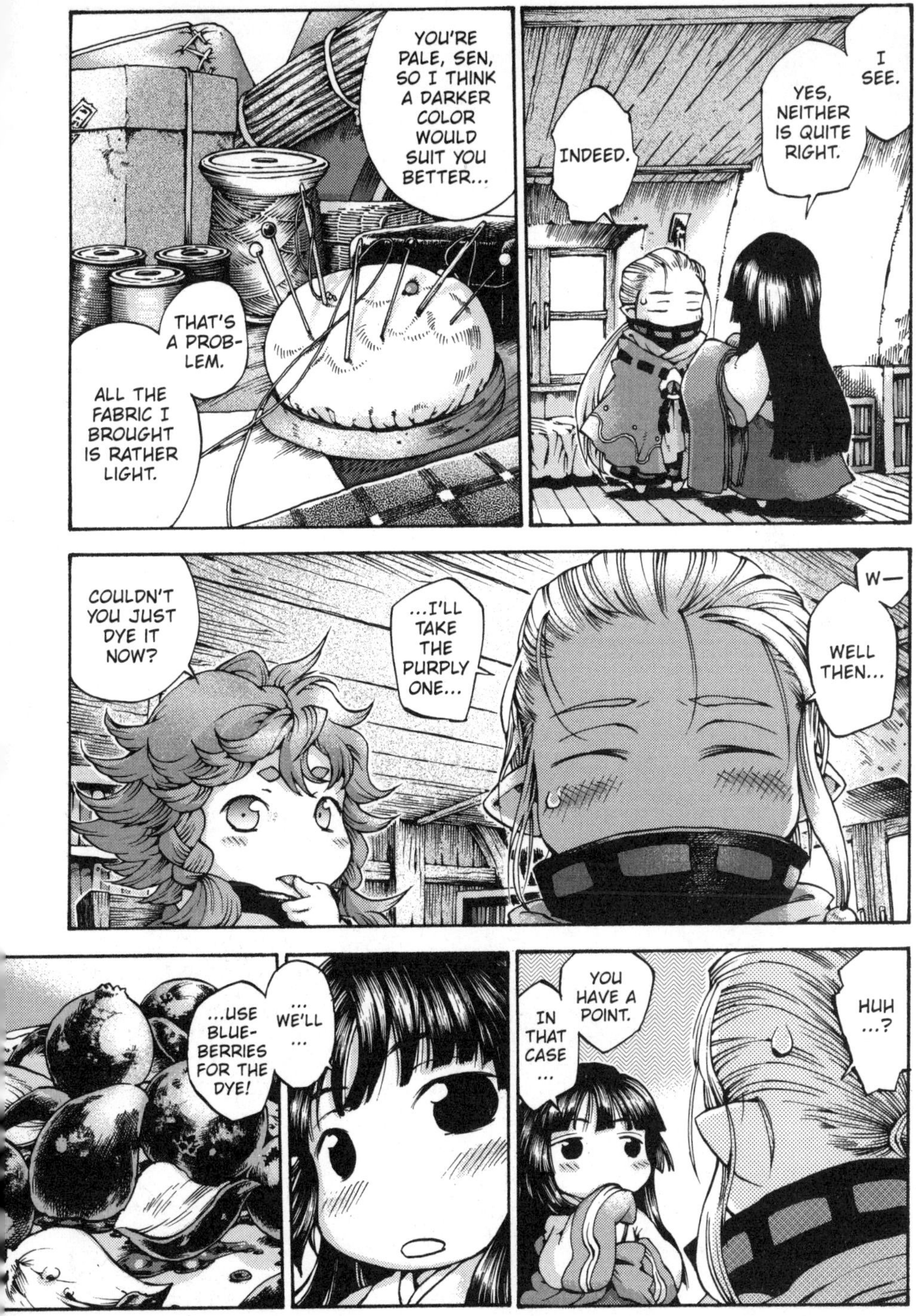
I SEE.
YES, NEITHER IS QUITE RIGHT.
INDEED.
YOU'RE PALE, SEN, SO I THINK A DARKER COLOR WOULD SUIT YOU BETTER...
THAT'S A PROB-LEM.
ALL THE FABRIC I BROUGHT IS RATHER LIGHT.
W—
WELL THEN...
...I'LL TAKE THE PURPLY ONE...
COULDN'T YOU JUST DYE IT NOW?
HUH ...?
YOU HAVE A POINT.
IN THAT CASE ...
... WE'LL ...
...USE BLUE-BERRIES FOR THE DYE!

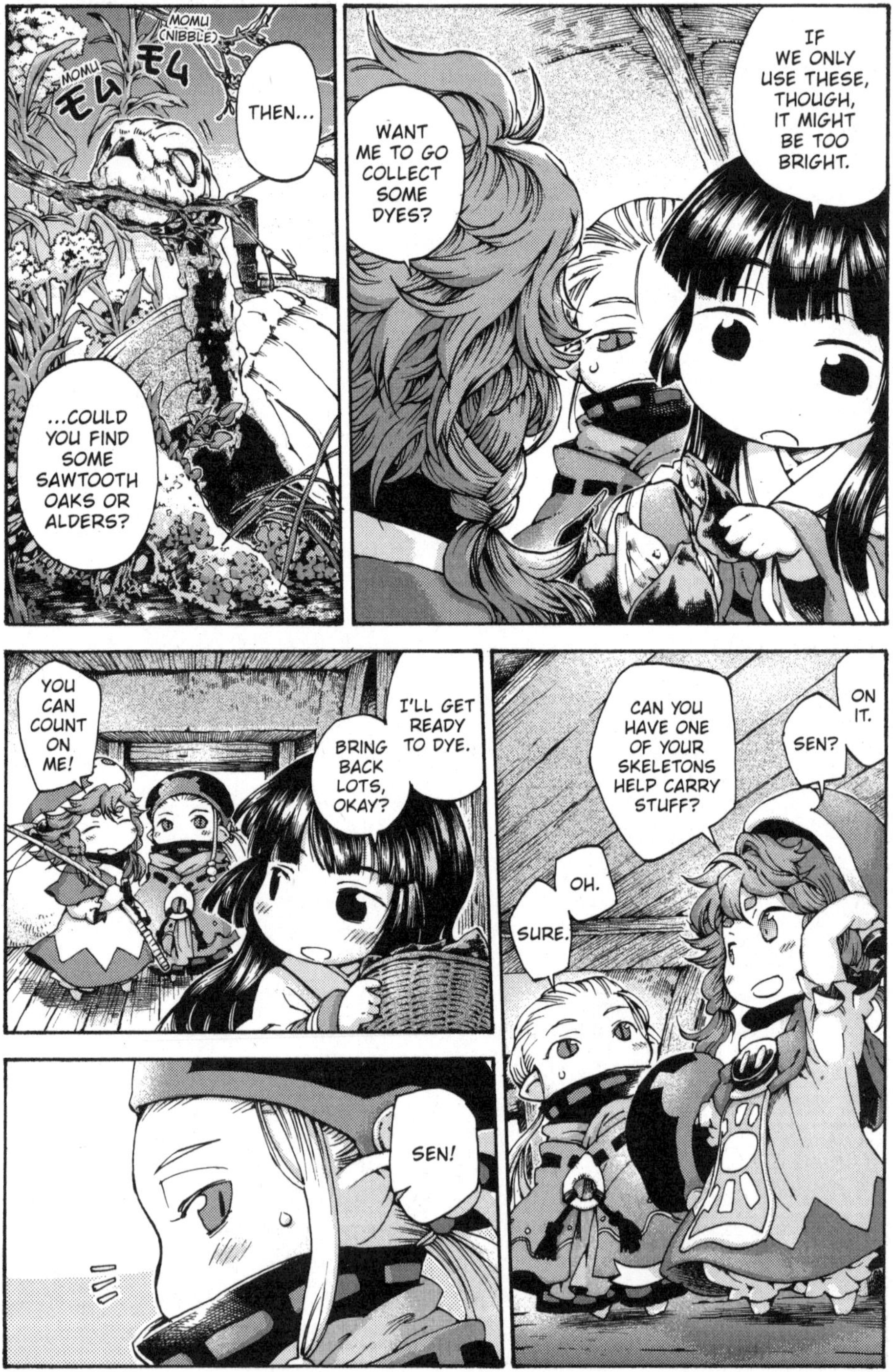
IF WE ONLY USE THESE, THOUGH, IT MIGHT BE TOO BRIGHT.
WANT ME TO GO COLLECT SOME DYES?
MOMU (NIBBLE)
モム モム
MOMU
THEN...
...COULD YOU FIND SOME SAWTOOTH OAKS OR ALDERS?
ON IT.
SEN?
CAN YOU HAVE ONE OF YOUR SKELETONS HELP CARRY STUFF?
OH.
SURE.
I'LL GET READY TO DYE.
BRING BACK LOTS, OKAY?
YOU CAN COUNT ON ME!
SEN!

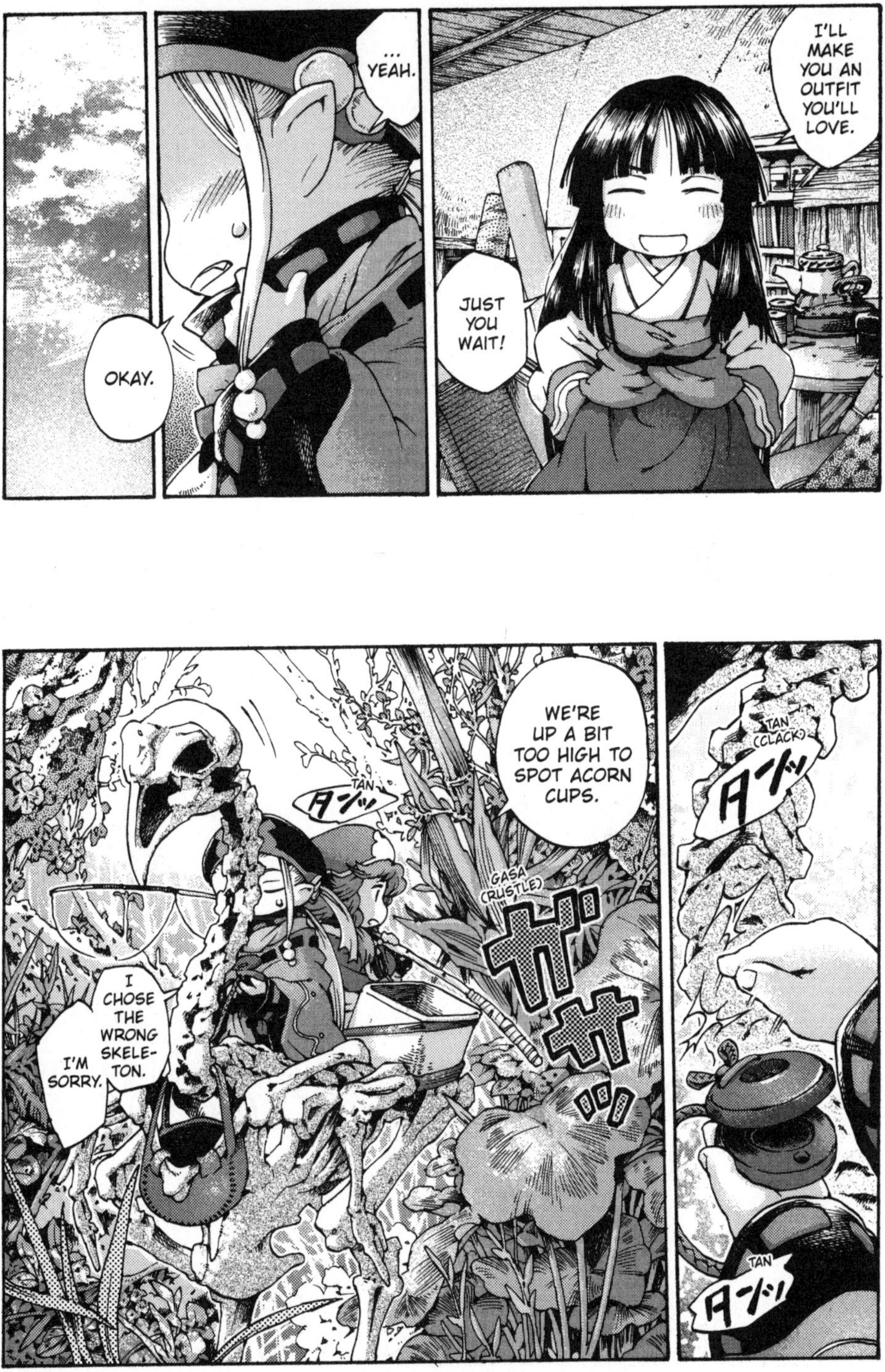
I'LL MAKE YOU AN OUTFIT YOU'LL LOVE.
JUST YOU WAIT!
... YEAH.
OKAY.
TAN (CLACK)
タンッ
TAN
タンッ
WE'RE UP A BIT TOO HIGH TO SPOT ACORN CUPS.
TAN
タンッ
GASA (RUSTLE)
ガサッ
I CHOSE THE WRONG SKELE-TON.
I'M SORRY.

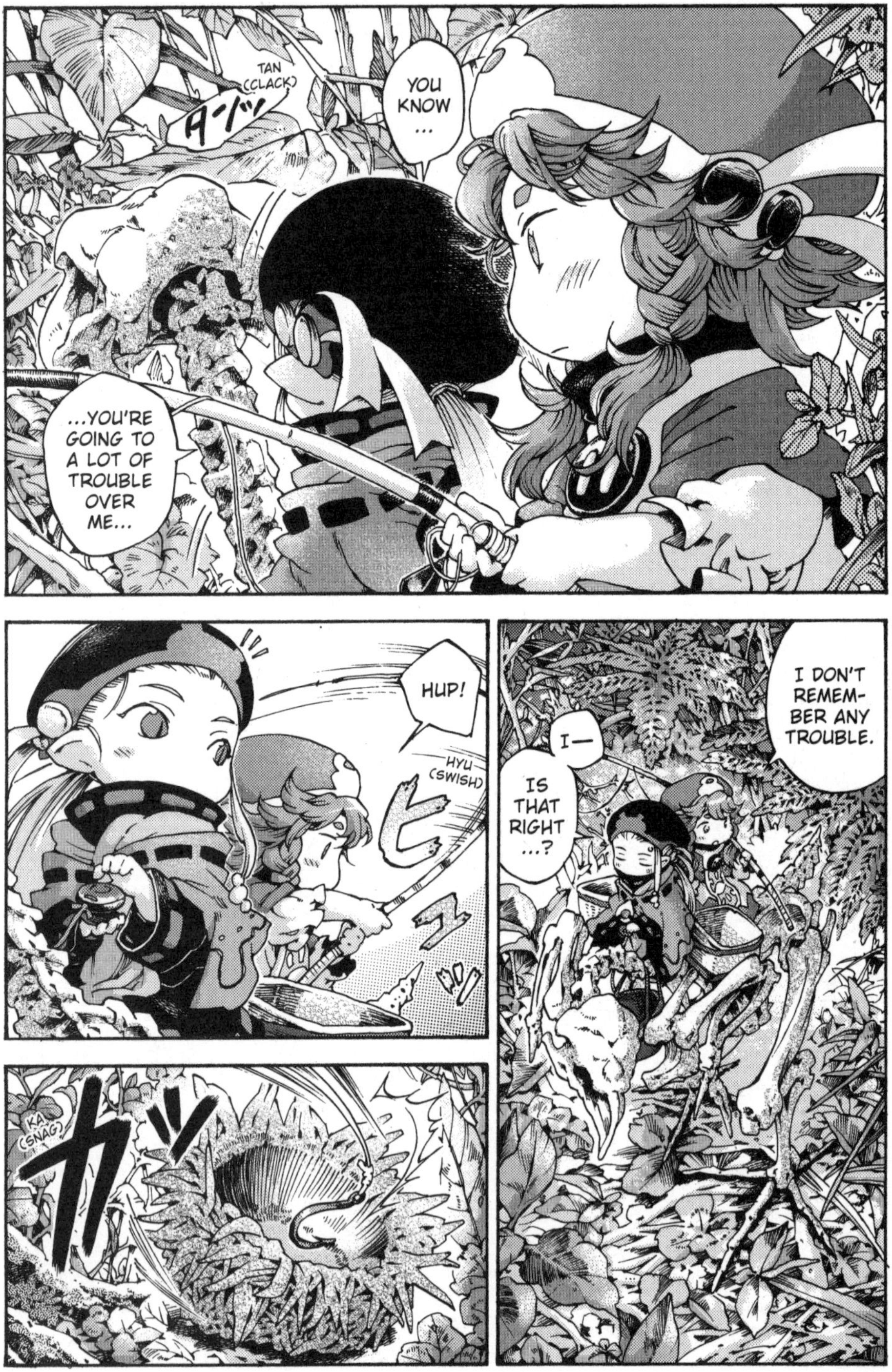
YOU KNOW ...
TAN (CLACK)
...YOU'RE GOING TO A LOT OF TROUBLE OVER ME...
I DON'T REMEMBER ANY TROUBLE.
I—
IS THAT RIGHT ...?
HUP!
HYU (SWISH)
KA (SNAG)

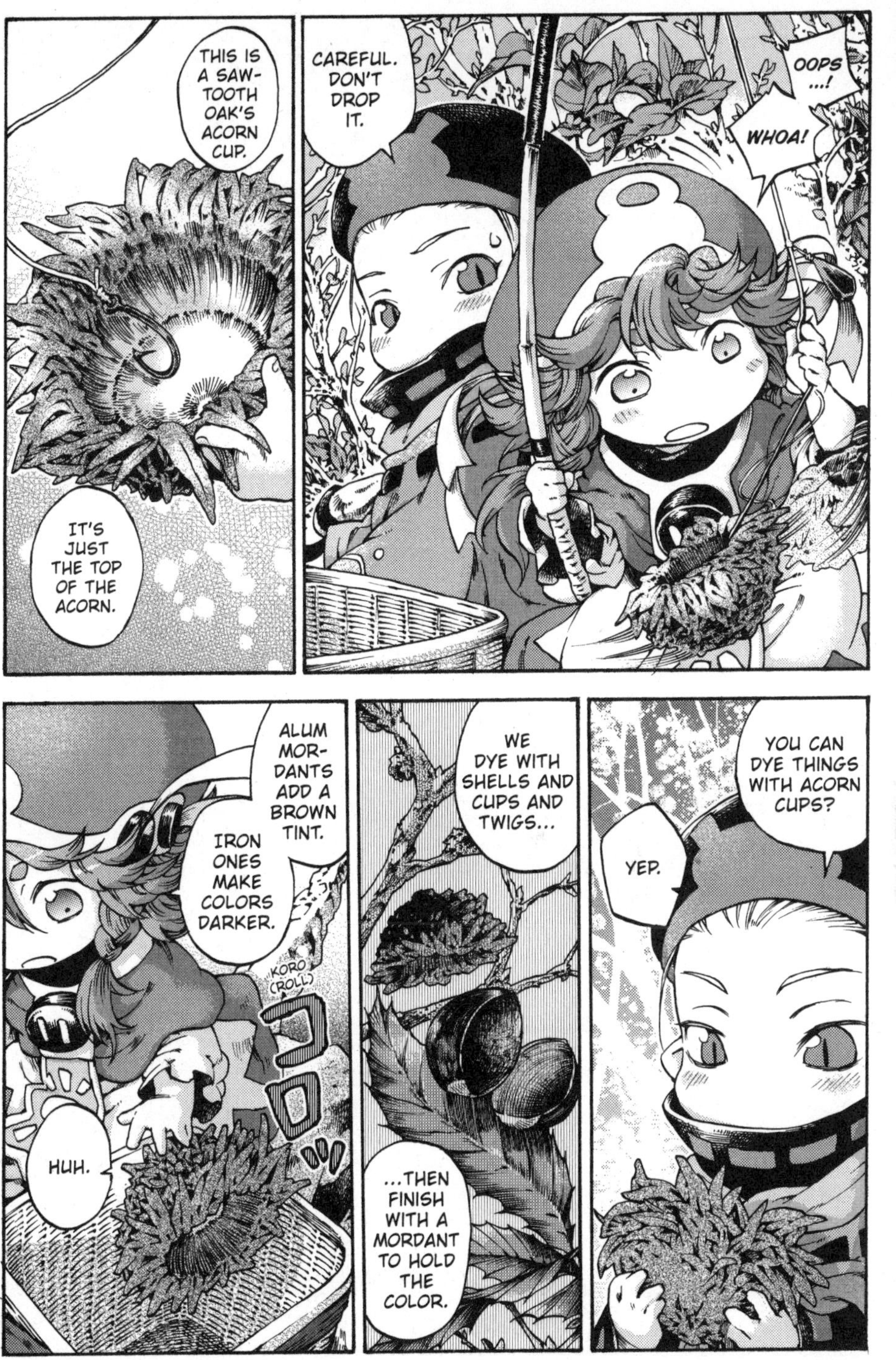
OOPS ...!
WHOA!
CAREFUL. DON'T DROP IT.
THIS IS A SAW-TOOTH OAK'S ACORN CUP.
IT'S JUST THE TOP OF THE ACORN.
YOU CAN DYE THINGS WITH ACORN CUPS?
YEP.
WE DYE WITH SHELLS AND CUPS AND TWIGS...
...THEN FINISH WITH A MORDANT TO HOLD THE COLOR.
ALUM MORDANTS ADD A BROWN TINT.
IRON ONES MAKE COLORS DARKER.
コロッ
KORO (ROLL)
HUH.

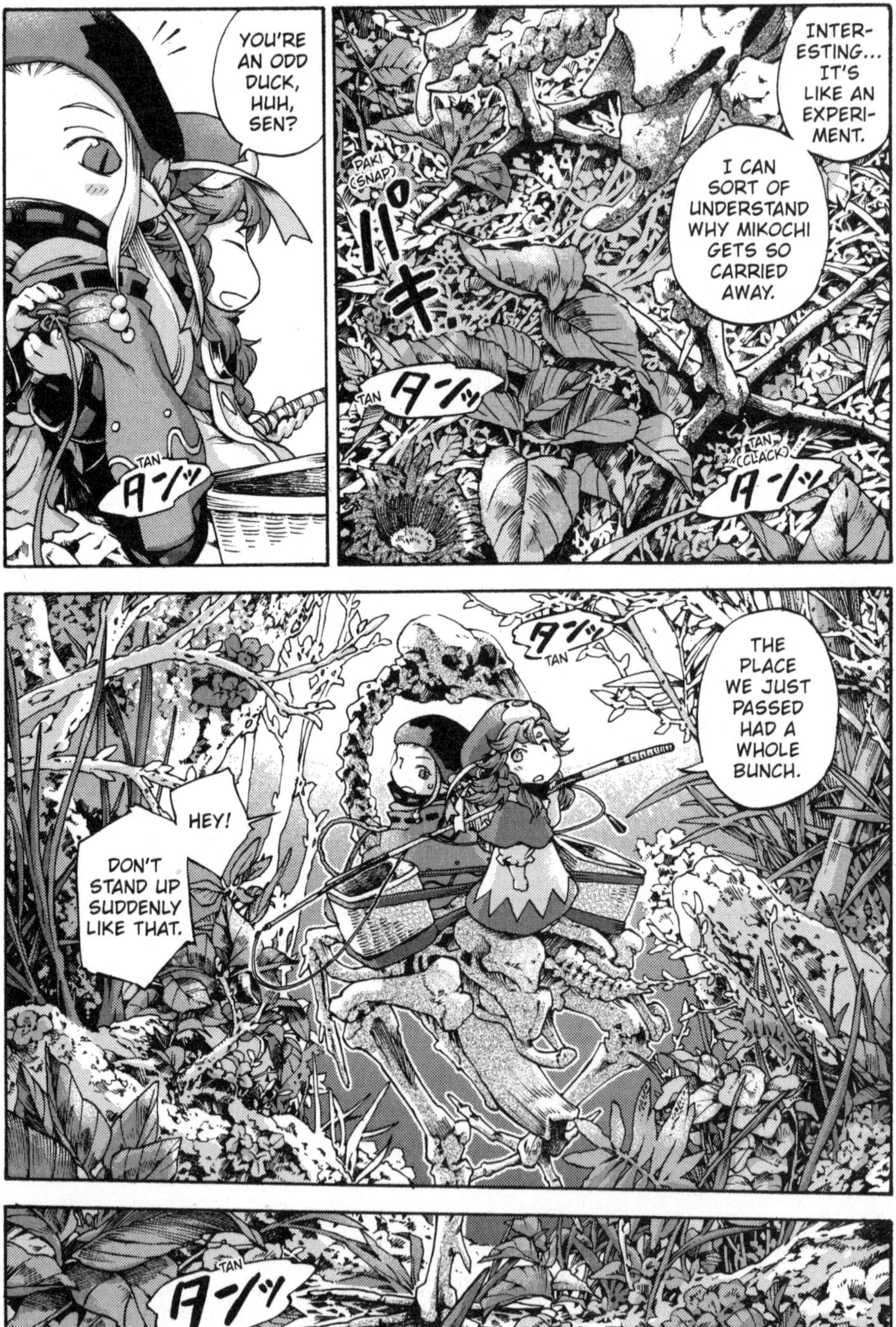
INTER-ESTING... IT'S LIKE AN EXPERI-MENT.
I CAN SORT OF UNDERSTAND WHY MIKOCHI GETS SO CARRIED AWAY.
PAKI (SNAP) パキ
TAN タンッ
TAN (CLACK) タンッ
YOU'RE AN ODD DUCK, HUH, SEN?
TAN タンッ
タンッ TAN
THE PLACE WE JUST PASSED HAD A WHOLE BUNCH.
HEY!
DON'T STAND UP SUDDENLY LIKE THAT.
TAN タンッ

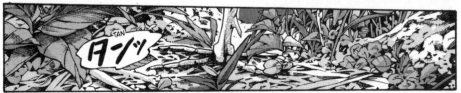

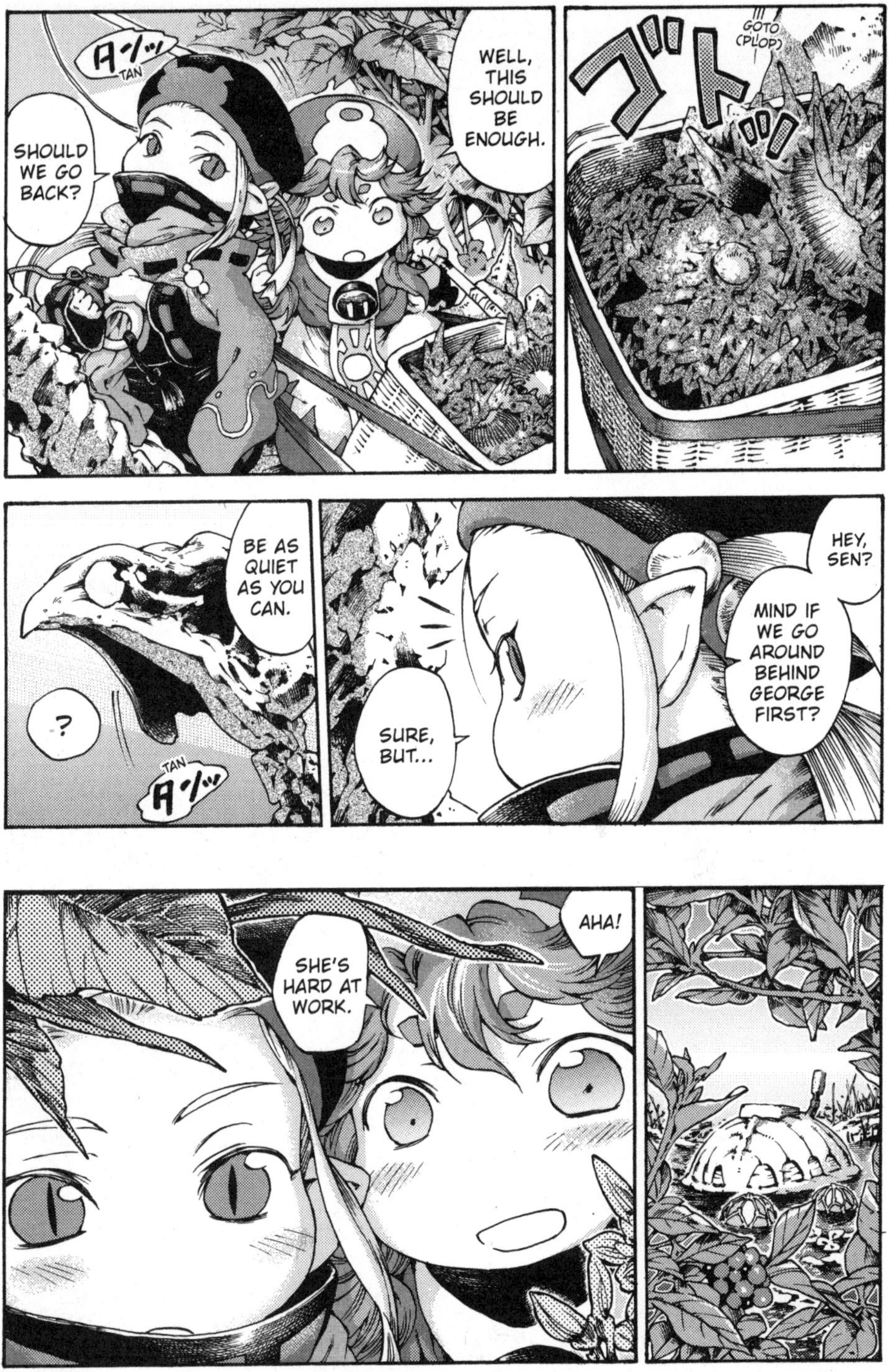
GOTO (PLOP)
WELL, THIS SHOULD BE ENOUGH.
SHOULD WE GO BACK?
TAN
HEY, SEN?
MIND IF WE GO AROUND BEHIND GEORGE FIRST?
SURE, BUT...
BE AS QUIET AS YOU CAN.
?
TAN
AHA!
SHE'S HARD AT WORK.

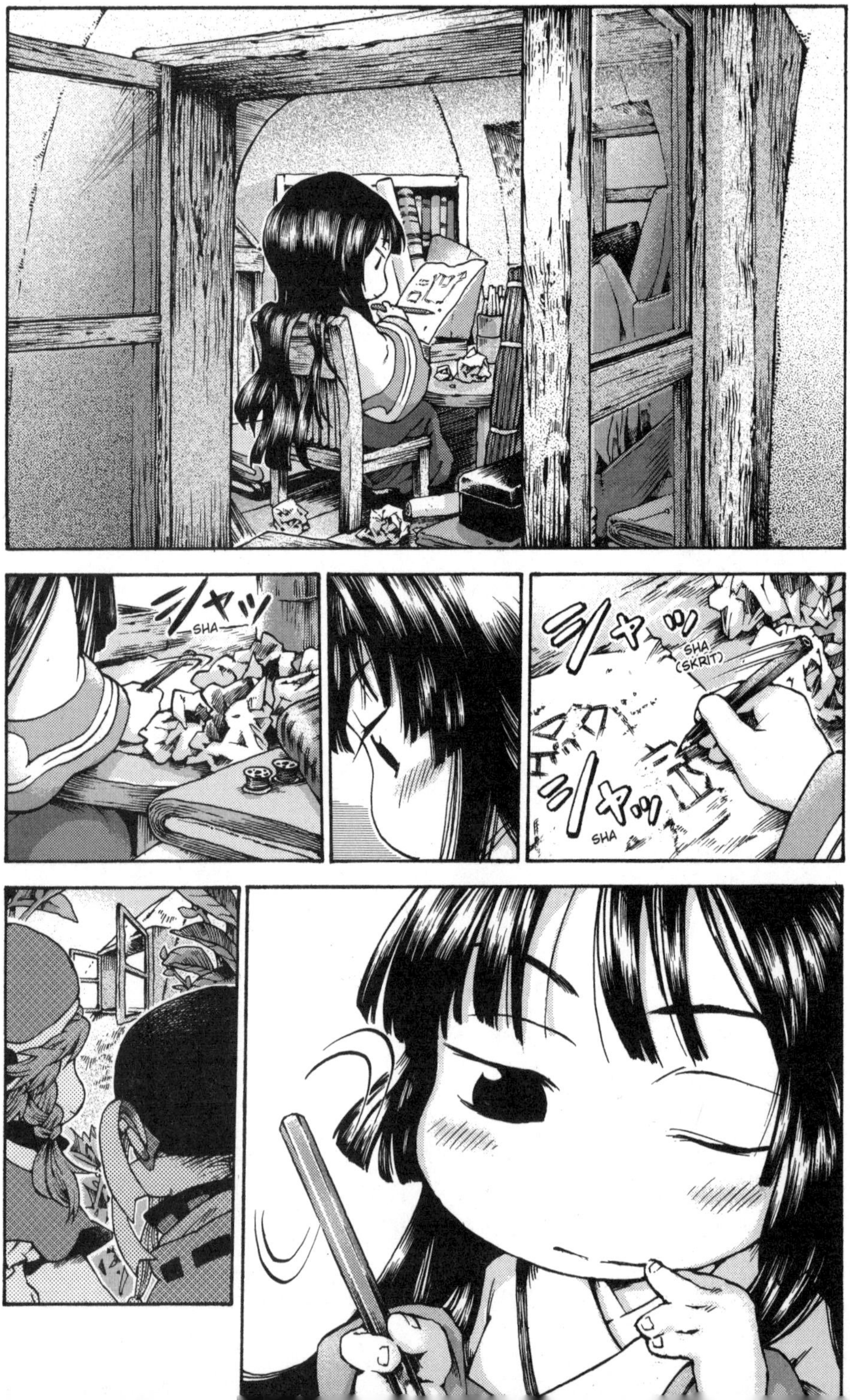
シャッ
SHA (SKRIT)
シャッ
SHA
シャッ
SHA

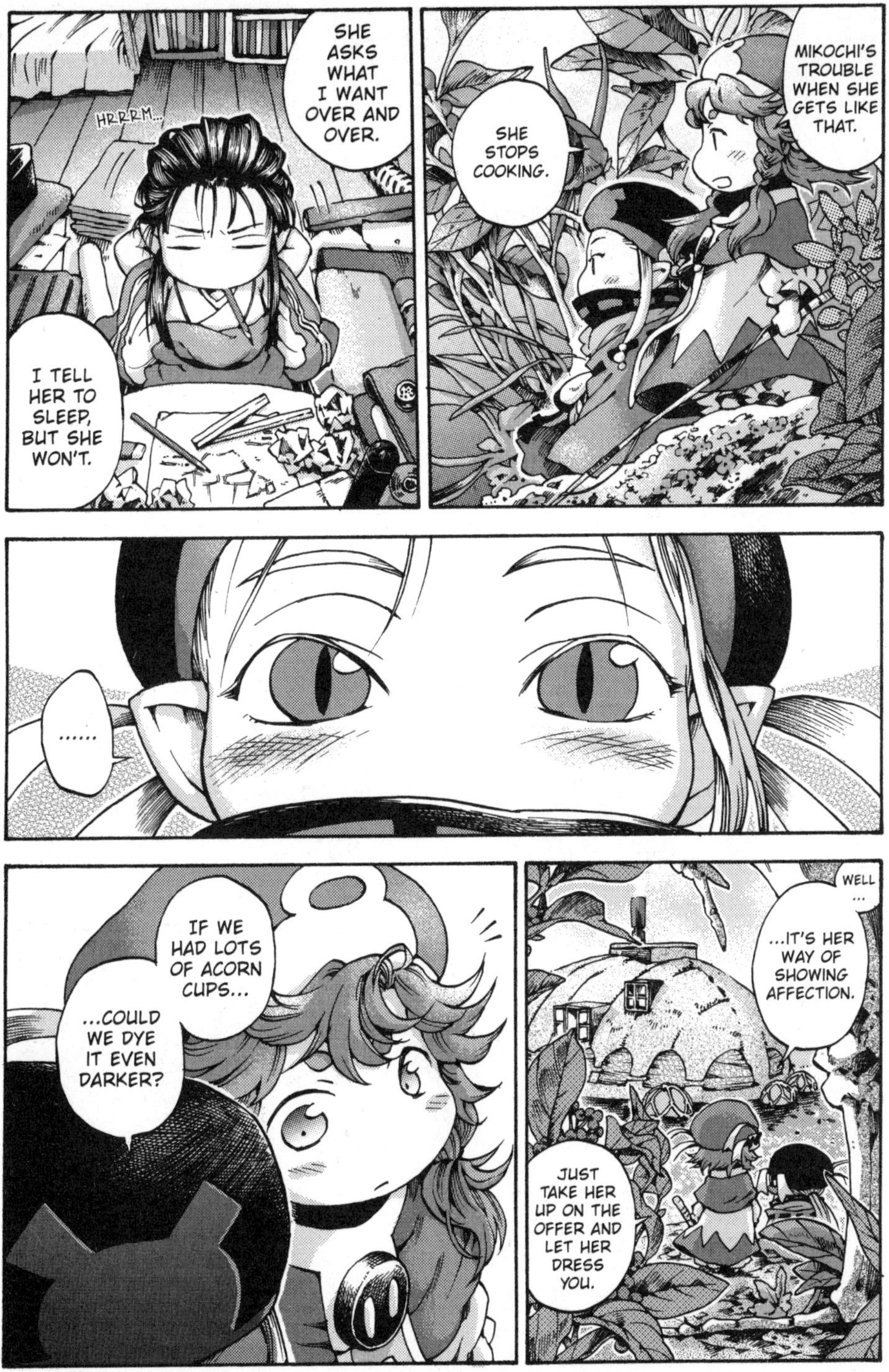
MIKOCHI'S TROUBLE WHEN SHE GETS LIKE THAT.
SHE STOPS COOKING.
SHE ASKS WHAT I WANT OVER AND OVER.
HRRRM...
I TELL HER TO SLEEP, BUT SHE WON'T.
......
WELL...
...IT'S HER WAY OF SHOWING AFFECTION.
JUST TAKE HER UP ON THE OFFER AND LET HER DRESS YOU.
IF WE HAD LOTS OF ACORN CUPS...
...COULD WE DYE IT EVEN DARKER?

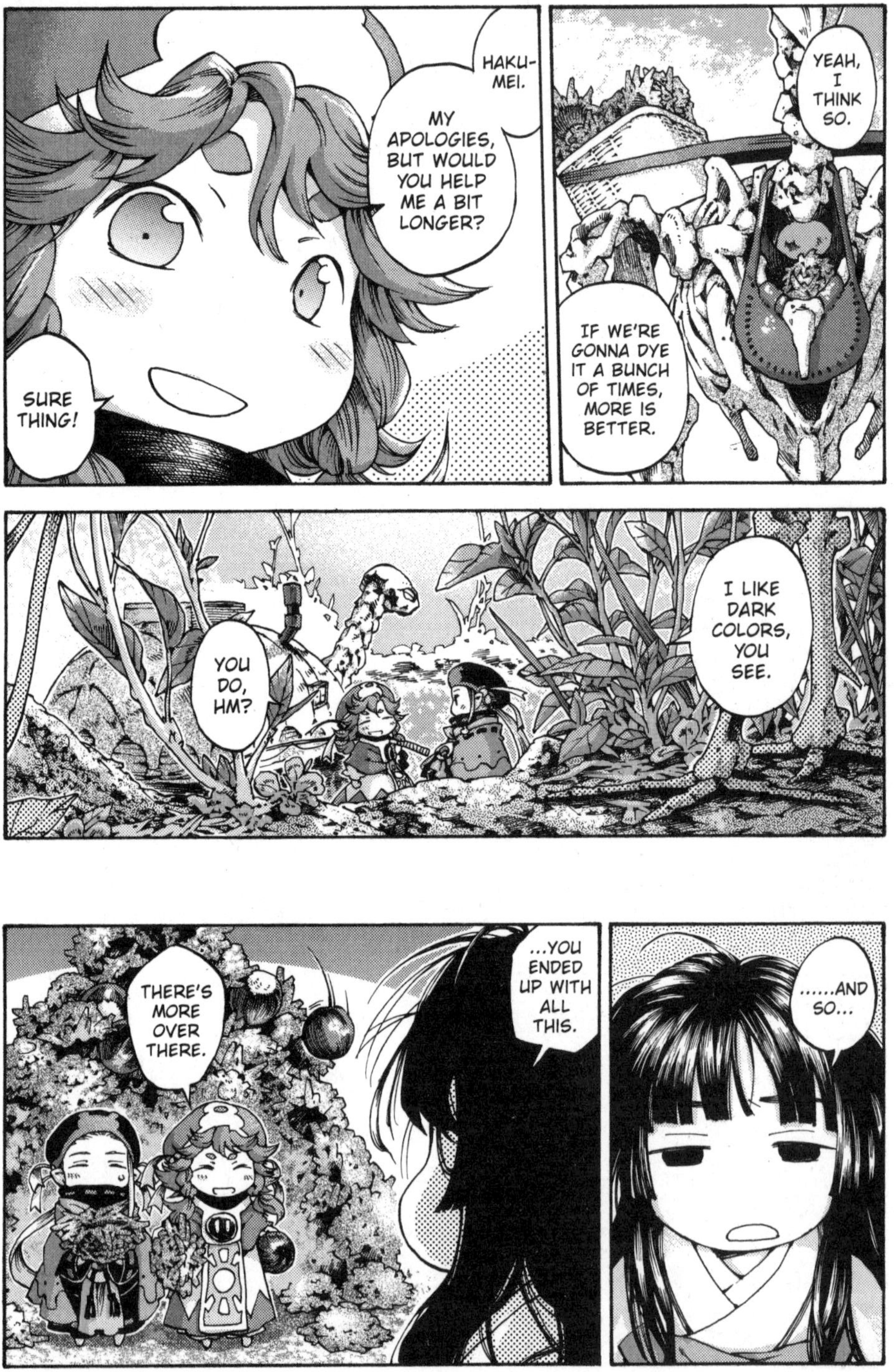
YEAH, I THINK SO.
IF WE'RE GONNA DYE IT A BUNCH OF TIMES, MORE IS BETTER.
HAKU-MEI.
MY APOLOGIES, BUT WOULD YOU HELP ME A BIT LONGER?
SURE THING!
I LIKE DARK COLORS, YOU SEE.
YOU DO, HM?
......AND SO...
...YOU ENDED UP WITH ALL THIS.
THERE'S MORE OVER THERE.

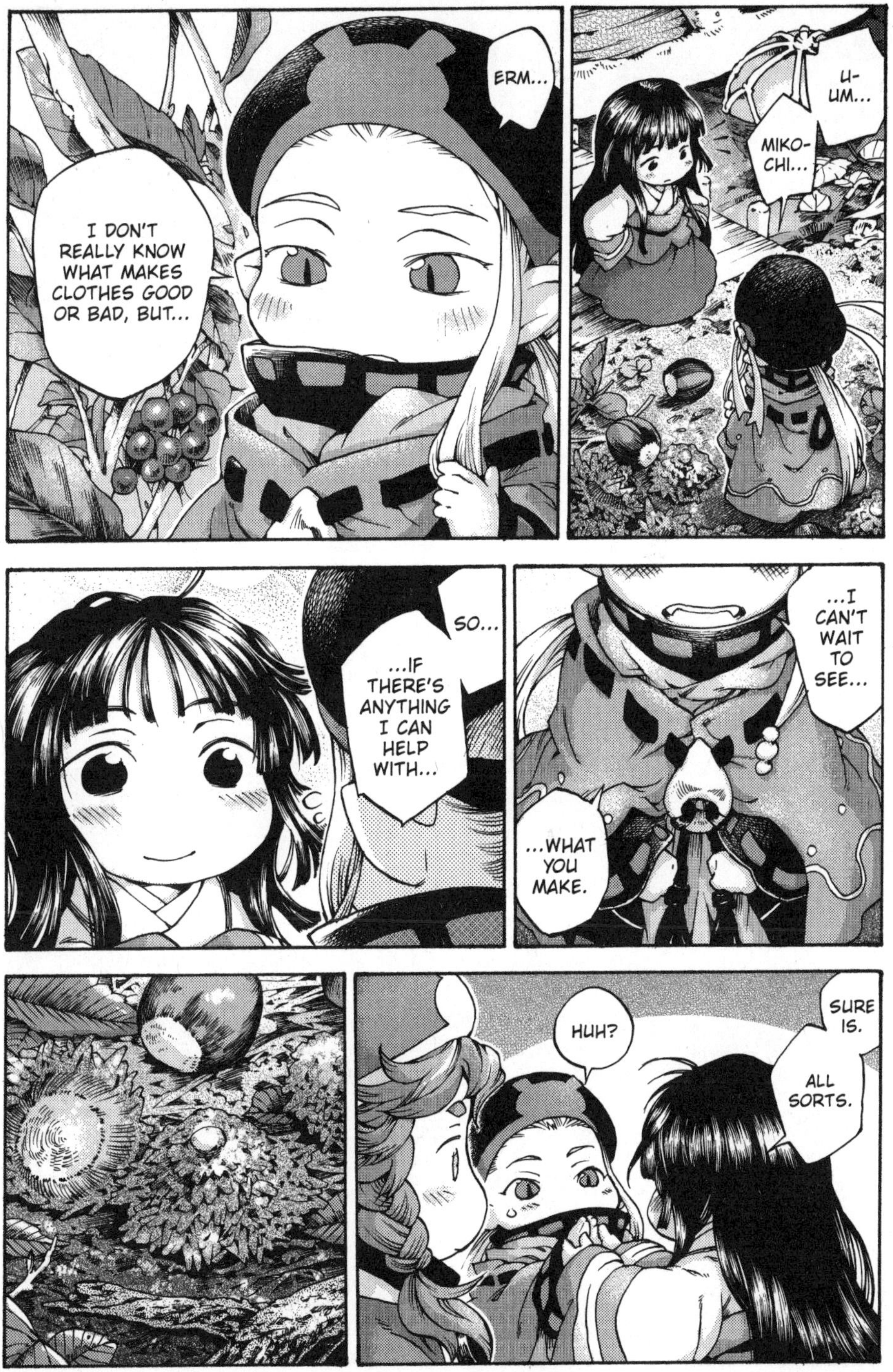
U-UM...
MIKO-CHI...
ERM...
I DON'T REALLY KNOW WHAT MAKES CLOTHES GOOD OR BAD, BUT...
...I CAN'T WAIT TO SEE...
...WHAT YOU MAKE.
SO...
...IF THERE'S ANYTHING I CAN HELP WITH...
SURE IS.
ALL SORTS.
HUH?

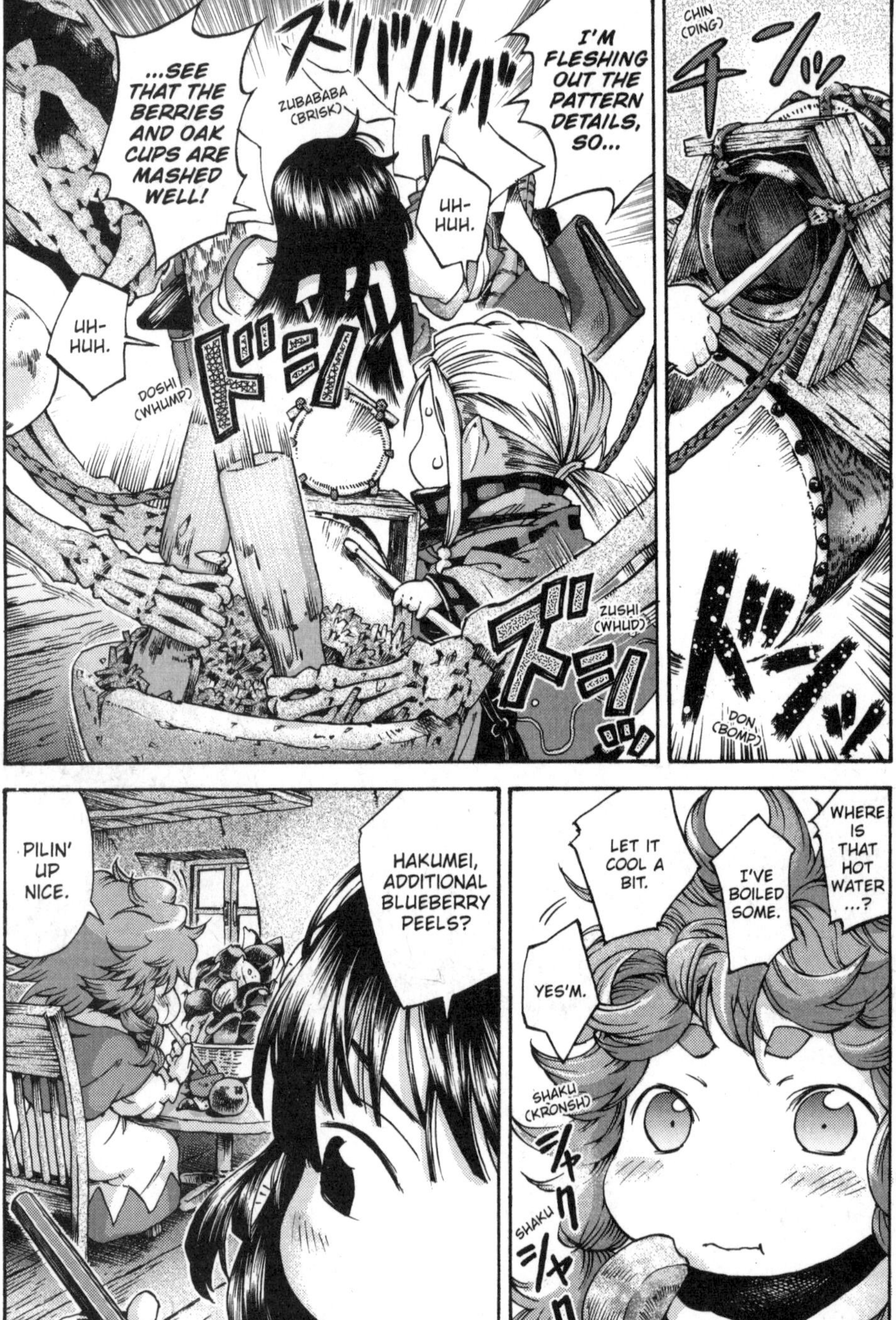
CHIN (DING)
DON (BOMP)
I'M FLESHING OUT THE PATTERN DETAILS, SO...
ZUBABABA (BRISK)
...SEE THAT THE BERRIES AND OAK CUPS ARE MASHED WELL!
UH-HUH.
UH-HUH.
DOSHI (WHUMP)
ZUSHI (WHUD)
WHERE IS THAT HOT WATER ...?
I'VE BOILED SOME.
LET IT COOL A BIT.
YES'M.
SHAKU (KRONSH)
SHAKU
HAKUMEI, ADDITIONAL BLUEBERRY PEELS?
PILIN' UP NICE.

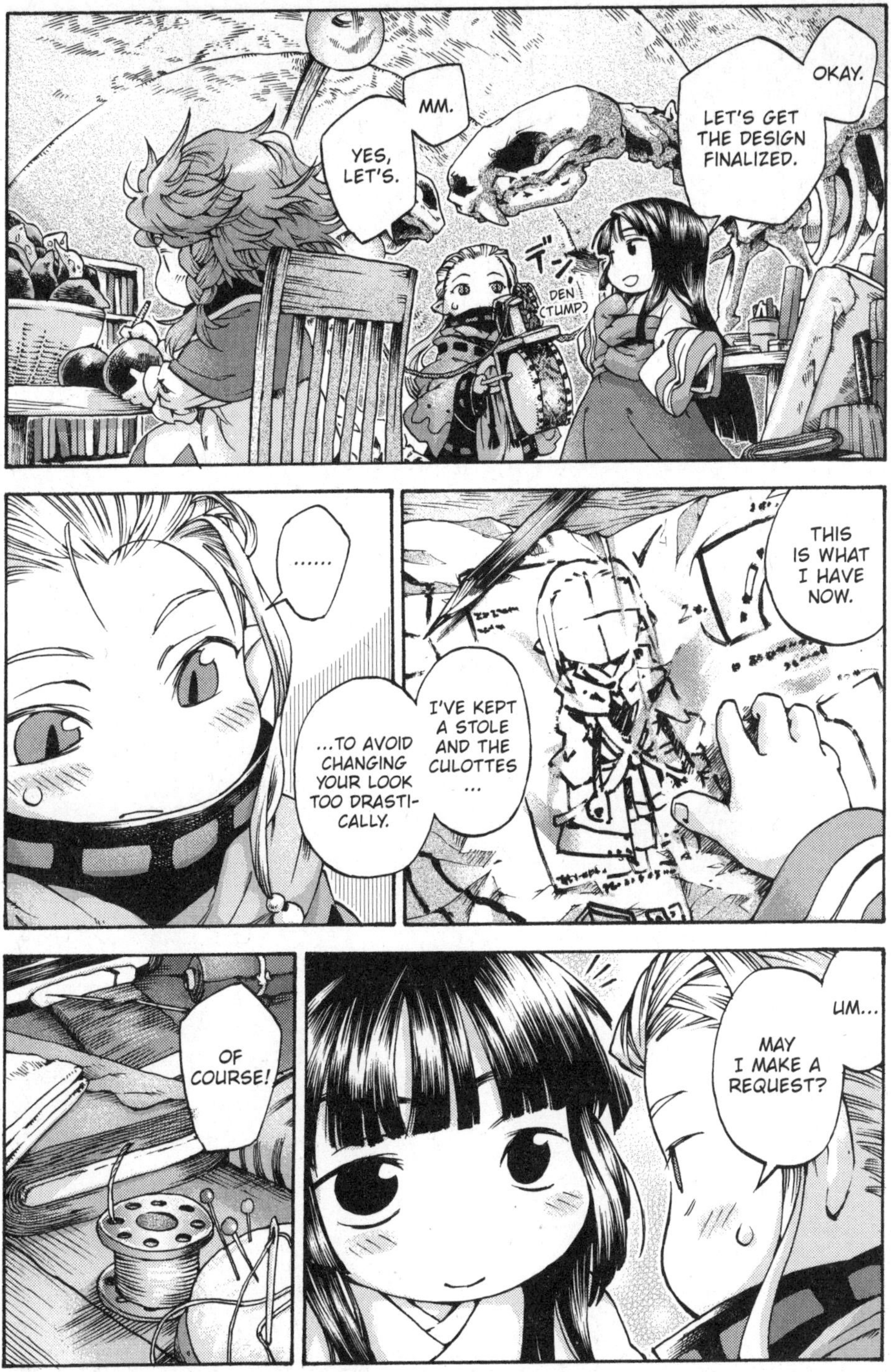
OKAY.
LET'S GET THE DESIGN FINALIZED.
MM.
YES, LET'S.
デン
DEN (TUMP)
THIS IS WHAT I HAVE NOW.
I'VE KEPT A STOLE AND THE CULOTTES ...
...TO AVOID CHANGING YOUR LOOK TOO DRASTICALLY.
......
UM...
MAY I MAKE A REQUEST?
OF COURSE!

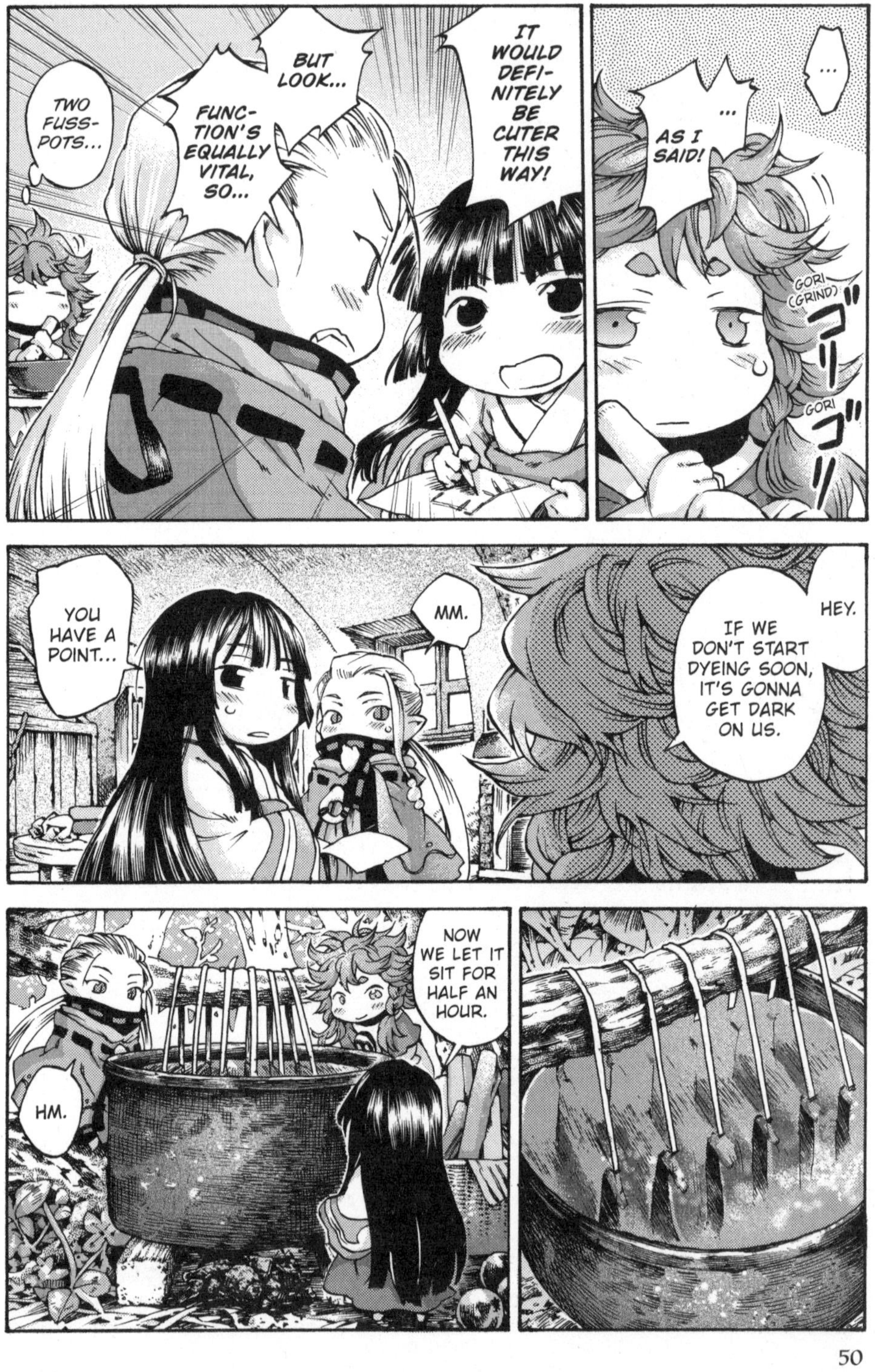
...
...
AS I SAID!
GORI (GRIND)
ゴリ
GORI
ゴリ
IT WOULD DEFINITELY BE CUTER THIS WAY!
BUT LOOK...
FUNCTION'S EQUALLY VITAL, SO...
TWO FUSS-POTS...
HEY.
IF WE DON'T START DYEING SOON, IT'S GONNA GET DARK ON US.
MM.
YOU HAVE A POINT...
NOW WE LET IT SIT FOR HALF AN HOUR.
HM.

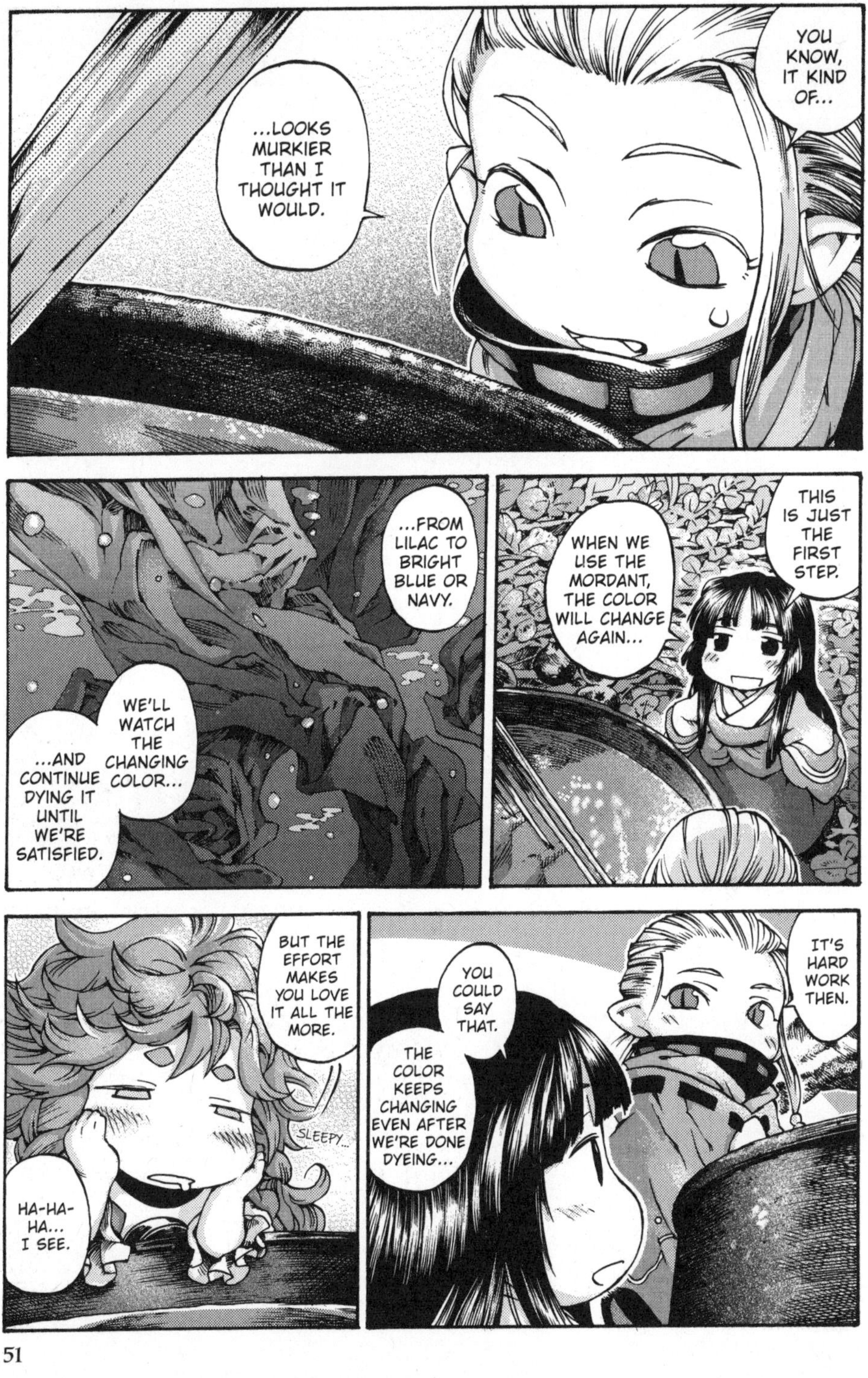
YOU KNOW, IT KIND OF...
...LOOKS MURKIER THAN I THOUGHT IT WOULD.
THIS IS JUST THE FIRST STEP.
WHEN WE USE THE MORDANT, THE COLOR WILL CHANGE AGAIN...
...FROM LILAC TO BRIGHT BLUE OR NAVY.
WE'LL WATCH THE CHANGING COLOR...
...AND CONTINUE DYING IT UNTIL WE'RE SATISFIED.
IT'S HARD WORK THEN.
YOU COULD SAY THAT.
THE COLOR KEEPS CHANGING EVEN AFTER WE'RE DONE DYEING...
BUT THE EFFORT MAKES YOU LOVE IT ALL THE MORE.
SLEEPY...
HA-HA-HA... I SEE.

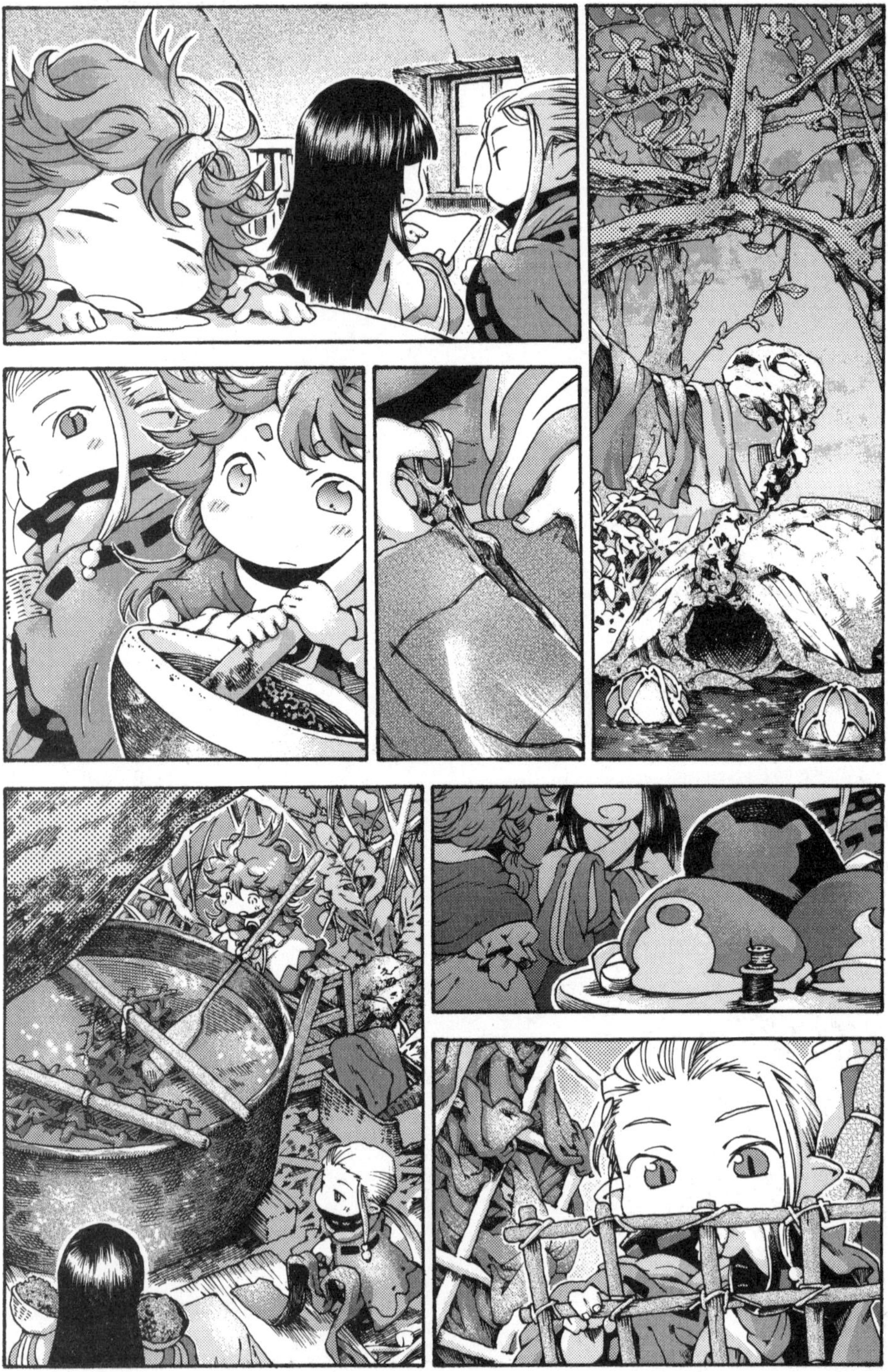

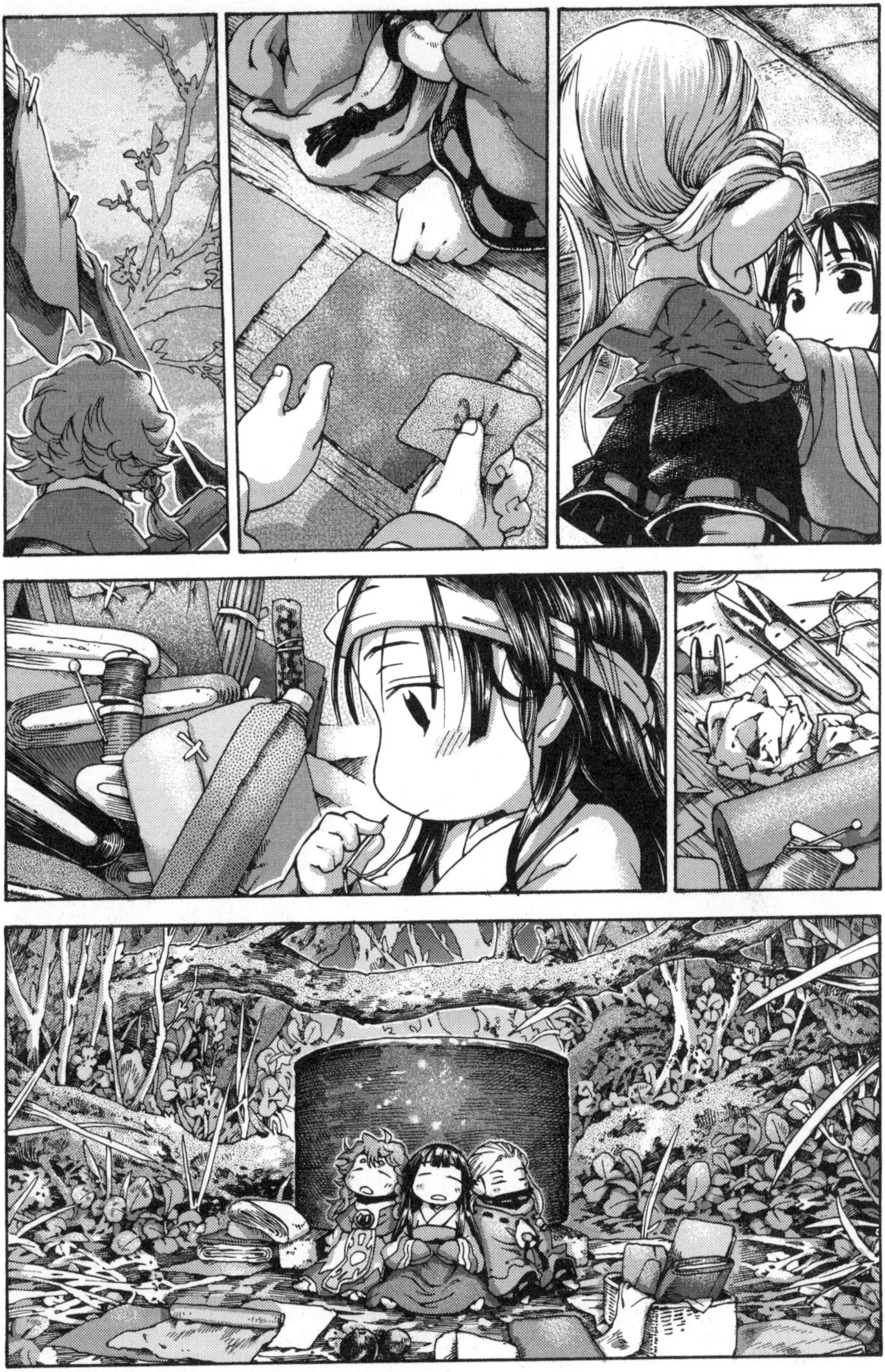

OKAY! IT'S DONE!

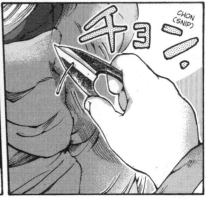

CHON (SNIP)

HOW...

...DOES IT LOOK?

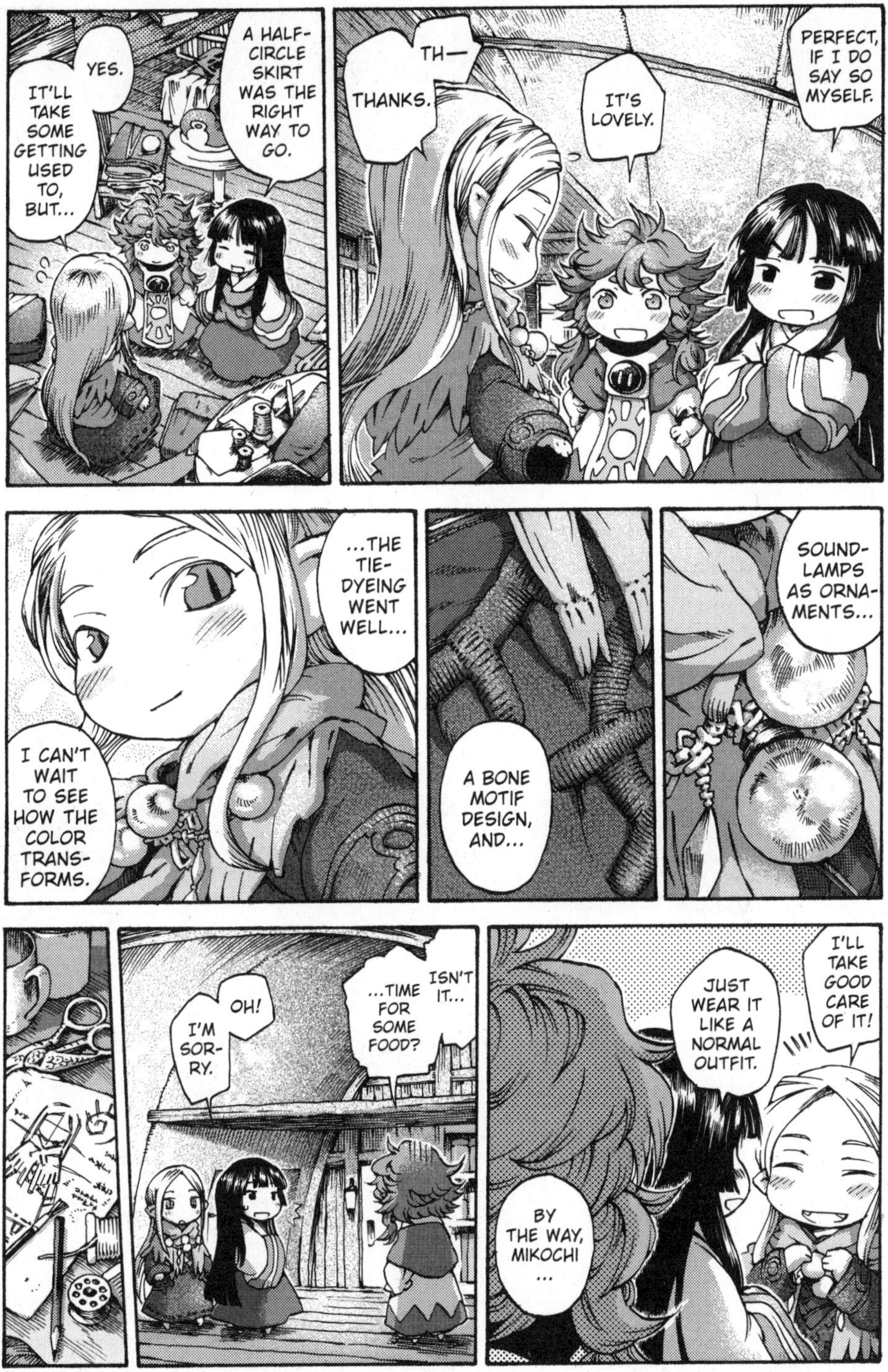
PERFECT, IF I DO SAY SO MYSELF.
IT'S LOVELY.
TH—
THANKS.
A HALF-CIRCLE SKIRT WAS THE RIGHT WAY TO GO.
YES.
IT'LL TAKE SOME GETTING USED TO, BUT...
SOUND-LAMPS AS ORNAMENTS...
A BONE MOTIF DESIGN, AND...
...THE TIE-DYEING WENT WELL...
I CAN'T WAIT TO SEE HOW THE COLOR TRANSFORMS.
I'LL TAKE GOOD CARE OF IT!
JUST WEAR IT LIKE A NORMAL OUTFIT.
BY THE WAY, MIKOCHI ...
ISN'T IT...
...TIME FOR SOME FOOD?
OH!
I'M SORRY.

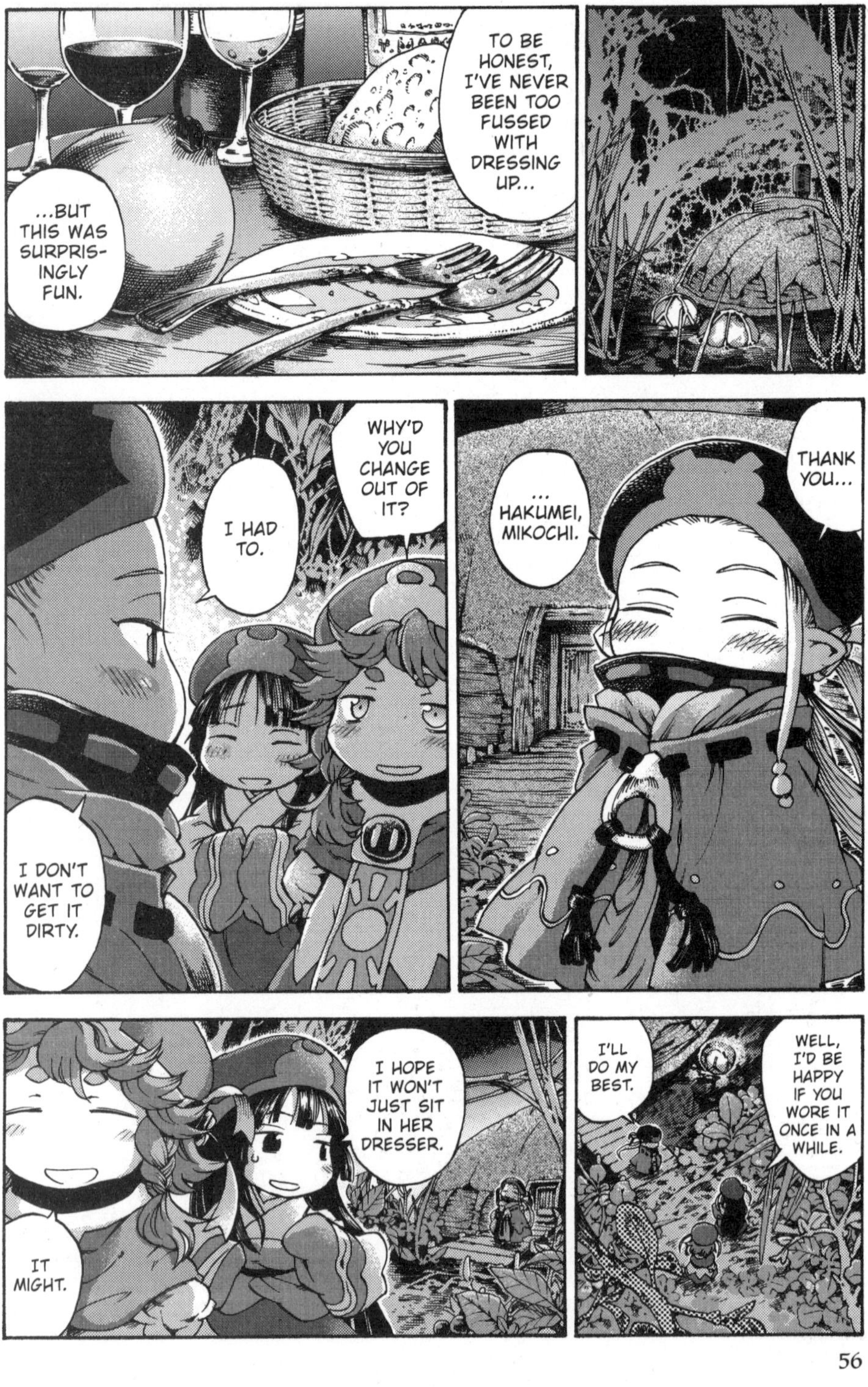
TO BE HONEST, I'VE NEVER BEEN TOO FUSSED WITH DRESSING UP...
...BUT THIS WAS SURPRIS-INGLY FUN.
THANK YOU...
...HAKUMEI, MIKOCHI.
WHY'D YOU CHANGE OUT OF IT?
I HAD TO.
I DON'T WANT TO GET IT DIRTY.
WELL, I'D BE HAPPY IF YOU WORE IT ONCE IN A WHILE.
I'LL DO MY BEST.
I HOPE IT WON'T JUST SIT IN HER DRESSER.
IT MIGHT.

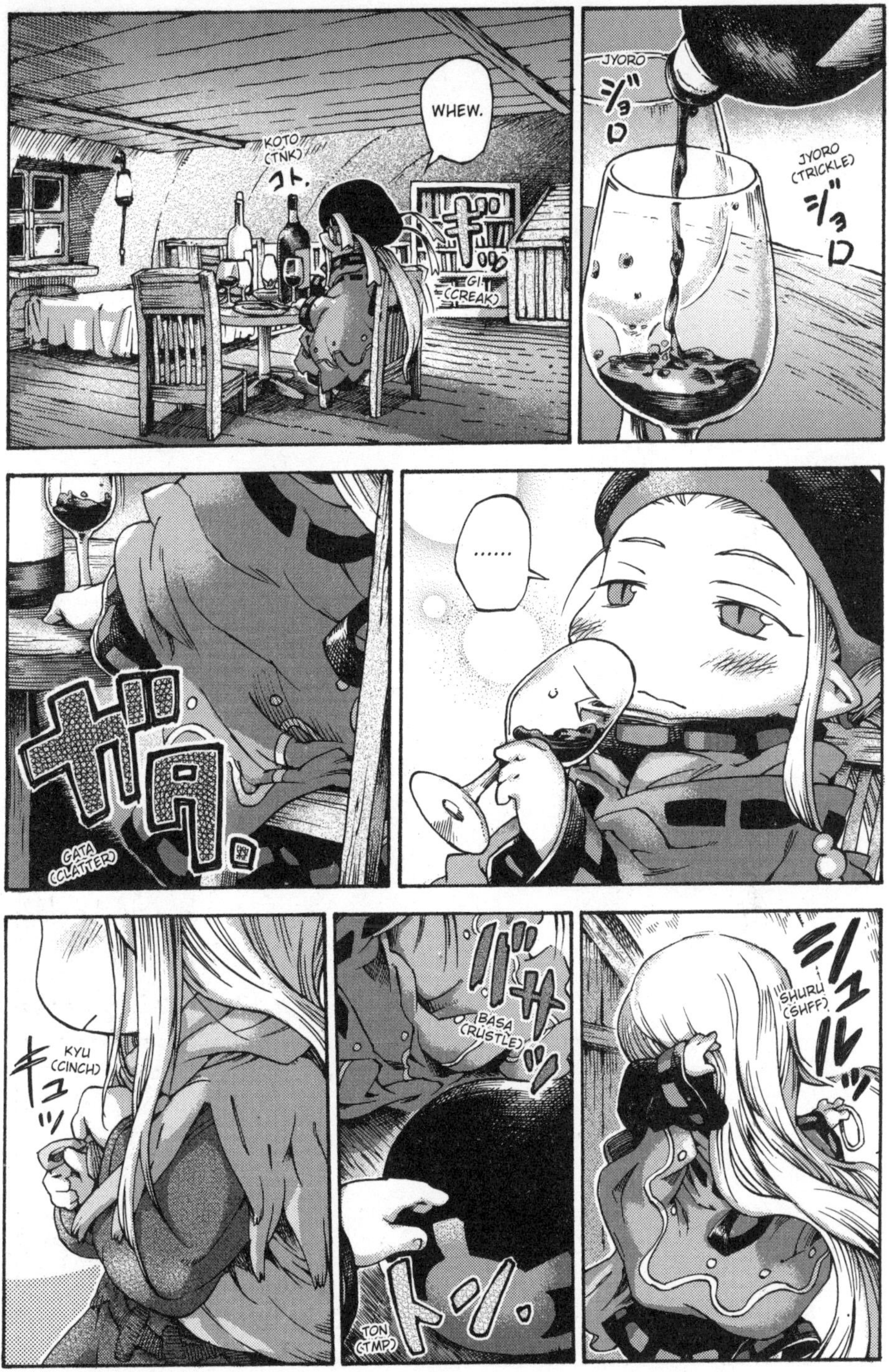
JYORO
ジョロ
JYORO (TRICKLE)
ジョロ
WHEW.
KOTO (TNK)
コト.
ギッ
GI (CREAK)
......
ガタ。
GATA (CLATTER)
シュルッ
SHURU (SHFF)
バサッ
BASA (RUSTLE)
トン.
TON (TMP)
KYU (CINCH)
キュッ

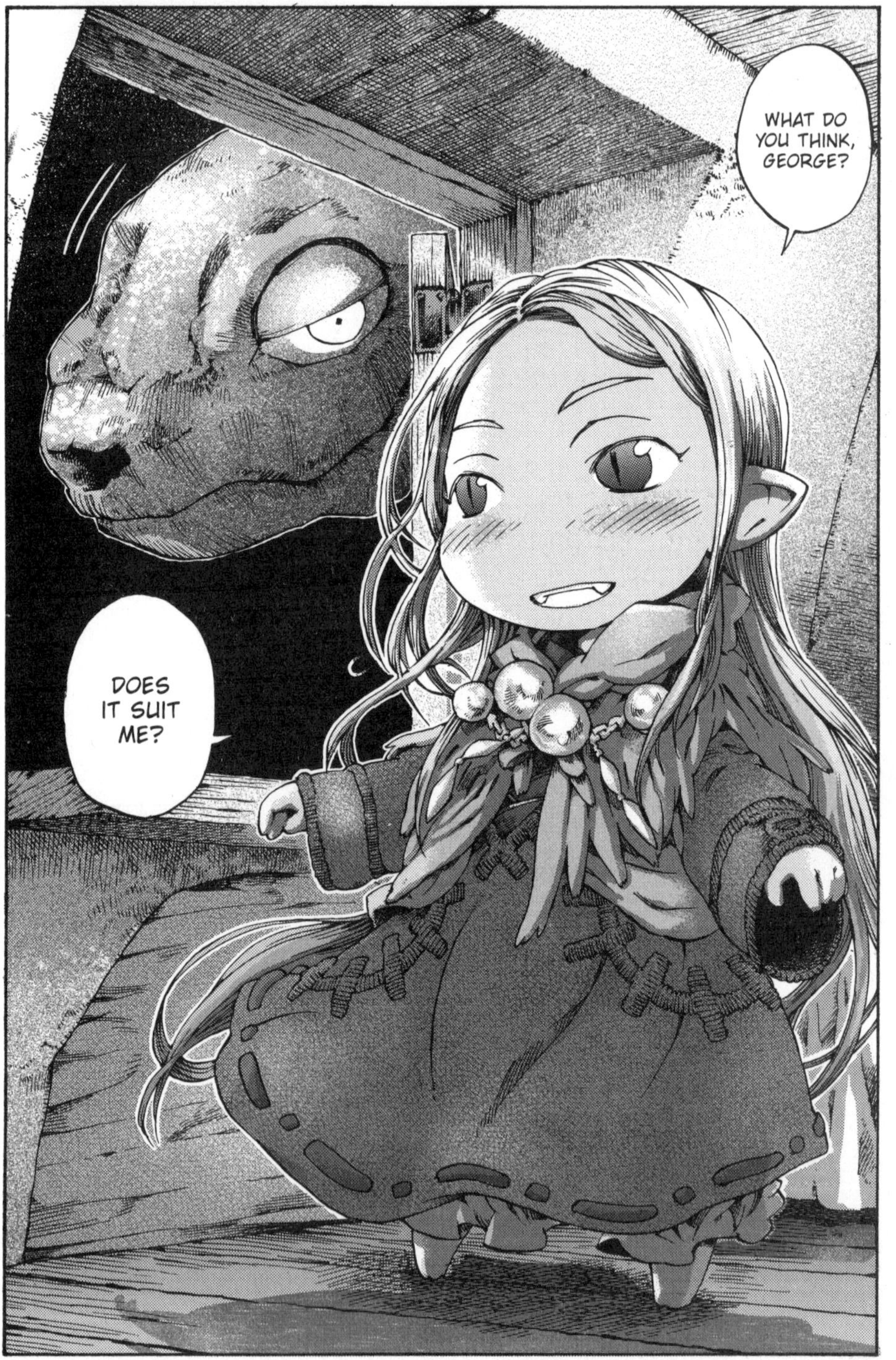
WHAT DO YOU THINK, GEORGE?
DOES IT SUIT ME?

"You have a fair complexion, Sen, so cool colors look good on you."

"D-do they?"

"On the other hand, we could go with one crisp, bold color all over..."

"Uh-huh."

"...Or use a lot of primary colors for a fitted look. That would be cute too."

"Oh...yeah?"

"We could even do a layered look with matte, translucent fabrics..."

"Lay—
What?"

"You know, I'd like to try making boyish clothes too."

"Go ahead and do whatever you like......"

Chapter 11
The Union Work Site

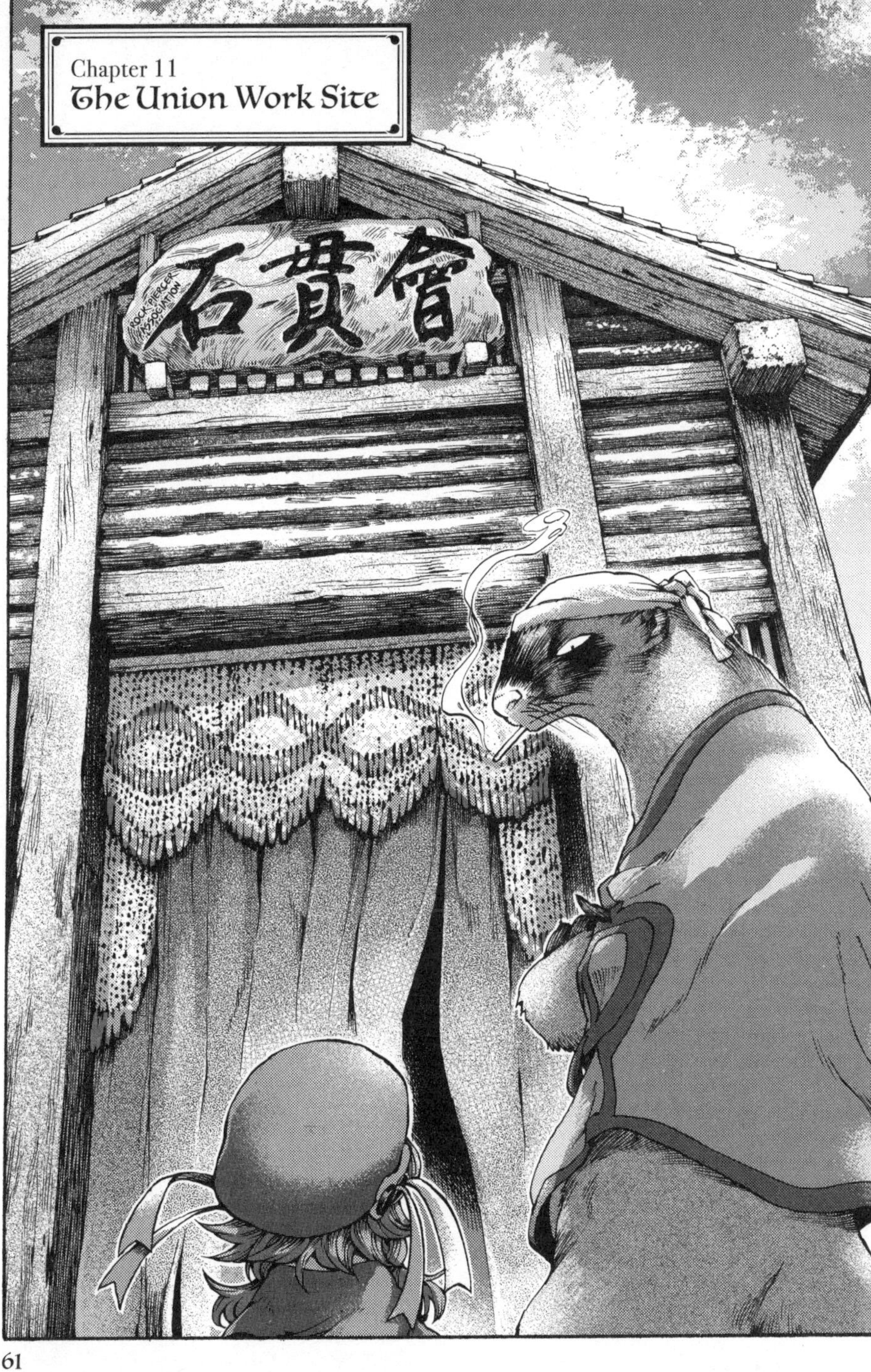
石貫會
ROCK PIERCER ASSOCIATION

SIGN: ROCK PIERCER ASSOCIATION

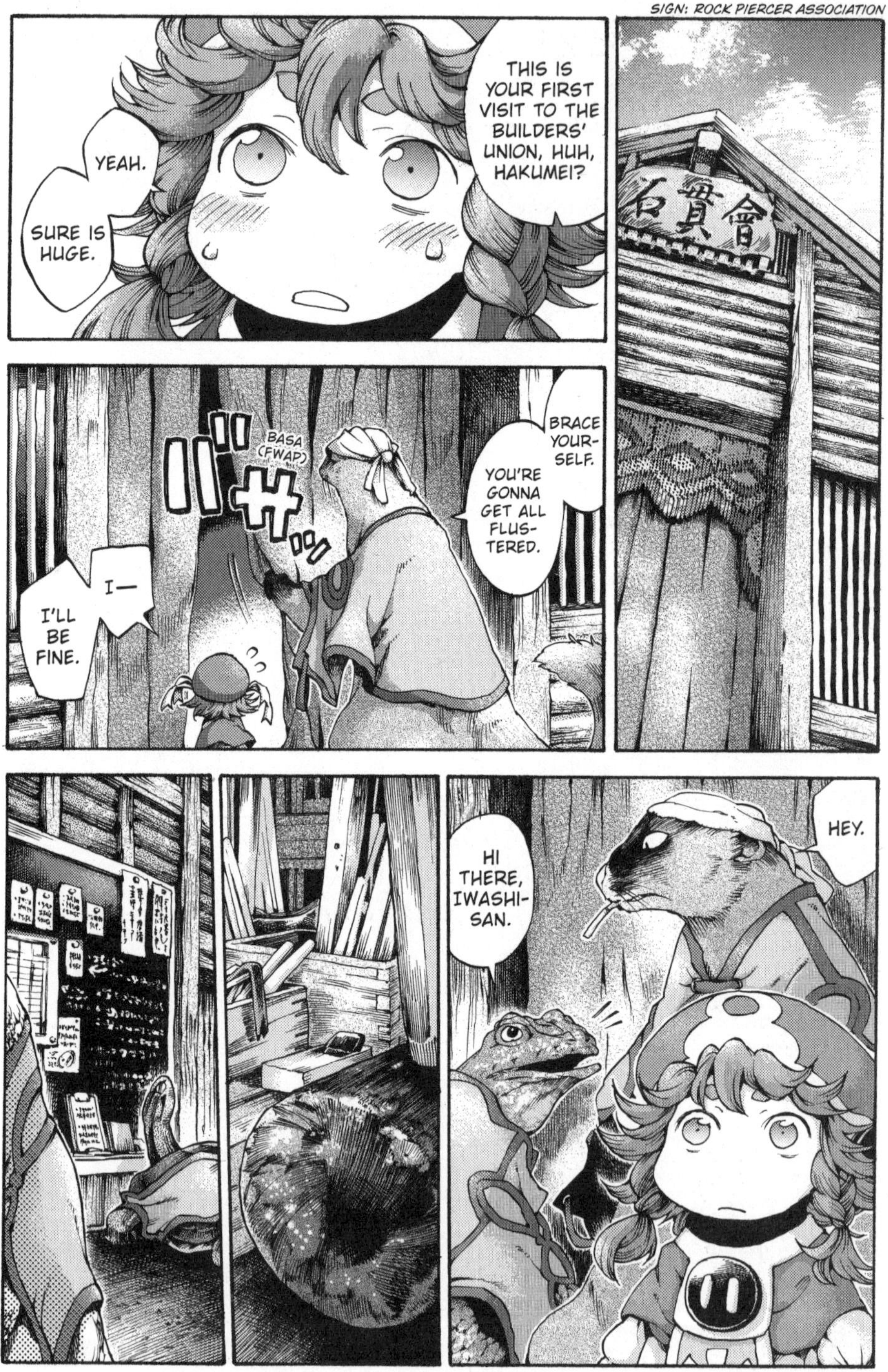
石貫會
THIS IS YOUR FIRST VISIT TO THE BUILDERS' UNION, HUH, HAKUMEI?
YEAH.
SURE IS HUGE.
BRACE YOURSELF.
YOU'RE GONNA GET ALL FLUSTERED.
BASA (FWAP)
I—
I'LL BE FINE.
HEY.
HI THERE, IWASHI-SAN.

SIGN: ROCK PIERCER ASSOCIATION

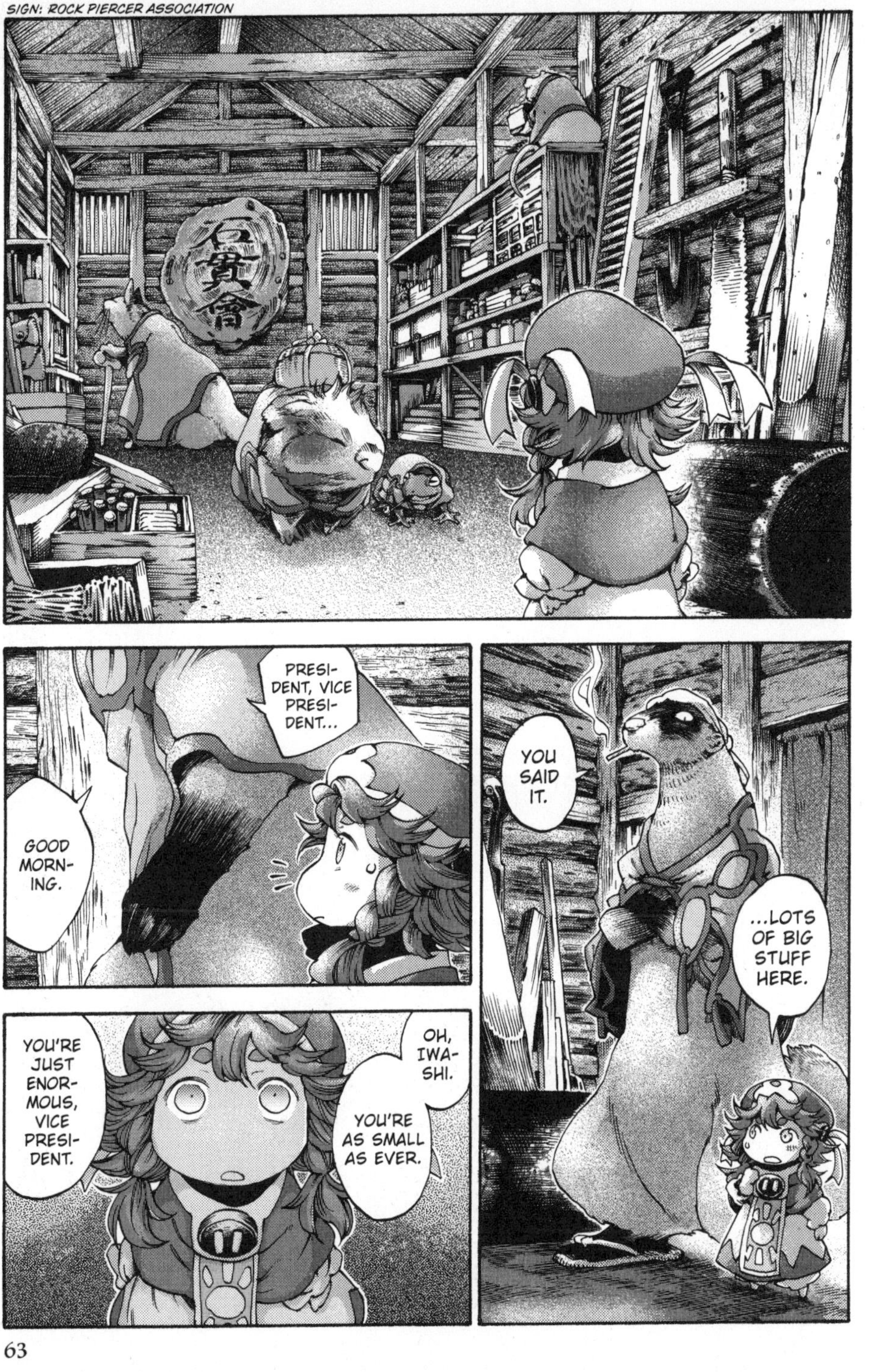
...LOTS OF BIG STUFF HERE.
YOU SAID IT.
PRESIDENT, VICE PRESIDENT...
GOOD MORNING.
OH, IWASHI.
YOU'RE AS SMALL AS EVER.
YOU'RE JUST ENORMOUS, VICE PRESIDENT.

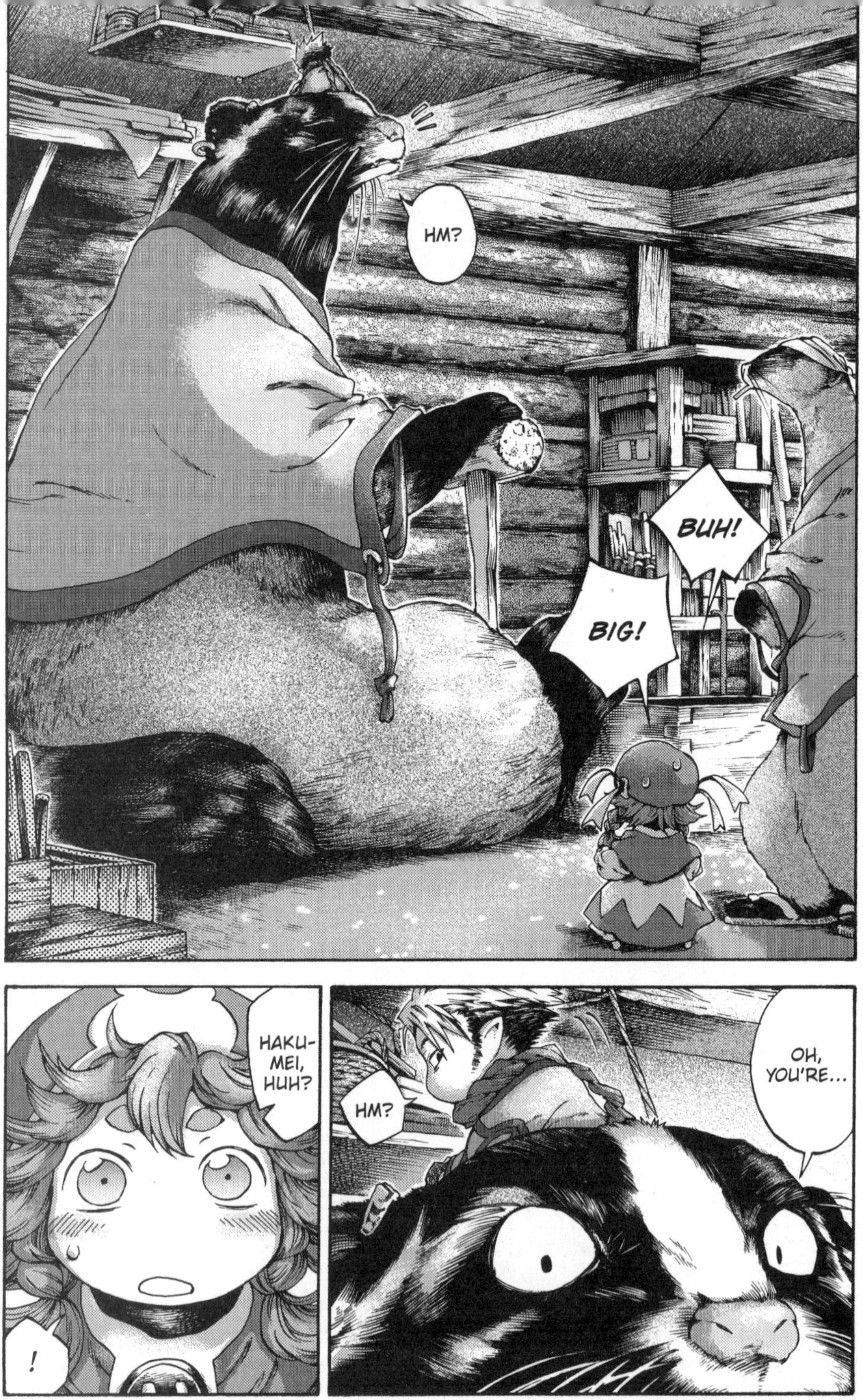
HM?
BUH!
BIG!
OH, YOU'RE...
HM?
HAKU-MEI, HUH?
!

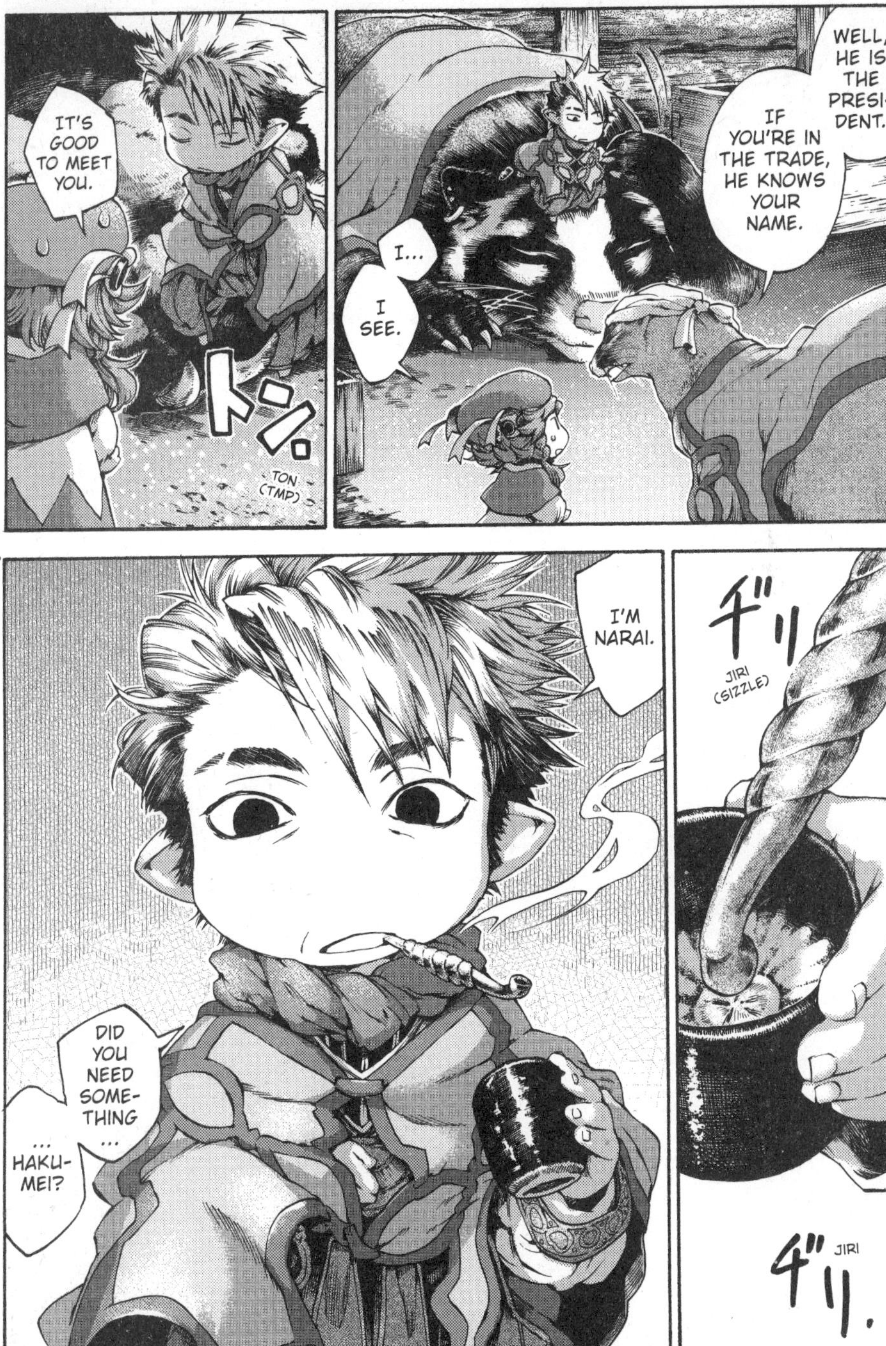
WELL, HE IS THE PRESI-DENT.
IF YOU'RE IN THE TRADE, HE KNOWS YOUR NAME.
I...
I SEE.
IT'S GOOD TO MEET YOU.
トン。
TON (TMP)
ヂリ
JIRI (SIZZLE)
ヂリ。
JIRI
I'M NARAI.
DID YOU NEED SOME-THING ...
... HAKU-MEI?

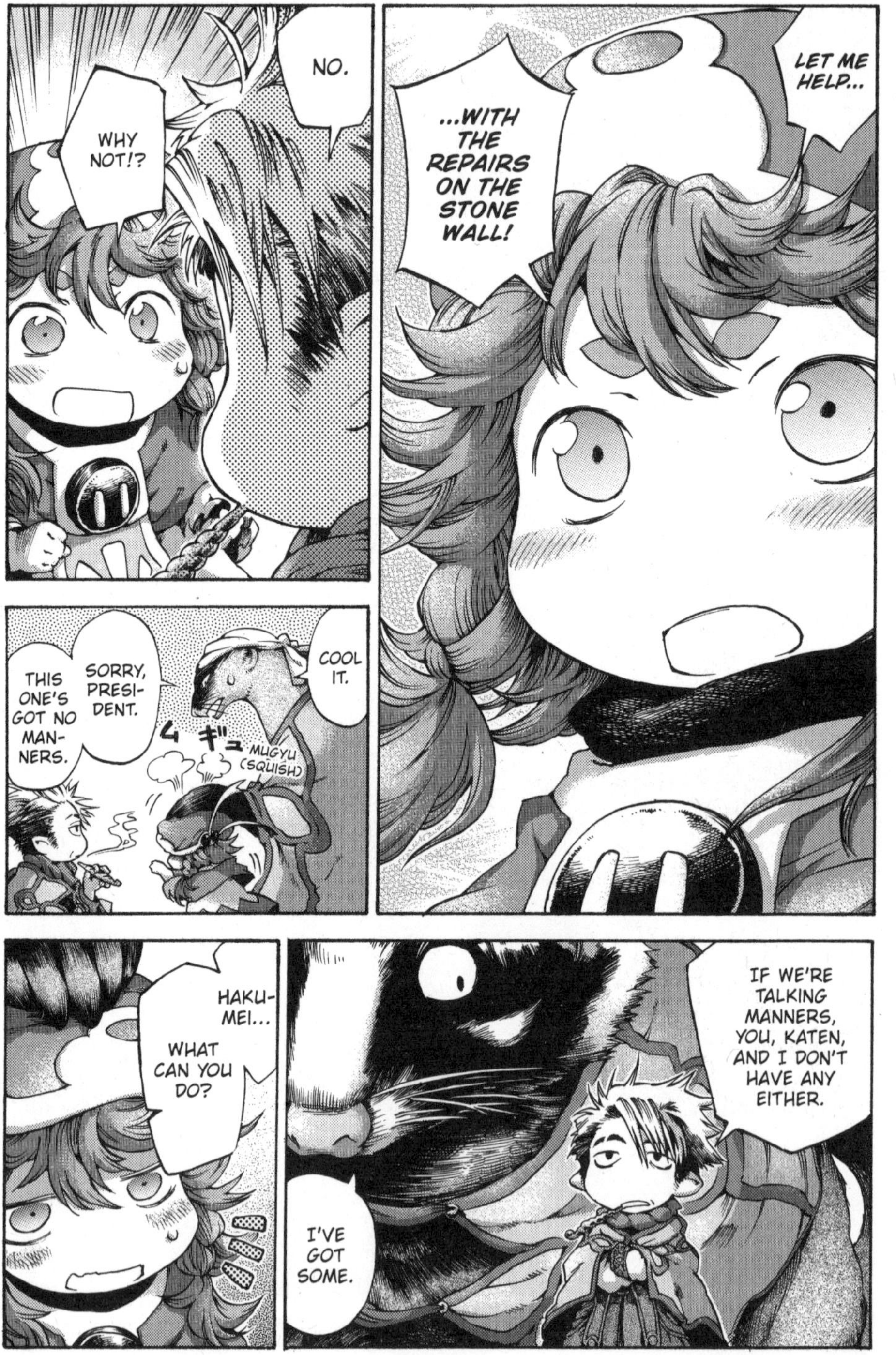
LET ME HELP...
...WITH THE REPAIRS ON THE STONE WALL!
NO.
WHY NOT!?
COOL IT.
SORRY, PRESIDENT.
THIS ONE'S GOT NO MANNERS.
ムギュ
MUGYU (SQUISH)
IF WE'RE TALKING MANNERS, YOU, KATEN, AND I DON'T HAVE ANY EITHER.
I'VE GOT SOME.
HAKUMEI...
WHAT CAN YOU DO?

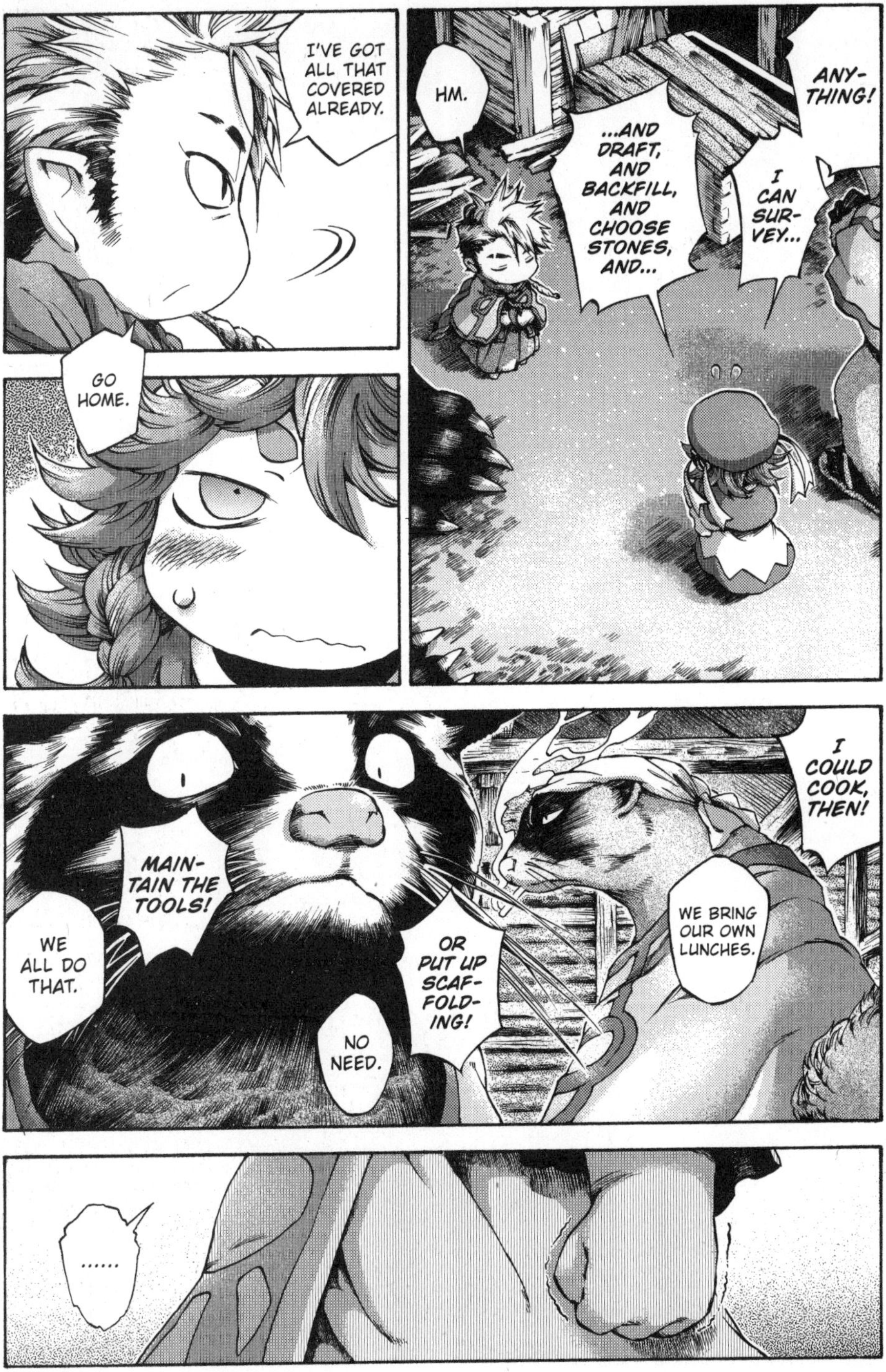
I CAN SUR-VEY...
...AND DRAFT, AND BACKFILL, AND CHOOSE STONES, AND...
ANY-THING!
HM.
I'VE GOT ALL THAT COVERED ALREADY.
GO HOME.
I COULD COOK, THEN!
WE BRING OUR OWN LUNCHES.
MAIN-TAIN THE TOOLS!
WE ALL DO THAT.
OR PUT UP SCAF-FOLD-ING!
NO NEED.
......

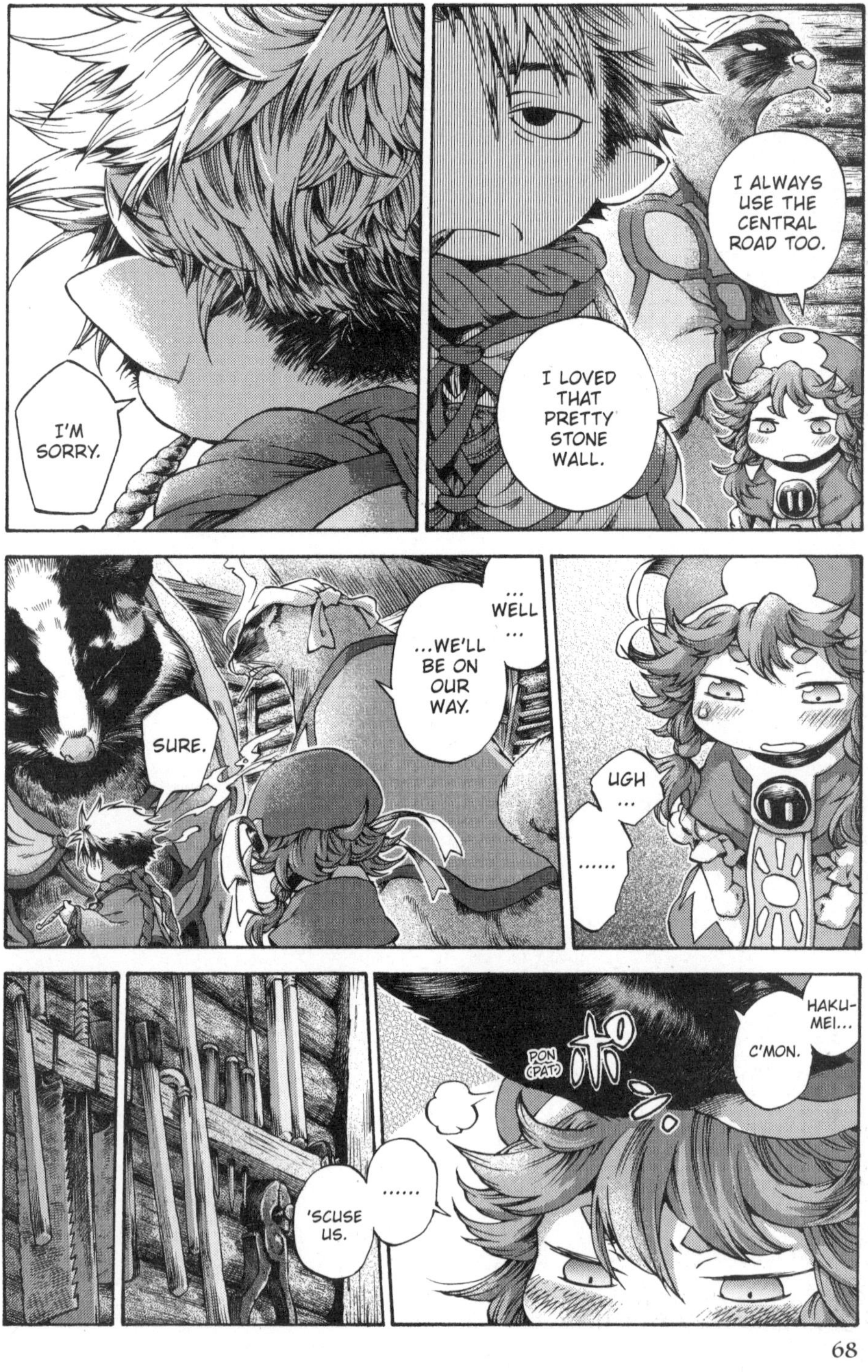
I ALWAYS USE THE CENTRAL ROAD TOO.
I LOVED THAT PRETTY STONE WALL.
I'M SORRY.
UGH ...
......
... WELL ...
...WE'LL BE ON OUR WAY.
SURE.
HAKU-MEI...
C'MON.
PON (PAT)
......
'SCUSE US.

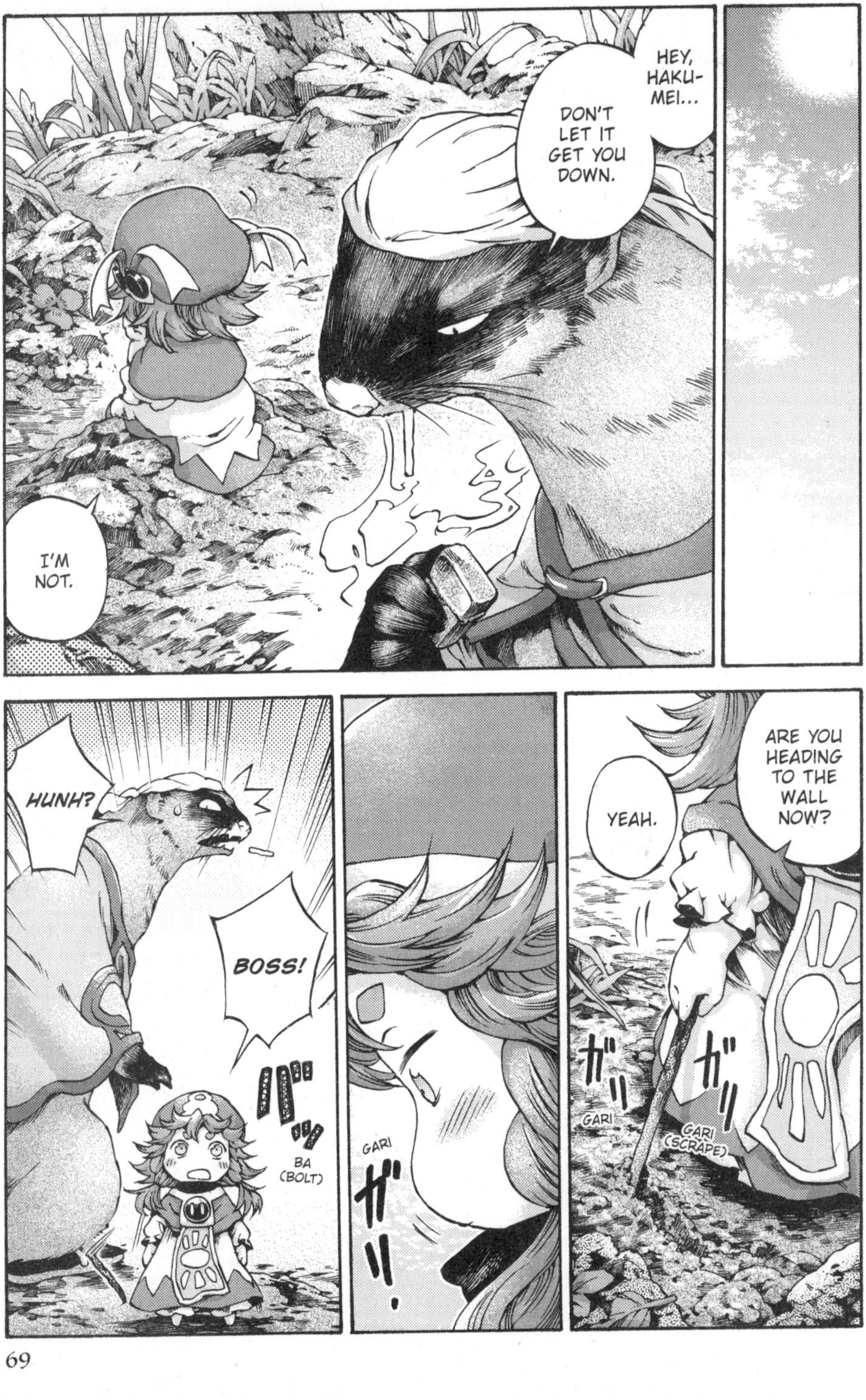
HEY, HAKU-MEI...
DON'T LET IT GET YOU DOWN.
I'M NOT.
ARE YOU HEADING TO THE WALL NOW?
YEAH.
GARI (SCRAPE)
GARI
GARI
HUNH?
BOSS!
BA (BOLT)

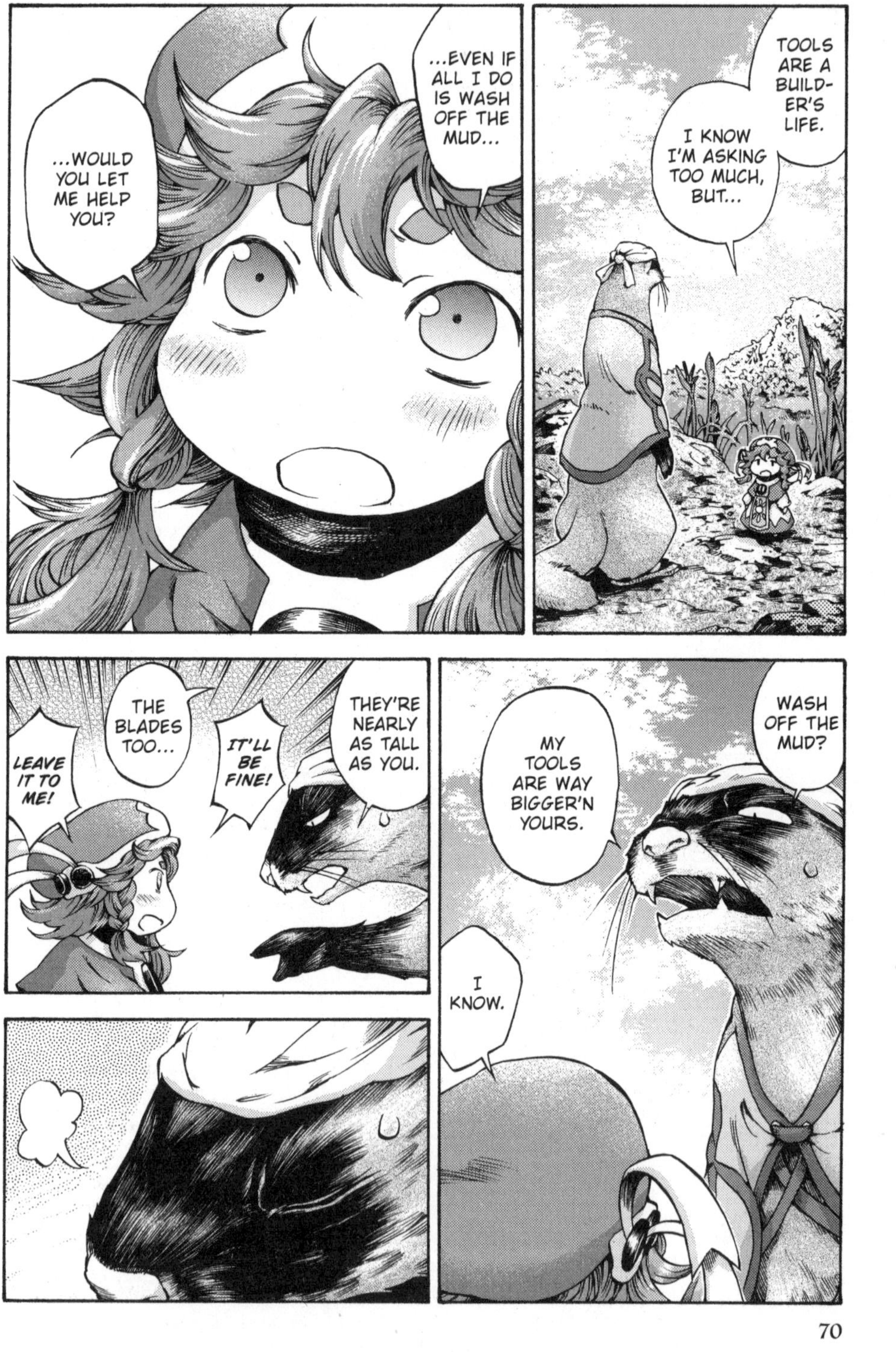
TOOLS ARE A BUILD-ER'S LIFE.
I KNOW I'M ASKING TOO MUCH, BUT...
...EVEN IF ALL I DO IS WASH OFF THE MUD...
...WOULD YOU LET ME HELP YOU?
WASH OFF THE MUD?
MY TOOLS ARE WAY BIGGER'N YOURS.
I KNOW.
THEY'RE NEARLY AS TALL AS YOU.
IT'LL BE FINE!
THE BLADES TOO...
LEAVE IT TO ME!

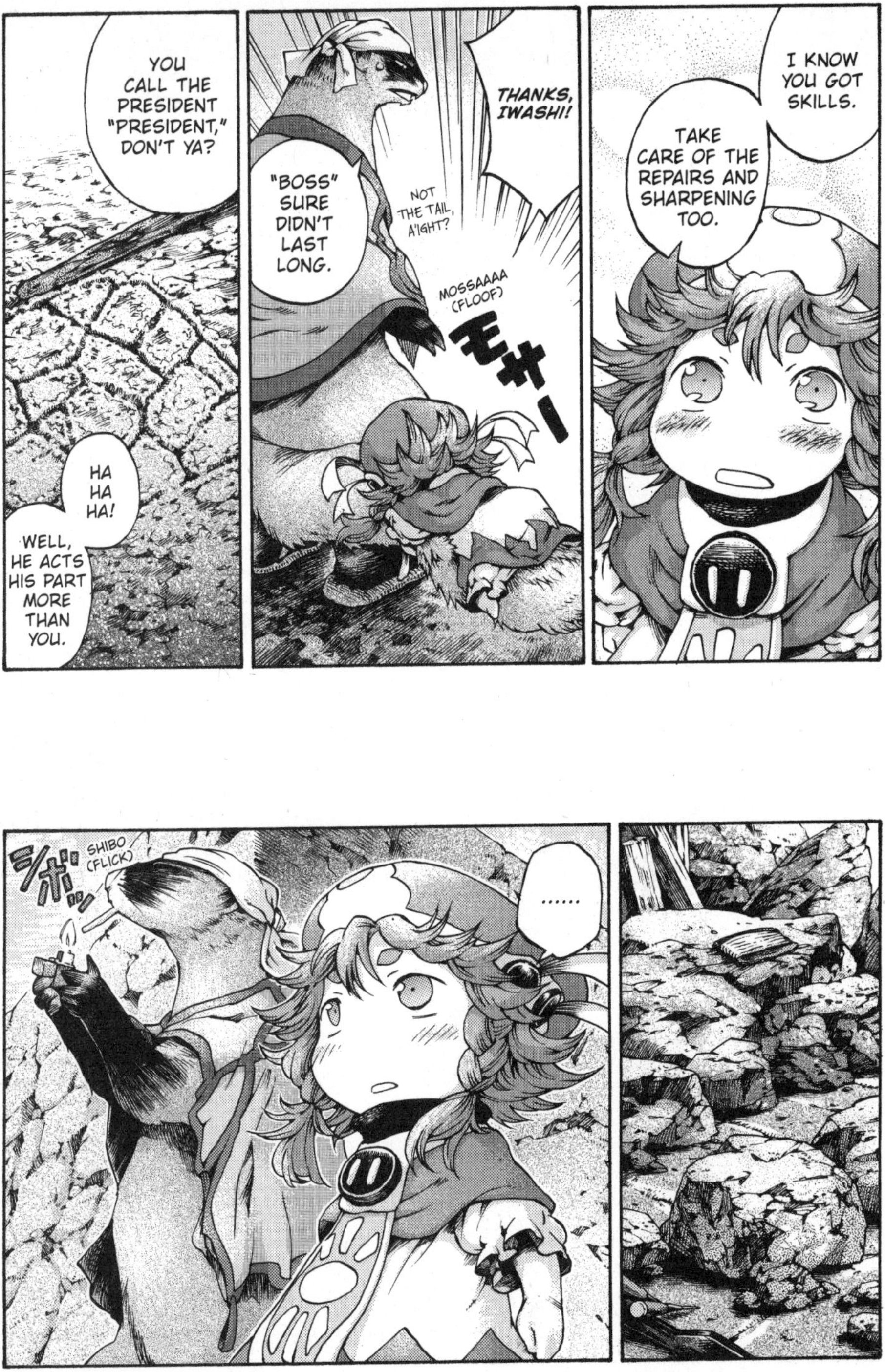
I KNOW YOU GOT SKILLS.
TAKE CARE OF THE REPAIRS AND SHARPENING TOO.
THANKS, IWASHI!
NOT THE TAIL, A'IGHT?
"BOSS" SURE DIDN'T LAST LONG.
MOSSAAAA (FLOOF)
モサー
YOU CALL THE PRESIDENT "PRESIDENT," DON'T YA?
HA HA HA!
WELL, HE ACTS HIS PART MORE THAN YOU.
......
シボッ
SHIBO (FLICK)

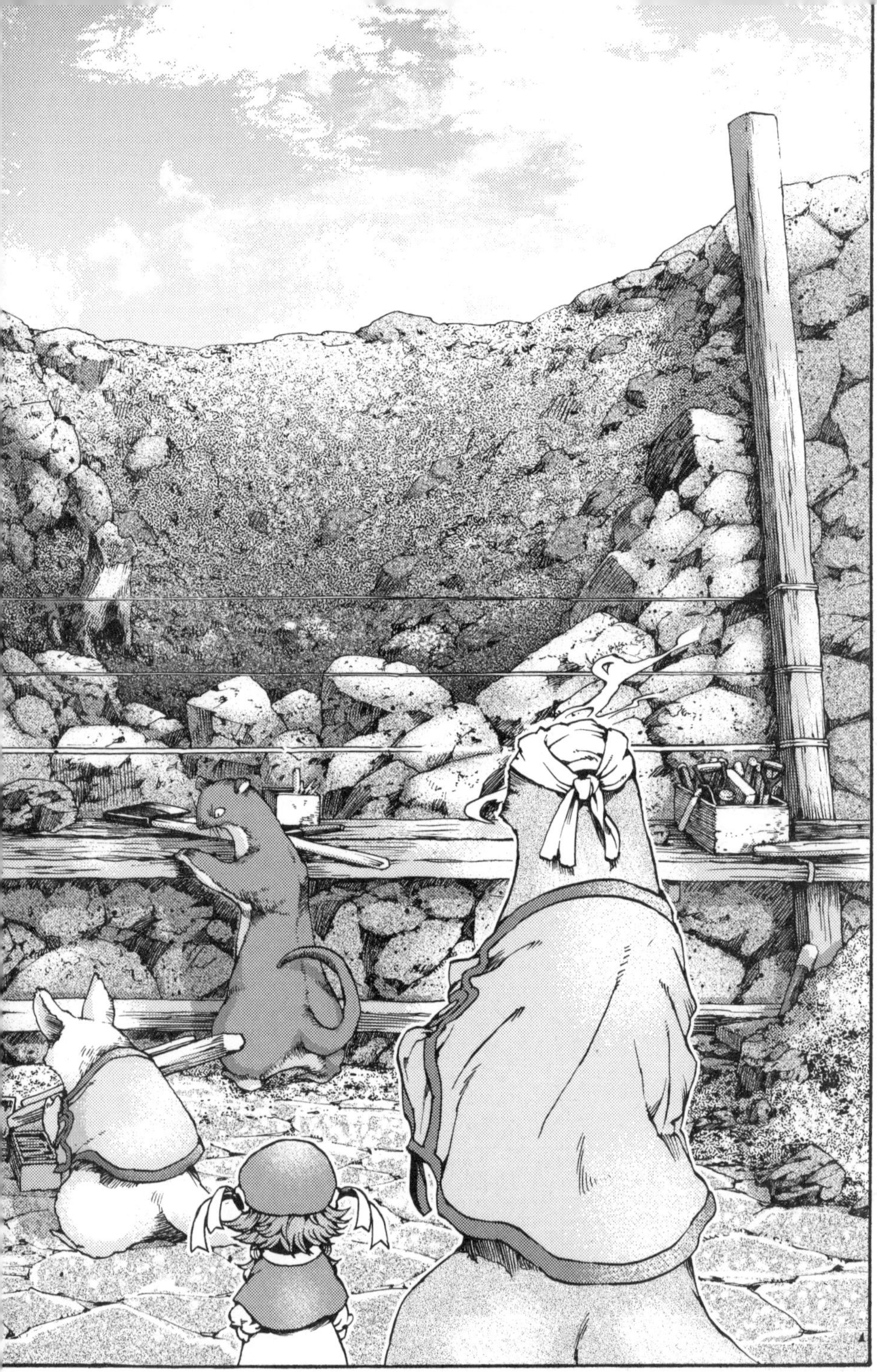

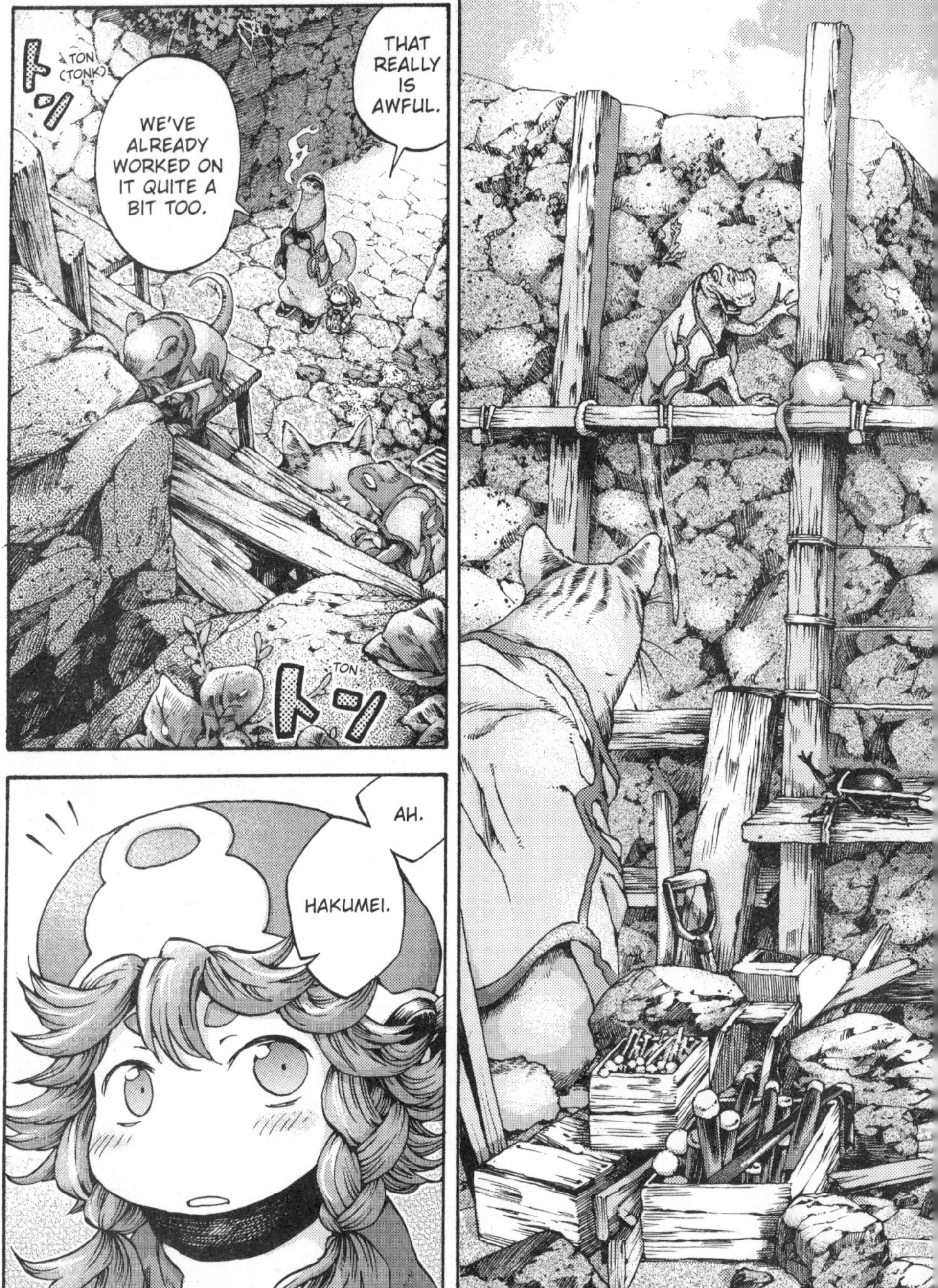
THAT REALLY IS AWFUL.
WE'VE ALREADY WORKED ON IT QUITE A BIT TOO.
トッ TON (TONK)
トッ TON
AH.
HAKUMEI.

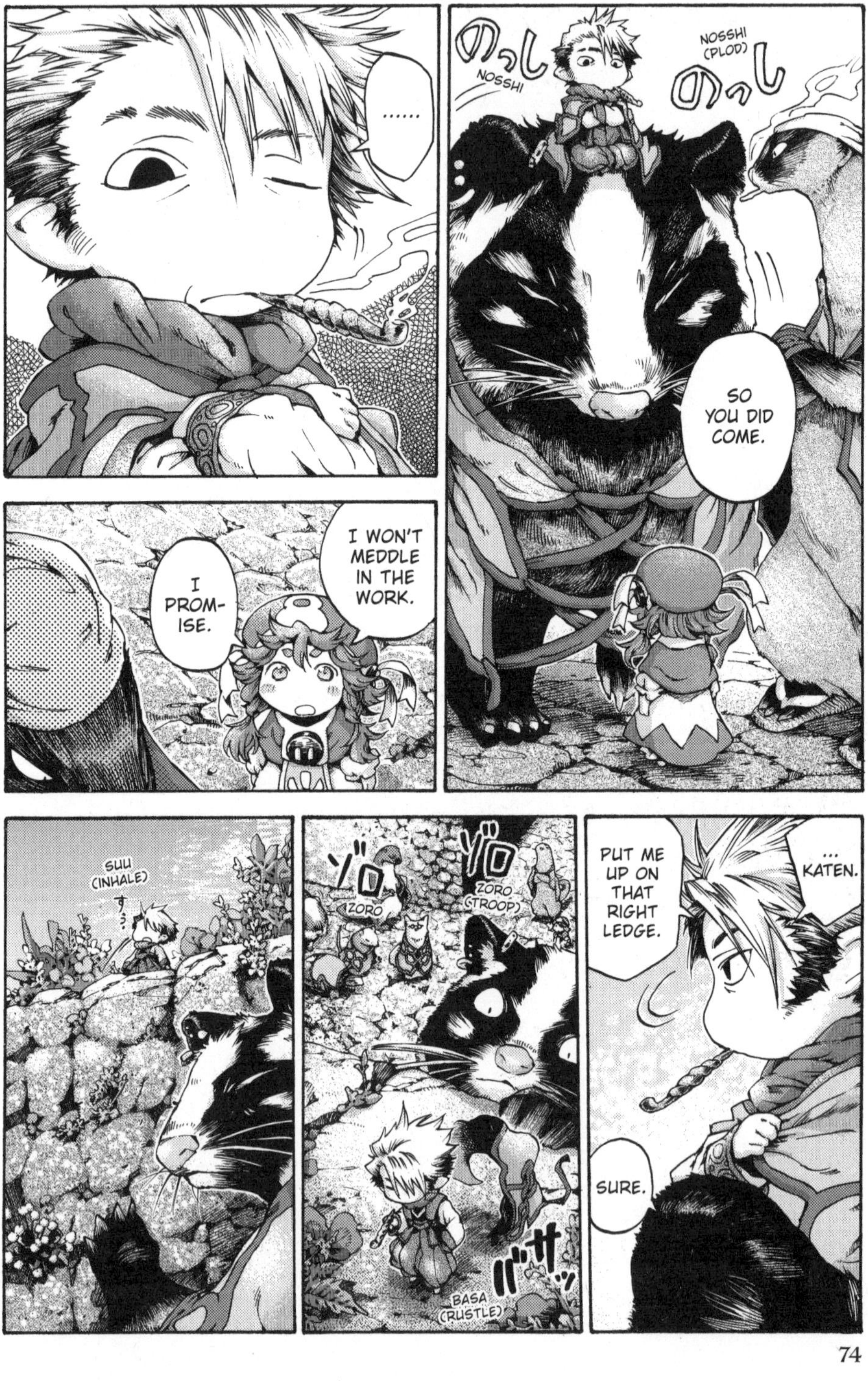
のっし
NOSSHI (PLOD)
のっし
NOSSHI
SO YOU DID COME.
......
I WON'T MEDDLE IN THE WORK.
I PROMISE.
... KATEN.
PUT ME UP ON THAT RIGHT LEDGE.
SURE.
ゾロ
ZORO (TROOP)
ゾロ
ZORO
バサッ
BASA (RUSTLE)
す...
SUU (INHALE)

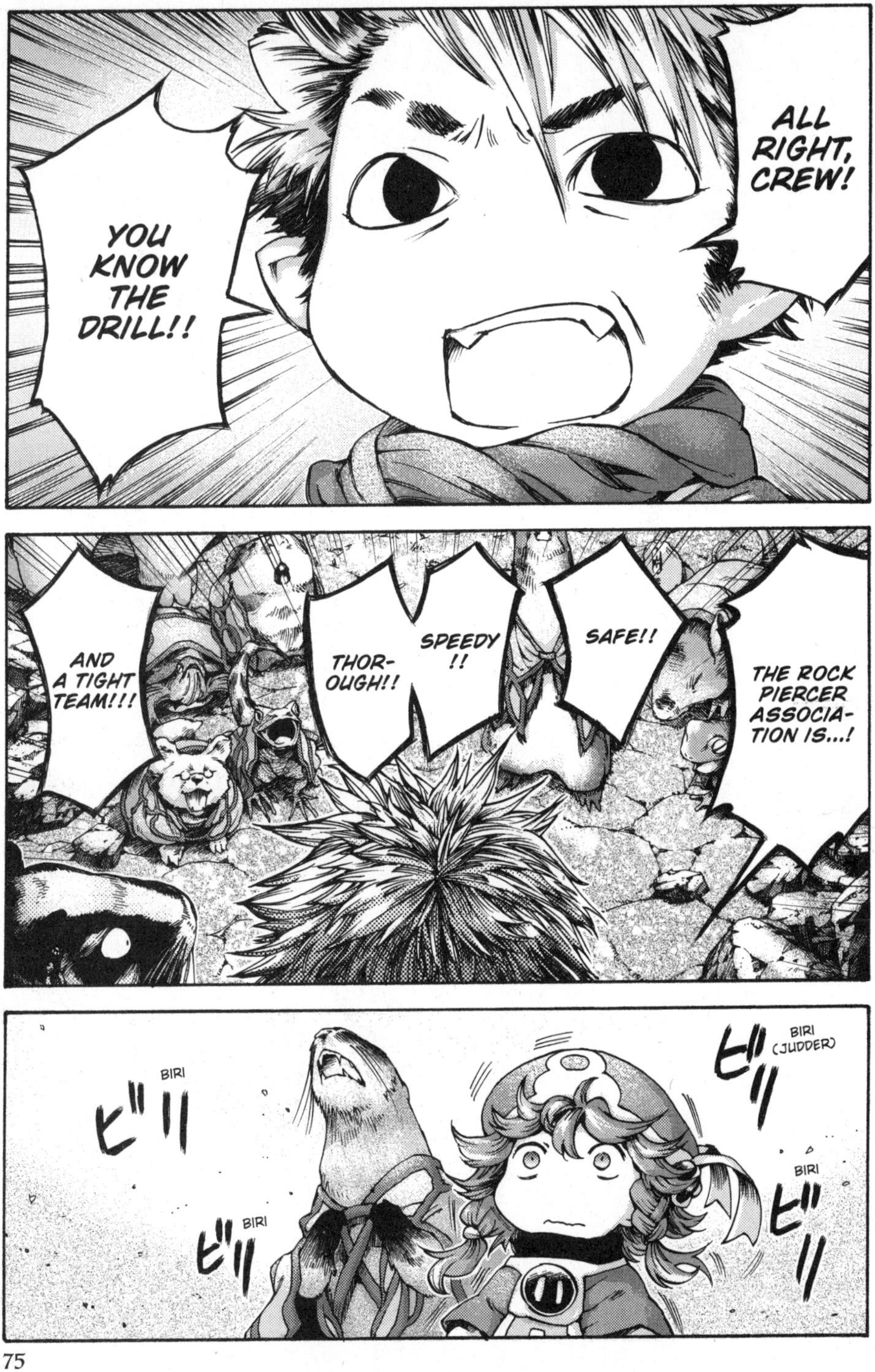
ALL RIGHT, CREW!
YOU KNOW THE DRILL!!
THE ROCK PIERCER ASSOCIATION IS...!
SAFE!!
SPEEDY!!
THOR-OUGH!!
AND A TIGHT TEAM!!!
ビリ
BIRI (JUDDER)
ビリ
BIRI
ビリ
BIRI
ビリ
BIRI

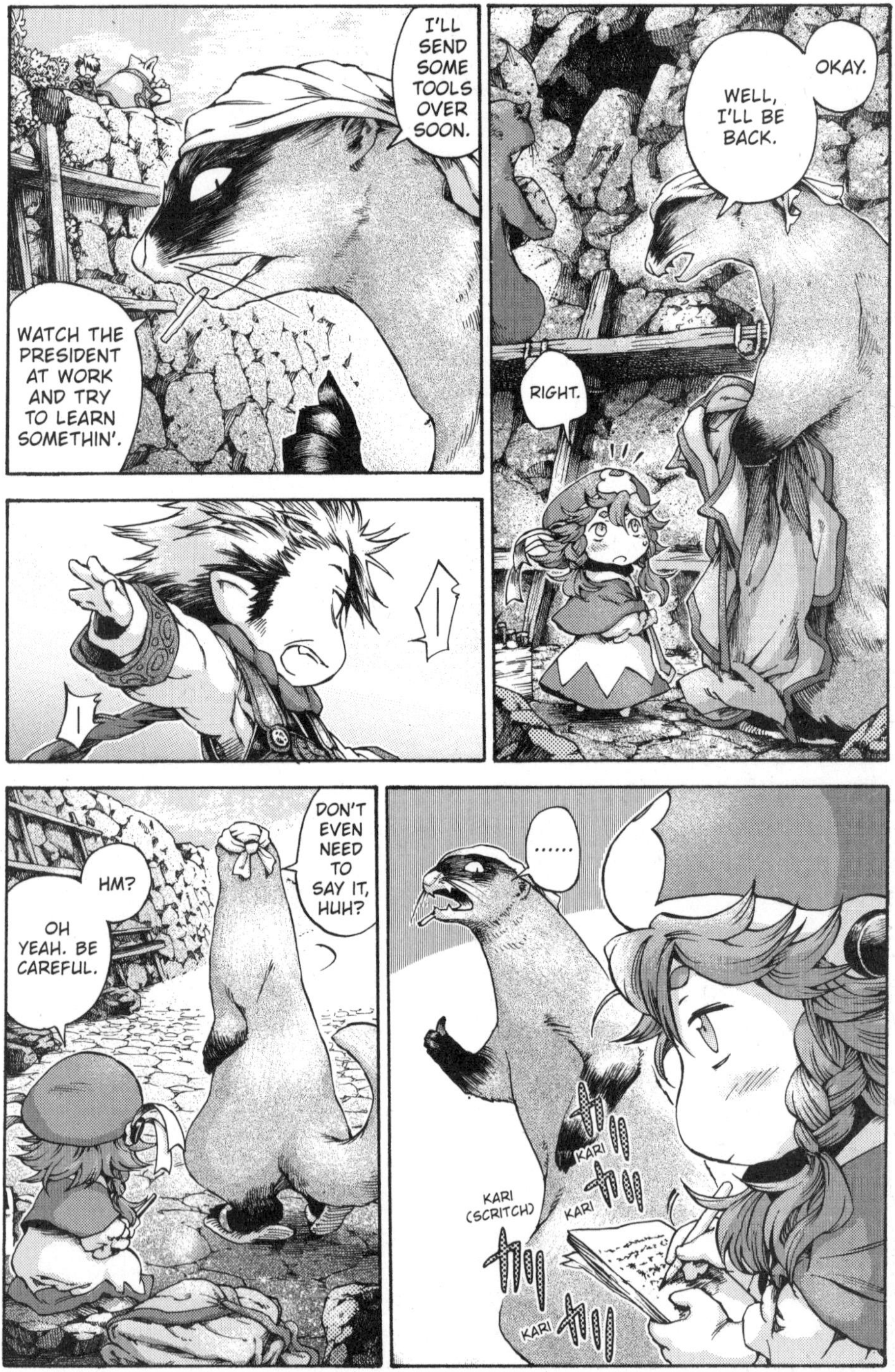
OKAY.
WELL, I'LL BE BACK.
RIGHT.
I'LL SEND SOME TOOLS OVER SOON.
WATCH THE PRESIDENT AT WORK AND TRY TO LEARN SOMETHIN'.
......
KARI
KARI
KARI (SCRITCH)
KARI
DON'T EVEN NEED TO SAY IT, HUH?
HM?
OH YEAH. BE CAREFUL.

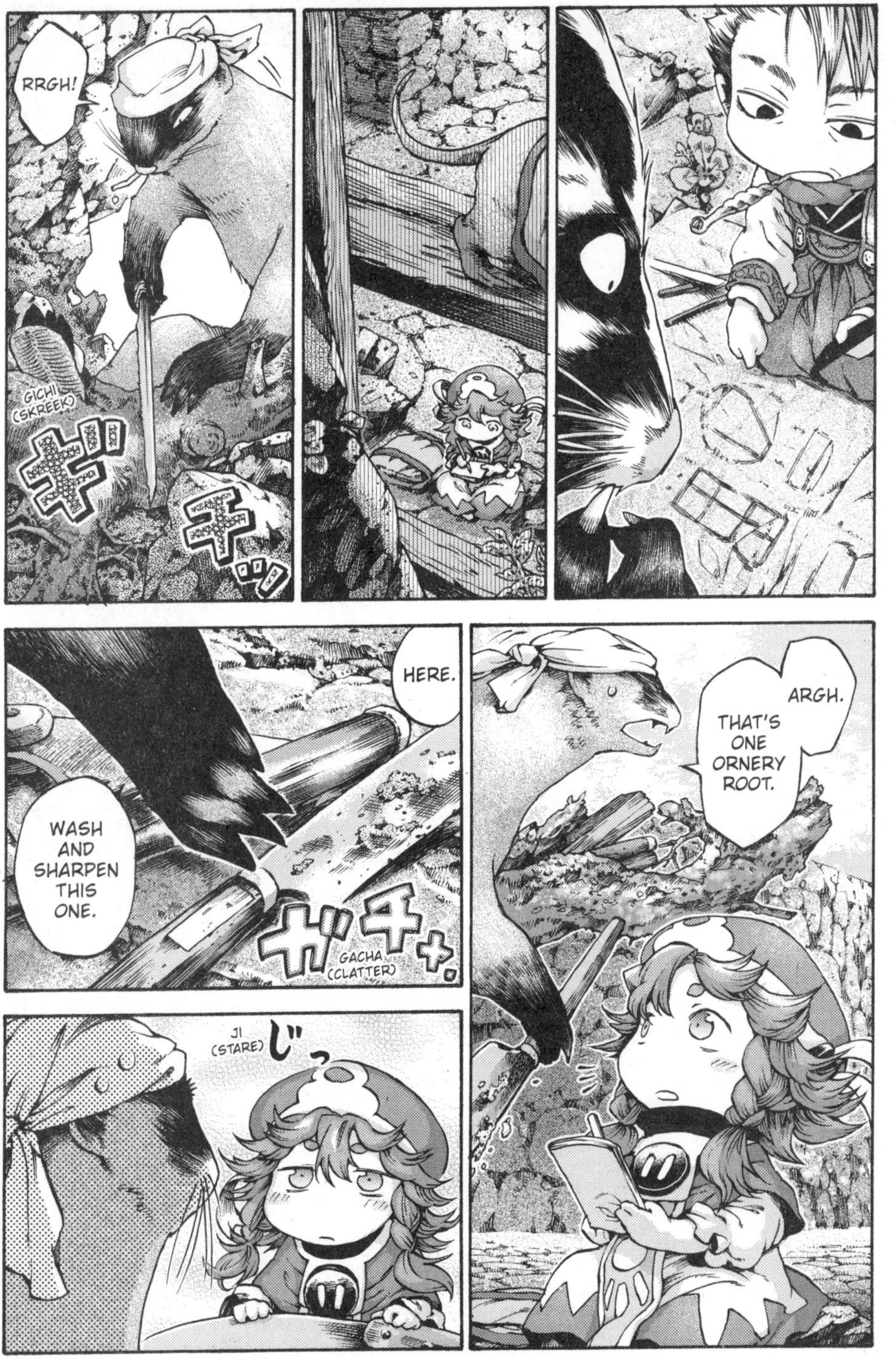
RRGH!
GICHI (SKREEK)
ギチッ
ARGH. THAT'S ONE ORNERY ROOT.
HERE.
WASH AND SHARPEN THIS ONE.
GACHA (CLATTER)
ガチャ
JI (STARE)
じっ

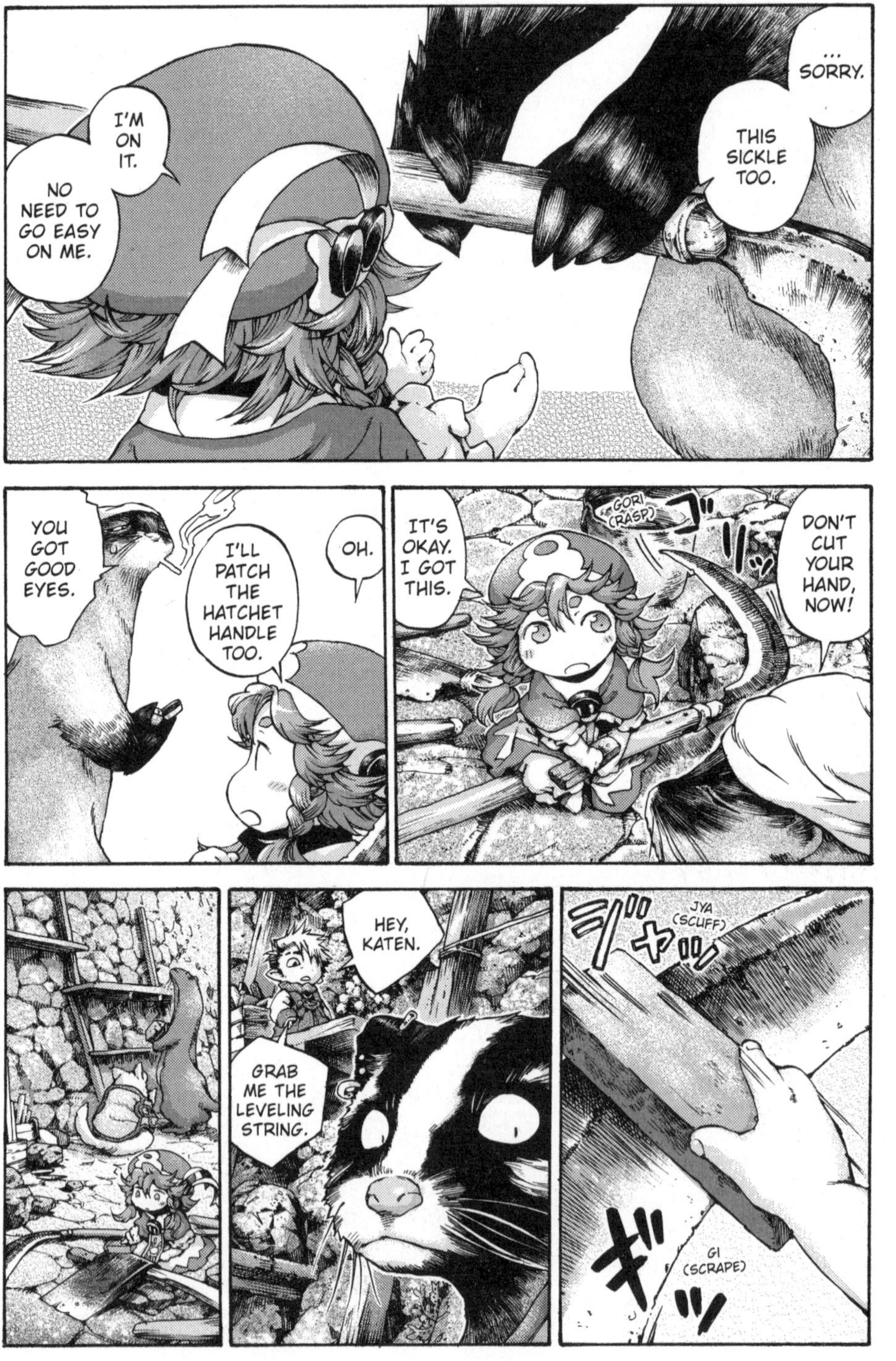
...SORRY.
THIS SICKLE TOO.
I'M ON IT.
NO NEED TO GO EASY ON ME.
DON'T CUT YOUR HAND, NOW!
GORI (RASP)
IT'S OKAY. I GOT THIS.
OH.
I'LL PATCH THE HATCHET HANDLE TOO.
YOU GOT GOOD EYES.
JYA (SCUFF)
GI (SCRAPE)
HEY, KATEN.
GRAB ME THE LEVELING STRING.

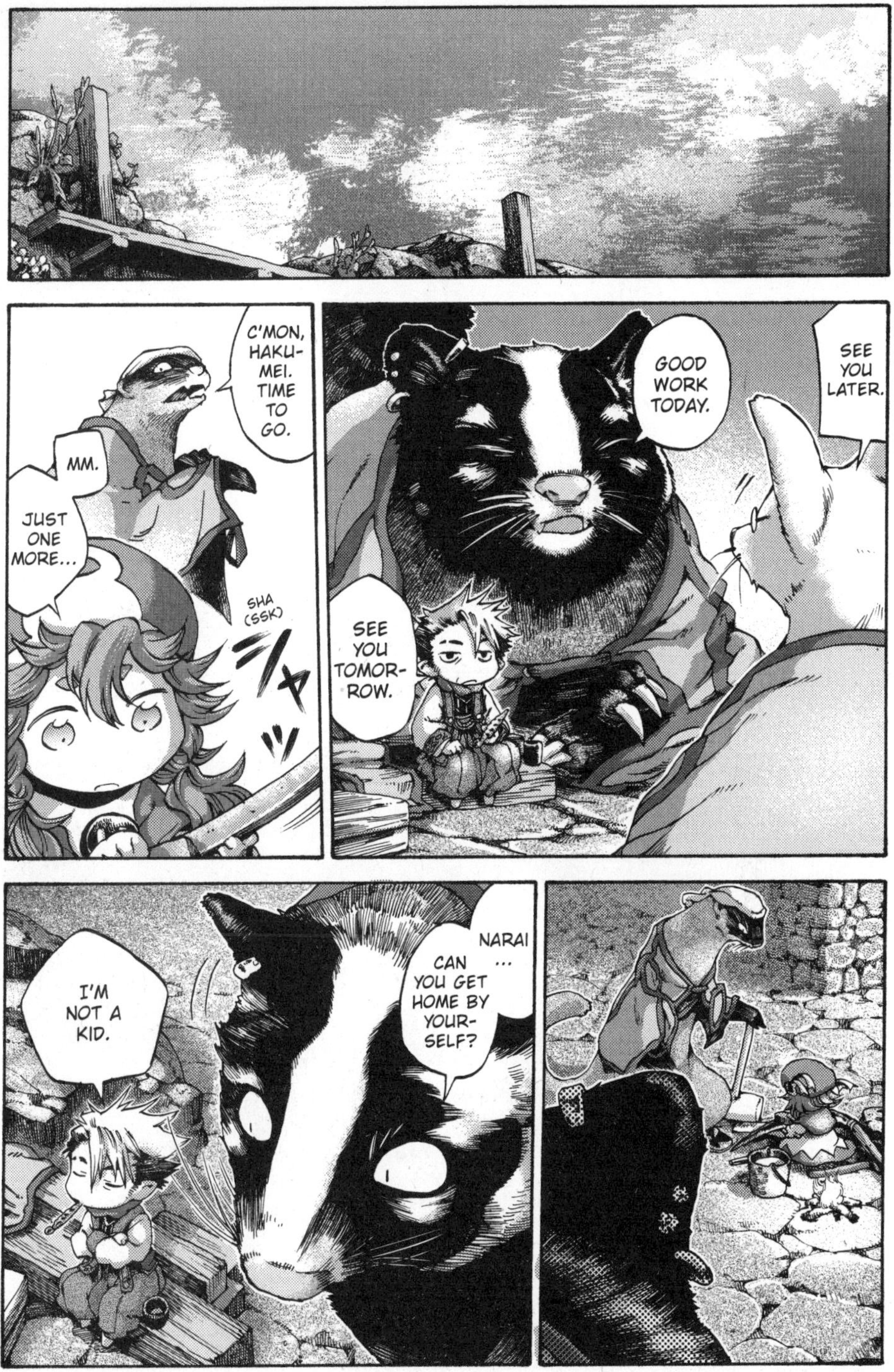
SEE YOU LATER.
GOOD WORK TODAY.
SEE YOU TOMORROW.
C'MON, HAKUMEI. TIME TO GO.
MM.
JUST ONE MORE...
SHA (SSK)
NARAI...
CAN YOU GET HOME BY YOURSELF?
I'M NOT A KID.

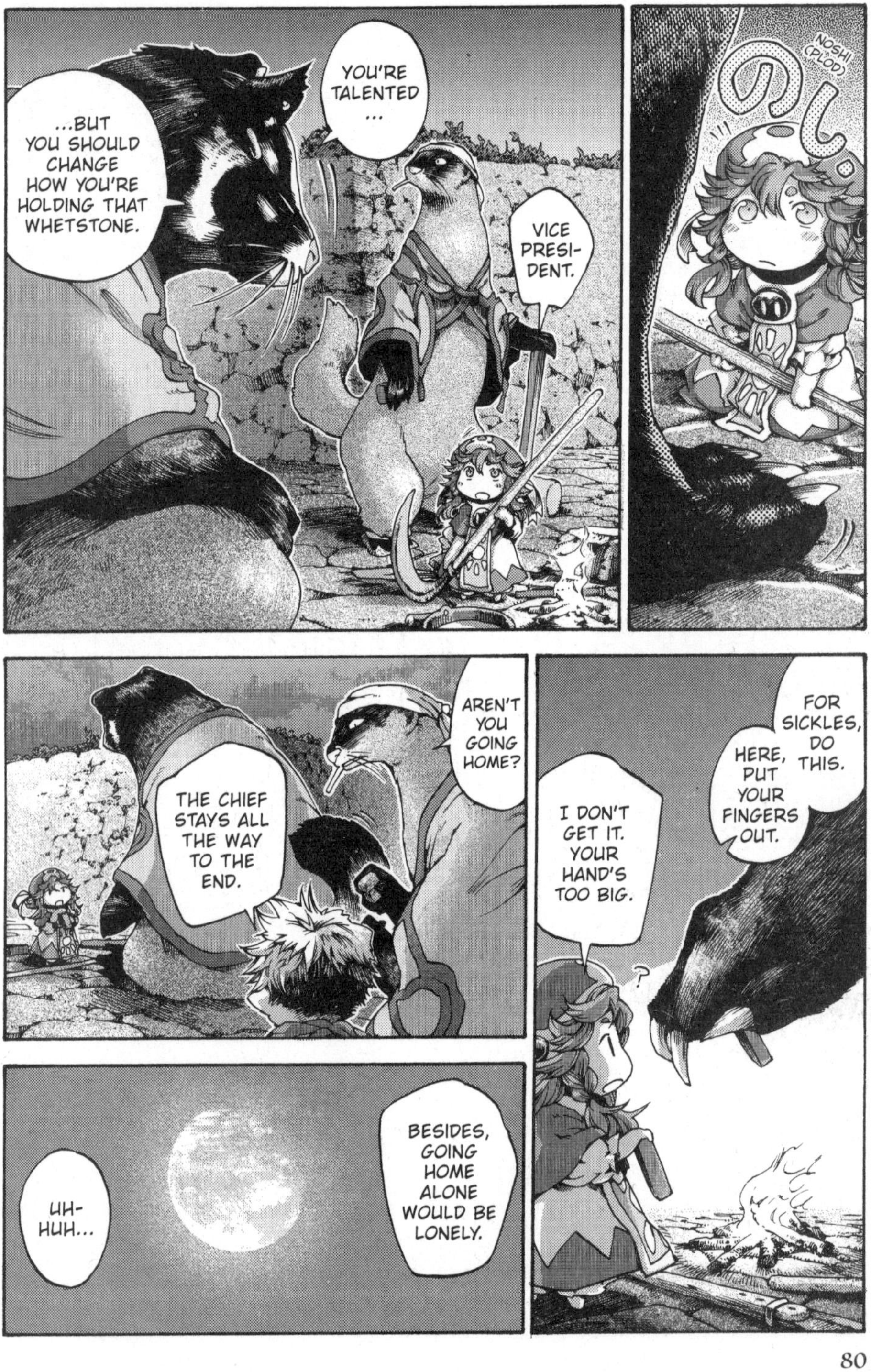
NOSHI (PLOD)
YOU'RE TALENTED ...
...BUT YOU SHOULD CHANGE HOW YOU'RE HOLDING THAT WHETSTONE.
VICE PRESI-DENT.
FOR SICKLES, DO THIS.
HERE, PUT YOUR FINGERS OUT.
I DON'T GET IT. YOUR HAND'S TOO BIG.
?
AREN'T YOU GOING HOME?
THE CHIEF STAYS ALL THE WAY TO THE END.
BESIDES, GOING HOME ALONE WOULD BE LONELY.
UH-HUH...

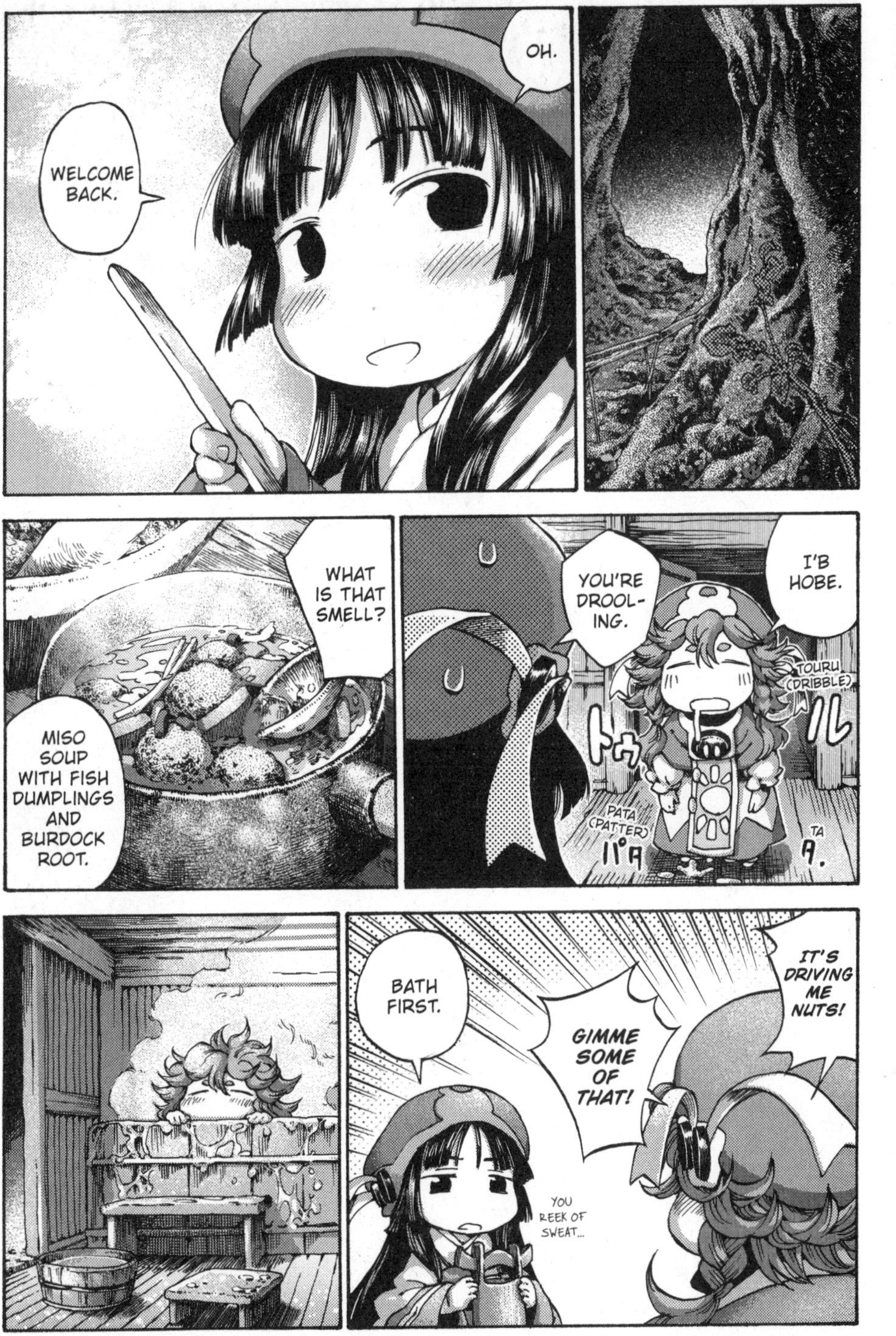
OH.
WELCOME BACK.
I'B HOBE.
YOU'RE DROOL-ING.
TOURU (DRIBBLE)
トゥル
PATA (PATTER)
パタ
TA
タ.
WHAT IS THAT SMELL?
MISO SOUP WITH FISH DUMPLINGS AND BURDOCK ROOT.
IT'S DRIVING ME NUTS!
GIMME SOME OF THAT!
BATH FIRST.
YOU REEK OF SWEAT...

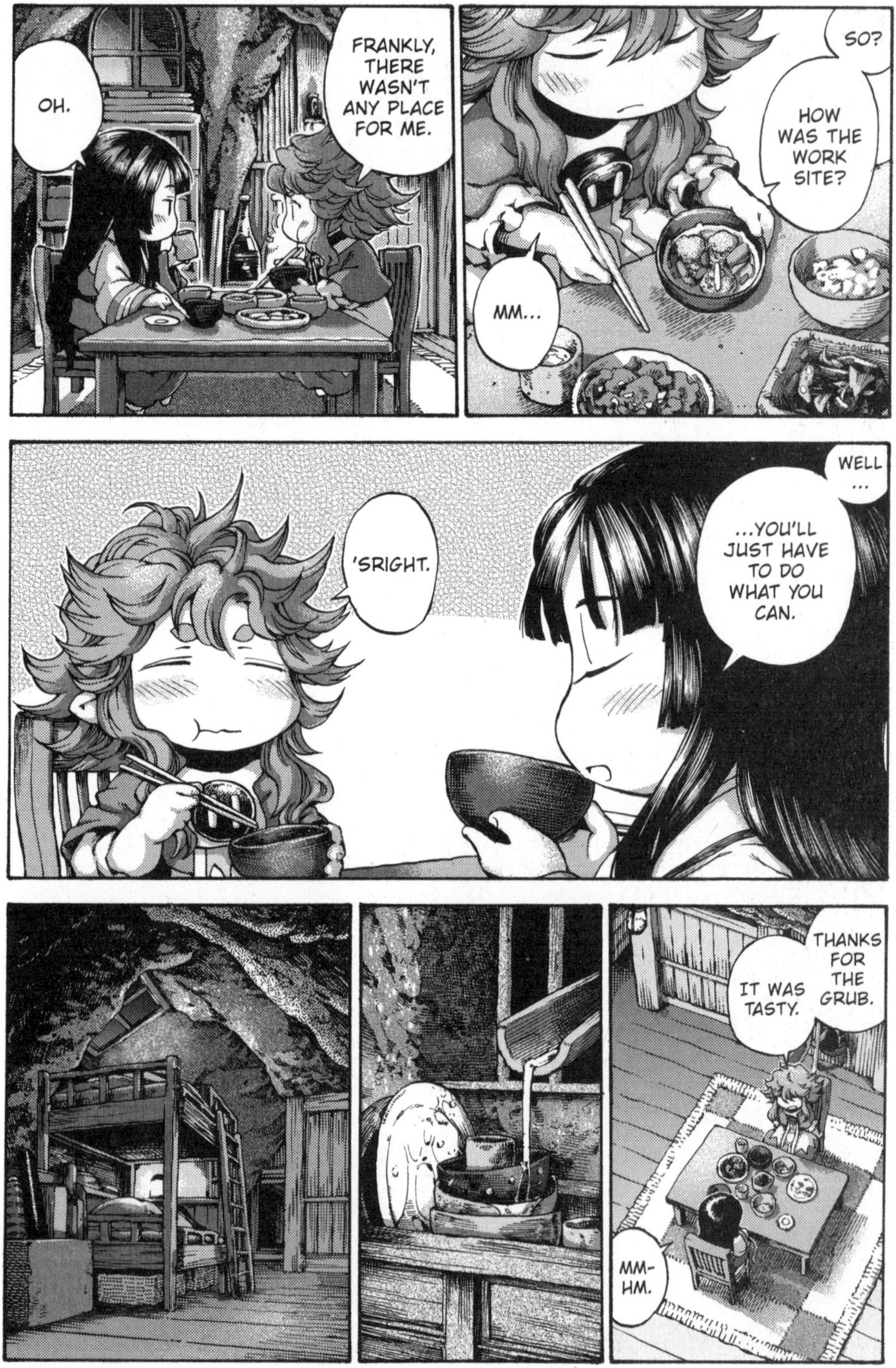
SO?
HOW WAS THE WORK SITE?
MM...
FRANKLY, THERE WASN'T ANY PLACE FOR ME.
OH.
WELL ...
...YOU'LL JUST HAVE TO DO WHAT YOU CAN.
'SRIGHT.
THANKS FOR THE GRUB.
IT WAS TASTY.
MM-HM.

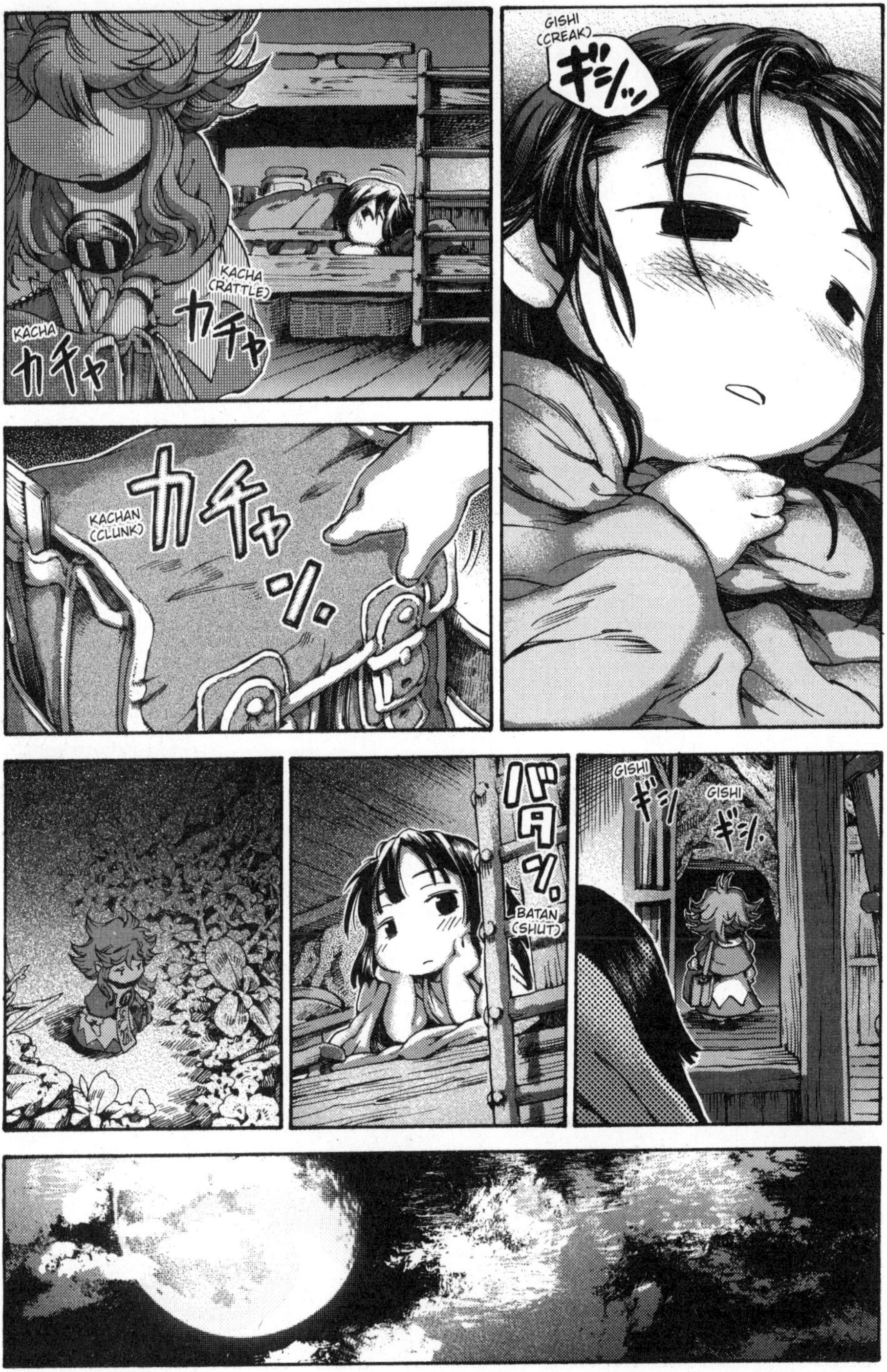
GISHI (CREAK)
ギシッ
KACHA (RATTLE)
カチャ
KACHA
カチャ
KACHAN (CLUNK)
カチャン
GISHI
ギシ
GISHI
ギシ
バタン
BATAN (SHUT)

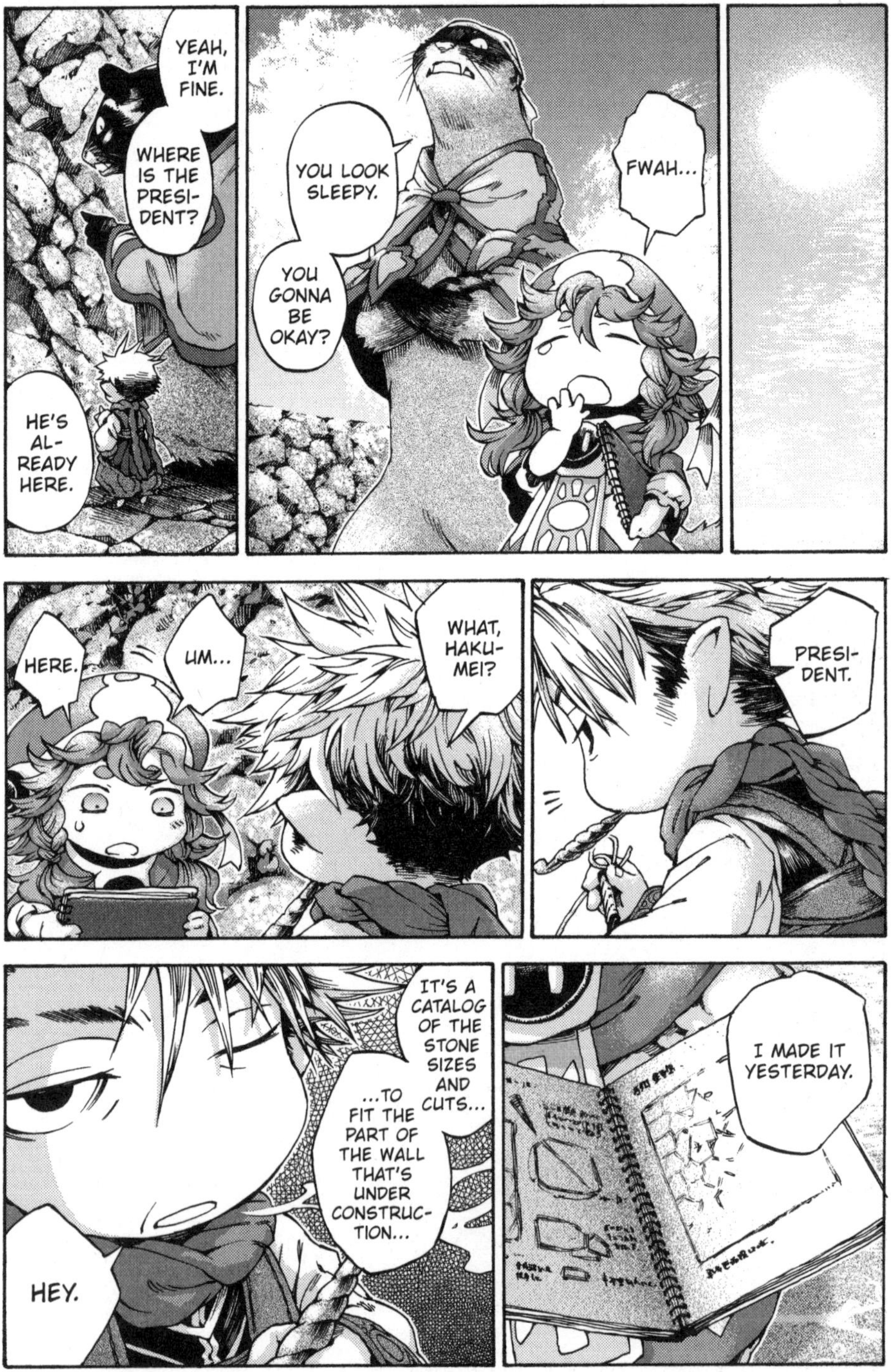
FWAH...
YOU LOOK SLEEPY.
YOU GONNA BE OKAY?
YEAH, I'M FINE.
WHERE IS THE PRESIDENT?
HE'S ALREADY HERE.
PRESIDENT.
WHAT, HAKUMEI?
UM...
HERE.
I MADE IT YESTERDAY.
IT'S A CATALOG OF THE STONE SIZES AND CUTS...
...TO FIT THE PART OF THE WALL THAT'S UNDER CONSTRUCTION...
HEY.

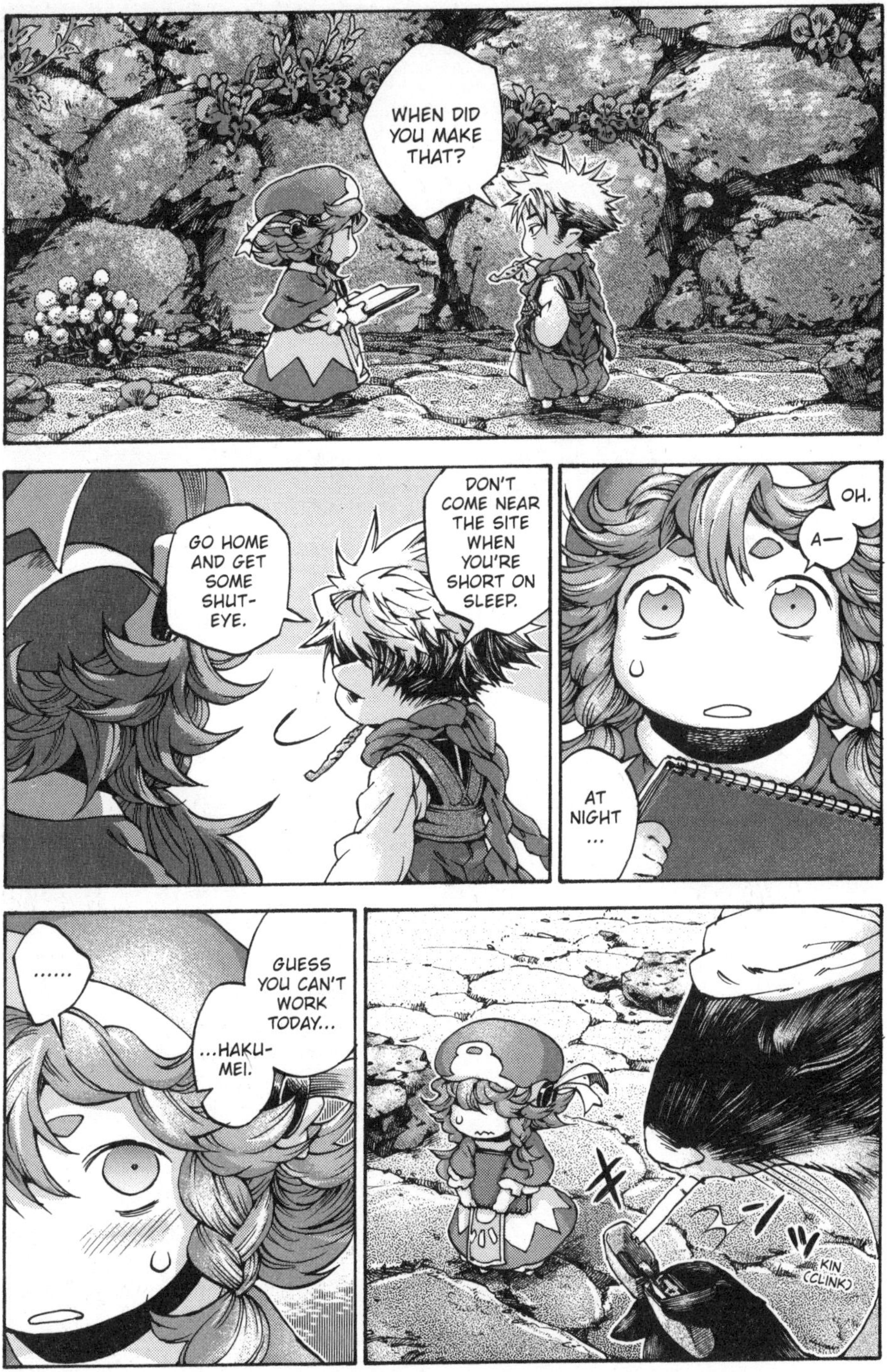
WHEN DID YOU MAKE THAT?
OH.
A—
AT NIGHT ...
DON'T COME NEAR THE SITE WHEN YOU'RE SHORT ON SLEEP.
GO HOME AND GET SOME SHUT-EYE.
KIN (CLINK)
GUESS YOU CAN'T WORK TODAY...
......
...HAKU-MEI.

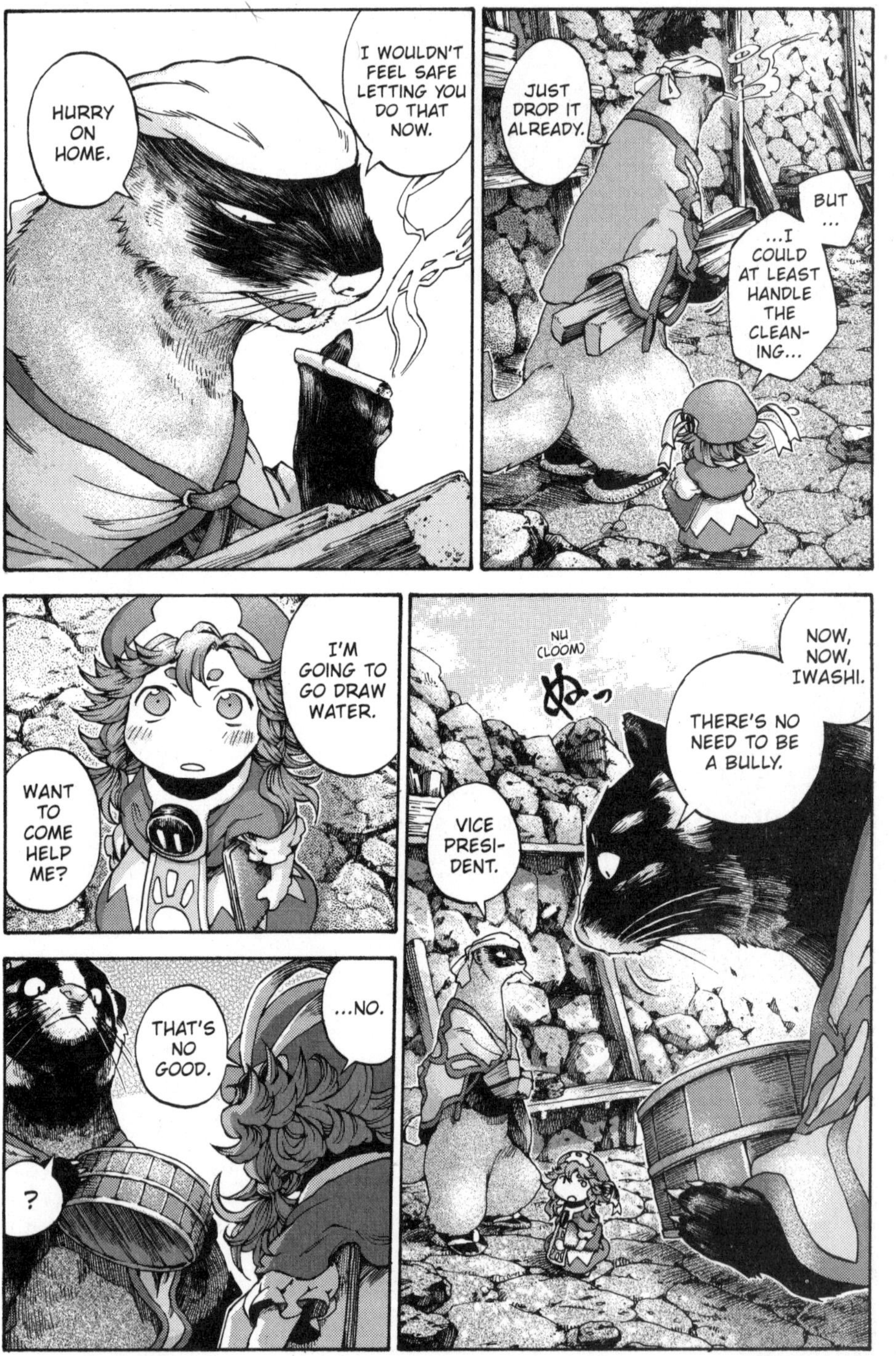
JUST DROP IT ALREADY.
BUT...
...I COULD AT LEAST HANDLE THE CLEANING...
I WOULDN'T FEEL SAFE LETTING YOU DO THAT NOW.
HURRY ON HOME.
NOW, NOW, IWASHI.
NU (LOOM)
ぬっ
THERE'S NO NEED TO BE A BULLY.
VICE PRESIDENT.
I'M GOING TO GO DRAW WATER.
WANT TO COME HELP ME?
...NO.
THAT'S NO GOOD.
?

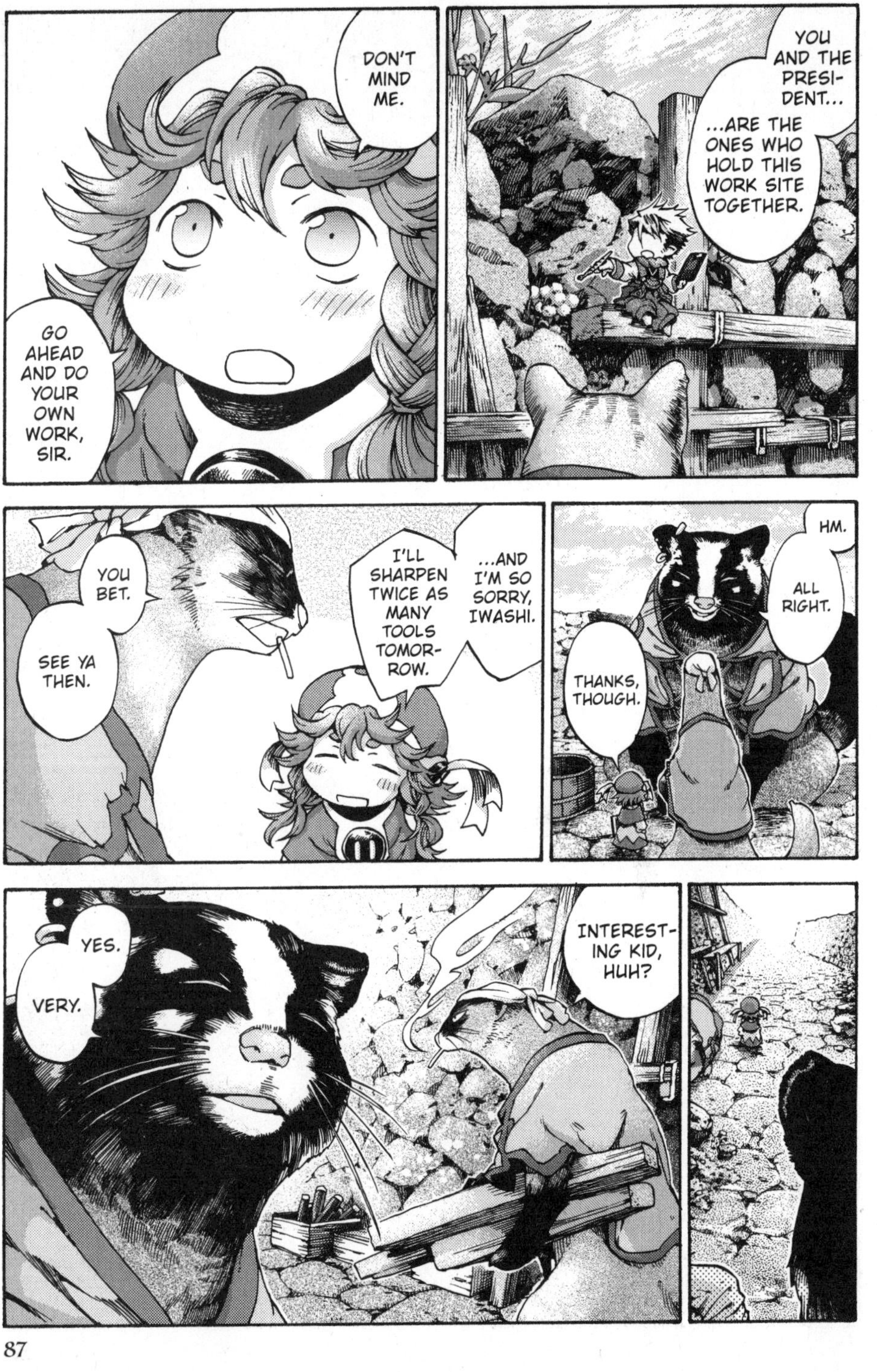
YOU AND THE PRESIDENT...
...ARE THE ONES WHO HOLD THIS WORK SITE TOGETHER.
DON'T MIND ME.
GO AHEAD AND DO YOUR OWN WORK, SIR.
HM.
ALL RIGHT.
THANKS, THOUGH.
...AND I'M SO SORRY, IWASHI.
I'LL SHARPEN TWICE AS MANY TOOLS TOMORROW.
YOU BET.
SEE YA THEN.
INTERESTING KID, HUH?
YES.
VERY.

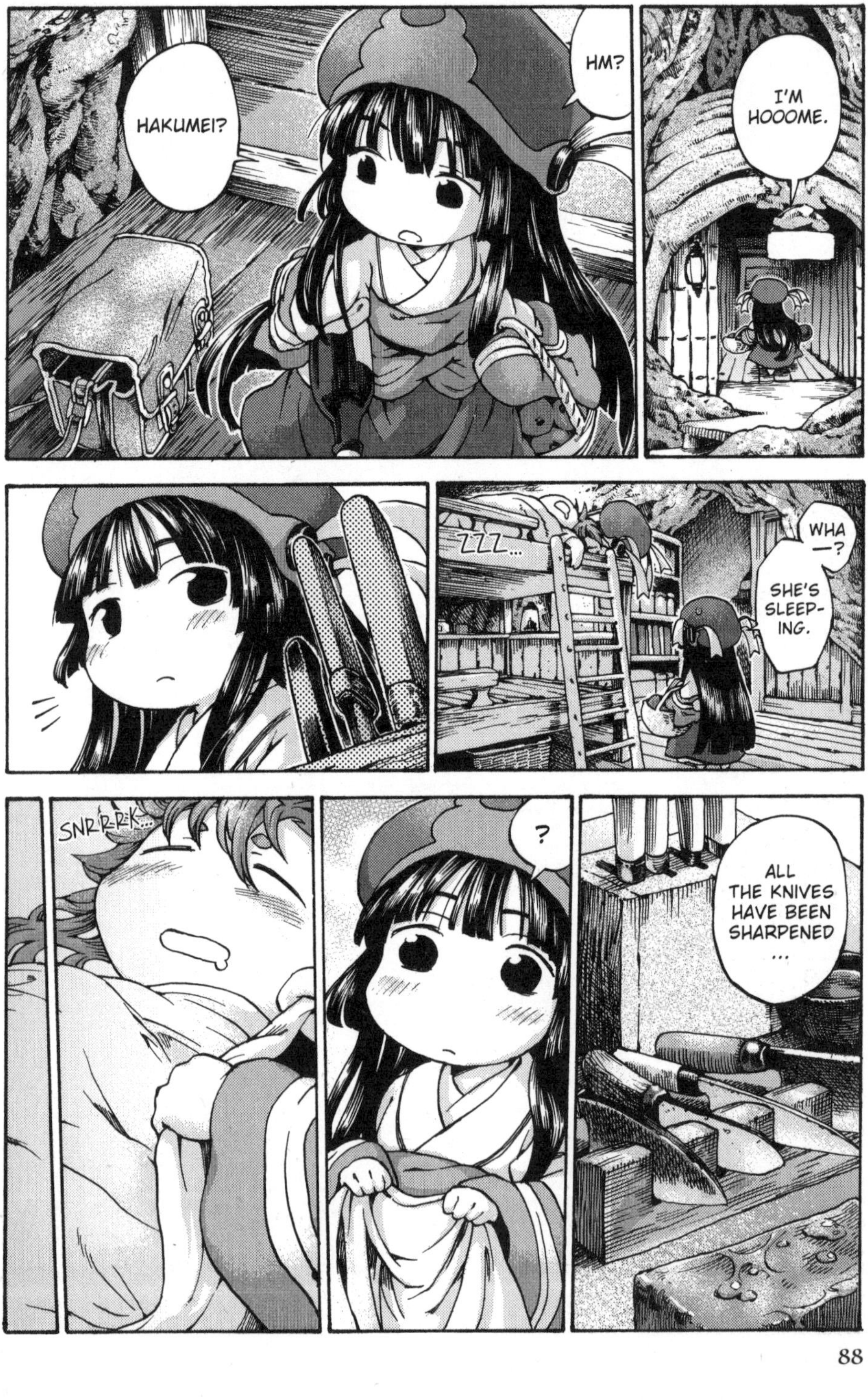
I'M HOOOME.
HM?
HAKUMEI?
WHA —?
ZZZ...
SHE'S SLEEP-ING.
ALL THE KNIVES HAVE BEEN SHARPENED ...
?
SNRRRK...

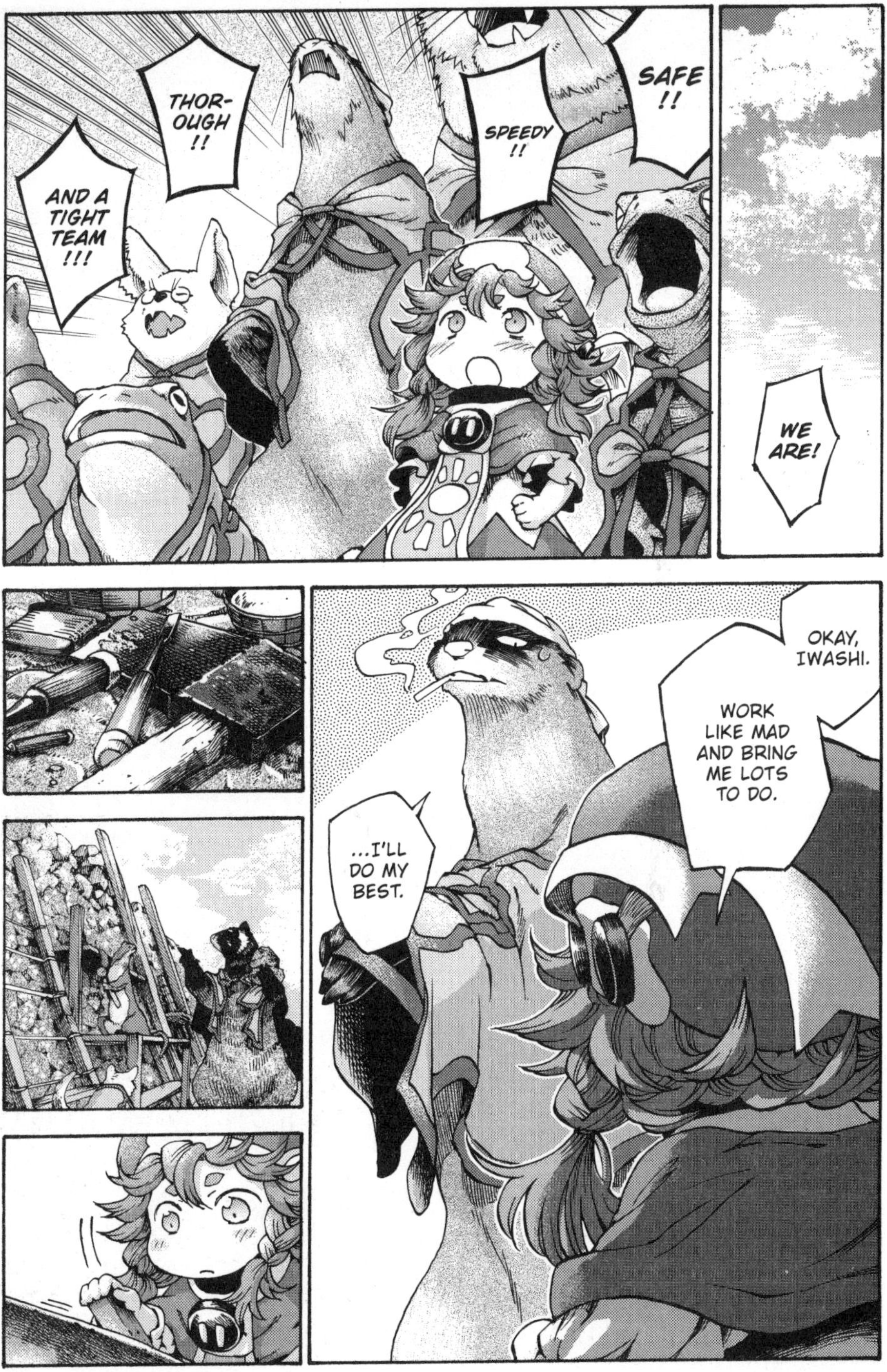
WE ARE!
SAFE !!
SPEEDY !!
THOR-OUGH !!
AND A TIGHT TEAM !!!
OKAY, IWASHI.
WORK LIKE MAD AND BRING ME LOTS TO DO.
...I'LL DO MY BEST.

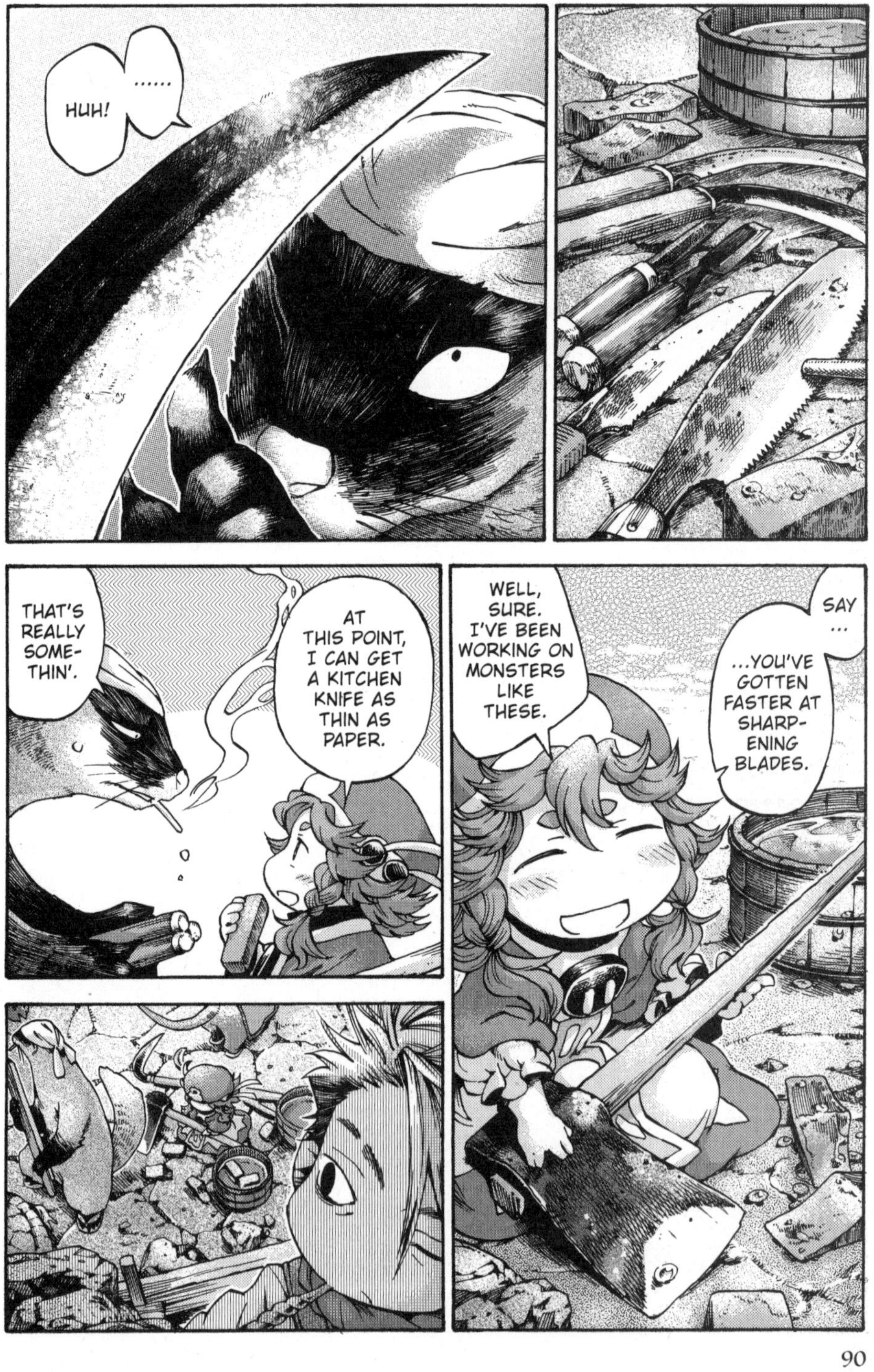
......
HUH!
SAY ...
...YOU'VE GOTTEN FASTER AT SHARP-ENING BLADES.
WELL, SURE. I'VE BEEN WORKING ON MONSTERS LIKE THESE.
AT THIS POINT, I CAN GET A KITCHEN KNIFE AS THIN AS PAPER.
THAT'S REALLY SOME-THIN'.

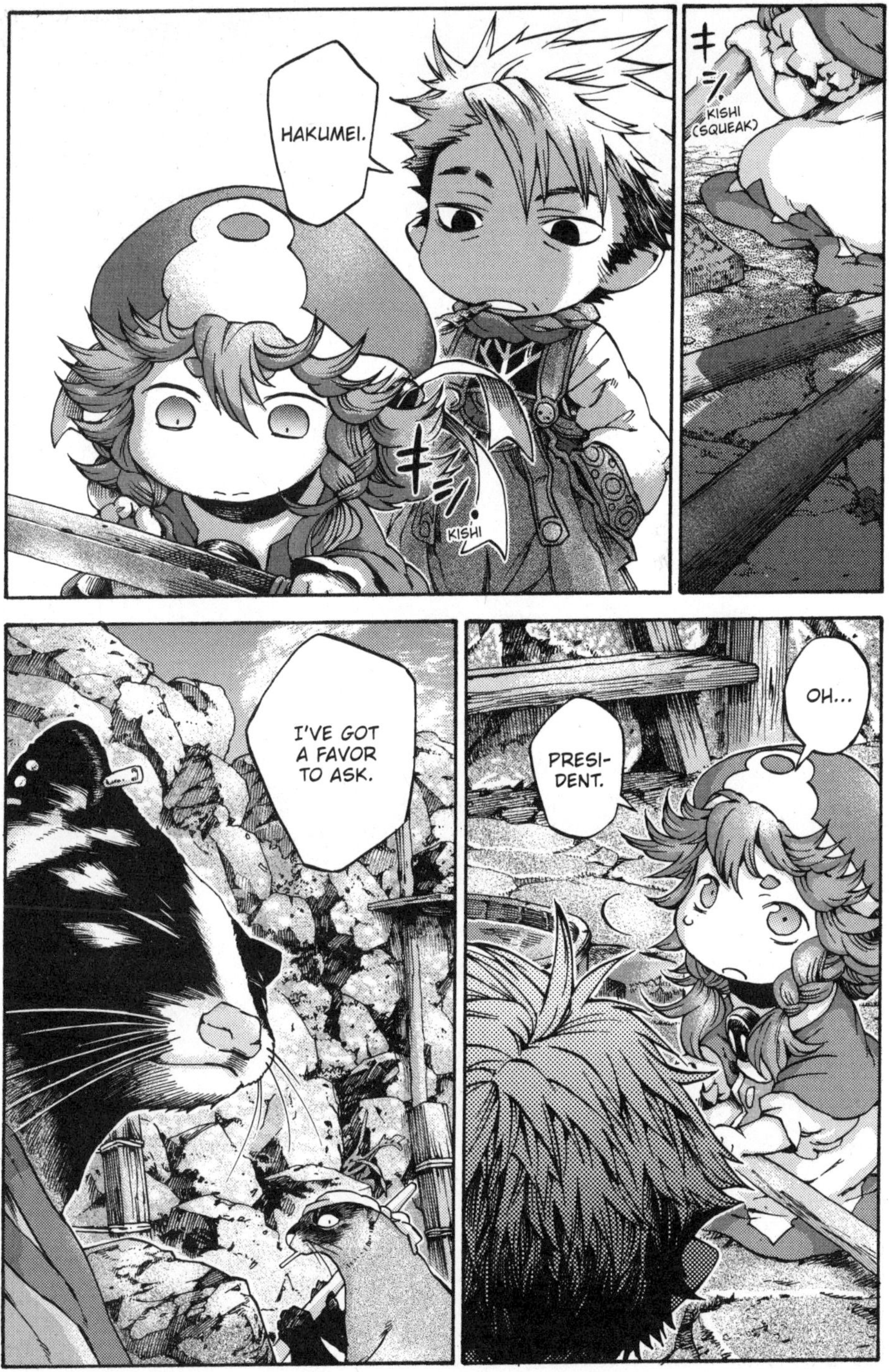
キシ
KISHI (SQUEAK)
HAKUMEI.
キシ
KISHI
OH...
PRESI-DENT.
I'VE GOT A FAVOR TO ASK.

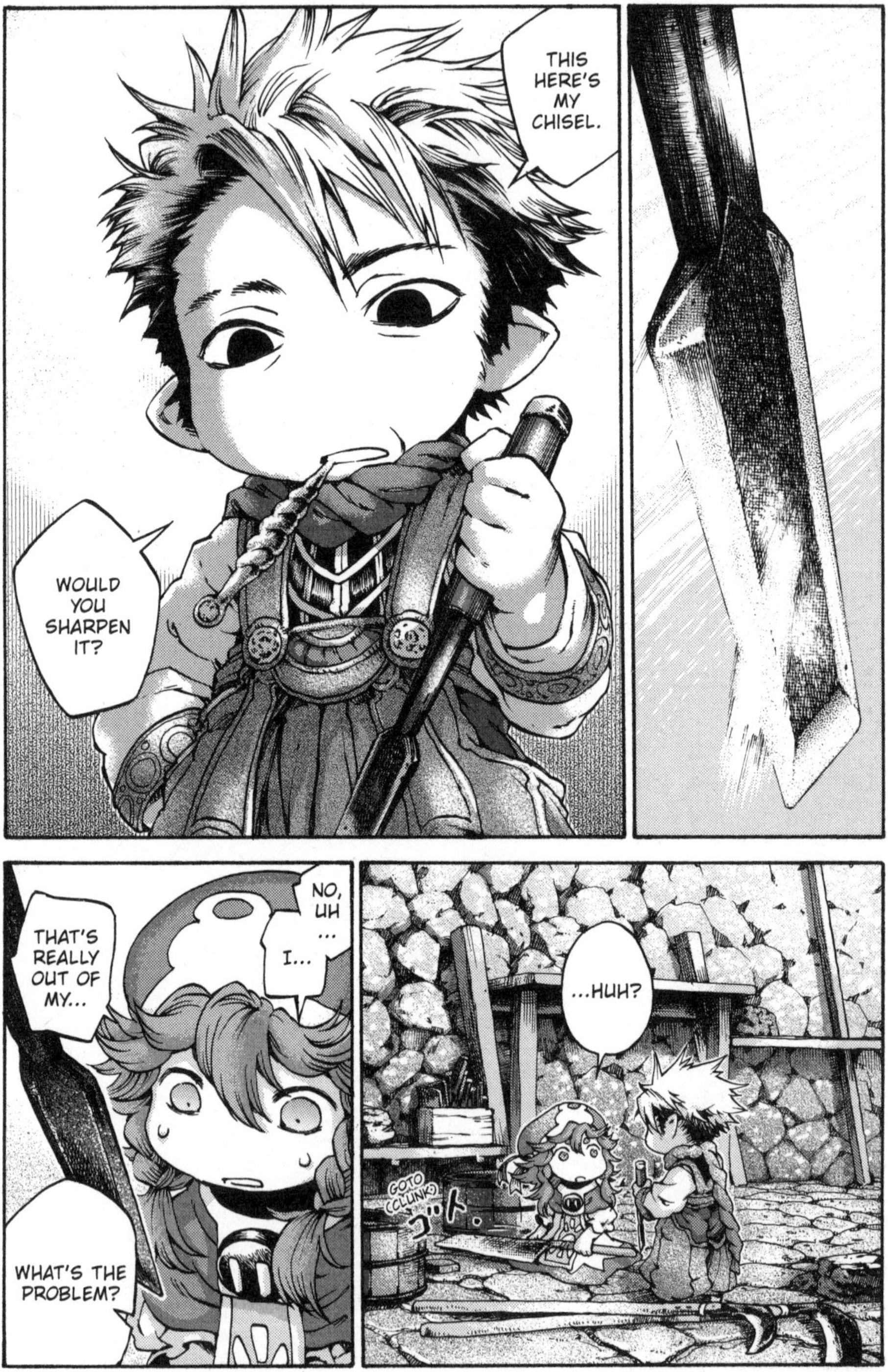
THIS HERE'S MY CHISEL.
WOULD YOU SHARPEN IT?
...HUH?
GOTO (CLUNK)
ゴト。
NO, UH ... I...
THAT'S REALLY OUT OF MY...
WHAT'S THE PROBLEM?

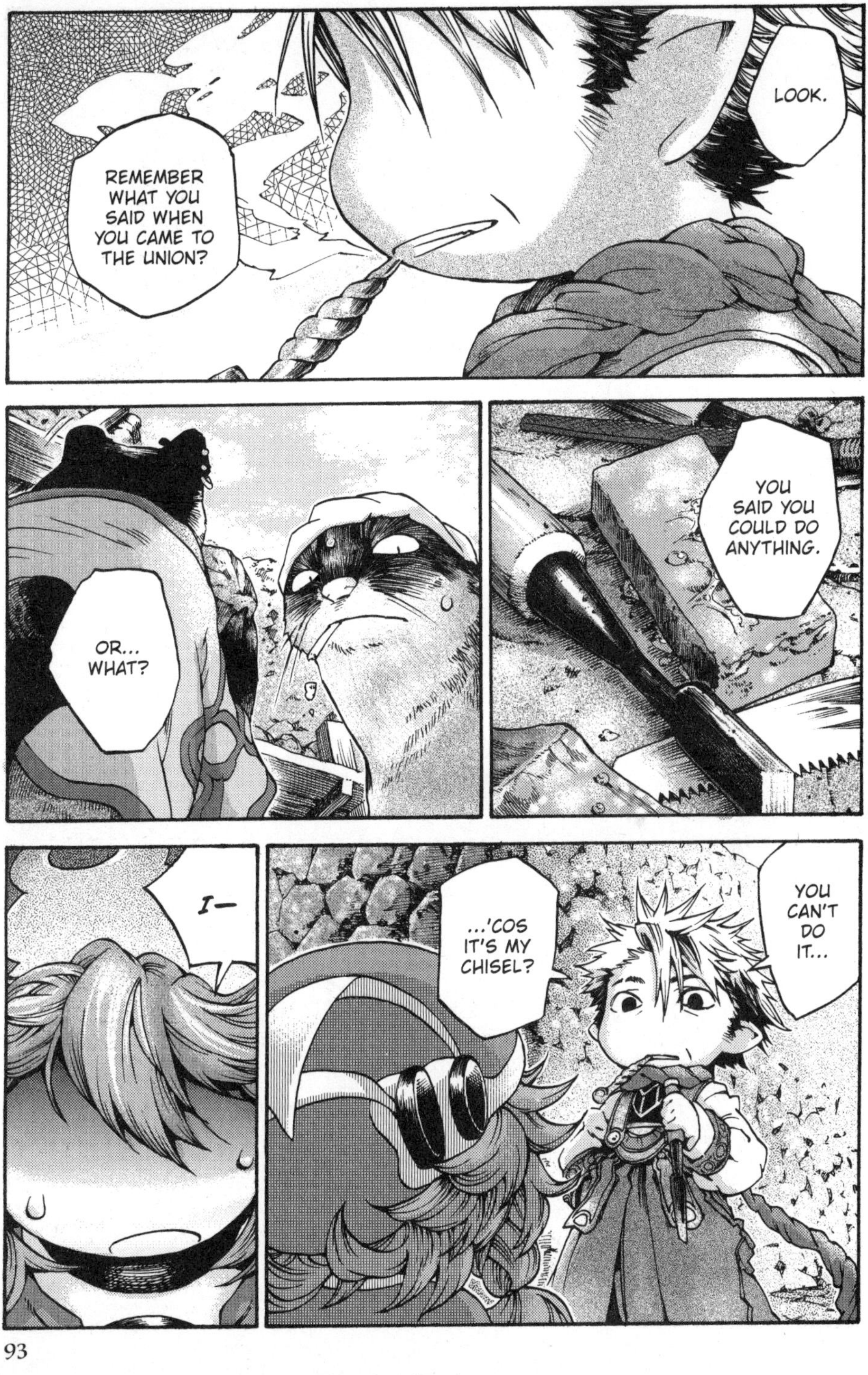
LOOK.
REMEMBER WHAT YOU SAID WHEN YOU CAME TO THE UNION?
YOU SAID YOU COULD DO ANYTHING.
OR... WHAT?
YOU CAN'T DO IT...
...'COS IT'S MY CHISEL?
I—

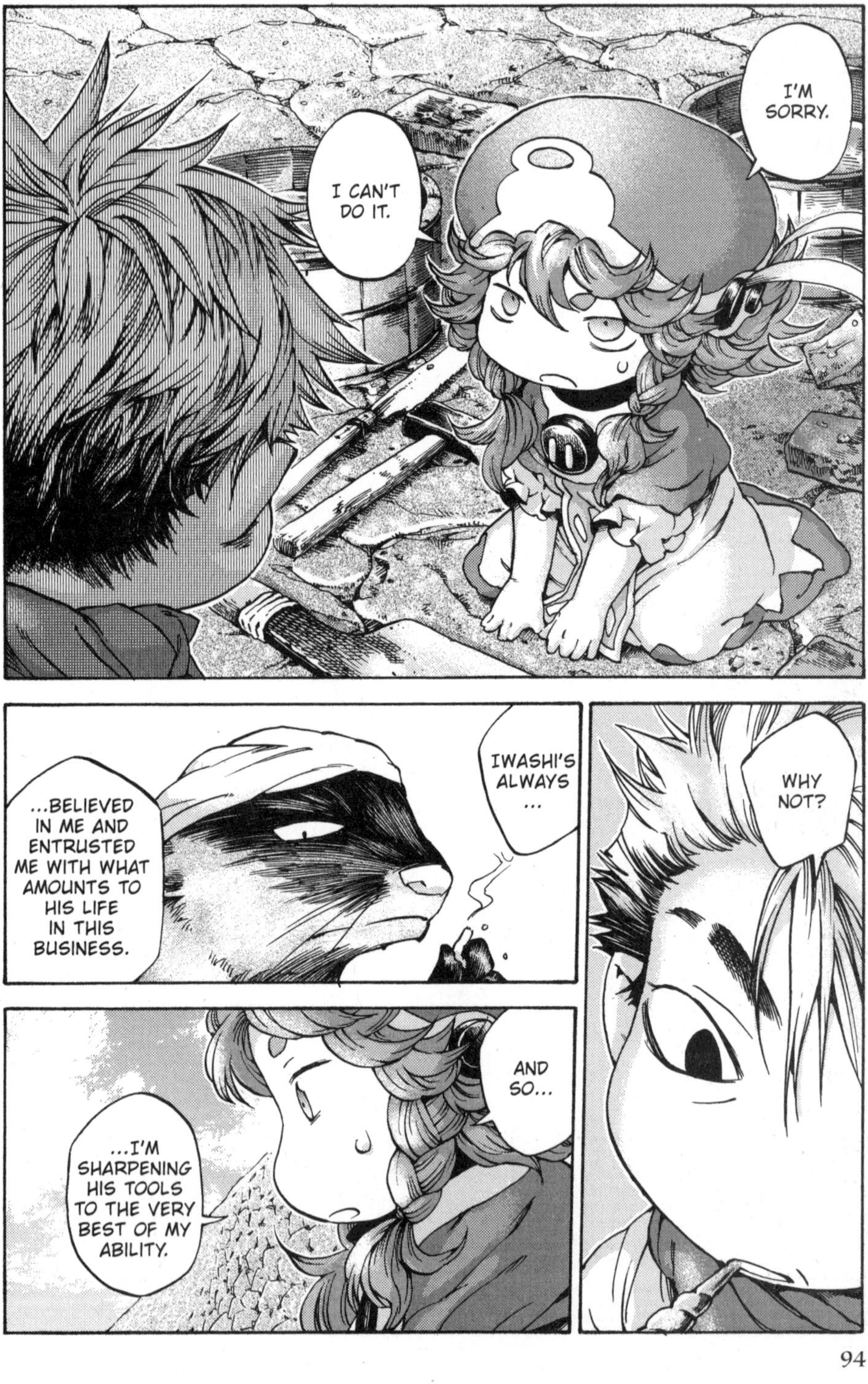
I'M SORRY.
I CAN'T DO IT.
WHY NOT?
IWASHI'S ALWAYS ...
...BELIEVED IN ME AND ENTRUSTED ME WITH WHAT AMOUNTS TO HIS LIFE IN THIS BUSINESS.
AND SO...
...I'M SHARPENING HIS TOOLS TO THE VERY BEST OF MY ABILITY.

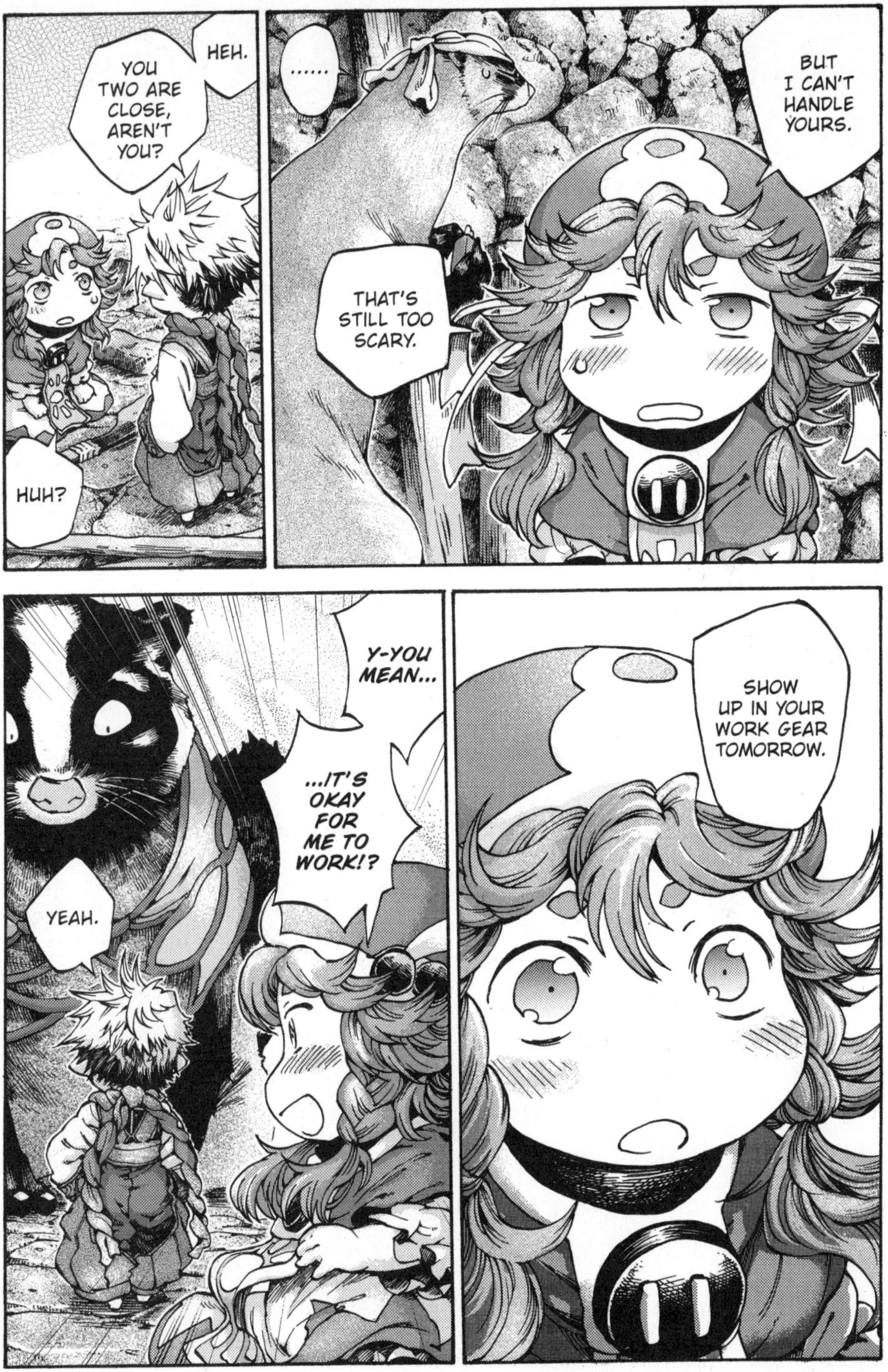
BUT I CAN'T HANDLE YOURS.
......
THAT'S STILL TOO SCARY.
HEH.
YOU TWO ARE CLOSE, AREN'T YOU?
HUH?
SHOW UP IN YOUR WORK GEAR TOMORROW.
Y-YOU MEAN...
...IT'S OKAY FOR ME TO WORK!?
YEAH.

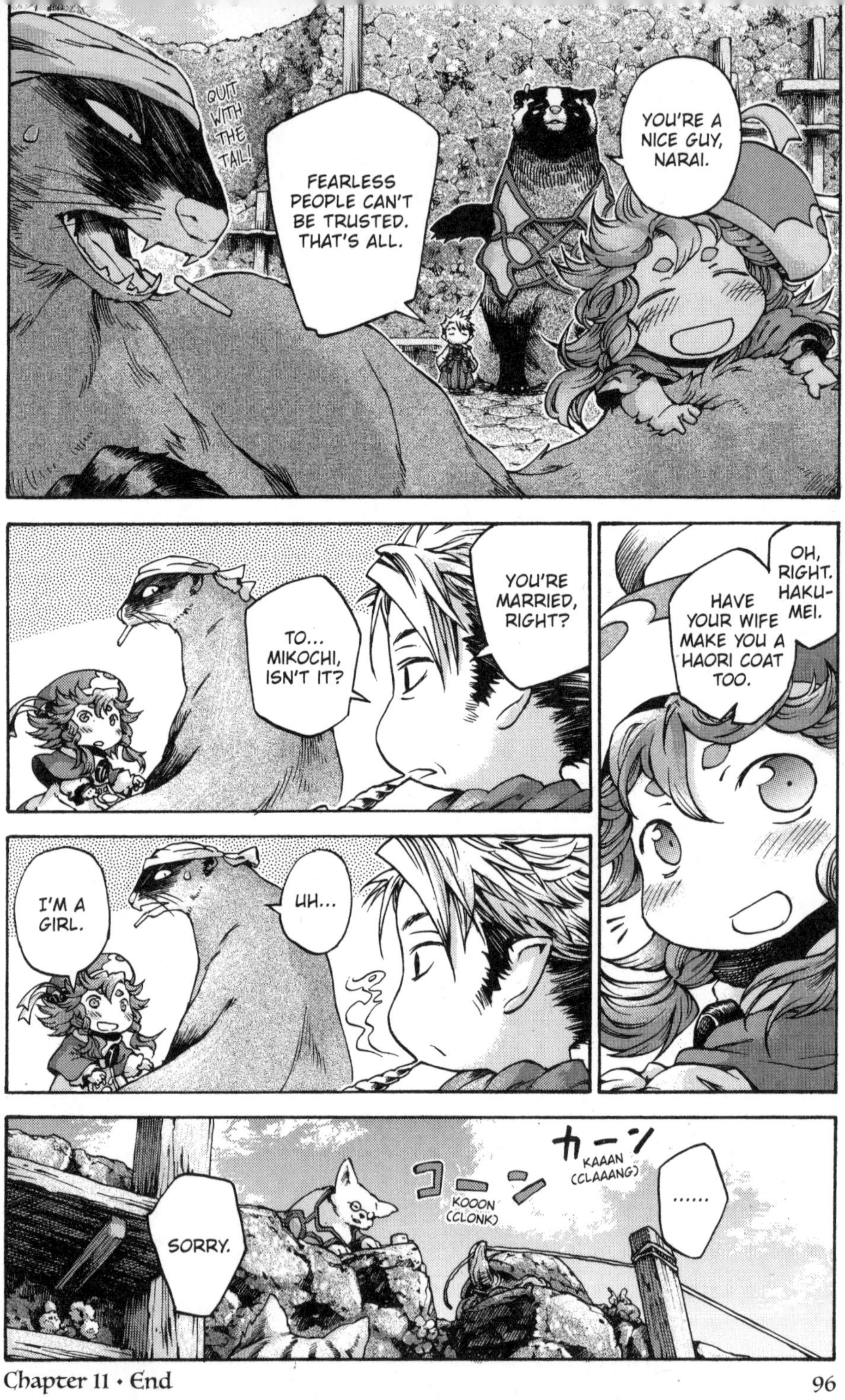
YOU'RE A NICE GUY, NARAI.
FEARLESS PEOPLE CAN'T BE TRUSTED. THAT'S ALL.
QUIT WITH THE TAIL!
OH, RIGHT. HAKU-MEI.
HAVE YOUR WIFE MAKE YOU A HAORI COAT TOO.
YOU'RE MARRIED, RIGHT?
TO... MIKOCHI, ISN'T IT?
UH...
I'M A GIRL.
......
カーン
KAAAN (CLAAANG)
コーン
KOOON (CLONK)
SORRY.

•*Column*• Underfoot Steps 11 / Two Men

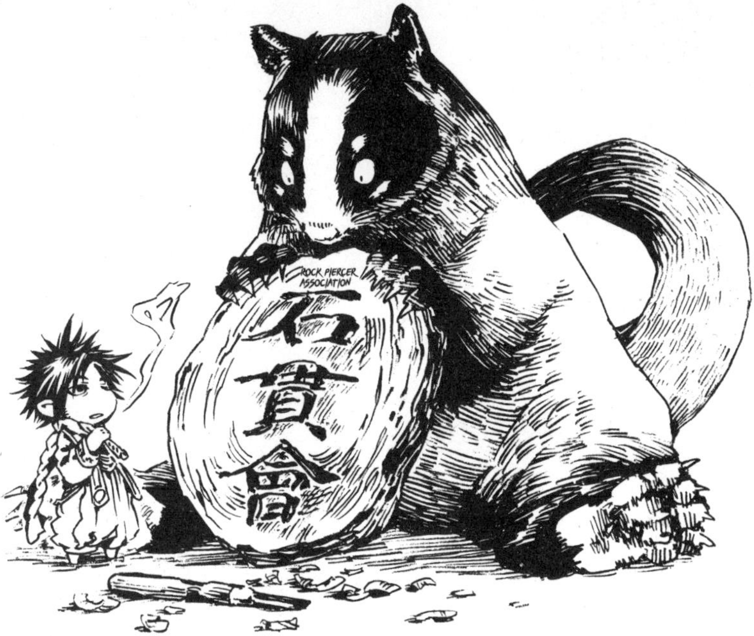
ROCK PIERCER ASSOCIATION
石貫會

Two men came to a builders' union that had been reduced to a shadow of its former glory.

The easygoing one brought in loads of lumber by himself in one go, a job normally reserved for several dozen men.
The one with the sharp eyes carried venerable old tools and exercised superb technique.

With exquisite teamwork, the pair plowed through unresolved requests that had been brought to the union, one after another. It was grueling, but they continued to work steadily, and it stirred the souls of many artisans and apprentices.

...And so the builders' union was revived.

–Excerpt from *The History of the Makinata Builders' Union*

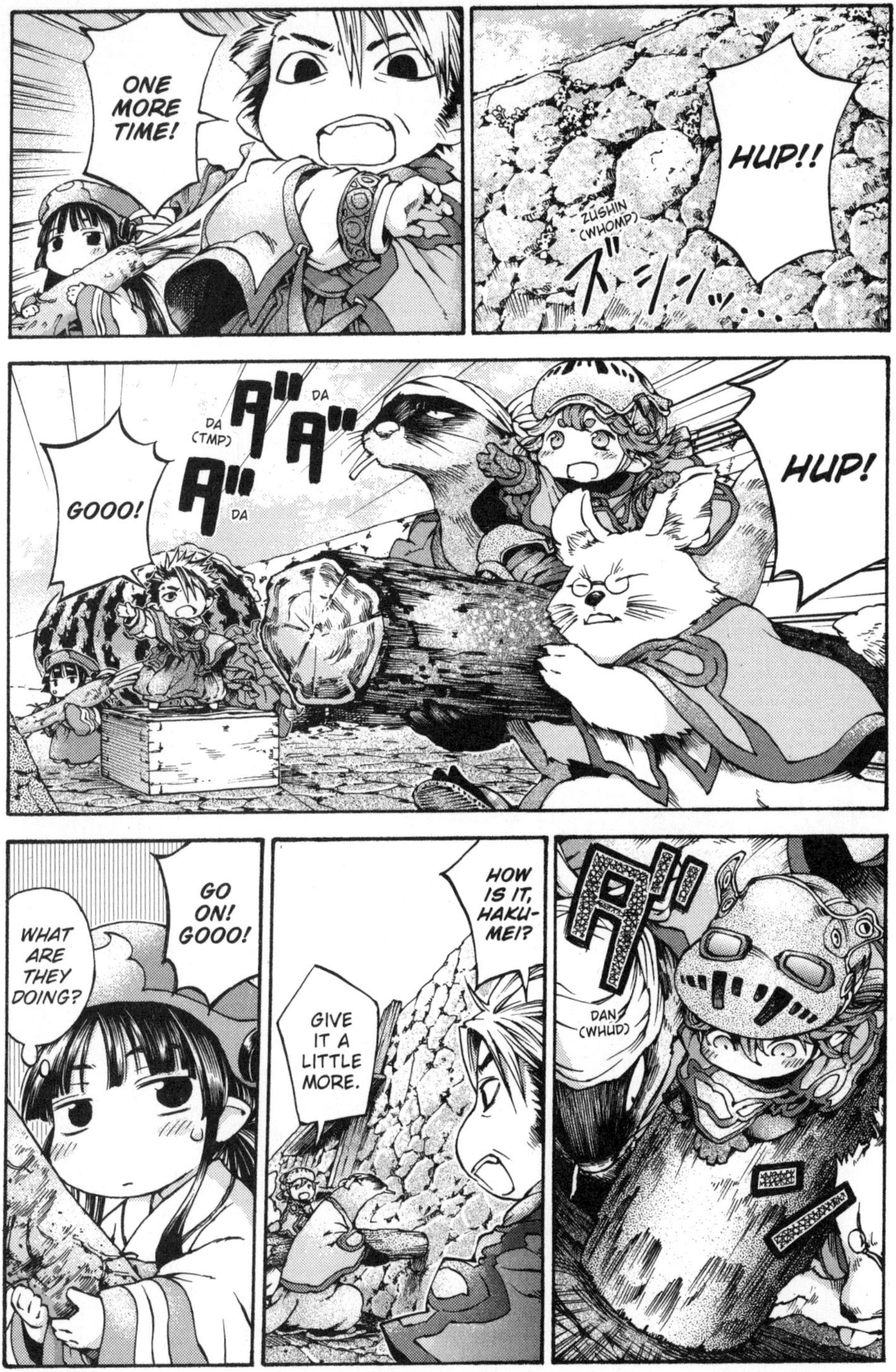
HUP!!
ZUSHIN (WHOMP)
ONE MORE TIME!
HUP!
DA
DA (TMP)
GOOO!
DA
DAN (WHUD)
HOW IS IT, HAKUMEI?
GIVE IT A LITTLE MORE.
GO ON! GOOO!
WHAT ARE THEY DOING?

Chapter 12
Boulder and Pinning Stones

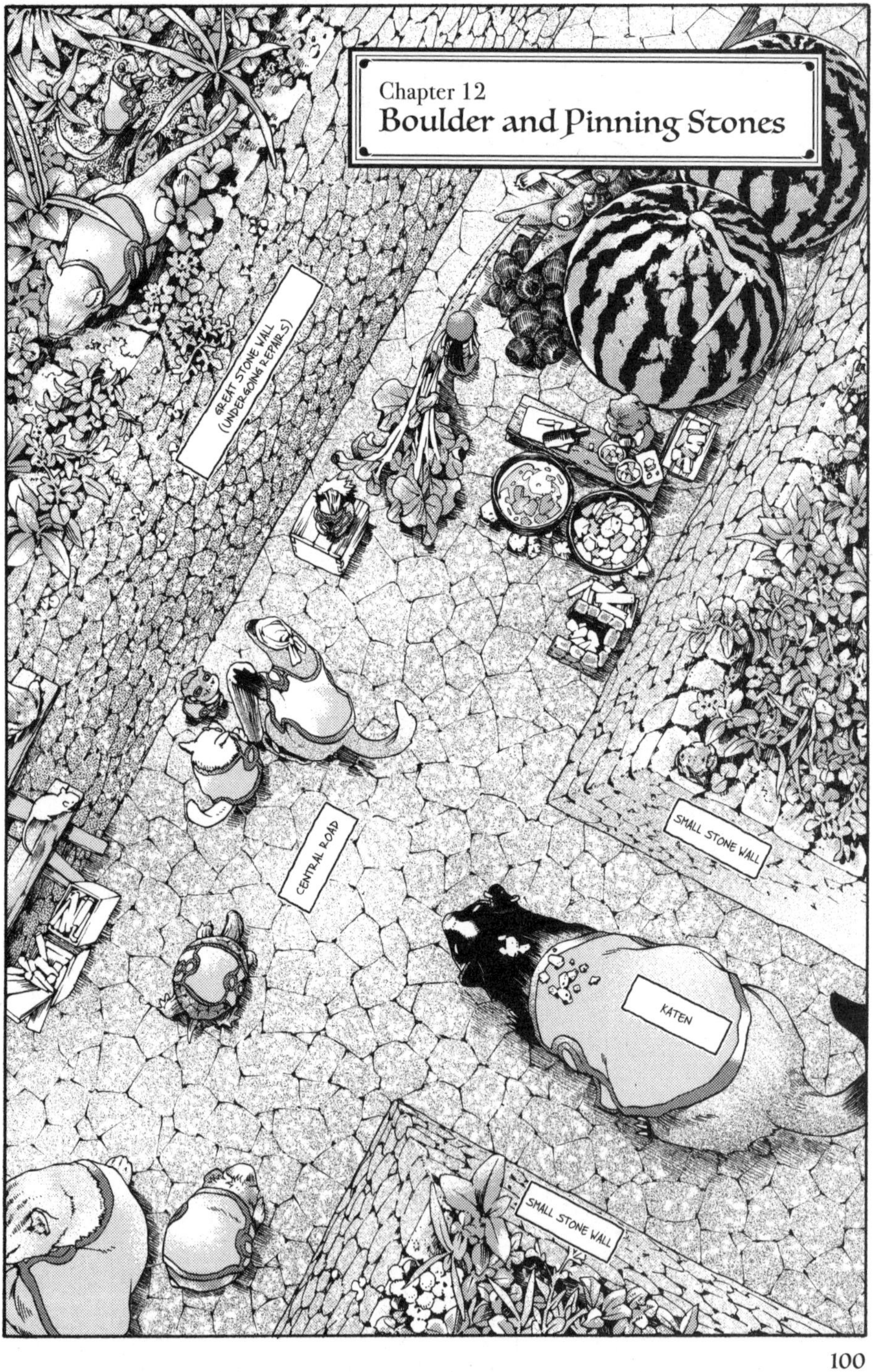
GREAT STONE WALL (UNDERGOING REPAIRS)
CENTRAL ROAD
SMALL STONE WALL
KATEN
SMALL STONE WALL

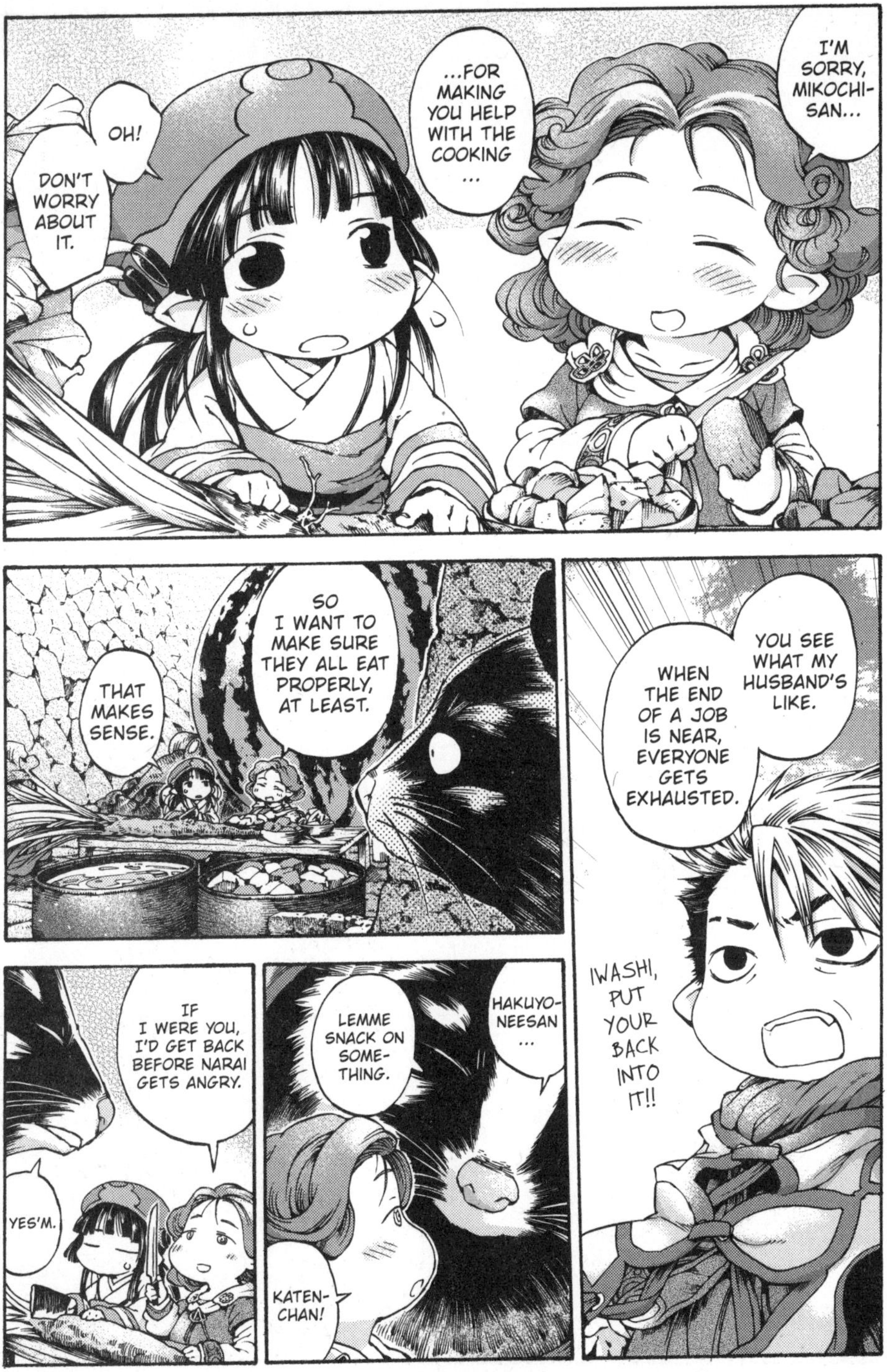
I'M SORRY, MIKOCHI-SAN...
...FOR MAKING YOU HELP WITH THE COOKING ...
OH!
DON'T WORRY ABOUT IT.
YOU SEE WHAT MY HUSBAND'S LIKE.
WHEN THE END OF A JOB IS NEAR, EVERYONE GETS EXHAUSTED.
IWASHI, PUT YOUR BACK INTO IT!!
SO I WANT TO MAKE SURE THEY ALL EAT PROPERLY, AT LEAST.
THAT MAKES SENSE.
HAKUYO-NEESAN ...
LEMME SNACK ON SOME-THING.
KATEN-CHAN!
IF I WERE YOU, I'D GET BACK BEFORE NARAI GETS ANGRY.
YES'M.

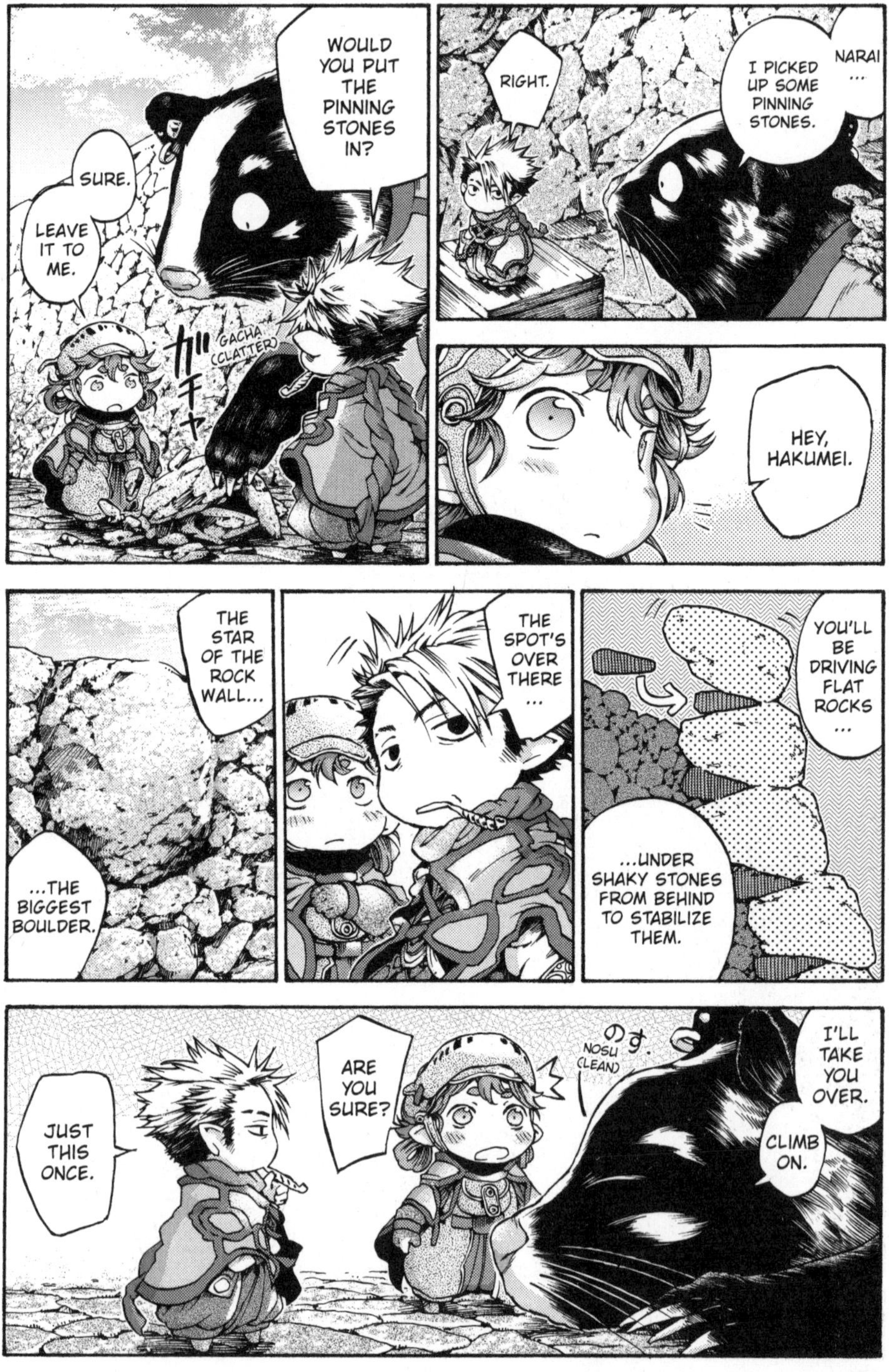
NARAI...
I PICKED UP SOME PINNING STONES.
RIGHT.
HEY, HAKUMEI.
WOULD YOU PUT THE PINNING STONES IN?
SURE.
LEAVE IT TO ME.
ガチャ
GACHA (CLATTER)
YOU'LL BE DRIVING FLAT ROCKS...
...UNDER SHAKY STONES FROM BEHIND TO STABILIZE THEM.
THE SPOT'S OVER THERE...
THE STAR OF THE ROCK WALL...
...THE BIGGEST BOULDER.
I'LL TAKE YOU OVER.
CLIMB ON.
のす.
NOSU (CLEAN)
ARE YOU SURE?
JUST THIS ONCE.

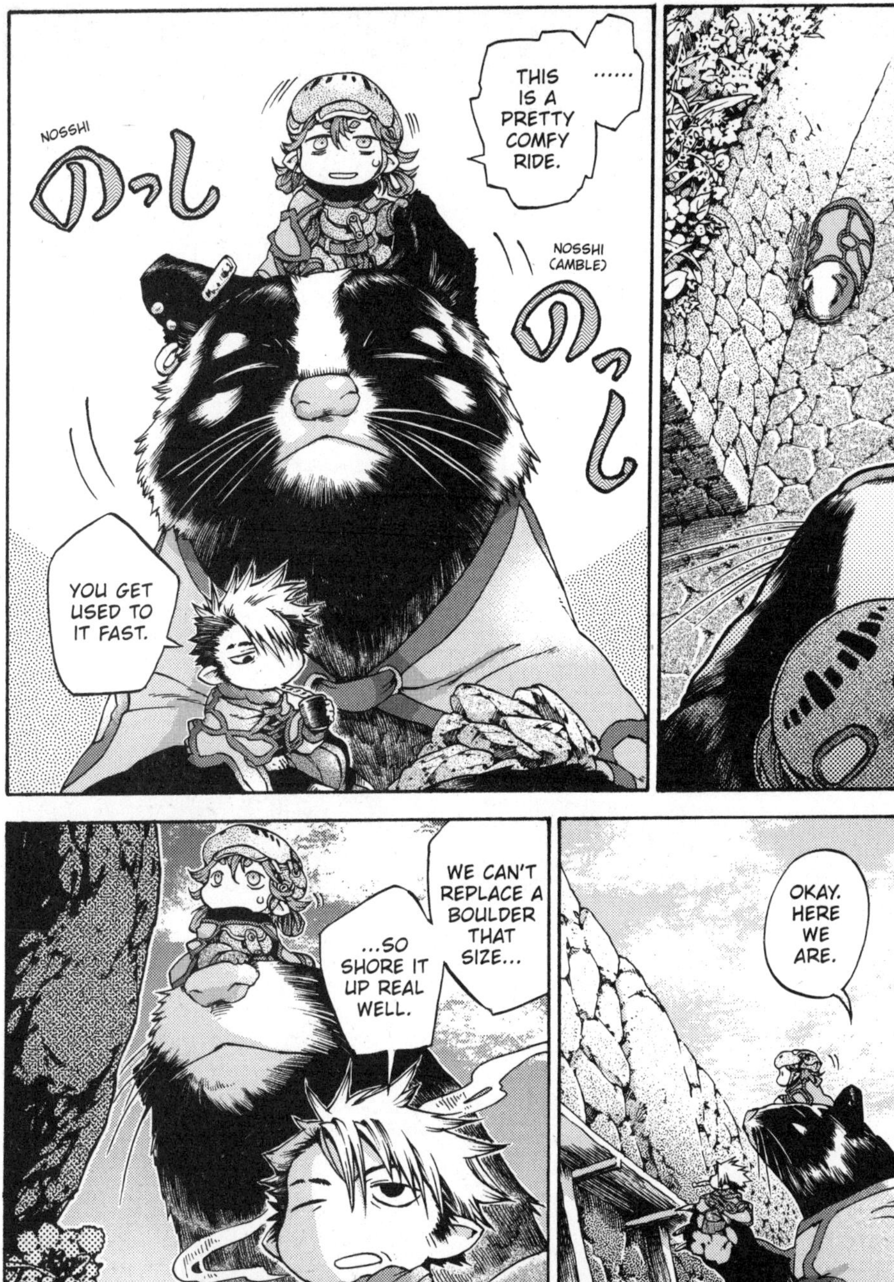
......
THIS IS A PRETTY COMFY RIDE.
NOSSHI (AMBLE)
のっし
NOSSHI
のっし
YOU GET USED TO IT FAST.
OKAY. HERE WE ARE.
WE CAN'T REPLACE A BOULDER THAT SIZE...
...SO SHORE IT UP REAL WELL.

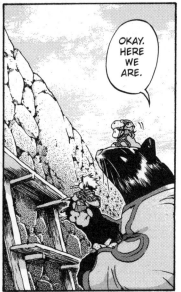

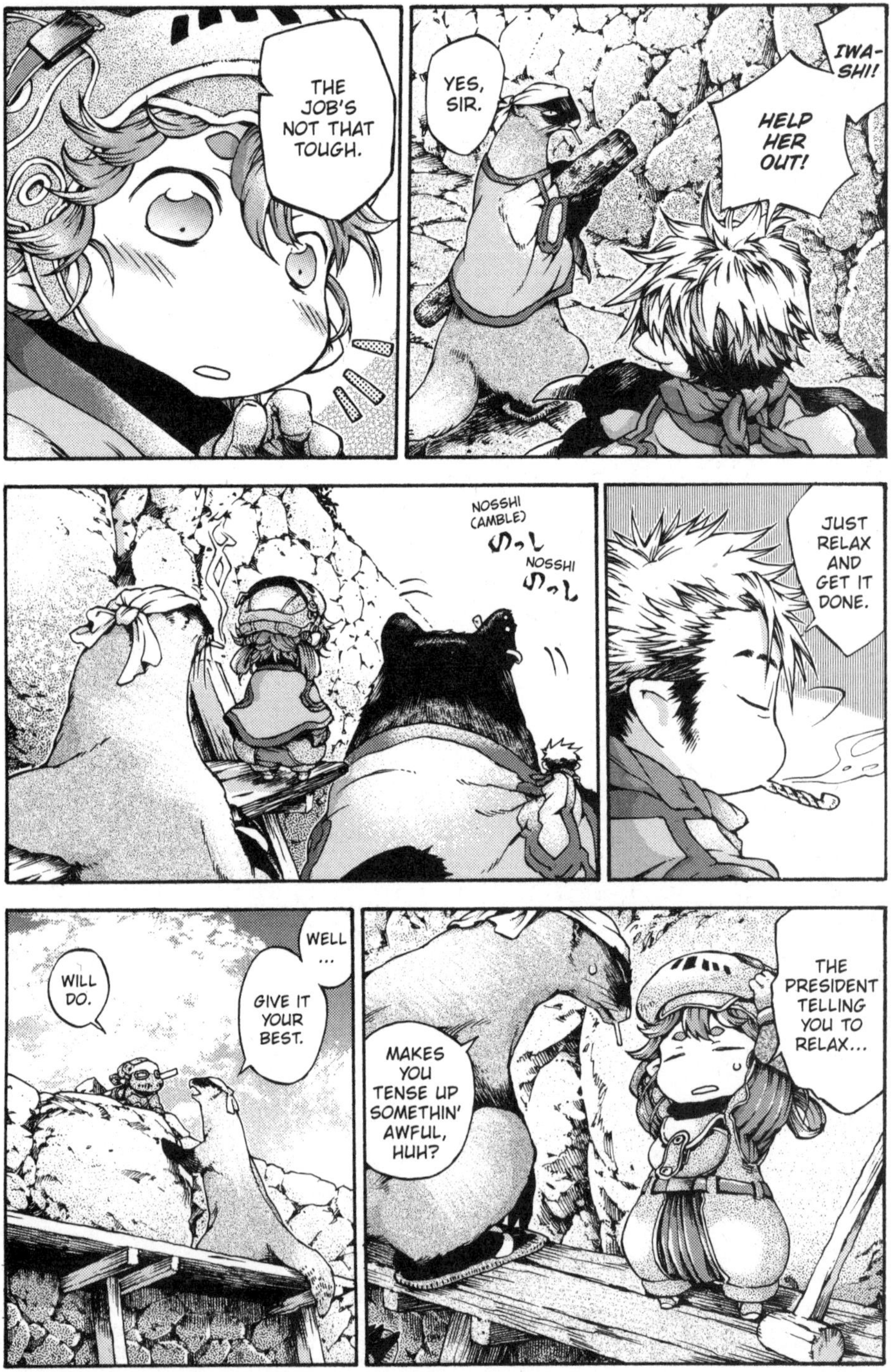
IWA-SHI!
HELP HER OUT!
YES, SIR.
THE JOB'S NOT THAT TOUGH.
JUST RELAX AND GET IT DONE.
NOSSHI (AMBLE) のっし
NOSSHI のっし
THE PRESIDENT TELLING YOU TO RELAX...
MAKES YOU TENSE UP SOMETHIN' AWFUL, HUH?
WELL...
GIVE IT YOUR BEST.
WILL DO.

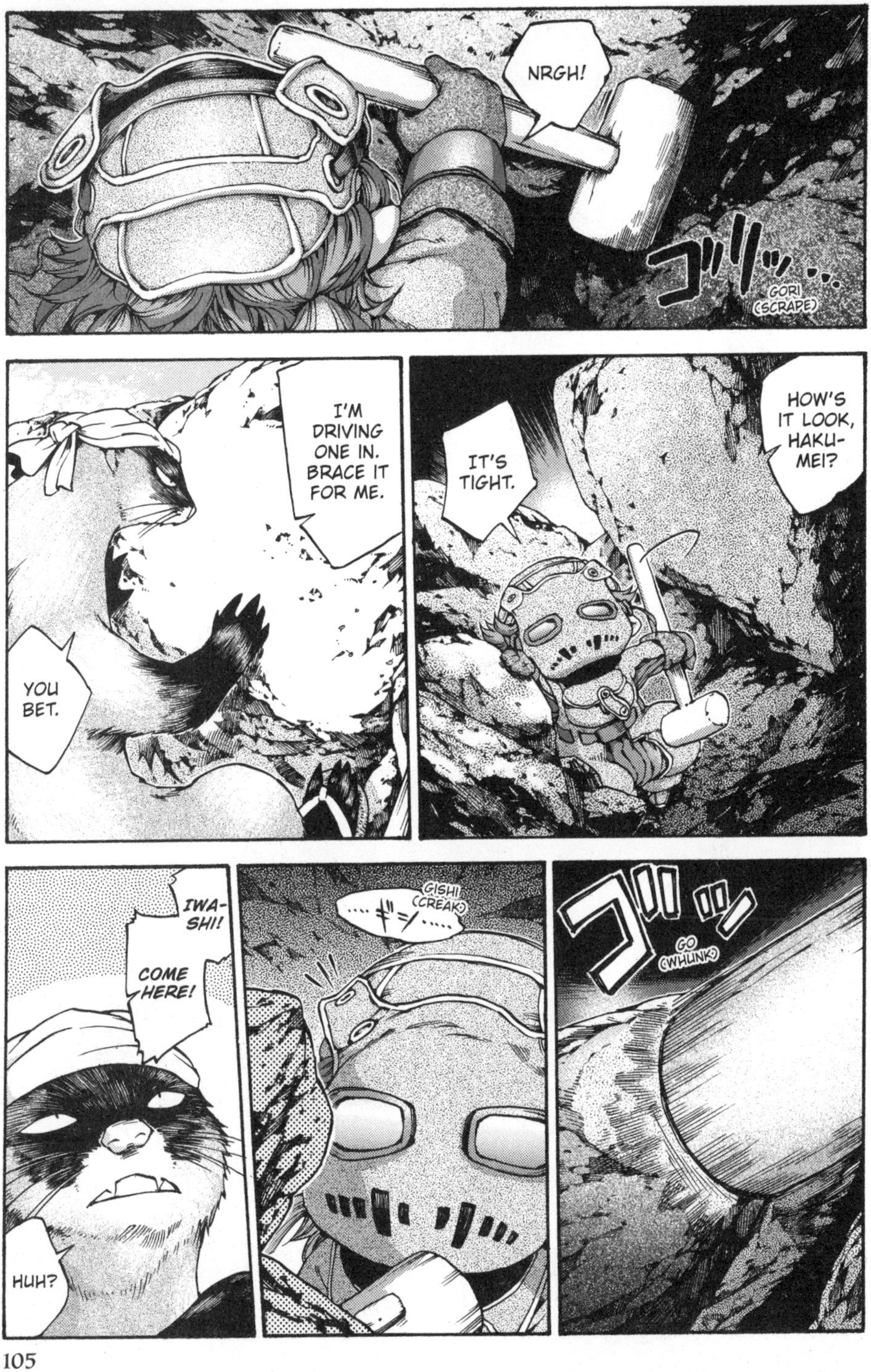
NRGH!
ゴリッ...
GORI (SCRAPE)
HOW'S IT LOOK, HAKU-MEI?
IT'S TIGHT.
I'M DRIVING ONE IN. BRACE IT FOR ME.
YOU BET.
ゴッ
GO (WHUNK)
GISHI (CREAK)
....ギシ....
IWA-SHI!
COME HERE!
HUH?

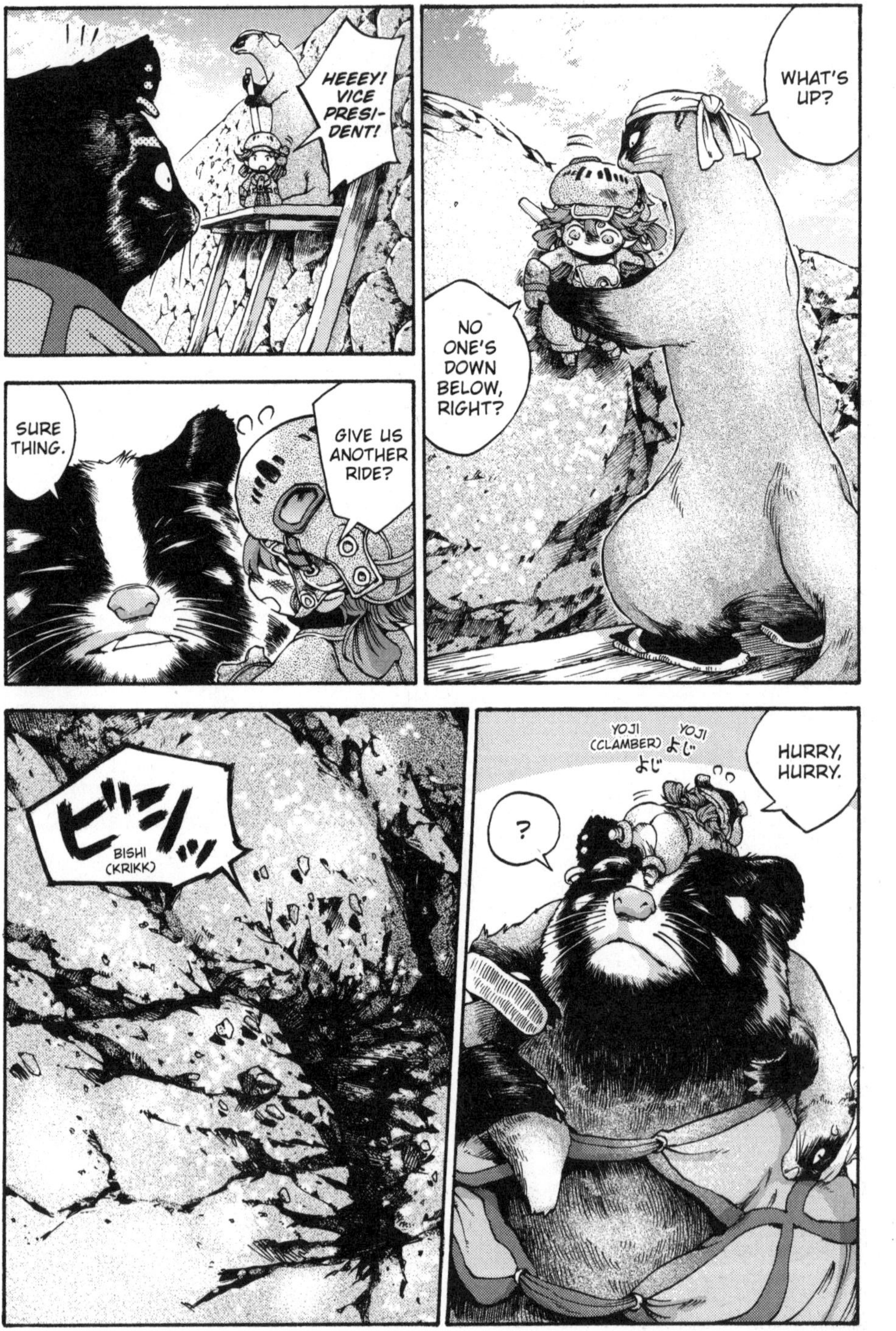
WHAT'S UP?
NO ONE'S DOWN BELOW, RIGHT?
HEEEY! VICE PRESI-DENT!
GIVE US ANOTHER RIDE?
SURE THING.
HURRY, HURRY.
YOJI (CLAMBER) よじ
YOJI よじ
?
ビシッ
BISHI (KRIKK)

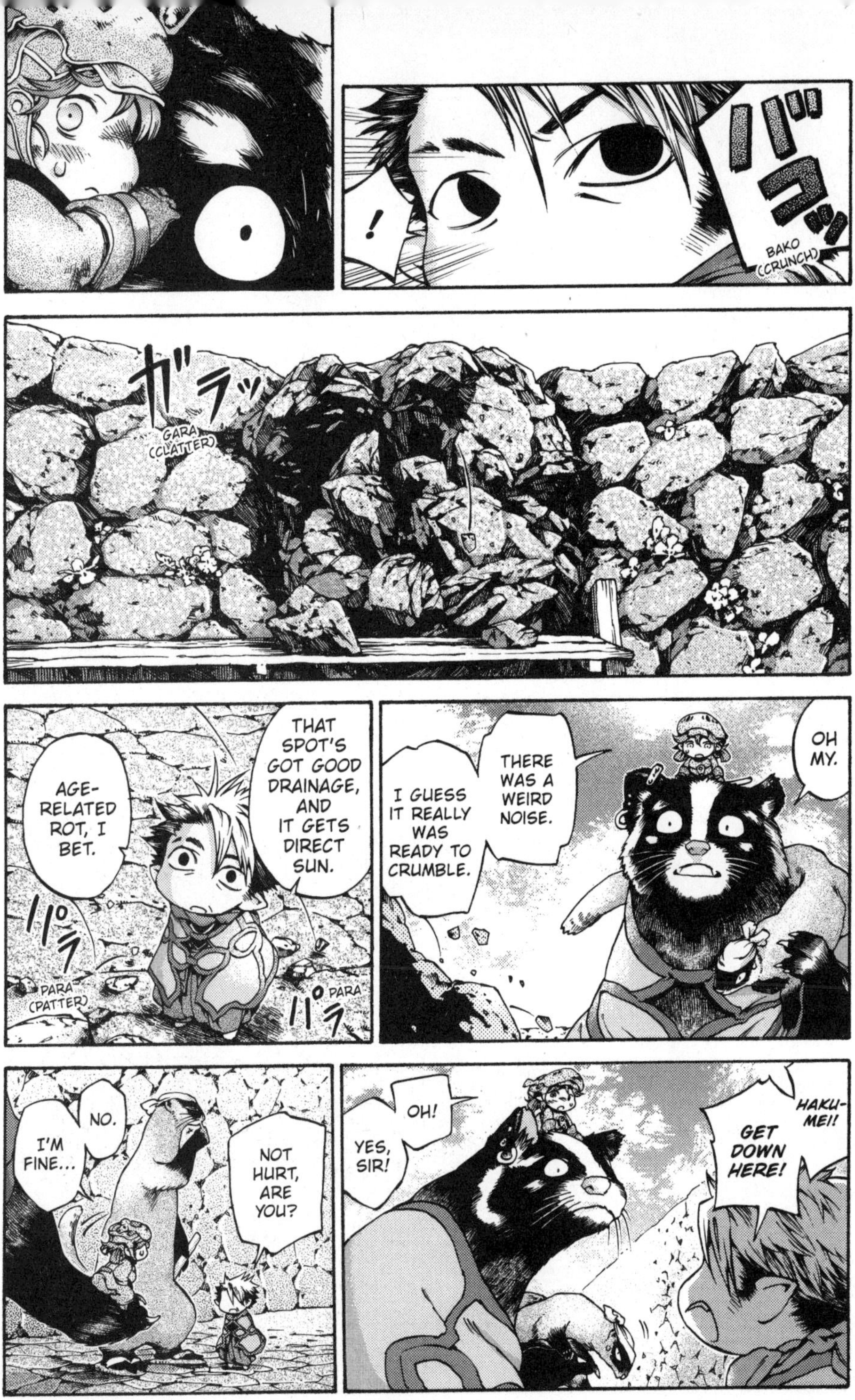

!
バコッ
BAKO (CRUNCH)
ガラッ
GARA (CLATTER)
OH MY.
THERE WAS A WEIRD NOISE.
I GUESS IT REALLY WAS READY TO CRUMBLE.
THAT SPOT'S GOT GOOD DRAINAGE, AND IT GETS DIRECT SUN.
AGE-RELATED ROT, I BET.
パラ
PARA (PATTER)
パラ
PARA
HAKUMEI!
GET DOWN HERE!
OH!
YES, SIR!
NOT HURT, ARE YOU?
NO.
I'M FINE...

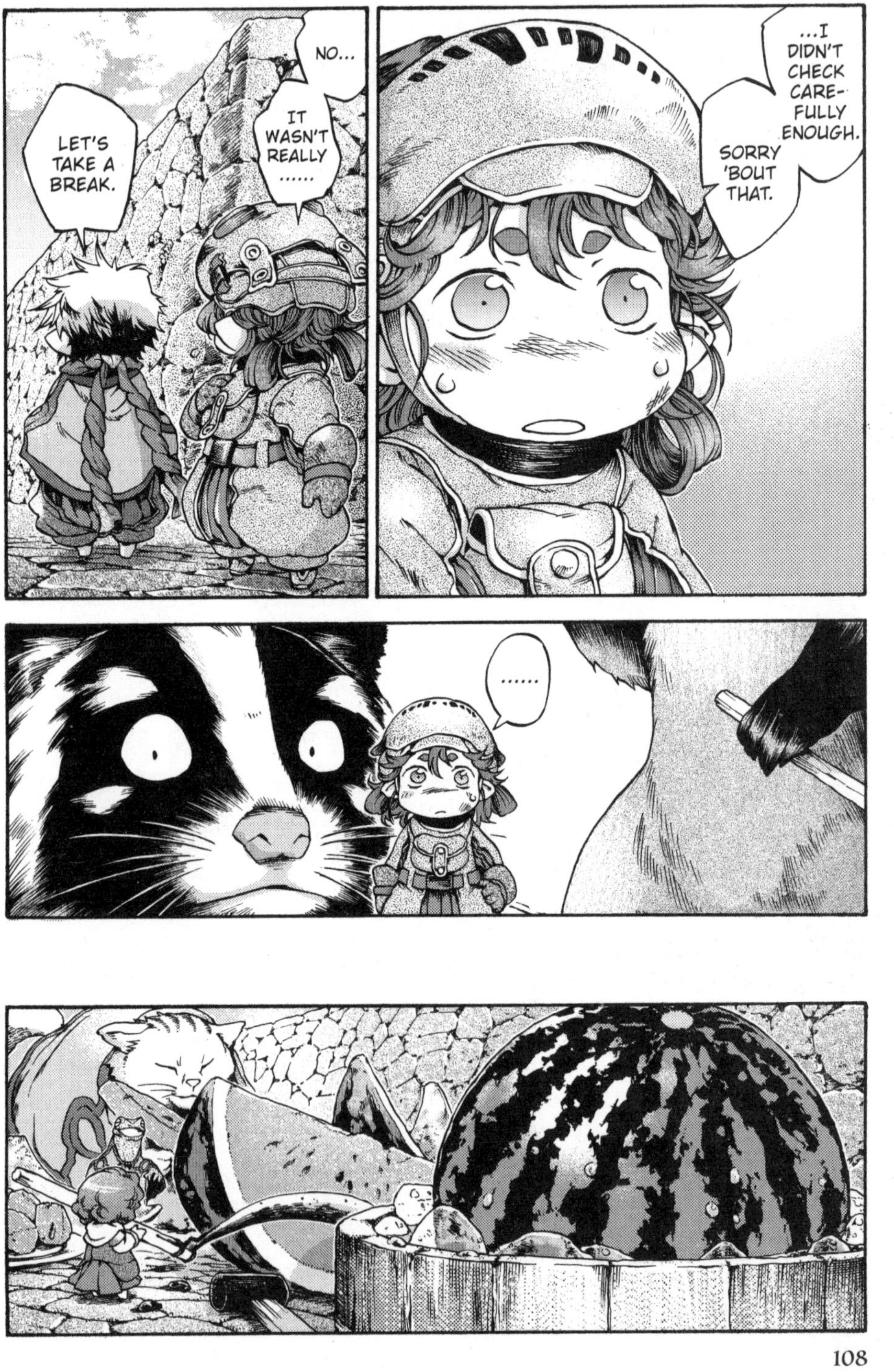
...I DIDN'T CHECK CARE-FULLY ENOUGH.
SORRY 'BOUT THAT.
NO...
IT WASN'T REALLY ......
LET'S TAKE A BREAK.
......

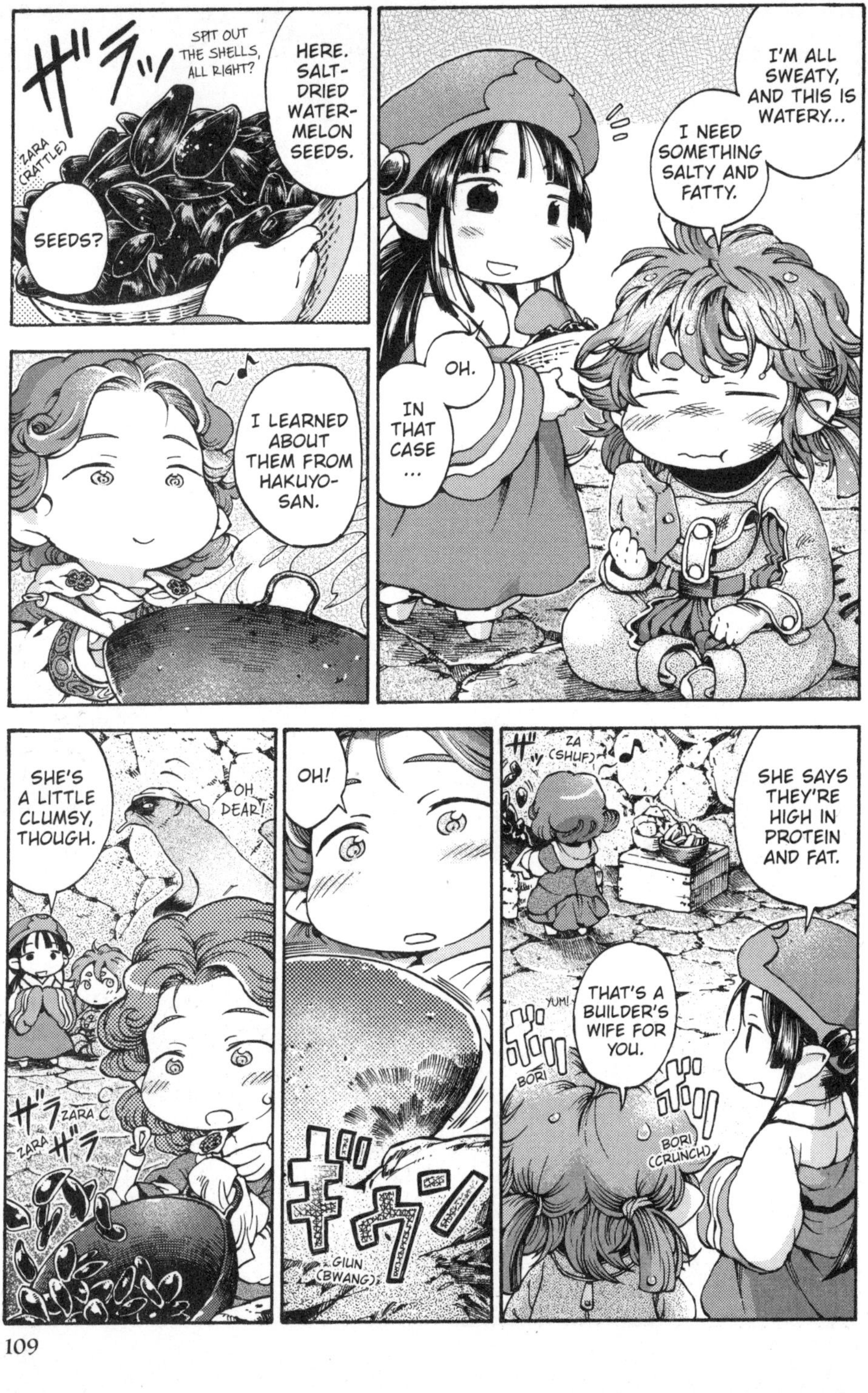
I'M ALL SWEATY, AND THIS IS WATERY...
I NEED SOMETHING SALTY AND FATTY.
OH.
IN THAT CASE ...
HERE. SALT-DRIED WATER-MELON SEEDS.
SPIT OUT THE SHELLS, ALL RIGHT?
ザラッ
ZARA (RATTLE)
SEEDS?
I LEARNED ABOUT THEM FROM HAKUYO-SAN.
SHE SAYS THEY'RE HIGH IN PROTEIN AND FAT.
ザッ
ZA (SHUF)
THAT'S A BUILDER'S WIFE FOR YOU.
YUM!
ボリ
BORI
ボリ
BORI (CRUNCH)
OH!
ギウン
GIUN (BWANG)
SHE'S A LITTLE CLUMSY, THOUGH.
OH DEAR!
ザラ
ZARA
ザラ
ZARA

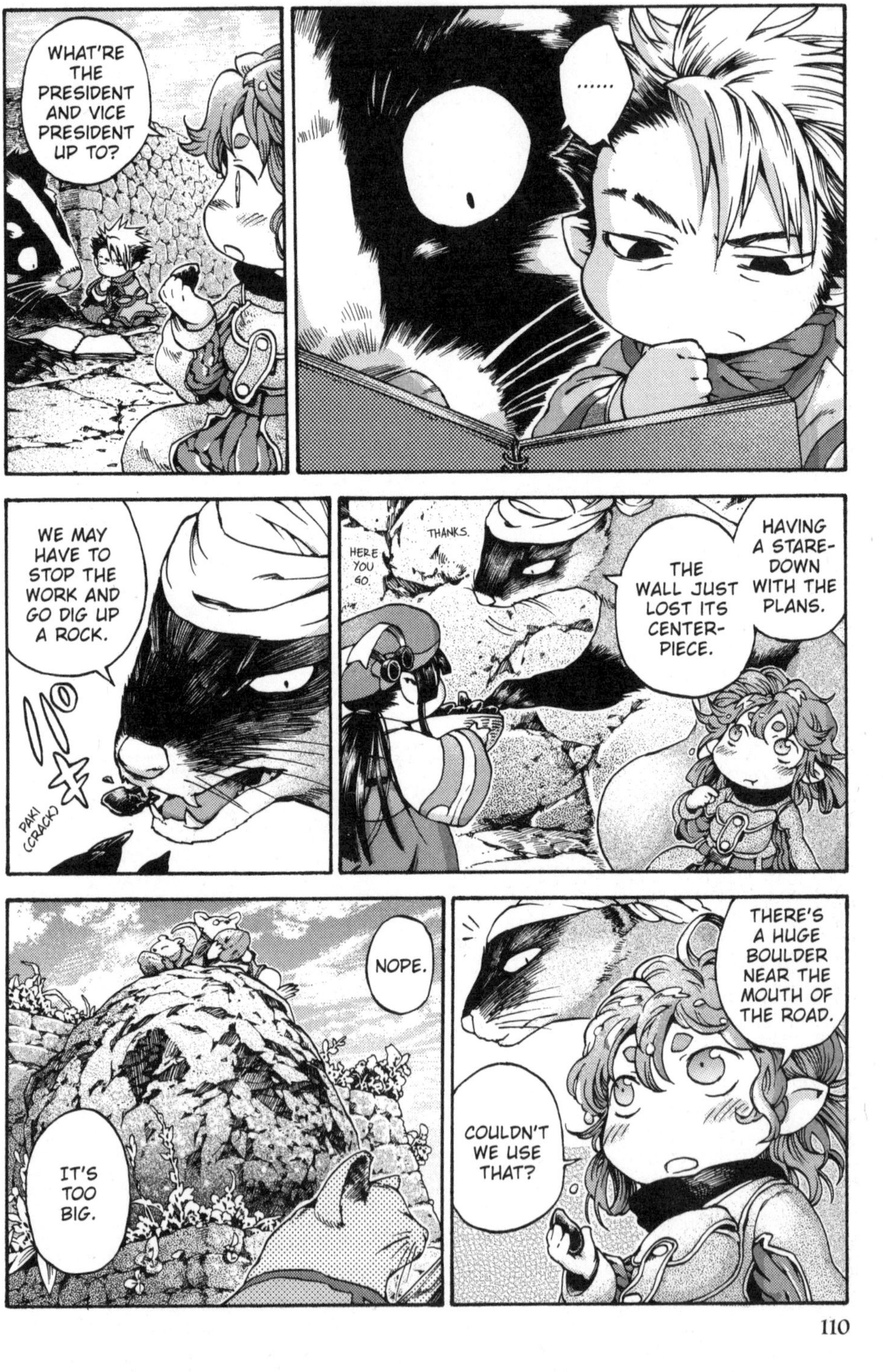
......
WHAT'RE THE PRESIDENT AND VICE PRESIDENT UP TO?
HAVING A STARE-DOWN WITH THE PLANS.
THE WALL JUST LOST ITS CENTER-PIECE.
THANKS.
HERE YOU GO.
WE MAY HAVE TO STOP THE WORK AND GO DIG UP A ROCK.
PAKI (CRACK)
THERE'S A HUGE BOULDER NEAR THE MOUTH OF THE ROAD.
COULDN'T WE USE THAT?
NOPE.
IT'S TOO BIG.

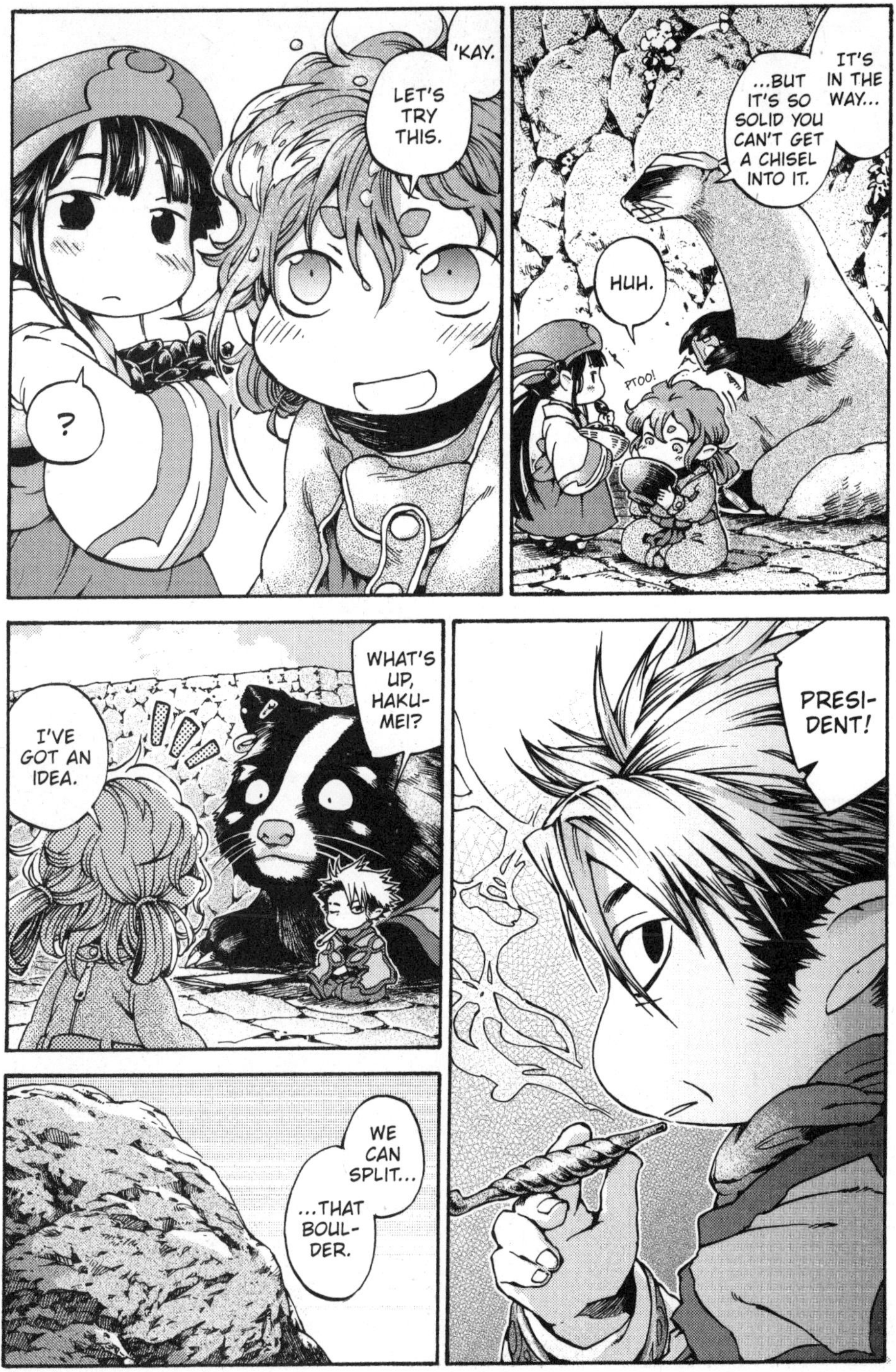
IT'S IN THE WAY...
...BUT IT'S SO SOLID YOU CAN'T GET A CHISEL INTO IT.
HUH.
PTOO!
'KAY.
LET'S TRY THIS.
?
PRESIDENT!
WHAT'S UP, HAKUMEI?
I'VE GOT AN IDEA.
WE CAN SPLIT...
...THAT BOULDER.

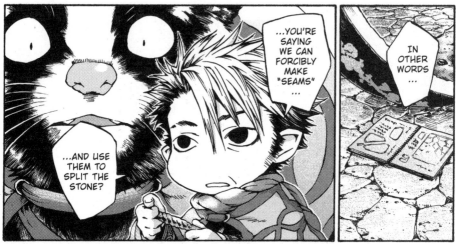

IN OTHER WORDS ...
...YOU'RE SAYING WE CAN FORCIBLY MAKE "SEAMS" ...
...AND USE THEM TO SPLIT THE STONE?
YOU BURN THE PLACES YOU WANNA SPLIT...
...THEN FREEZE THEM QUICK WITH ICE WATER. THAT MAKES THEM CRACK.
THEN WE'LL SPLIT IT WITH YOUR CHISEL...
...SO THAT IT DOESN'T CRUMBLE TOO MUCH.
HOW'LL WE KEEP THE FIRE GOING THAT LONG?
I HAVE A PLAN FOR THAT TOO.

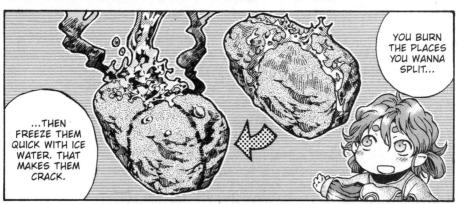

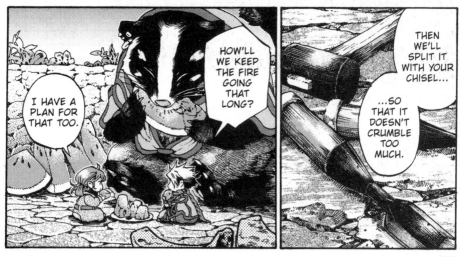

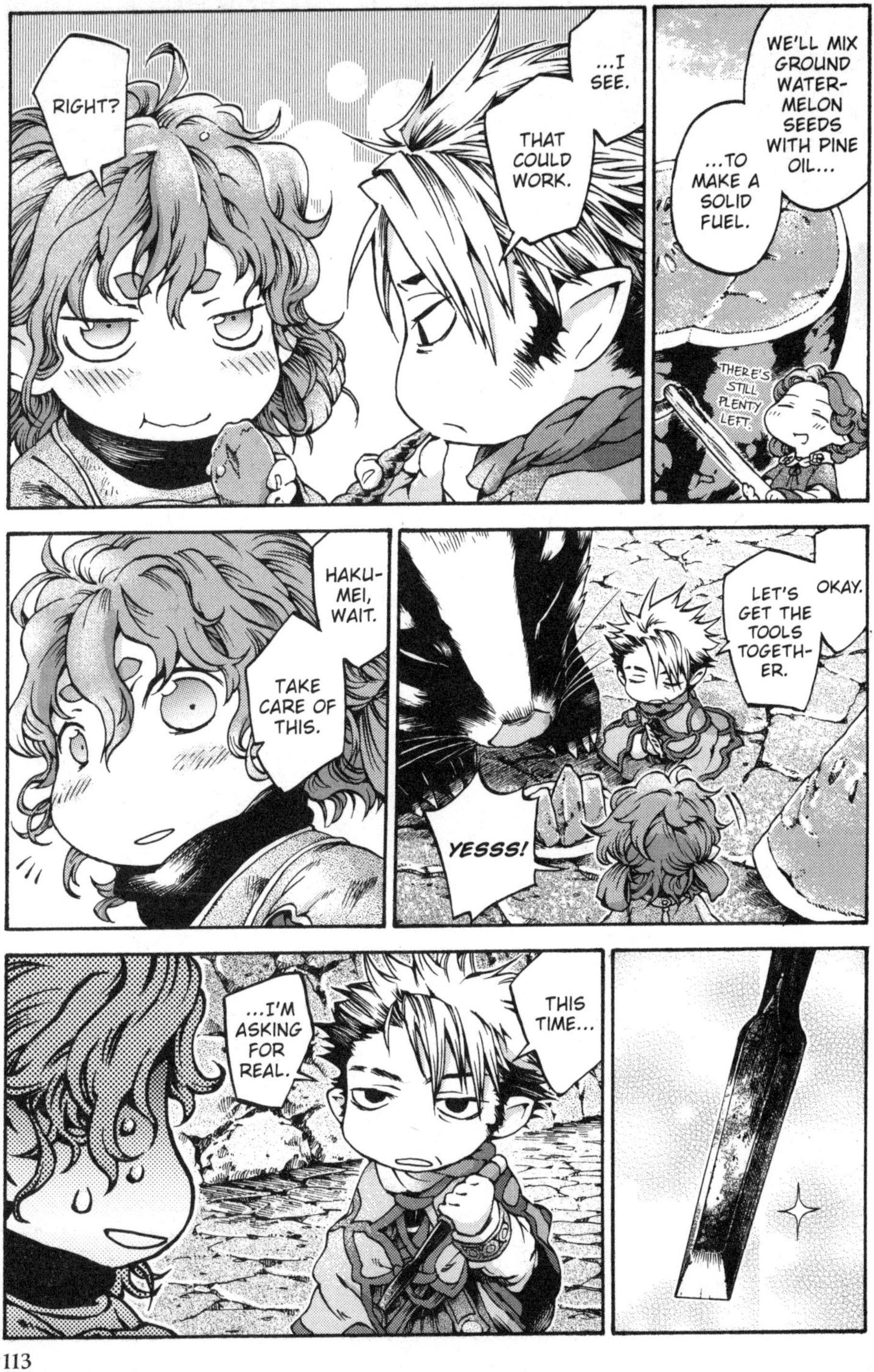
WE'LL MIX GROUND WATER-MELON SEEDS WITH PINE OIL...
...TO MAKE A SOLID FUEL.
THERE'S STILL PLENTY LEFT.
...I SEE.
THAT COULD WORK.
RIGHT?
OKAY.
LET'S GET THE TOOLS TOGETH-ER.
YESSS!
HAKU-MEI, WAIT.
TAKE CARE OF THIS.
THIS TIME...
...I'M ASKING FOR REAL.

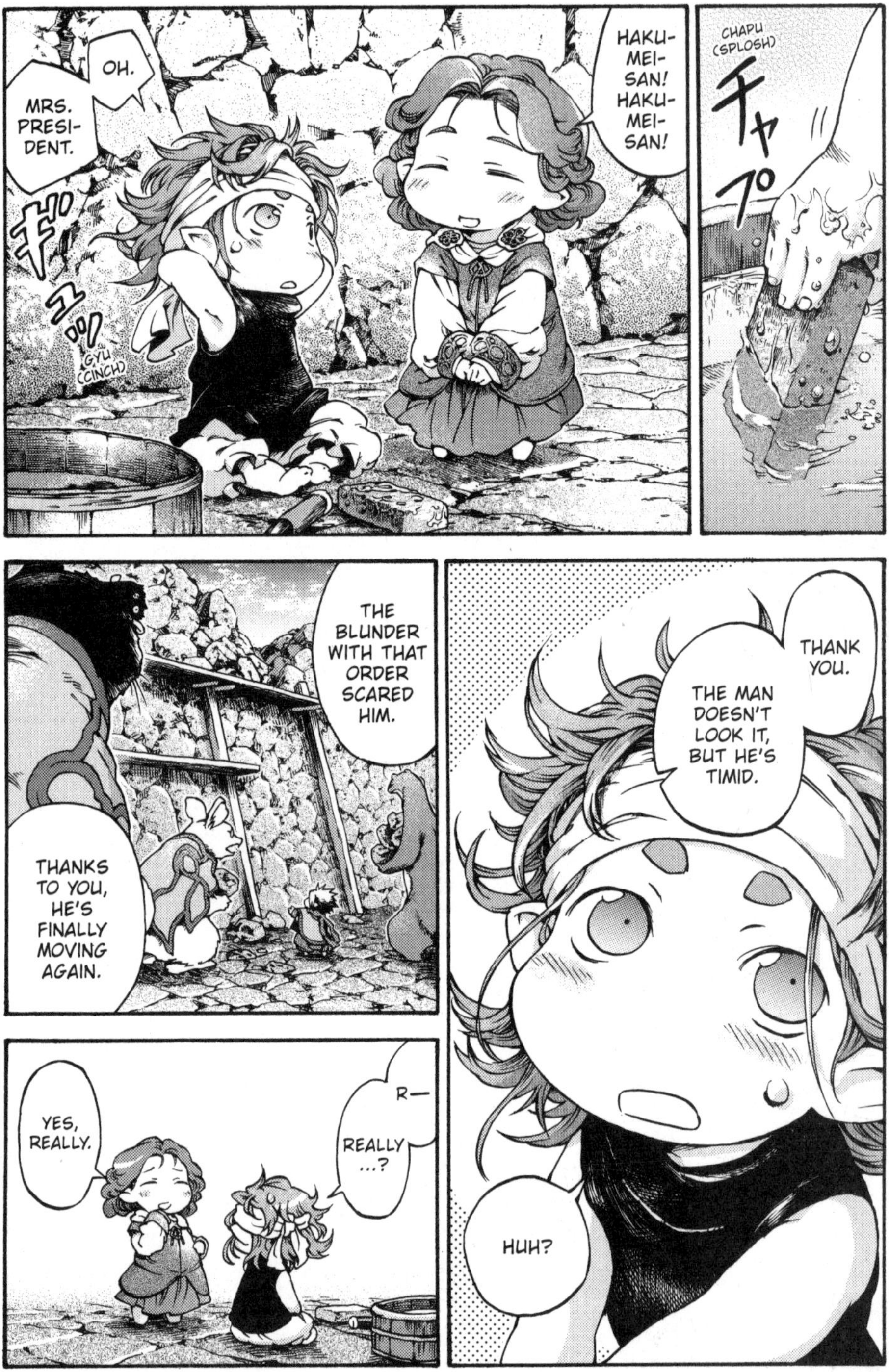
CHAPU (SPLOSH)
チャプ
HAKU-MEI-SAN! HAKU-MEI-SAN!
OH.
MRS. PRESI-DENT.
ギュッ
GYU (CINCH)
THANK YOU.
THE MAN DOESN'T LOOK IT, BUT HE'S TIMID.
HUH?
THE BLUNDER WITH THAT ORDER SCARED HIM.
THANKS TO YOU, HE'S FINALLY MOVING AGAIN.
R— REALLY ...?
YES, REALLY.

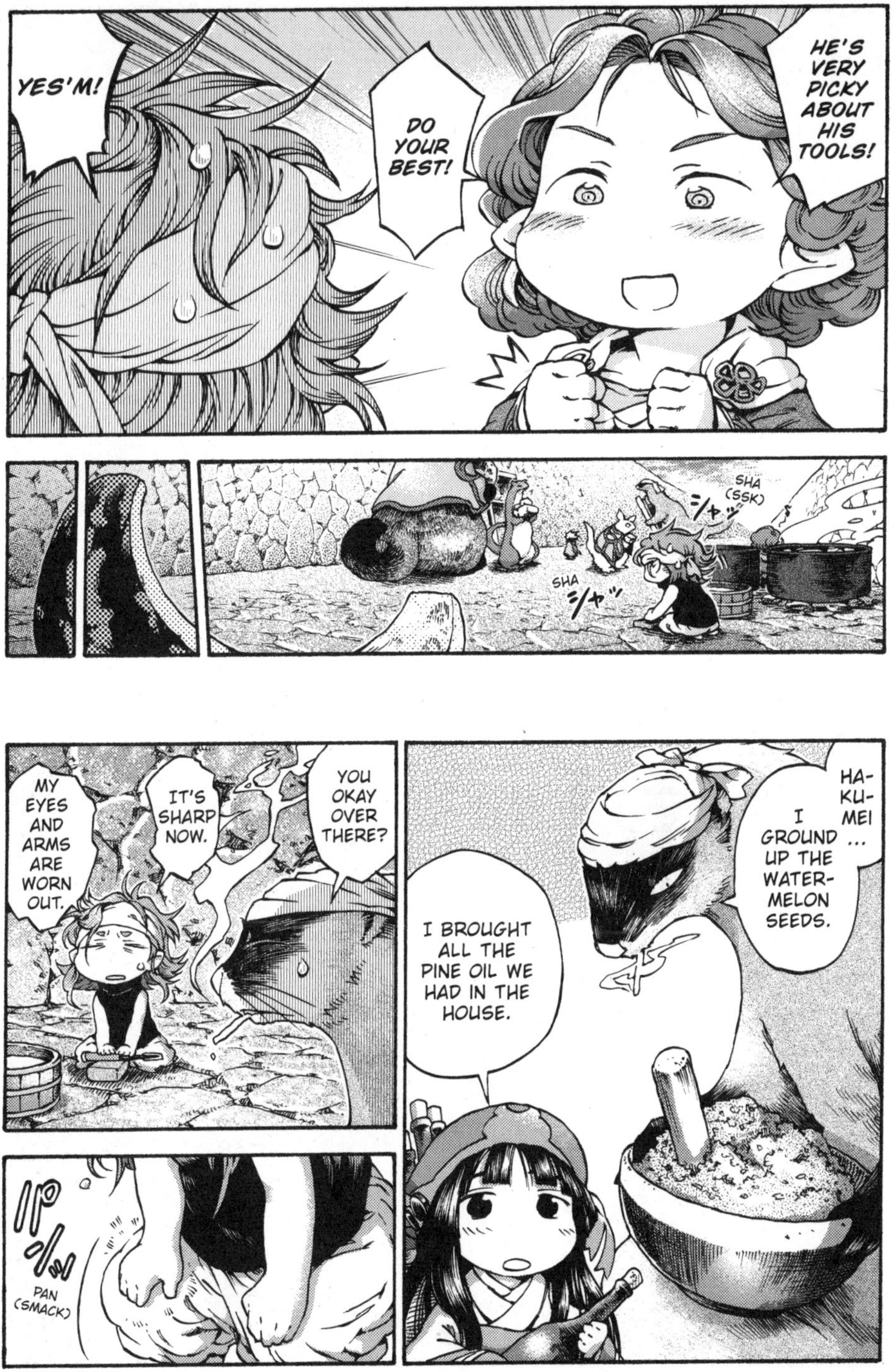
HE'S VERY PICKY ABOUT HIS TOOLS!
DO YOUR BEST!
YES'M!
SHA (SSK)
シャッ
SHA
シャッ
HAKUMEI...
I GROUND UP THE WATERMELON SEEDS.
I BROUGHT ALL THE PINE OIL WE HAD IN THE HOUSE.
YOU OKAY OVER THERE?
IT'S SHARP NOW.
MY EYES AND ARMS ARE WORN OUT.
パン
PAN (SMACK)

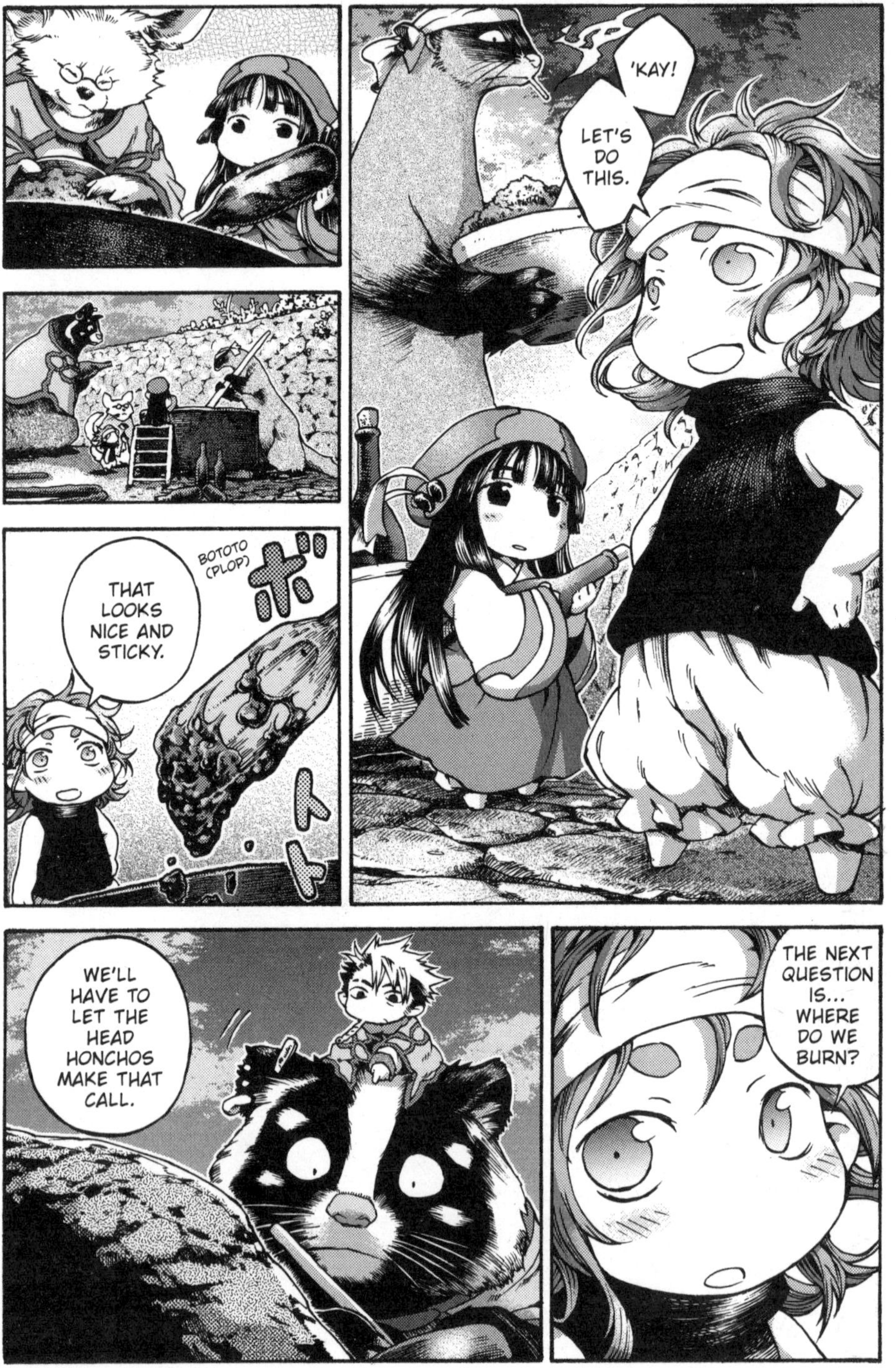
'KAY!
LET'S DO THIS.
BOTOTO (PLOP)
ボトト
THAT LOOKS NICE AND STICKY.
THE NEXT QUESTION IS... WHERE DO WE BURN?
WE'LL HAVE TO LET THE HEAD HONCHOS MAKE THAT CALL.

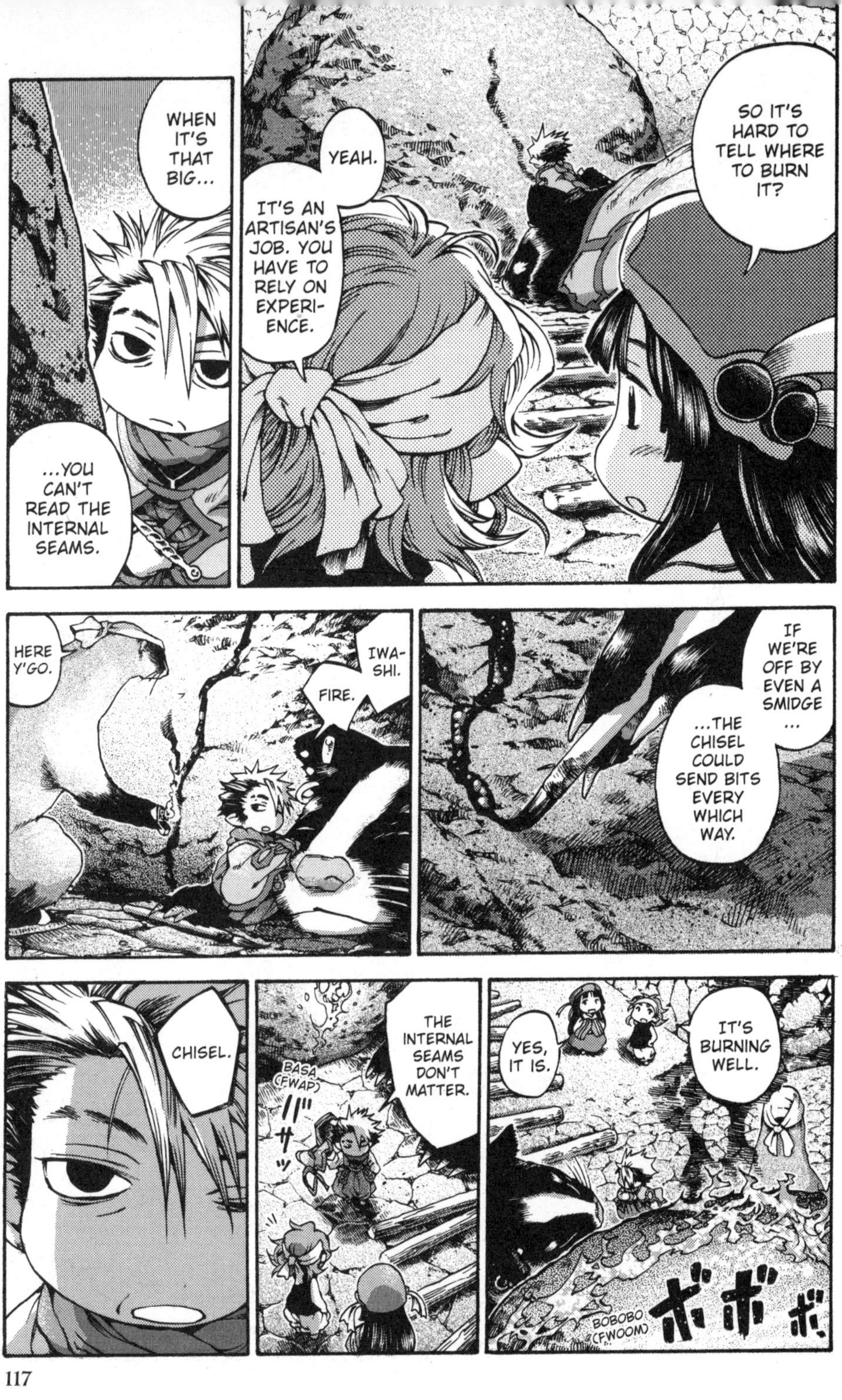
SO IT'S HARD TO TELL WHERE TO BURN IT?
YEAH.
IT'S AN ARTISAN'S JOB. YOU HAVE TO RELY ON EXPERIENCE.
WHEN IT'S THAT BIG...
...YOU CAN'T READ THE INTERNAL SEAMS.
IF WE'RE OFF BY EVEN A SMIDGE ...
...THE CHISEL COULD SEND BITS EVERY WHICH WAY.
IWASHI.
FIRE.
HERE Y'GO.
IT'S BURNING WELL.
YES, IT IS.
ボボボ
BOBOBO (FWOOM)
THE INTERNAL SEAMS DON'T MATTER.
BASA (FWAP)
バサッ
CHISEL.

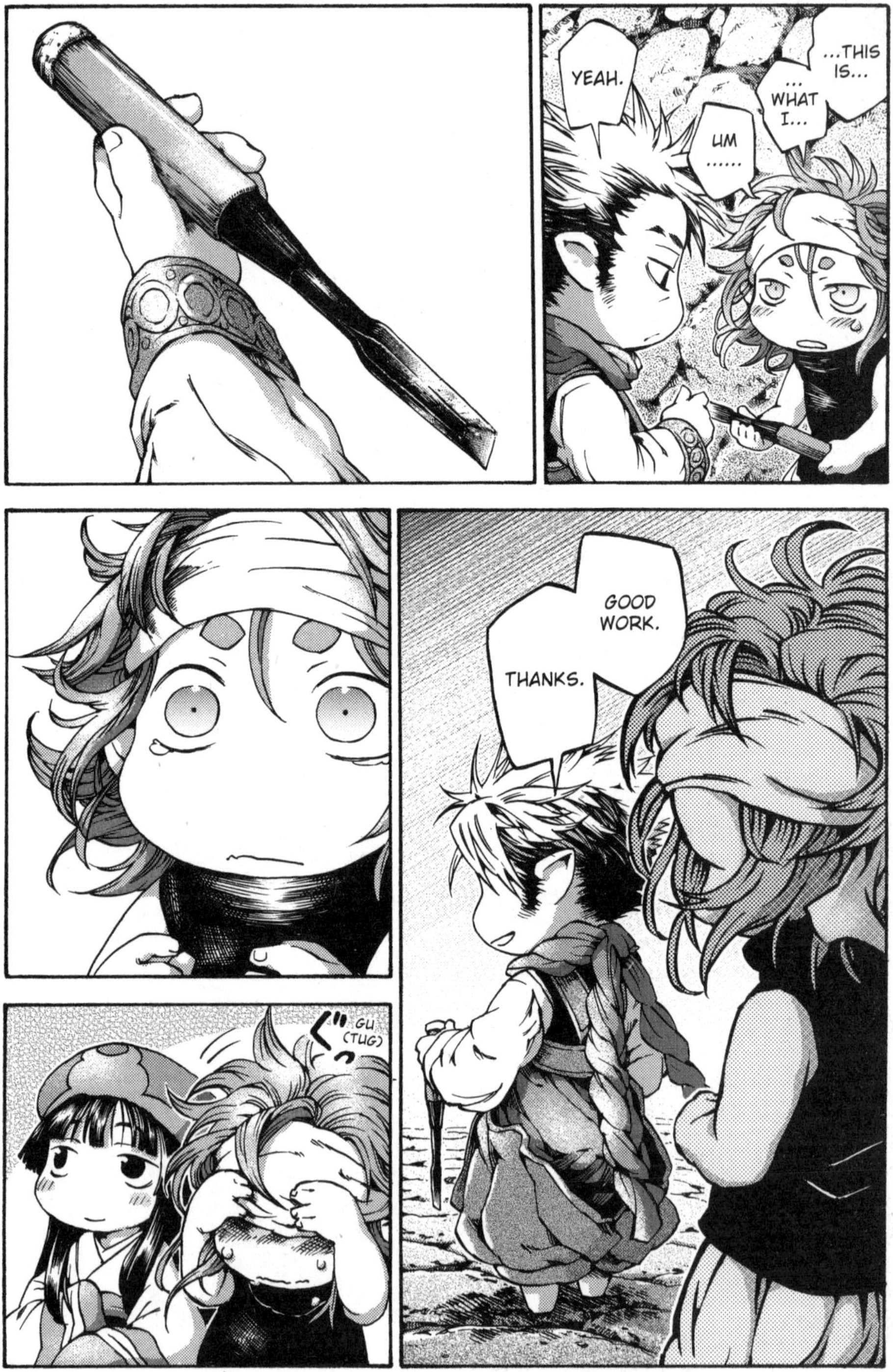
...THIS IS...
... WHAT I...
UM ......
YEAH.
GOOD WORK.
THANKS.
ぐっ
GU (TUG)

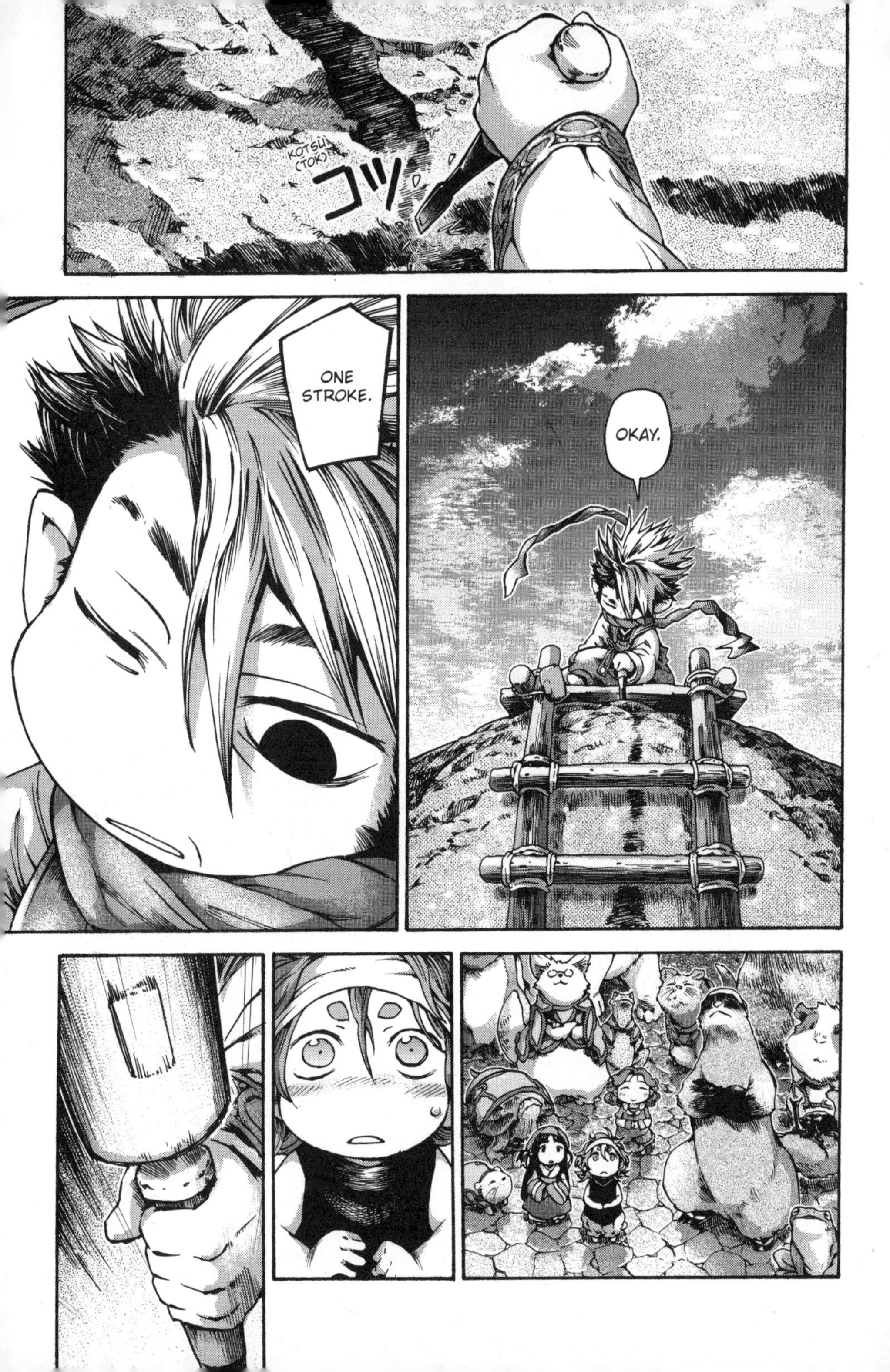
KOTSU (TOK)
コツ
OKAY.
ONE STROKE.

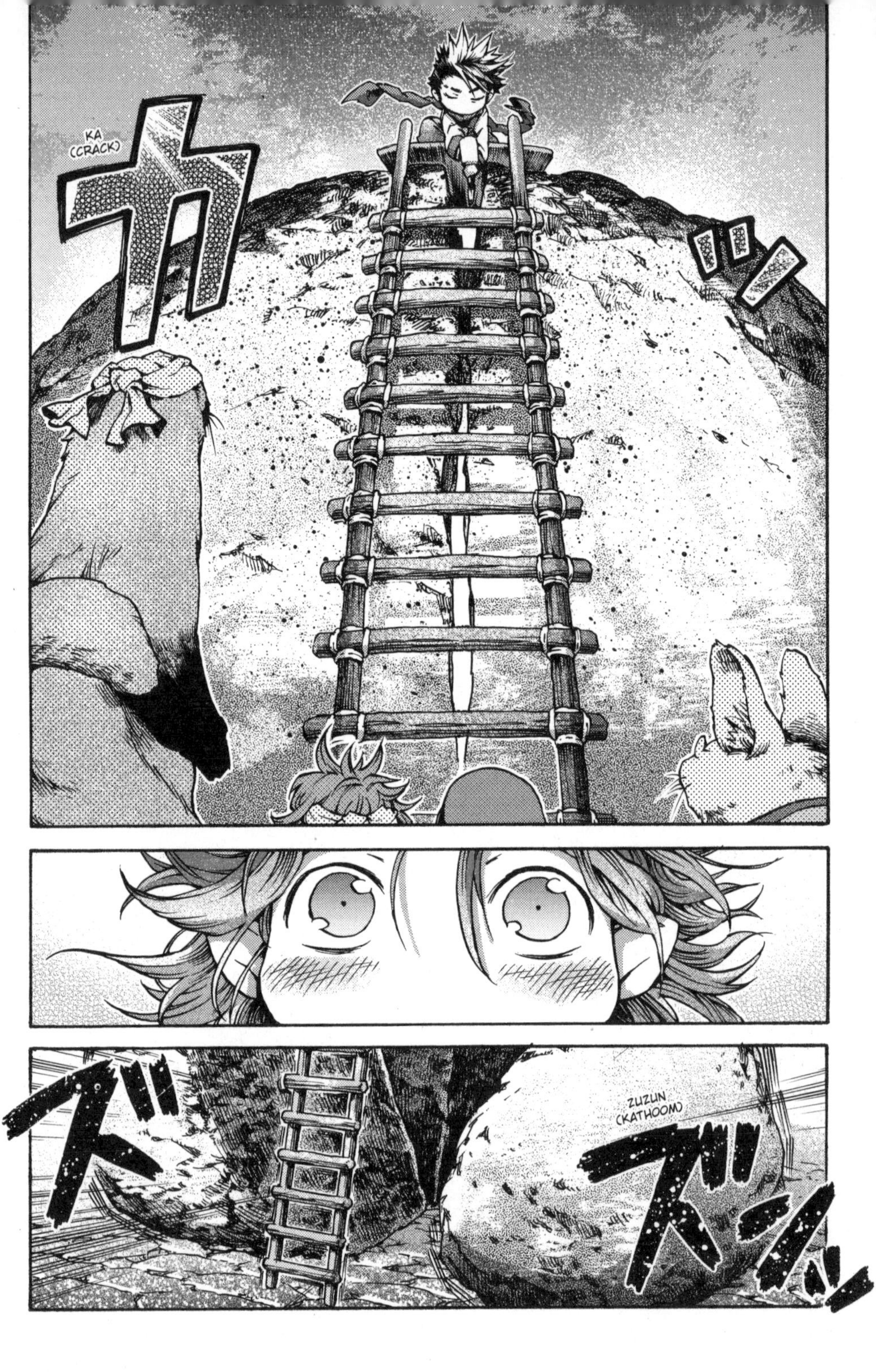
KA (CRACK)
ZUZUN (KATHOOM)

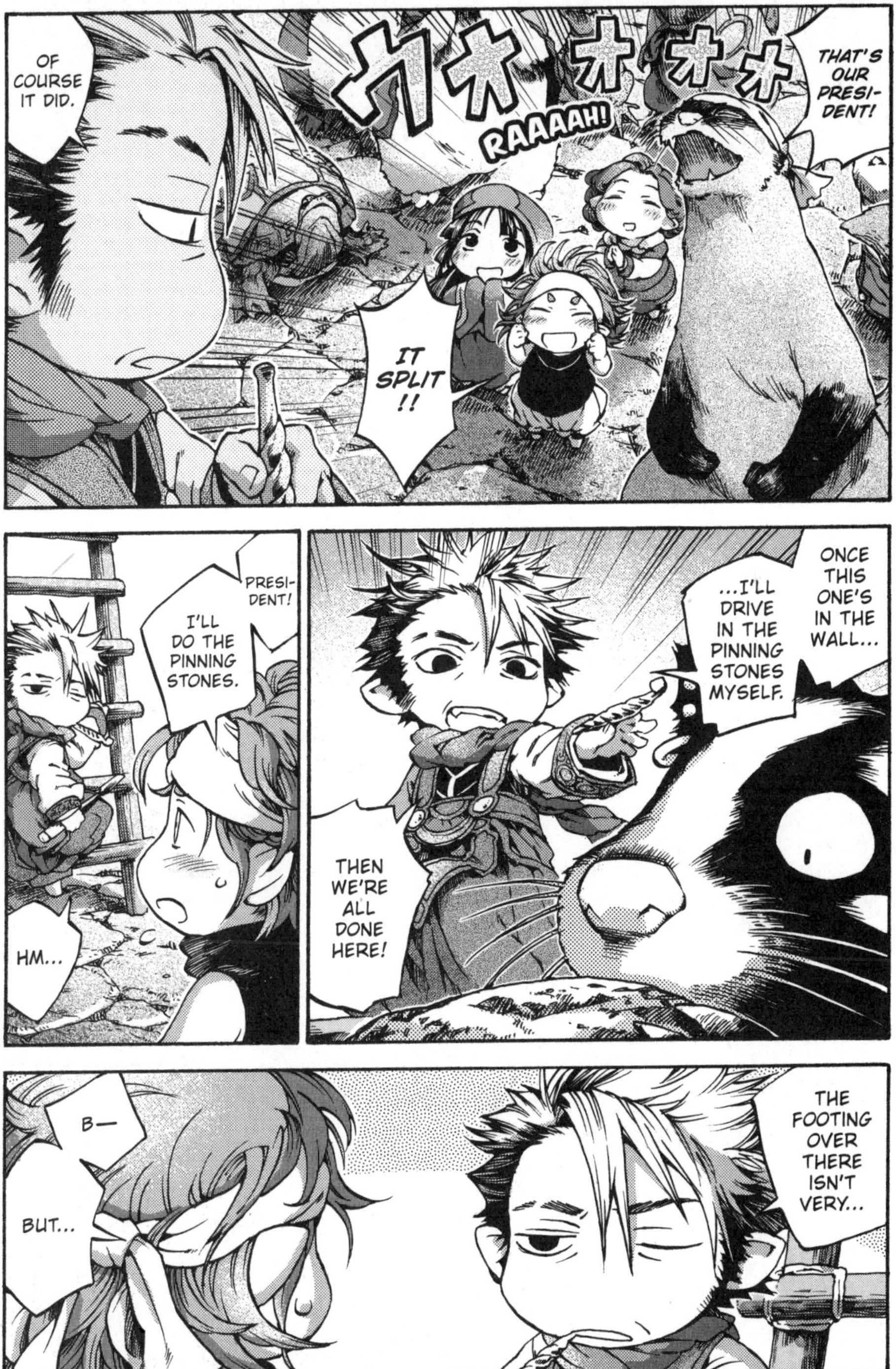
THAT'S OUR PRESI-DENT!
ウオオオオ
RAAAAH!
IT SPLIT !!
OF COURSE IT DID.
ONCE THIS ONE'S IN THE WALL...
...I'LL DRIVE IN THE PINNING STONES MYSELF.
THEN WE'RE ALL DONE HERE!
PRESI-DENT!
I'LL DO THE PINNING STONES.
HM...
THE FOOTING OVER THERE ISN'T VERY...
B—
BUT...

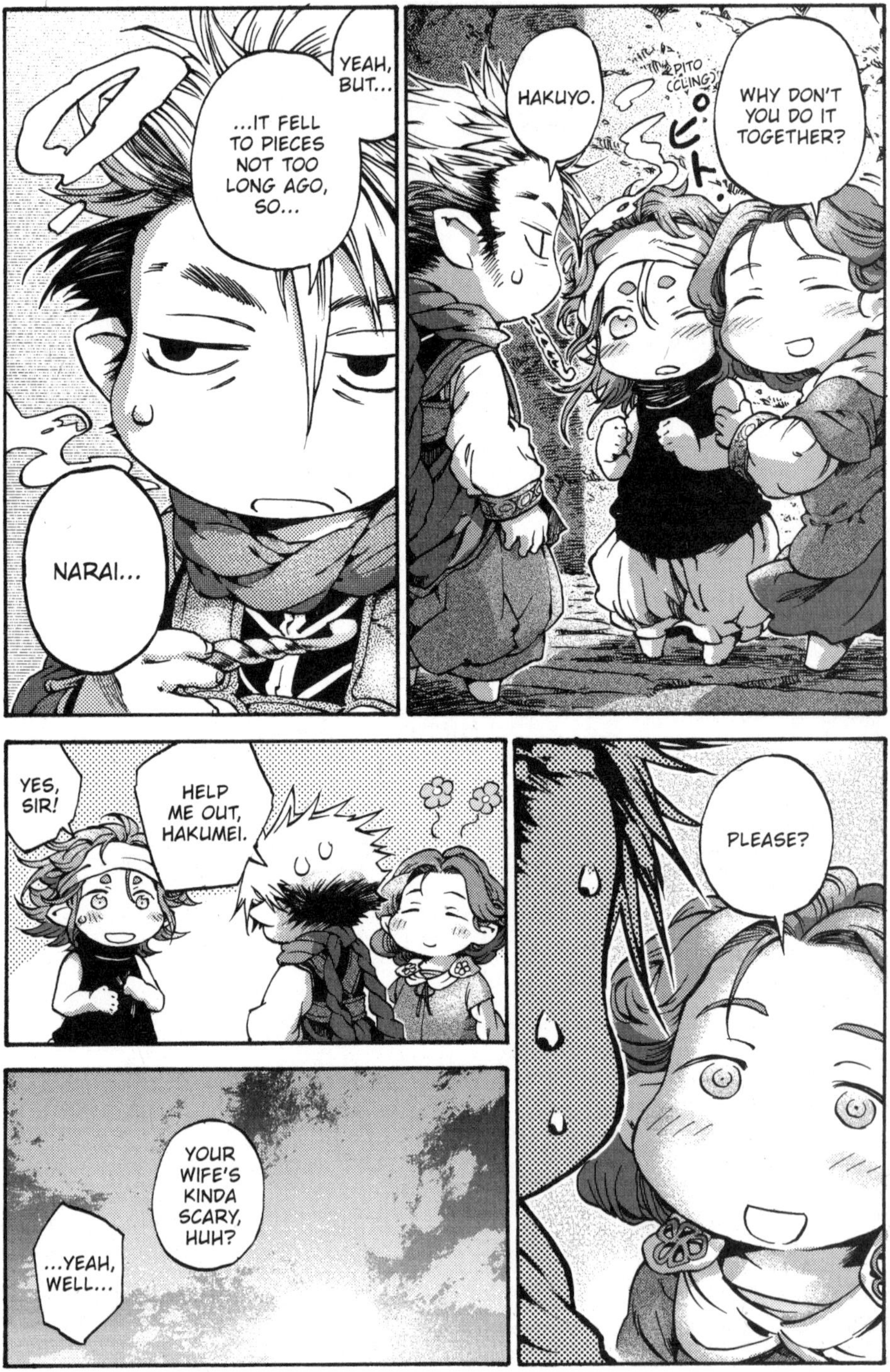
WHY DON'T YOU DO IT TOGETHER?
PITO (CLING)
ピトッ
HAKUYO.
YEAH, BUT...
...IT FELL TO PIECES NOT TOO LONG AGO, SO...
NARAI...
PLEASE?
HELP ME OUT, HAKUMEI.
YES, SIR!
YOUR WIFE'S KINDA SCARY, HUH?
...YEAH, WELL...

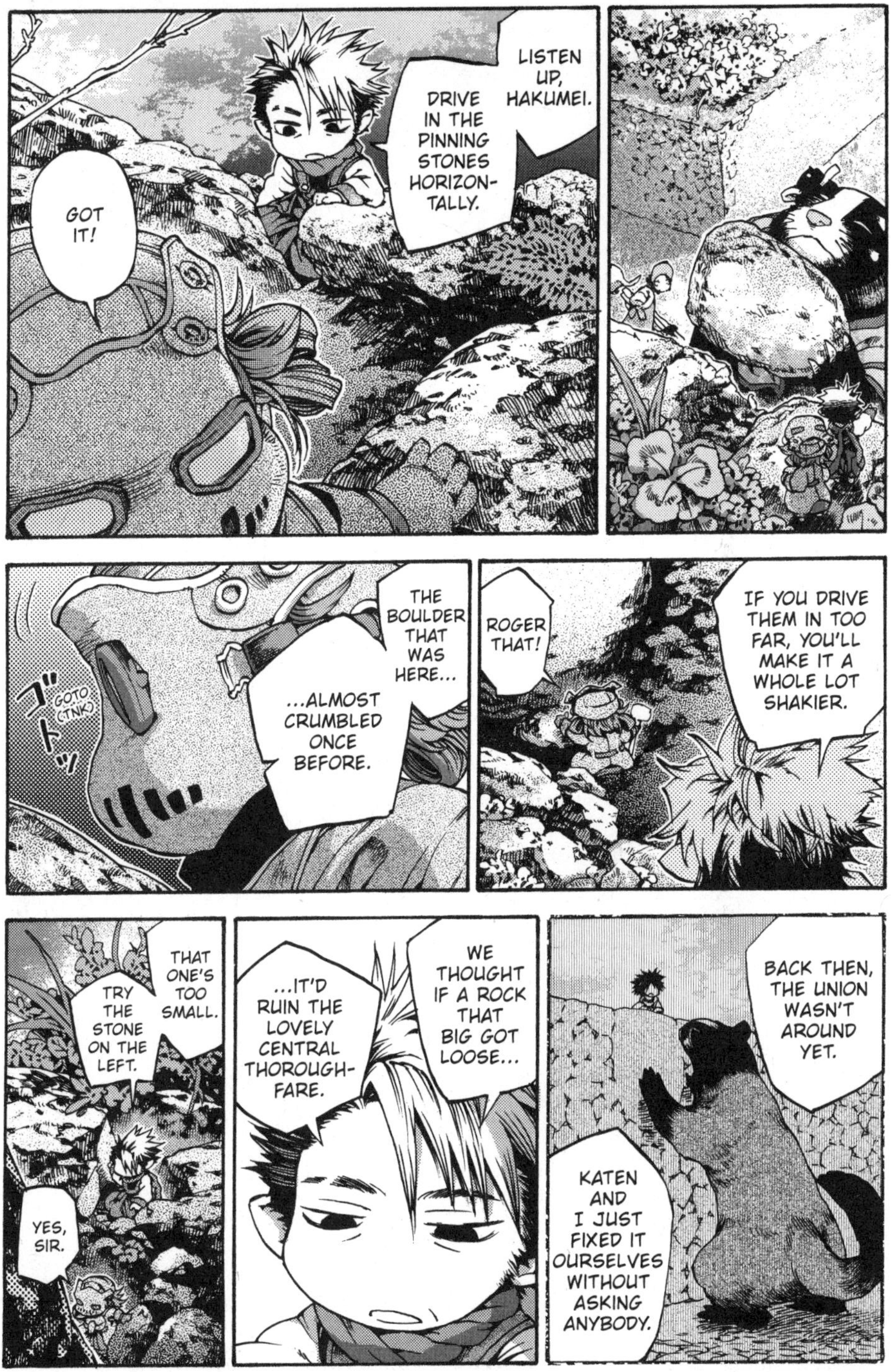
LISTEN UP, HAKUMEI.
DRIVE IN THE PINNING STONES HORIZONTALLY.
GOT IT!
IF YOU DRIVE THEM IN TOO FAR, YOU'LL MAKE IT A WHOLE LOT SHAKIER.
ROGER THAT!
THE BOULDER THAT WAS HERE...
...ALMOST CRUMBLED ONCE BEFORE.
ゴトッ GOTO (TNK)
BACK THEN, THE UNION WASN'T AROUND YET.
KATEN AND I JUST FIXED IT OURSELVES WITHOUT ASKING ANYBODY.
WE THOUGHT IF A ROCK THAT BIG GOT LOOSE...
...IT'D RUIN THE LOVELY CENTRAL THOROUGHFARE.
THAT ONE'S TOO SMALL.
TRY THE STONE ON THE LEFT.
YES, SIR.

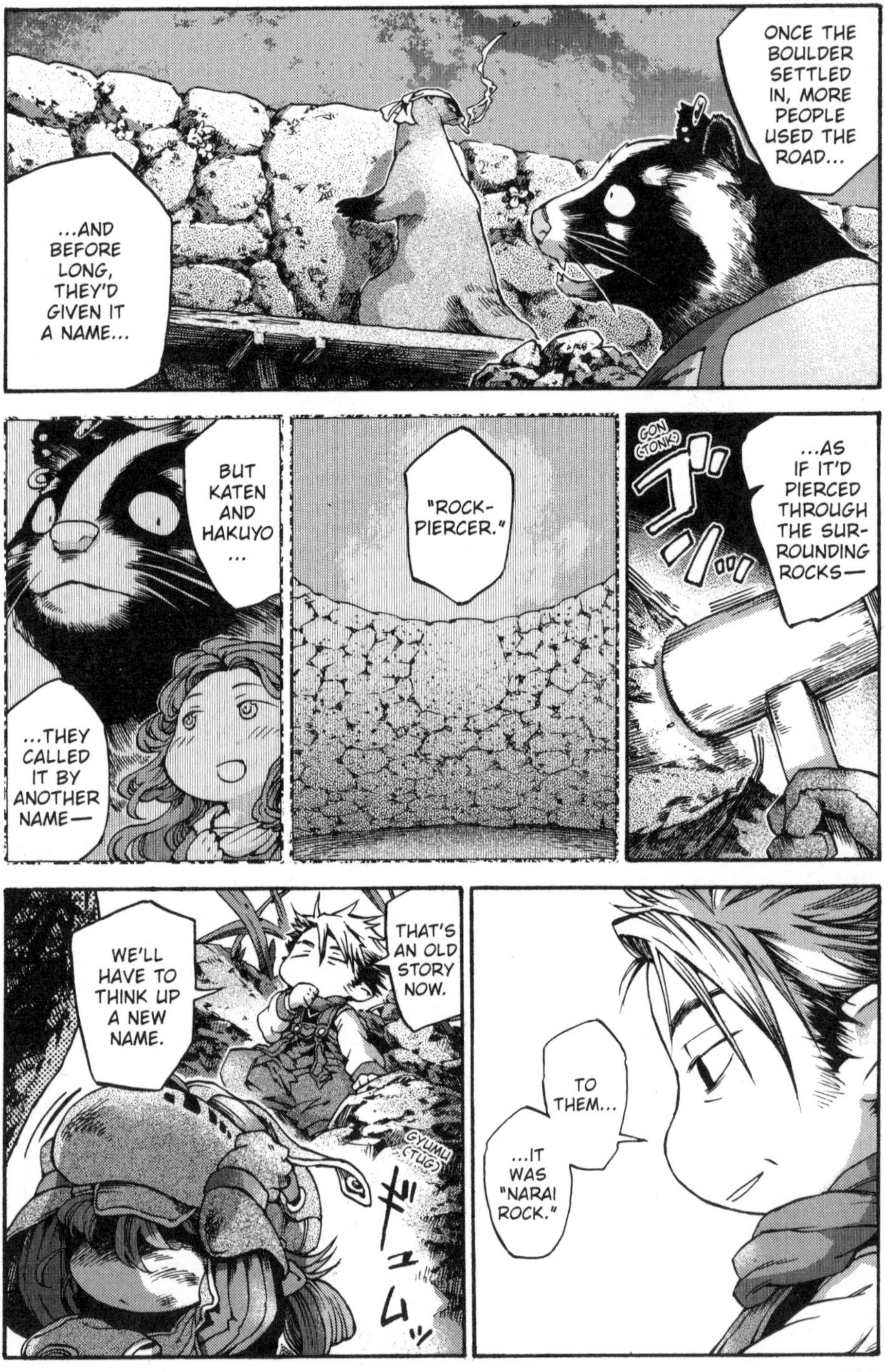
ONCE THE BOULDER SETTLED IN, MORE PEOPLE USED THE ROAD...
...AND BEFORE LONG, THEY'D GIVEN IT A NAME...
GON (TONK)
...AS IF IT'D PIERCED THROUGH THE SUR-ROUNDING ROCKS—
"ROCK-PIERCER."
BUT KATEN AND HAKUYO...
...THEY CALLED IT BY ANOTHER NAME—
TO THEM...
...IT WAS "NARAI ROCK."
THAT'S AN OLD STORY NOW.
WE'LL HAVE TO THINK UP A NEW NAME.
GYUMU (TUG)

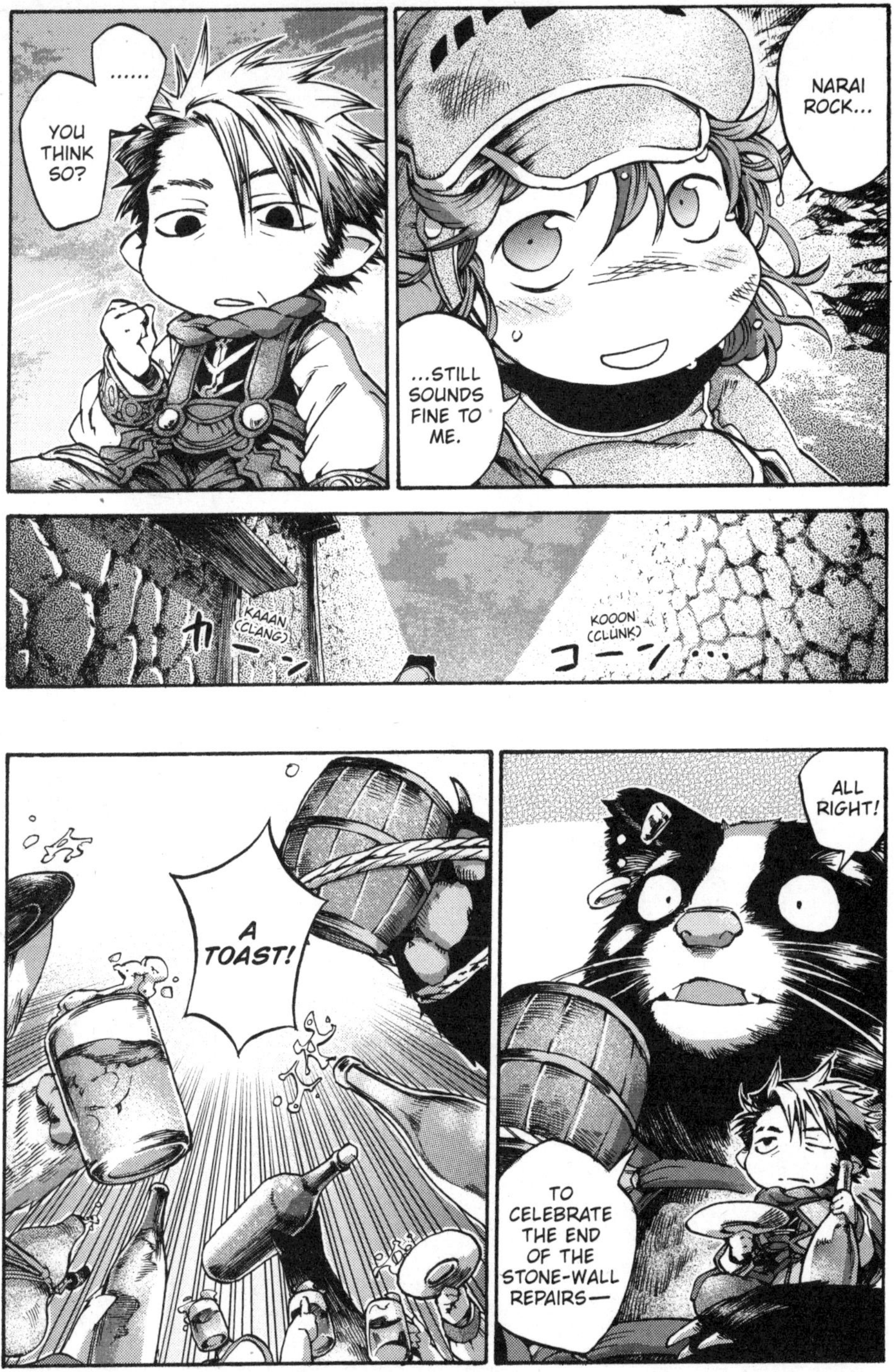
NARAI ROCK...
...STILL SOUNDS FINE TO ME.
......
YOU THINK SO?
KAAAN (CLANG)
KOOON (CLUNK)
ALL RIGHT!
TO CELEBRATE THE END OF THE STONE-WALL REPAIRS—
A TOAST!

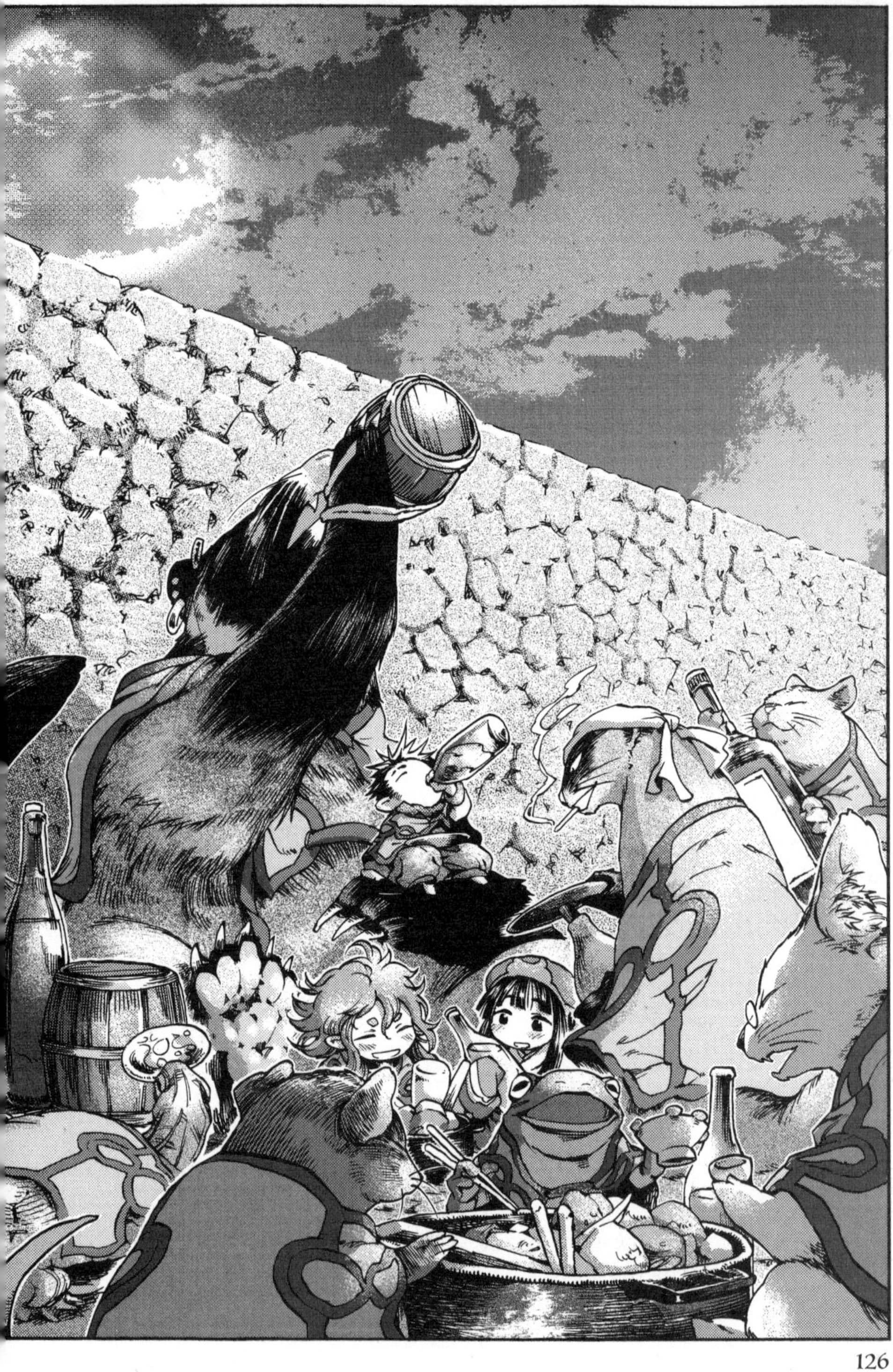

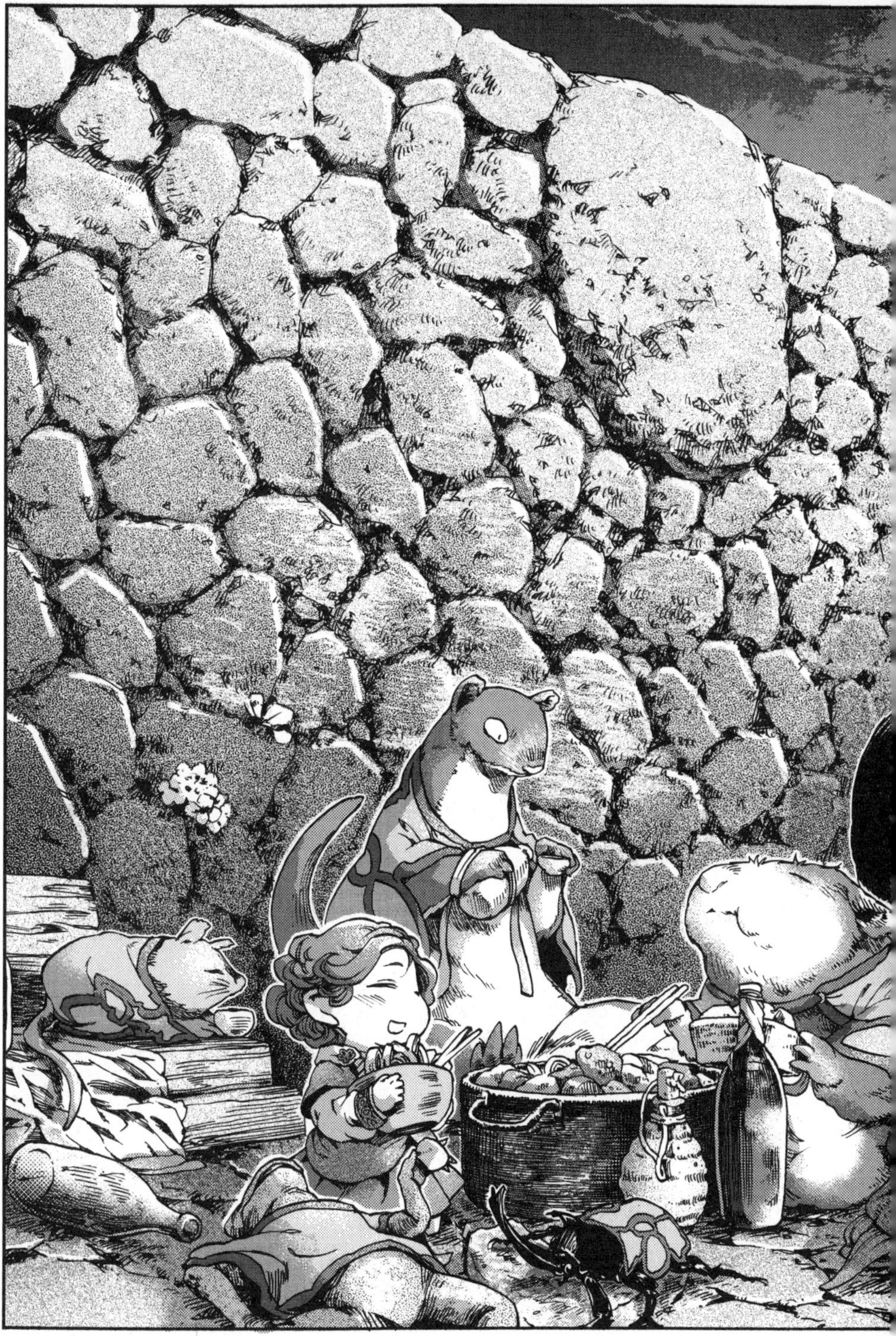

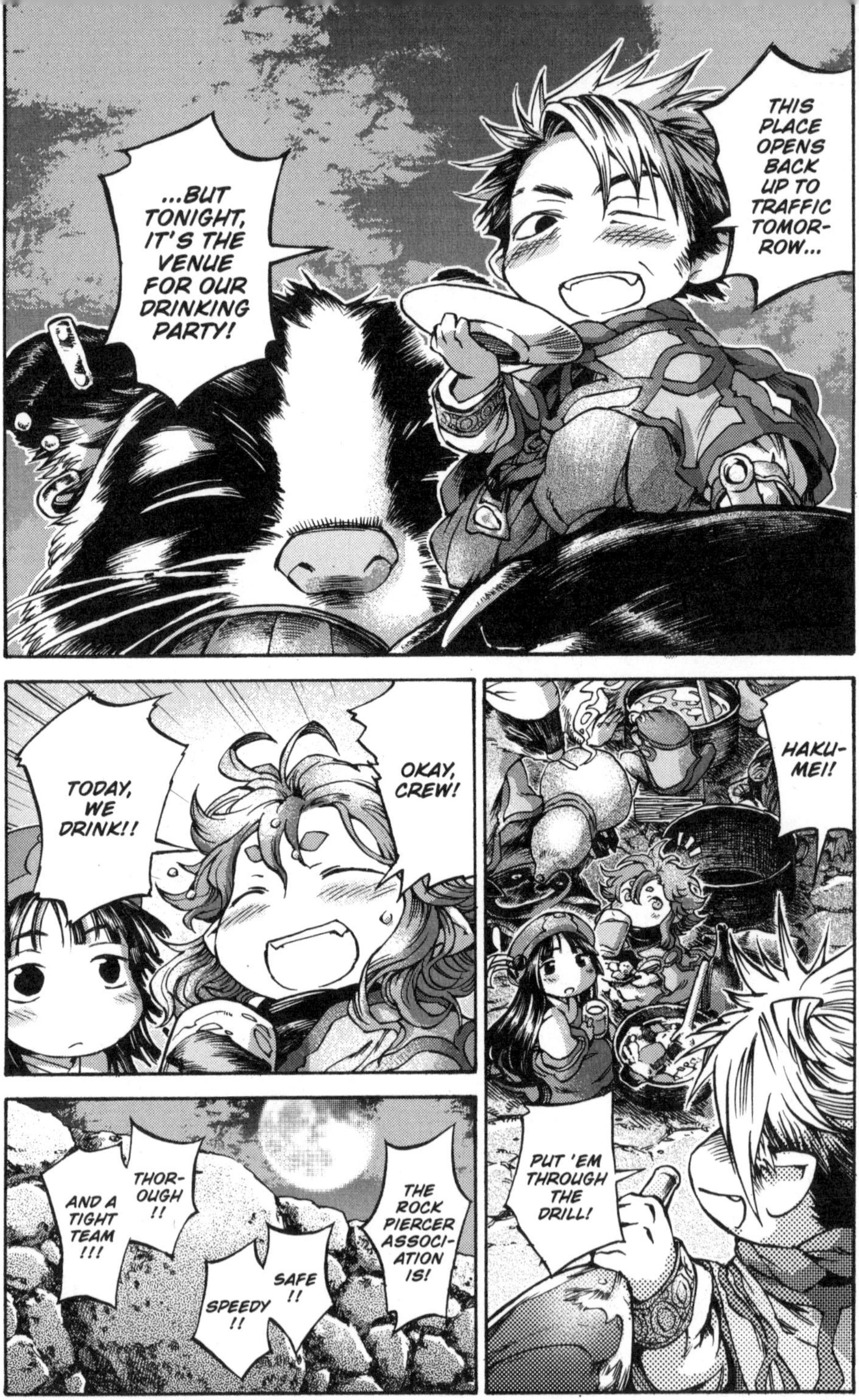
THIS PLACE OPENS BACK UP TO TRAFFIC TOMOR-ROW...
...BUT TONIGHT, IT'S THE VENUE FOR OUR DRINKING PARTY!
HAKU-MEI!
PUT 'EM THROUGH THE DRILL!
OKAY, CREW!
TODAY, WE DRINK!!
THE ROCK PIERCER ASSOCI-ATION IS!
SAFE !!
SPEEDY !!
THOR-OUGH !!
AND A TIGHT TEAM !!!

•*Column*• Underfoot Steps 12 / The RPA's Most Formidable Member

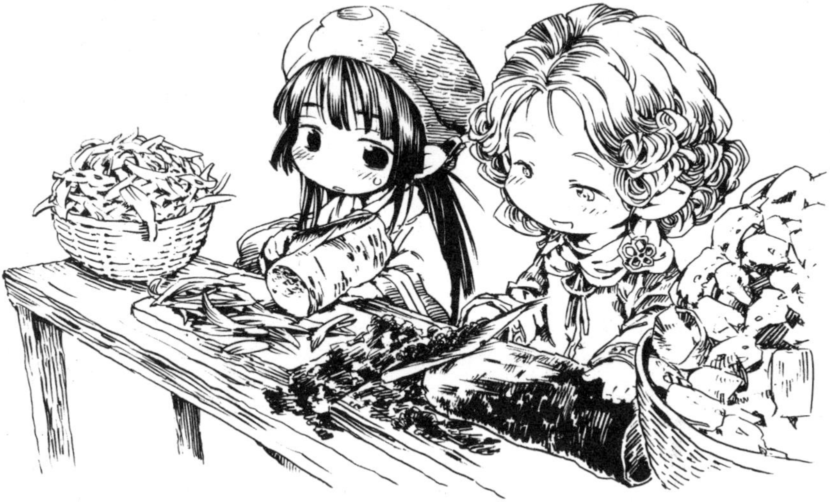

"Narai doesn't care for burdock root, you see. He's always making Katen-chan eat it on the sly. I've nagged and nagged, saying, 'Eat it. It's good for you,' but he says childish things about how he gets enough of tree roots and the taste of dirt at work. Everyone's watching him today, though, and he can't very well look petty in front of them, can he? And so I bought a magnificent burdock root. It still has its leaves, and it looks as if it should be quite stinky, so I'm sure it's very nutritious. Oh, cut it just a little finer...There's a dear."

She's talking, and yet her fingers are never at rest...

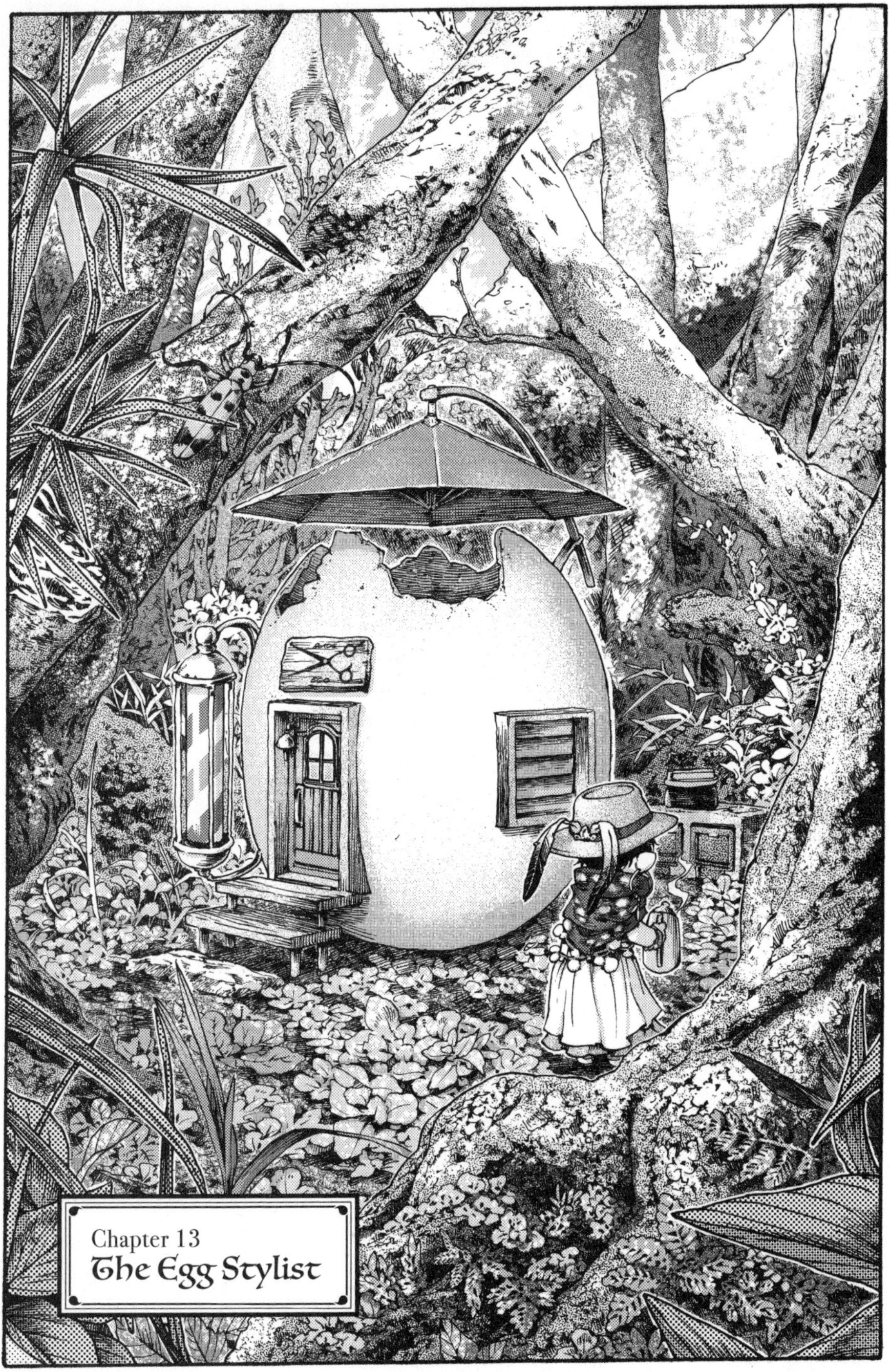
Chapter 13
The Egg Stylist

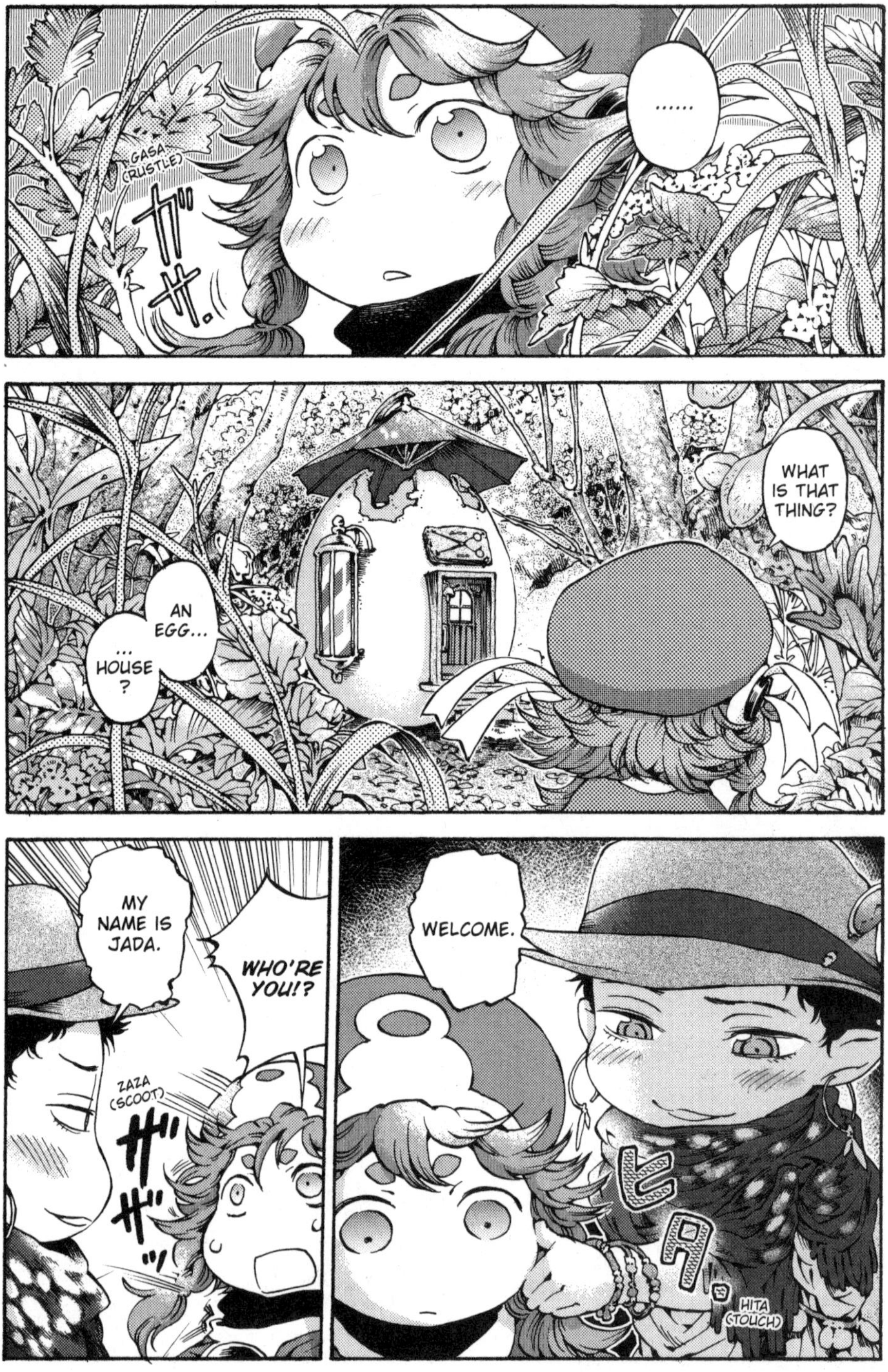
......
GASA (RUSTLE)
WHAT IS THAT THING?
AN EGG... ...HOUSE?
WELCOME.
HITA (TOUCH)
WHO'RE YOU!?
MY NAME IS JADA.
ZAZA (SCOOT)

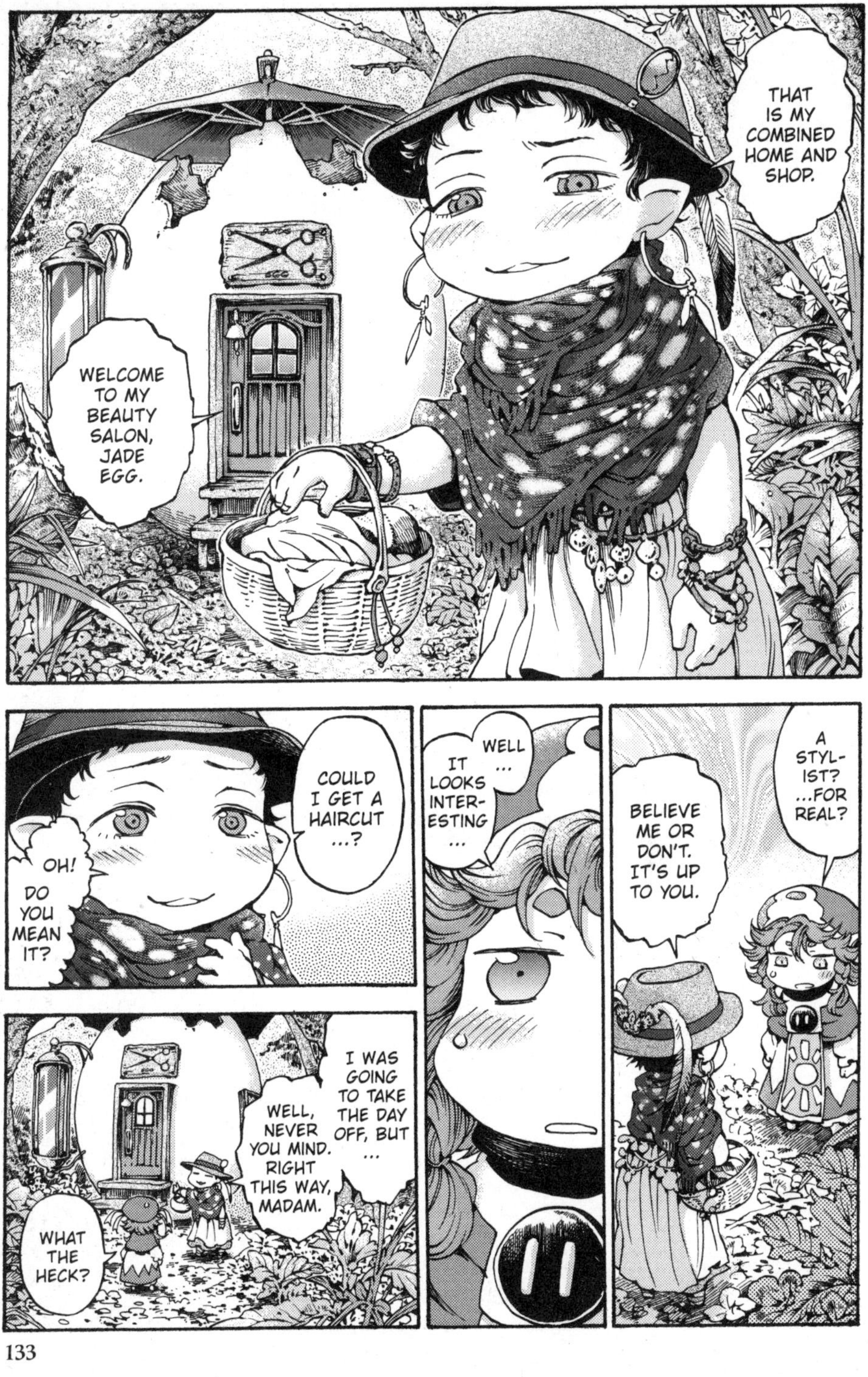
THAT IS MY COMBINED HOME AND SHOP.
WELCOME TO MY BEAUTY SALON, JADE EGG.
A STYLIST? ...FOR REAL?
BELIEVE ME OR DON'T. IT'S UP TO YOU.
WELL ... IT LOOKS INTERESTING ...
COULD I GET A HAIRCUT ...?
OH! DO YOU MEAN IT?
I WAS GOING TO TAKE THE DAY OFF, BUT ...
WELL, NEVER YOU MIND. RIGHT THIS WAY, MADAM.
WHAT THE HECK?

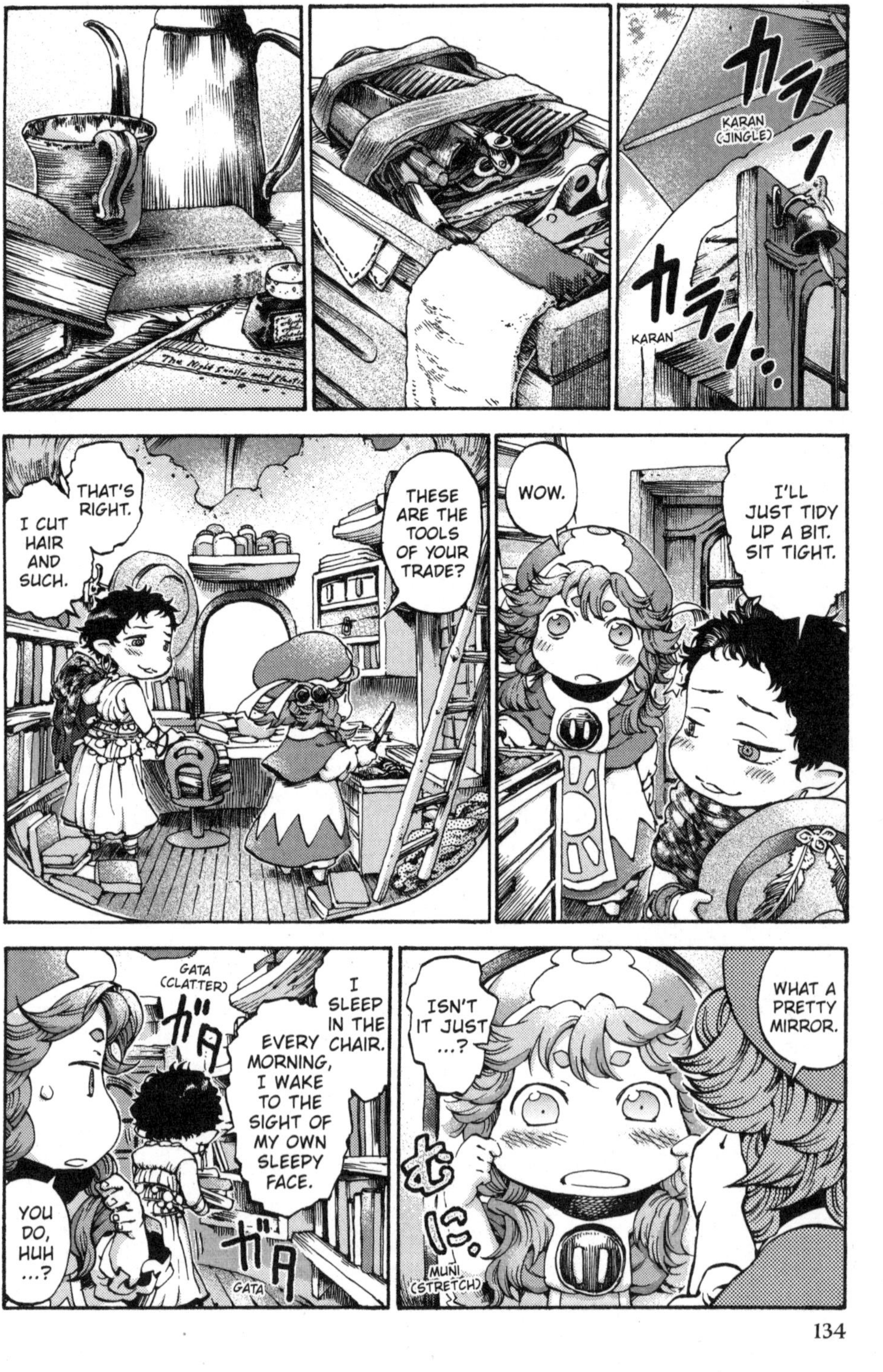
KARAN (JINGLE)
KARAN
I'LL JUST TIDY UP A BIT. SIT TIGHT.
WOW.
THESE ARE THE TOOLS OF YOUR TRADE?
THAT'S RIGHT.
I CUT HAIR AND SUCH.
WHAT A PRETTY MIRROR.
ISN'T IT JUST ...?
MUNI (STRETCH)
GATA (CLATTER)
I SLEEP IN THE CHAIR.
EVERY MORNING, I WAKE TO THE SIGHT OF MY OWN SLEEPY FACE.
GATA
YOU DO, HUH ...?

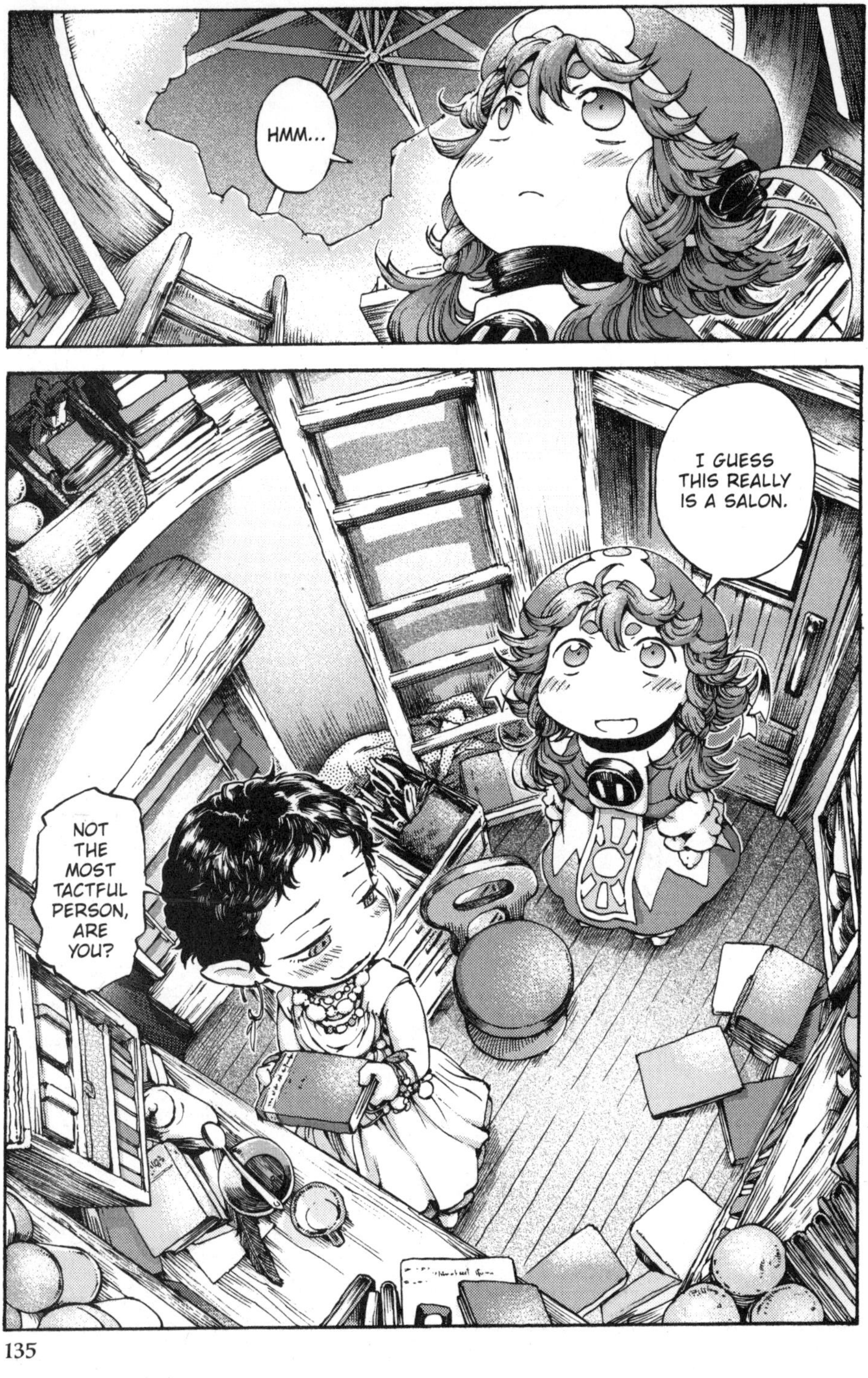
HMM...
I GUESS THIS REALLY IS A SALON.
NOT THE MOST TACTFUL PERSON, ARE YOU?

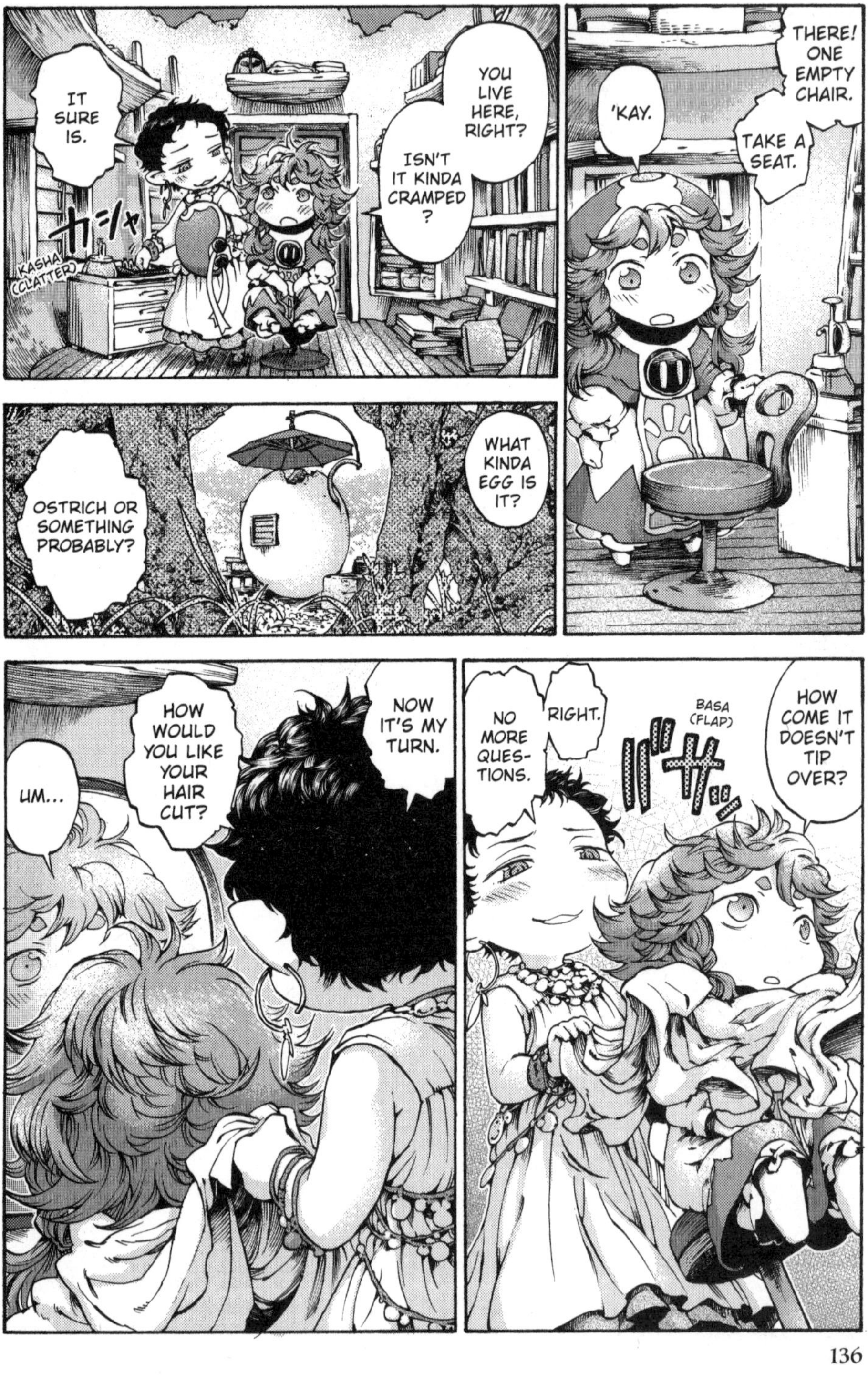
THERE! ONE EMPTY CHAIR.
TAKE A SEAT.
'KAY.
YOU LIVE HERE, RIGHT?
ISN'T IT KINDA CRAMPED?
IT SURE IS.
カシャ
KASHA (CLATTER)
WHAT KINDA EGG IS IT?
OSTRICH OR SOMETHING PROBABLY?
HOW COME IT DOESN'T TIP OVER?
バサッ
BASA (FLAP)
RIGHT.
NO MORE QUES-TIONS.
NOW IT'S MY TURN.
HOW WOULD YOU LIKE YOUR HAIR CUT?
UM...

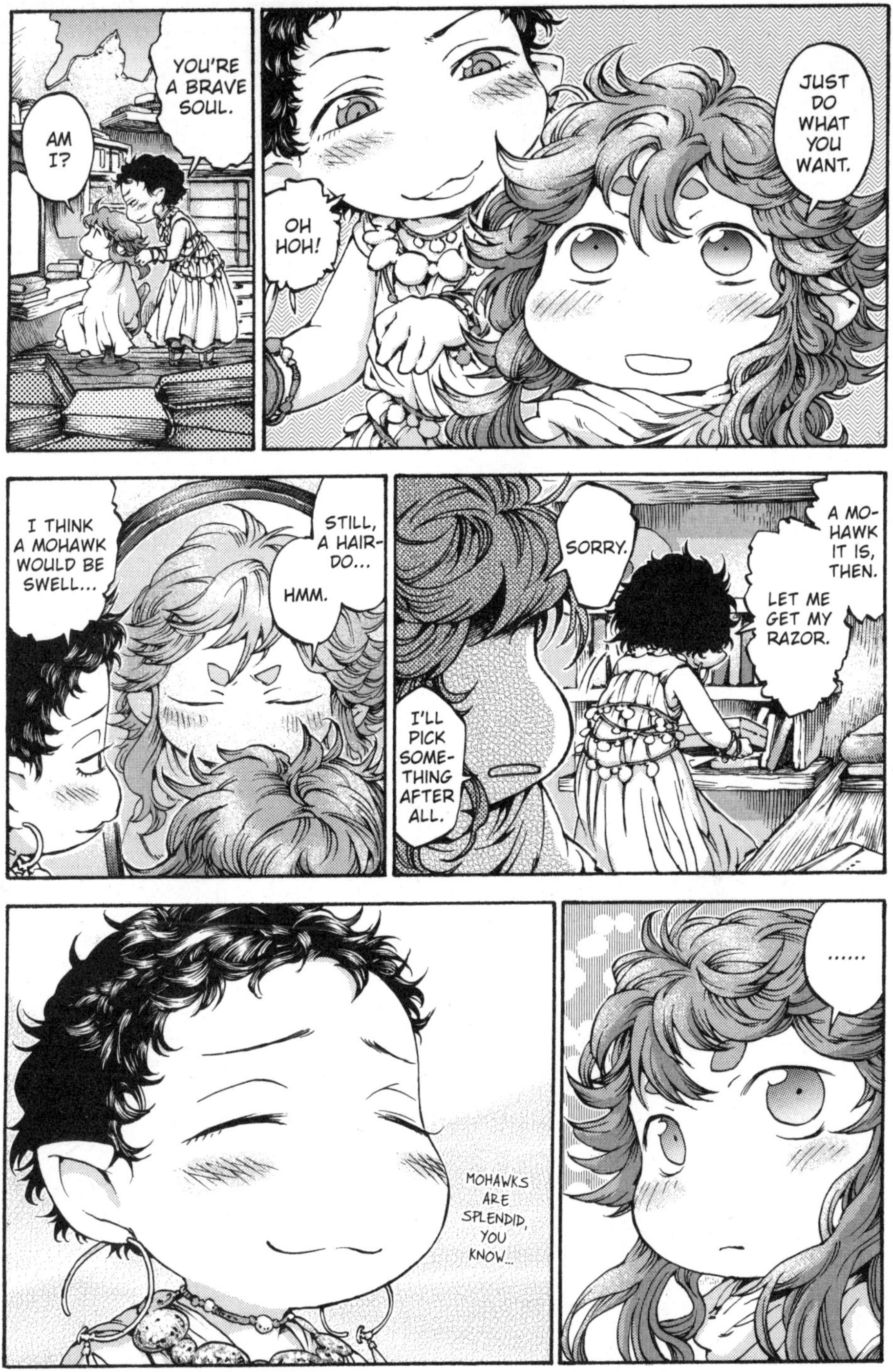
JUST DO WHAT YOU WANT.
OH HOH!
YOU'RE A BRAVE SOUL.
AM I?
A MO-HAWK IT IS, THEN.
LET ME GET MY RAZOR.
SORRY.
I'LL PICK SOME-THING AFTER ALL.
STILL, A HAIR-DO...
HMM.
I THINK A MOHAWK WOULD BE SWELL...
......
MOHAWKS ARE SPLENDID, YOU KNOW...

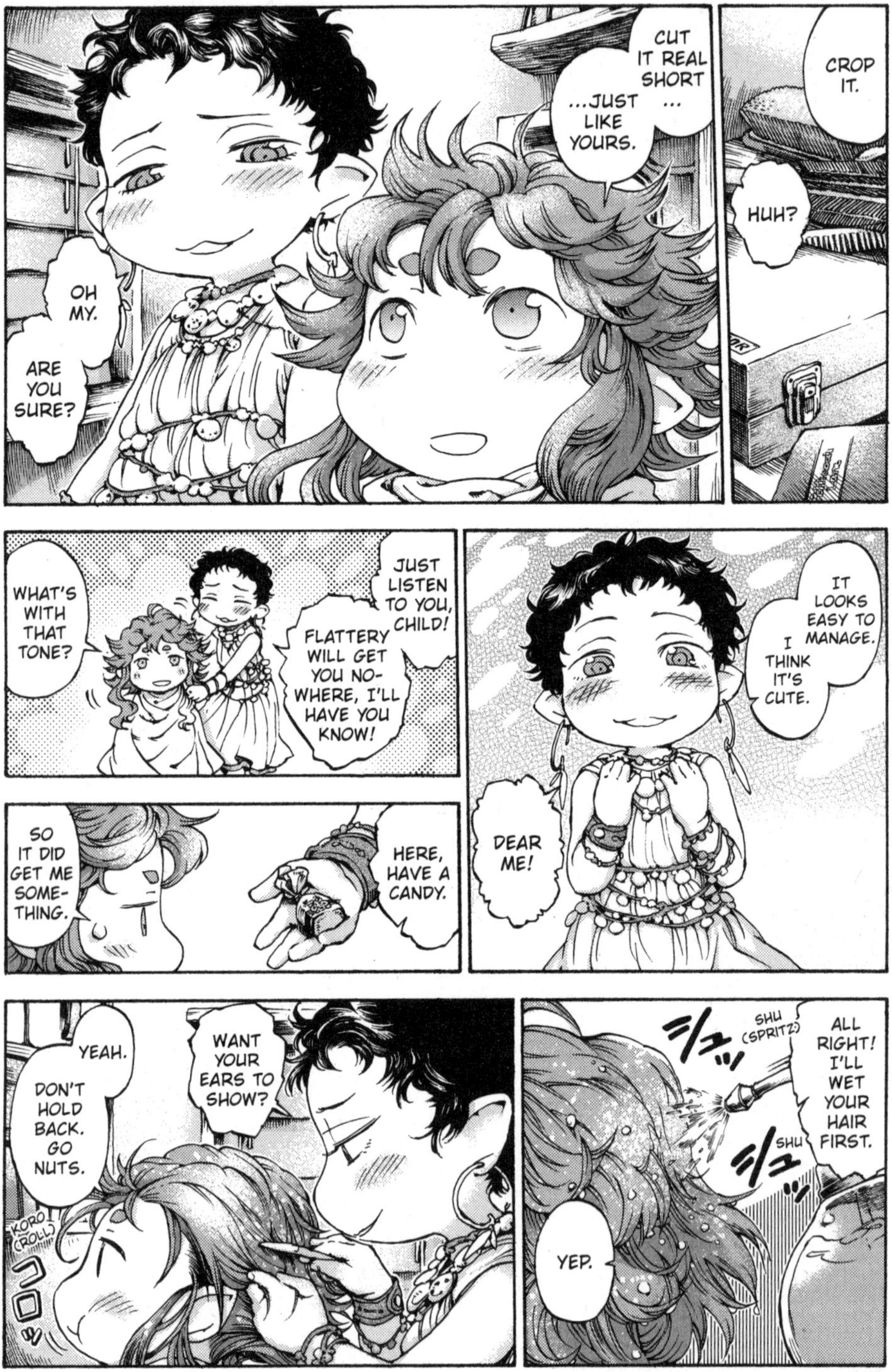
CROP IT.
HUH?
CUT IT REAL SHORT ...
...JUST LIKE YOURS.
OH MY.
ARE YOU SURE?
IT LOOKS EASY TO MANAGE.
I THINK IT'S CUTE.
DEAR ME!
JUST LISTEN TO YOU, CHILD!
FLATTERY WILL GET YOU NO-WHERE, I'LL HAVE YOU KNOW!
WHAT'S WITH THAT TONE?
HERE, HAVE A CANDY.
SO IT DID GET ME SOME-THING.
SHU (SPRITZ)
ALL RIGHT! I'LL WET YOUR HAIR FIRST.
SHU
YEP.
WANT YOUR EARS TO SHOW?
YEAH.
DON'T HOLD BACK. GO NUTS.
KORO (ROLL)

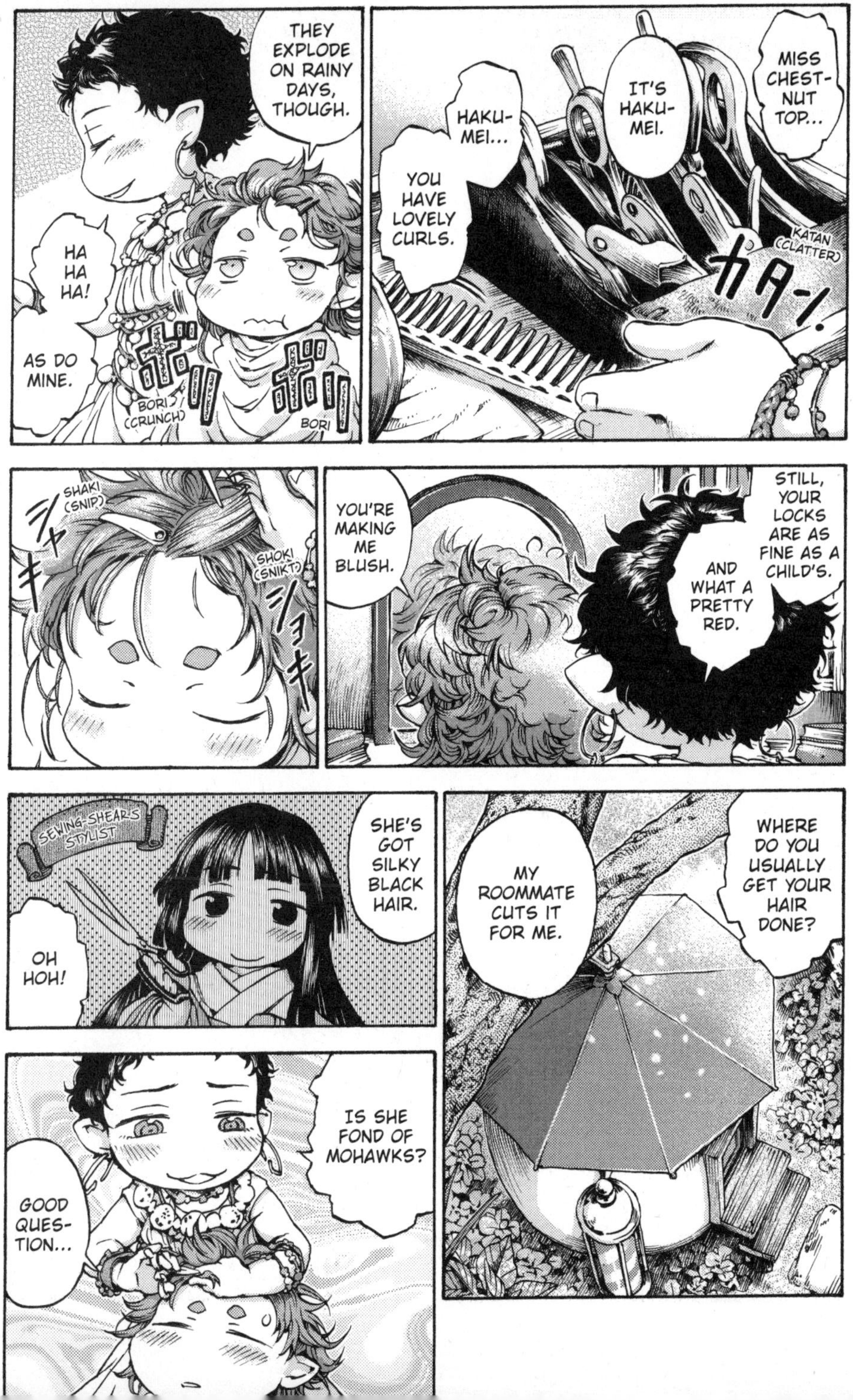
MISS CHEST-NUT TOP...
IT'S HAKU-MEI.
HAKU-MEI...
YOU HAVE LOVELY CURLS.
KATAN (CLATTER)
THEY EXPLODE ON RAINY DAYS, THOUGH.
HA HA HA!
AS DO MINE.
BORI (CRUNCH)
BORI
STILL, YOUR LOCKS ARE AS FINE AS A CHILD'S.
AND WHAT A PRETTY RED.
YOU'RE MAKING ME BLUSH.
SHAKI (SNIP)
SHOKI (SNIKT)
WHERE DO YOU USUALLY GET YOUR HAIR DONE?
MY ROOMMATE CUTS IT FOR ME.
SEWING-SHEARS STYLIST
SHE'S GOT SILKY BLACK HAIR.
OH HOH!
IS SHE FOND OF MOHAWKS?
GOOD QUES-TION...

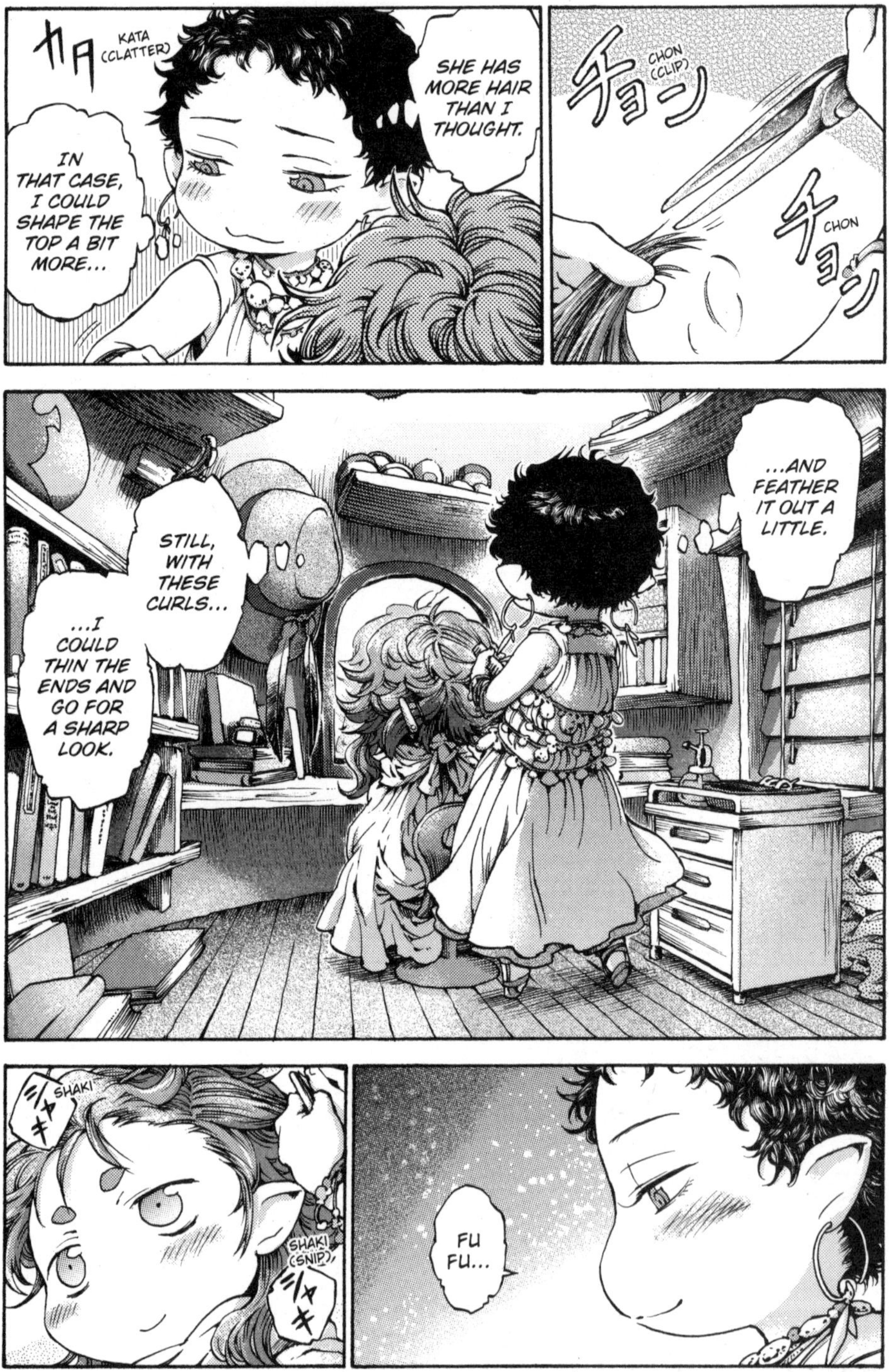
チョン
CHON (CLIP)
チョン
CHON
SHE HAS MORE HAIR THAN I THOUGHT.
カタ
KATA (CLATTER)
IN THAT CASE, I COULD SHAPE THE TOP A BIT MORE...
...AND FEATHER IT OUT A LITTLE.
STILL, WITH THESE CURLS...
...I COULD THIN THE ENDS AND GO FOR A SHARP LOOK.
FU FU...
シャキ
SHAKI
SHAKI (SNIP)
シャキ

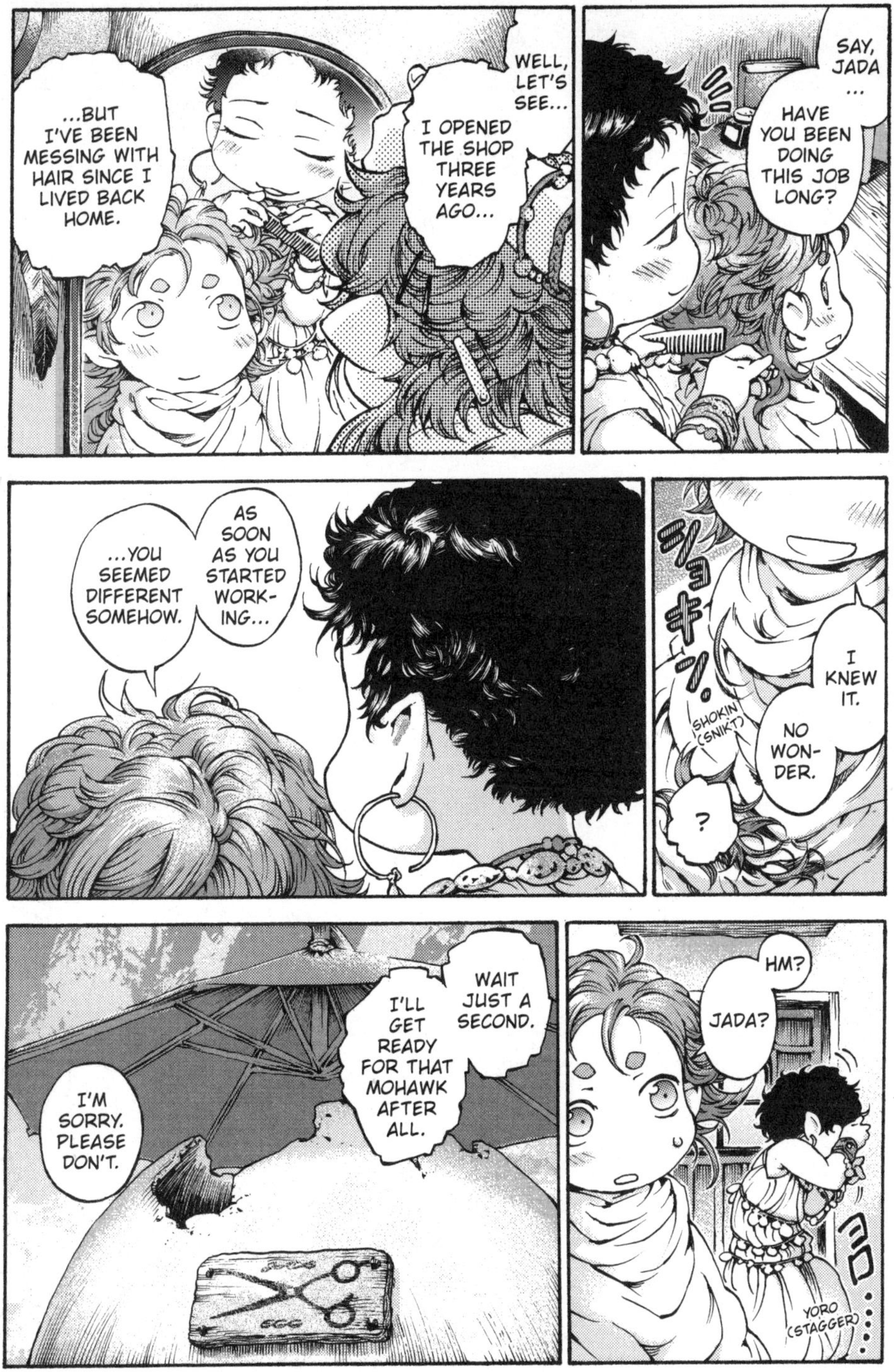
SAY, JADA...
HAVE YOU BEEN DOING THIS JOB LONG?
WELL, LET'S SEE...
I OPENED THE SHOP THREE YEARS AGO...
...BUT I'VE BEEN MESSING WITH HAIR SINCE I LIVED BACK HOME.
I KNEW IT.
NO WONDER.
ショキン
SHOKIN (SNIKT)
?
AS SOON AS YOU STARTED WORKING...
...YOU SEEMED DIFFERENT SOMEHOW.
HM?
JADA?
ヨロ...
YORO (STAGGER)
WAIT JUST A SECOND.
I'LL GET READY FOR THAT MOHAWK AFTER ALL.
I'M SORRY. PLEASE DON'T.

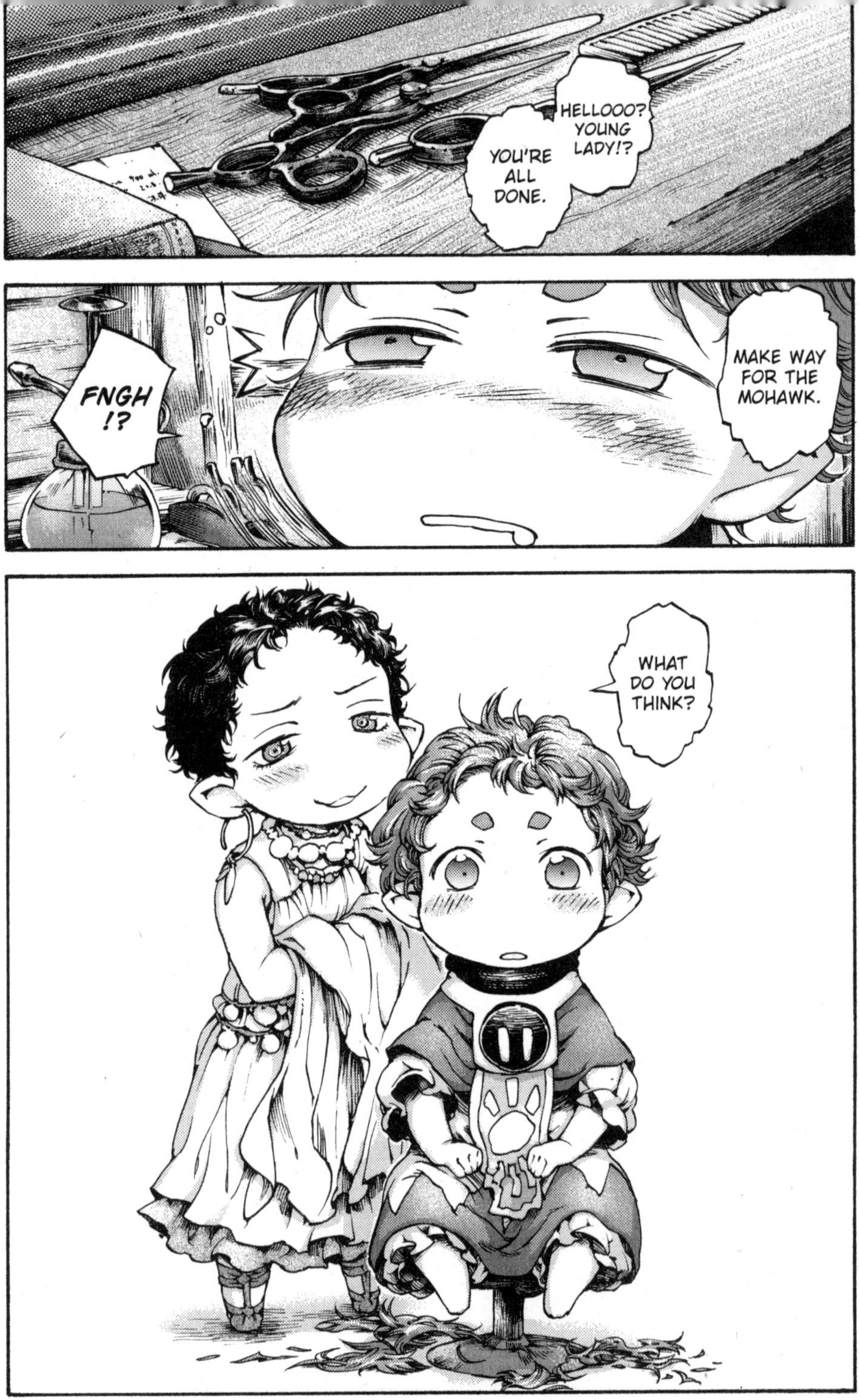
HELLOOO? YOUNG LADY!?
YOU'RE ALL DONE.
MAKE WAY FOR THE MOHAWK.
FNGH !?
WHAT DO YOU THINK?

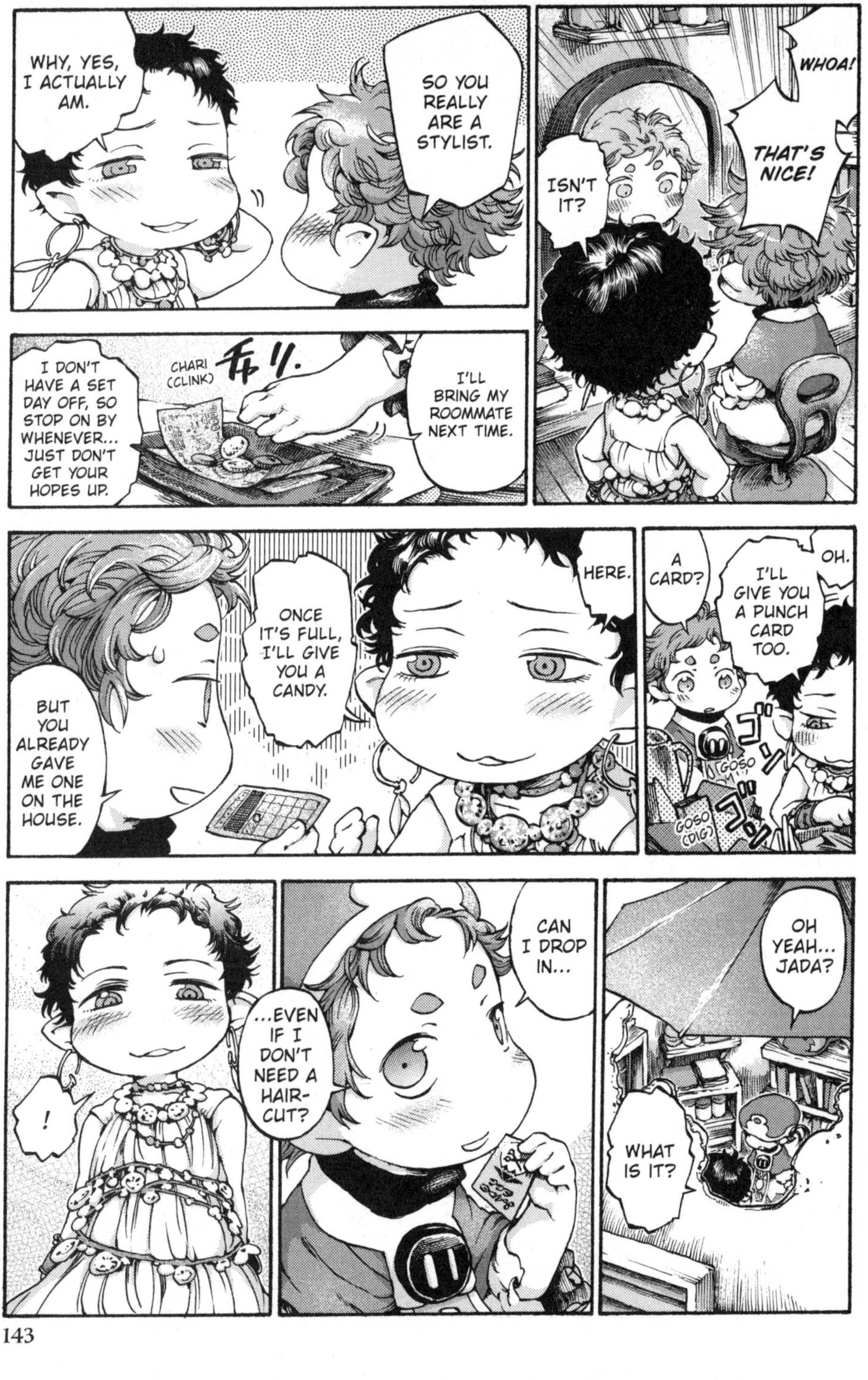

WHOA!
THAT'S NICE!
ISN'T IT?
SO YOU REALLY ARE A STYLIST.
WHY, YES, I ACTUALLY AM.
I'LL BRING MY ROOMMATE NEXT TIME.
CHARI (CLINK)
I DON'T HAVE A SET DAY OFF, SO STOP ON BY WHENEVER... JUST DON'T GET YOUR HOPES UP.
OH.
I'LL GIVE YOU A PUNCH CARD TOO.
A CARD?
GOSO
GOSO (DIG)
HERE.
ONCE IT'S FULL, I'LL GIVE YOU A CANDY.
BUT YOU ALREADY GAVE ME ONE ON THE HOUSE.
OH YEAH... JADA?
WHAT IS IT?
CAN I DROP IN...
...EVEN IF I DON'T NEED A HAIR-CUT?
!

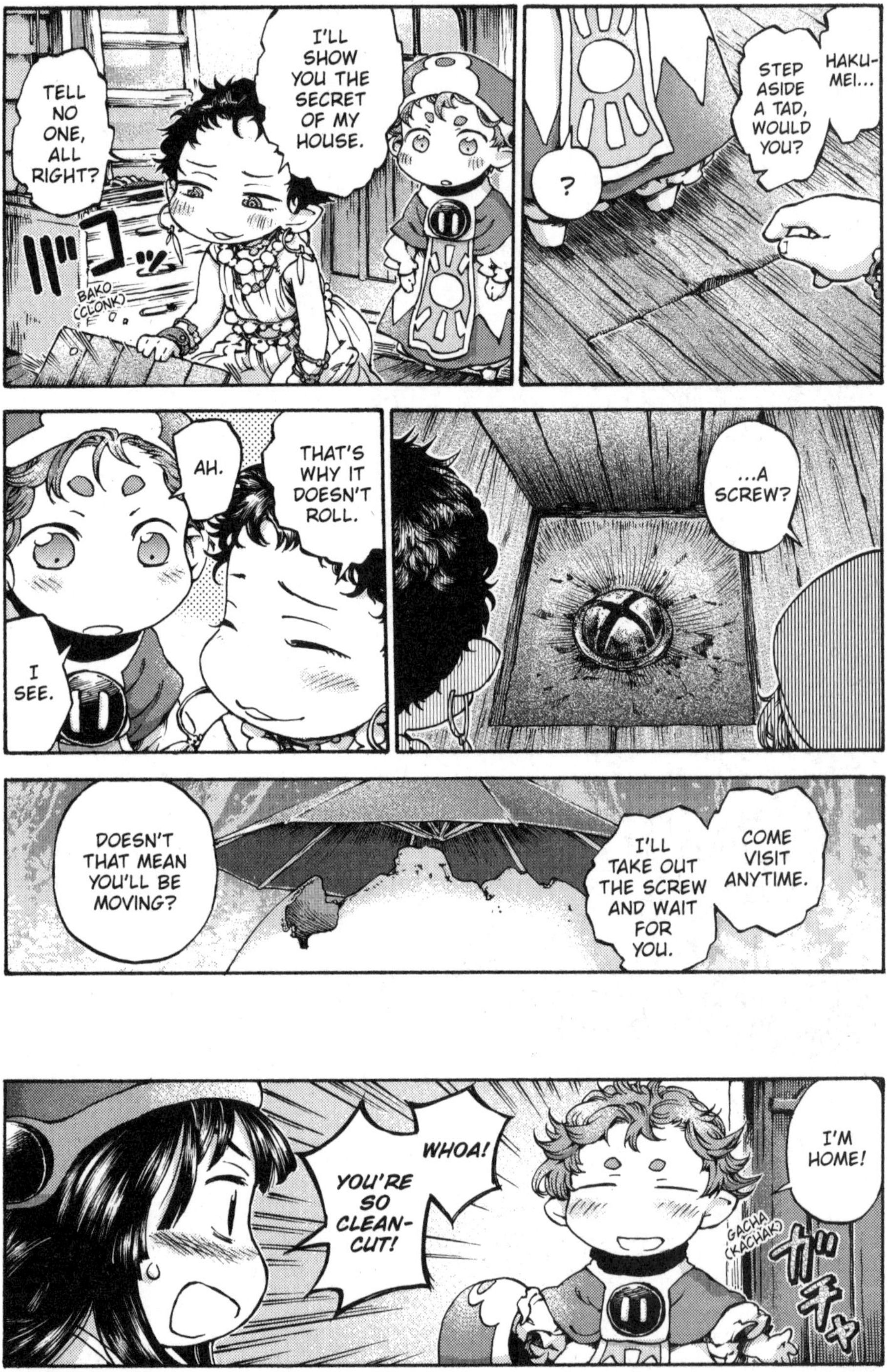
HAKU-MEI...
STEP ASIDE A TAD, WOULD YOU?
?
I'LL SHOW YOU THE SECRET OF MY HOUSE.
TELL NO ONE, ALL RIGHT?
BAKO (CLONK)
...A SCREW?
THAT'S WHY IT DOESN'T ROLL.
AH.
I SEE.
COME VISIT ANYTIME.
I'LL TAKE OUT THE SCREW AND WAIT FOR YOU.
DOESN'T THAT MEAN YOU'LL BE MOVING?
I'M HOME!
GACHA (KACHAK)
WHOA!
YOU'RE SO CLEAN-CUT!

To Be Continued

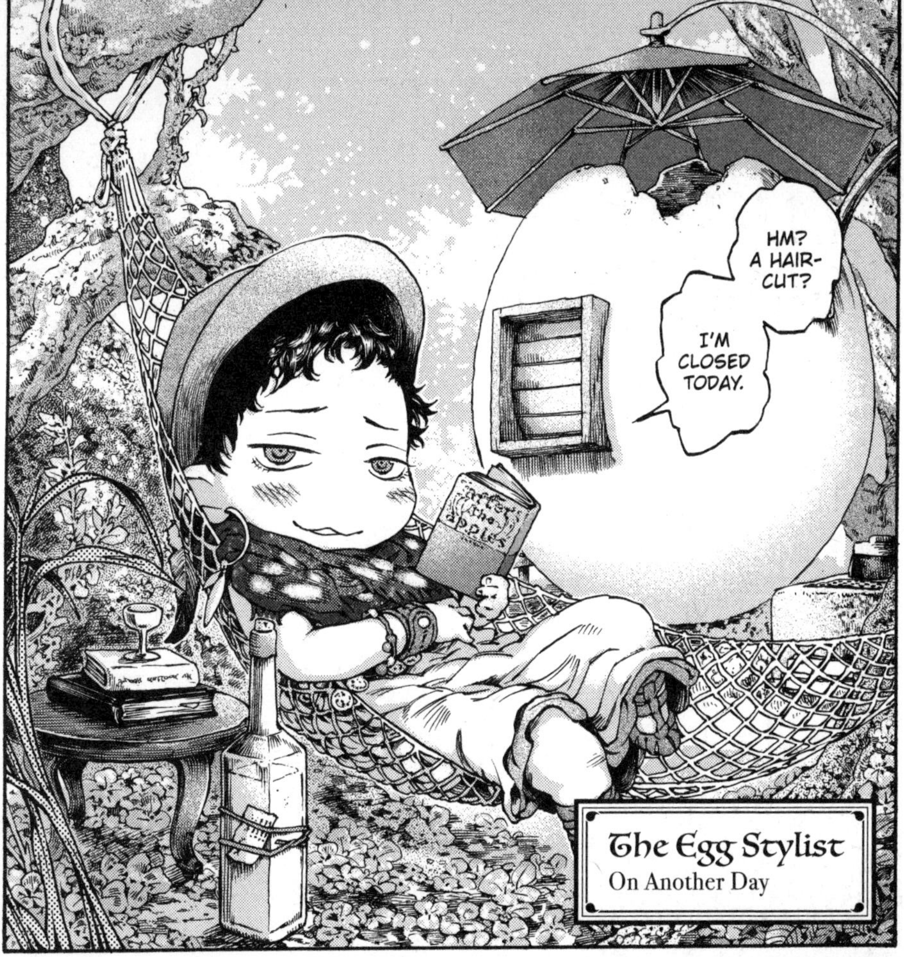
HM? A HAIR-CUT?
I'M CLOSED TODAY.
The Egg Stylist
On Another Day

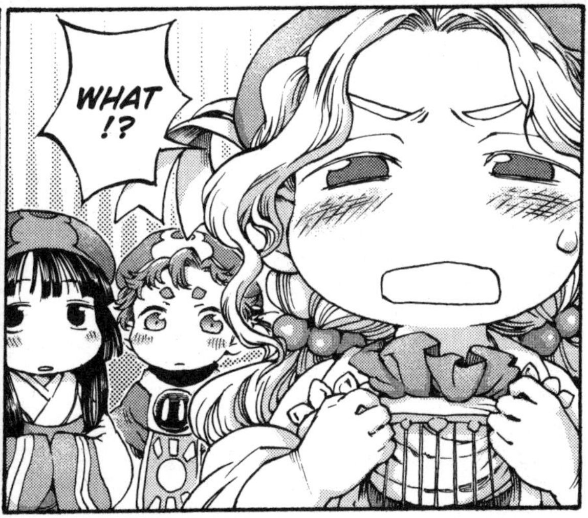
WHAT!?

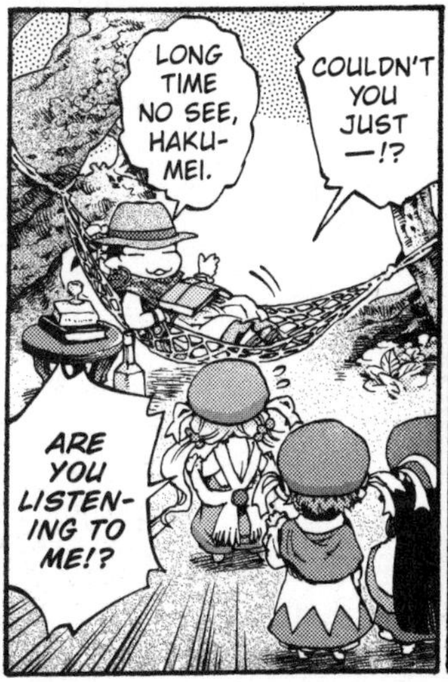
COULDN'T YOU JUST —!?
LONG TIME NO SEE, HAKU-MEI.
ARE YOU LISTEN-ING TO ME!?

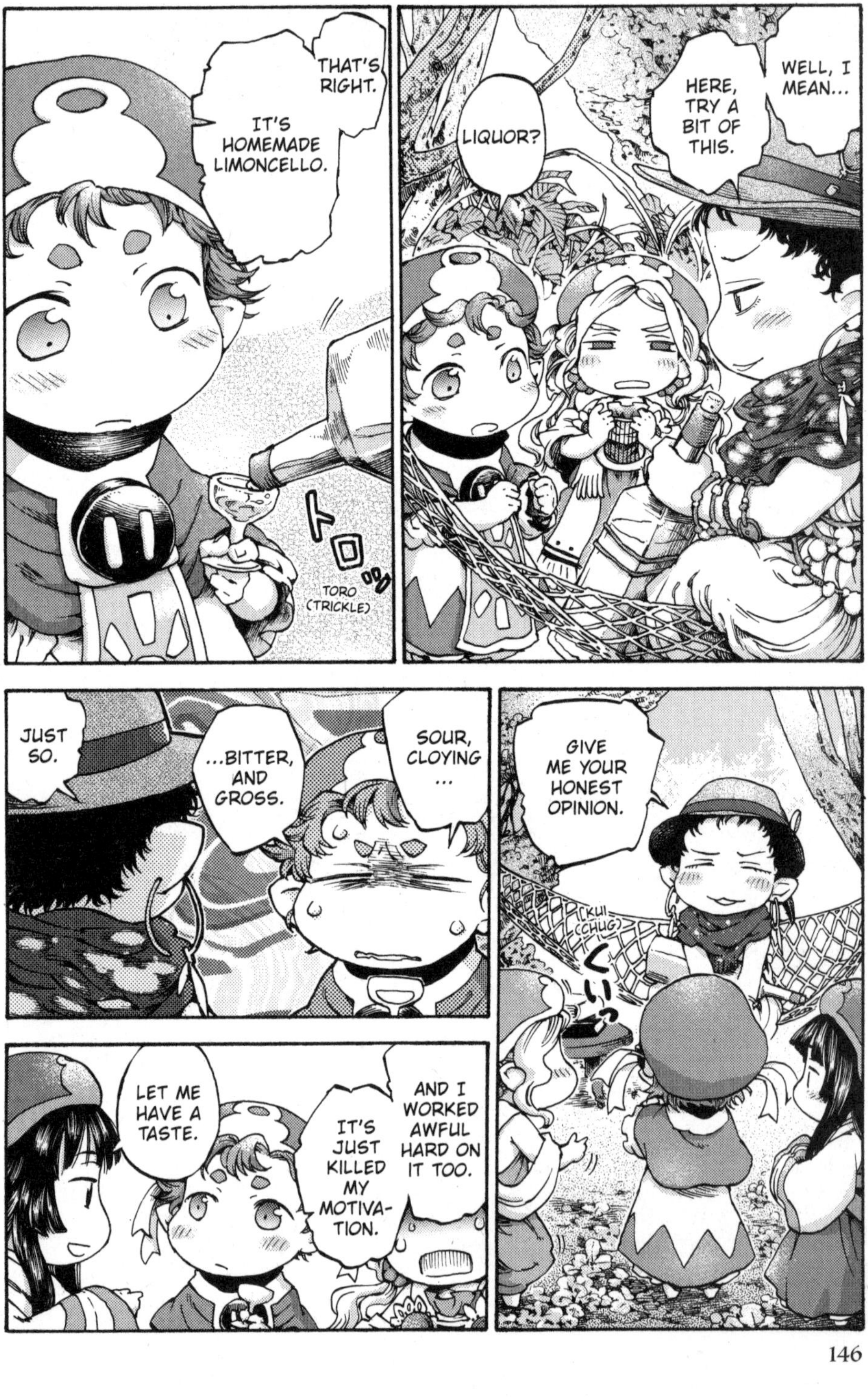

WELL, I MEAN...
HERE, TRY A BIT OF THIS.
LIQUOR?
THAT'S RIGHT.
IT'S HOMEMADE LIMONCELLO.
トロ
TORO (TRICKLE)
GIVE ME YOUR HONEST OPINION.
KUI (CHUG)
くいっ
SOUR, CLOYING...
...BITTER, AND GROSS.
JUST SO.
AND I WORKED AWFUL HARD ON IT TOO.
IT'S JUST KILLED MY MOTIVATION.
LET ME HAVE A TASTE.

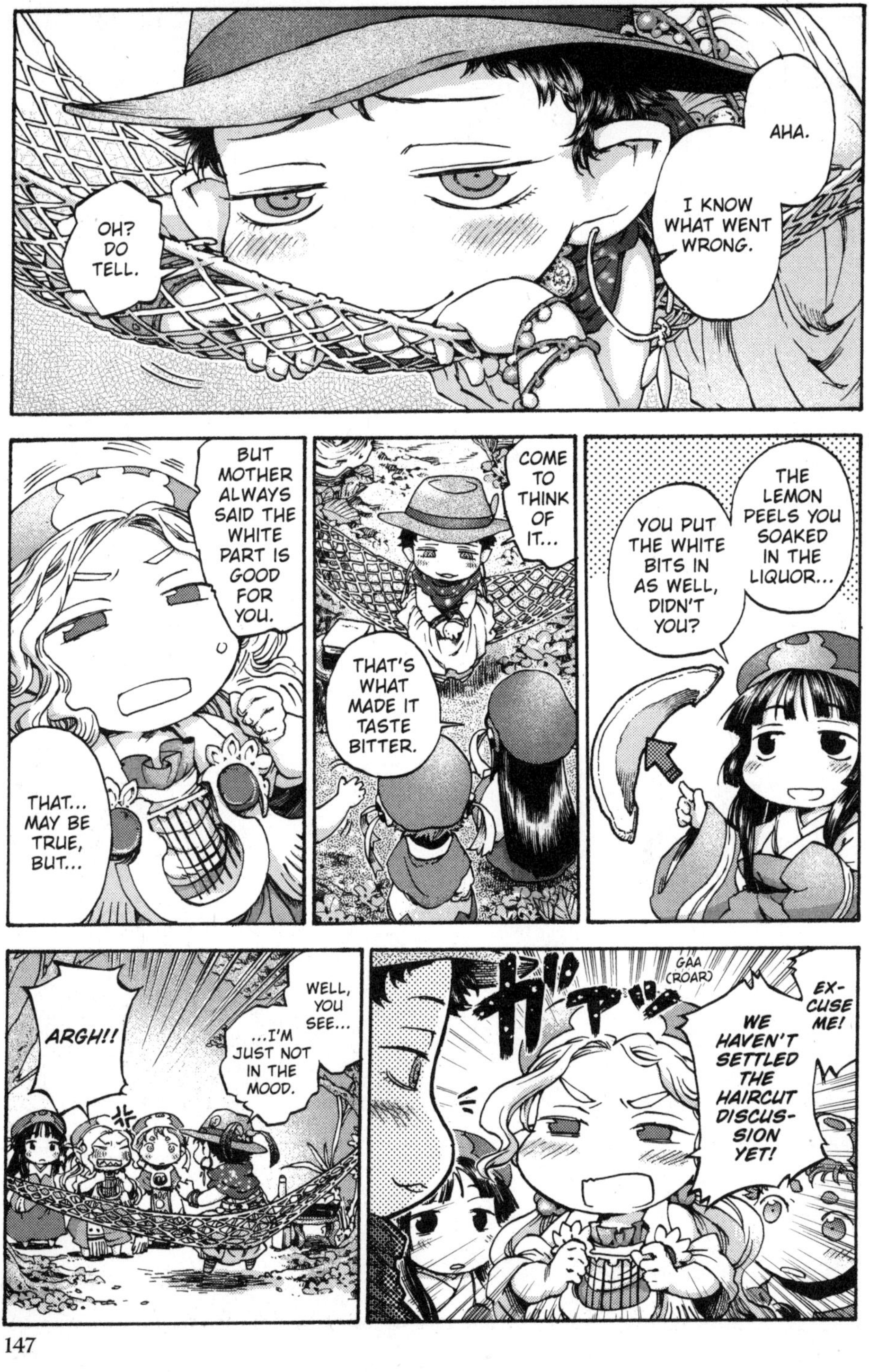
AHA.
I KNOW WHAT WENT WRONG.
OH? DO TELL.
THE LEMON PEELS YOU SOAKED IN THE LIQUOR...
YOU PUT THE WHITE BITS IN AS WELL, DIDN'T YOU?
COME TO THINK OF IT...
THAT'S WHAT MADE IT TASTE BITTER.
BUT MOTHER ALWAYS SAID THE WHITE PART IS GOOD FOR YOU.
THAT... MAY BE TRUE, BUT...
GAA (ROAR)
EX-CUSE ME!
WE HAVEN'T SETTLED THE HAIRCUT DISCUS-SION YET!
WELL, YOU SEE...
...I'M JUST NOT IN THE MOOD.
ARGH!!

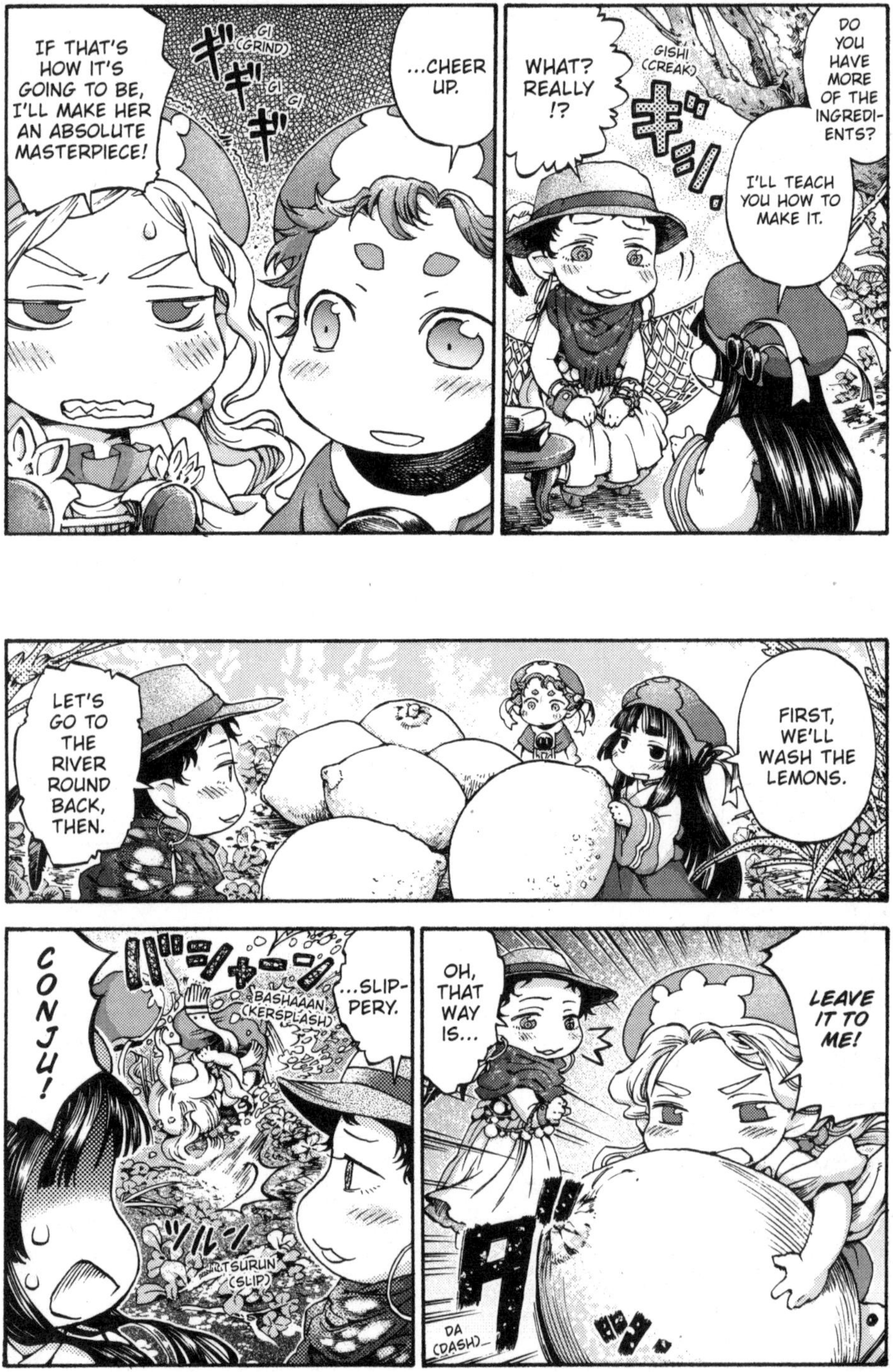
DO YOU HAVE MORE OF THE INGREDIENTS?
I'LL TEACH YOU HOW TO MAKE IT.
GISHI (CREAK)
WHAT? REALLY!?
...CHEER UP.
GI (GRIND) GI GI
IF THAT'S HOW IT'S GOING TO BE, I'LL MAKE HER AN ABSOLUTE MASTERPIECE!
FIRST, WE'LL WASH THE LEMONS.
LET'S GO TO THE RIVER ROUND BACK, THEN.
LEAVE IT TO ME!
OH, THAT WAY IS...
DA (DASH)
...SLIPPERY.
BASHAAAN (KERSPLASH)
TSURUN (SLIP)
CONJU!

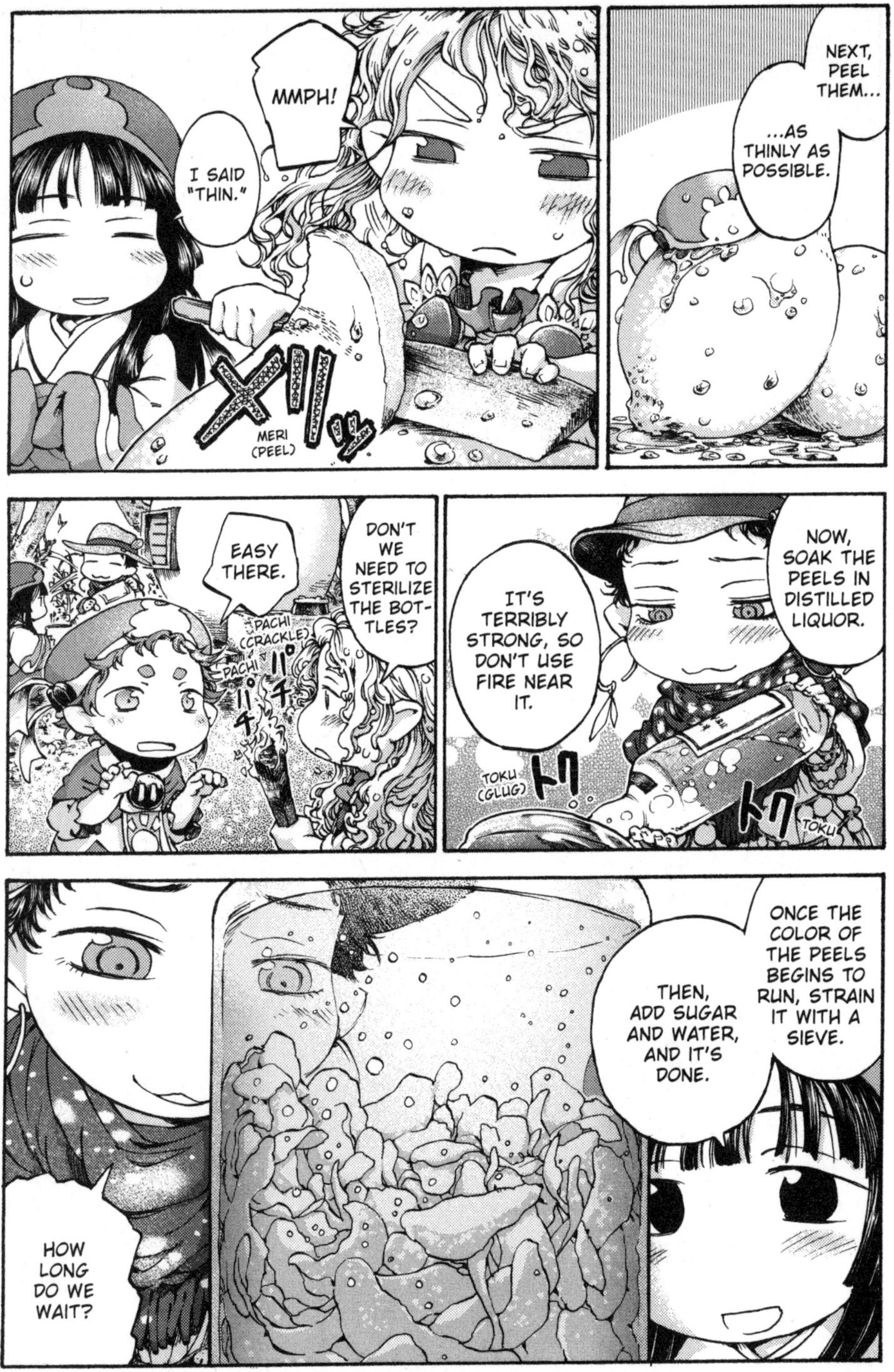
NEXT, PEEL THEM...
...AS THINLY AS POSSIBLE.
MMPH!
I SAID "THIN."
MERI (PEEL)
NOW, SOAK THE PEELS IN DISTILLED LIQUOR.
IT'S TERRIBLY STRONG, SO DON'T USE FIRE NEAR IT.
TOKU (GLUG)
TOKU
DON'T WE NEED TO STERILIZE THE BOT-TLES?
EASY THERE.
PACHI (CRACKLE)
PACHI
ONCE THE COLOR OF THE PEELS BEGINS TO RUN, STRAIN IT WITH A SIEVE.
THEN, ADD SUGAR AND WATER, AND IT'S DONE.
HOW LONG DO WE WAIT?

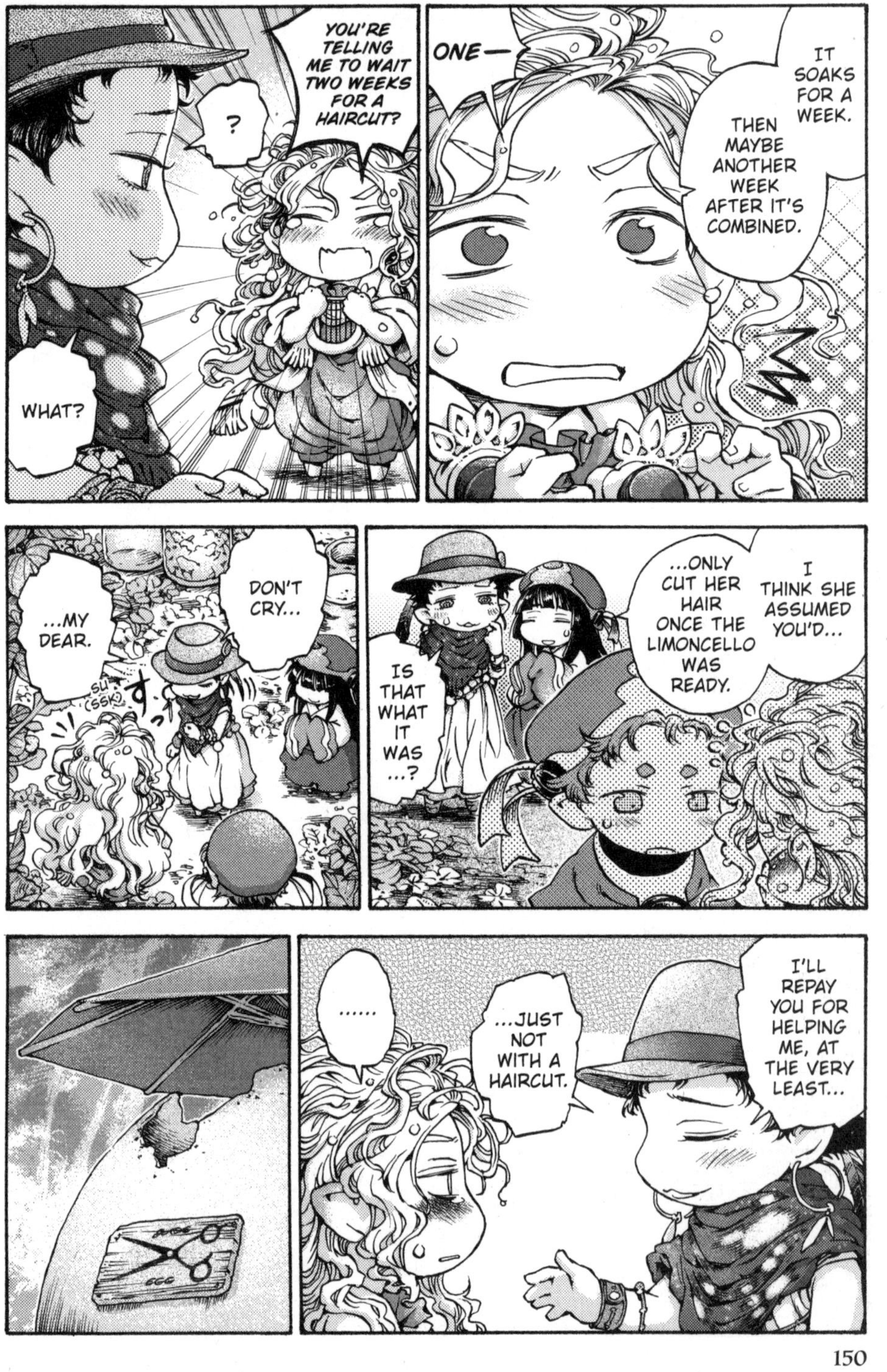
IT SOAKS FOR A WEEK.
THEN MAYBE ANOTHER WEEK AFTER IT'S COMBINED.
ONE—
YOU'RE TELLING ME TO WAIT TWO WEEKS FOR A HAIRCUT?
?
WHAT?
I THINK SHE ASSUMED YOU'D...
...ONLY CUT HER HAIR ONCE THE LIMONCELLO WAS READY.
IS THAT WHAT IT WAS...?
DON'T CRY...
...MY DEAR.
SU (SSK)
I'LL REPAY YOU FOR HELPING ME, AT THE VERY LEAST...
...JUST NOT WITH A HAIRCUT.
......

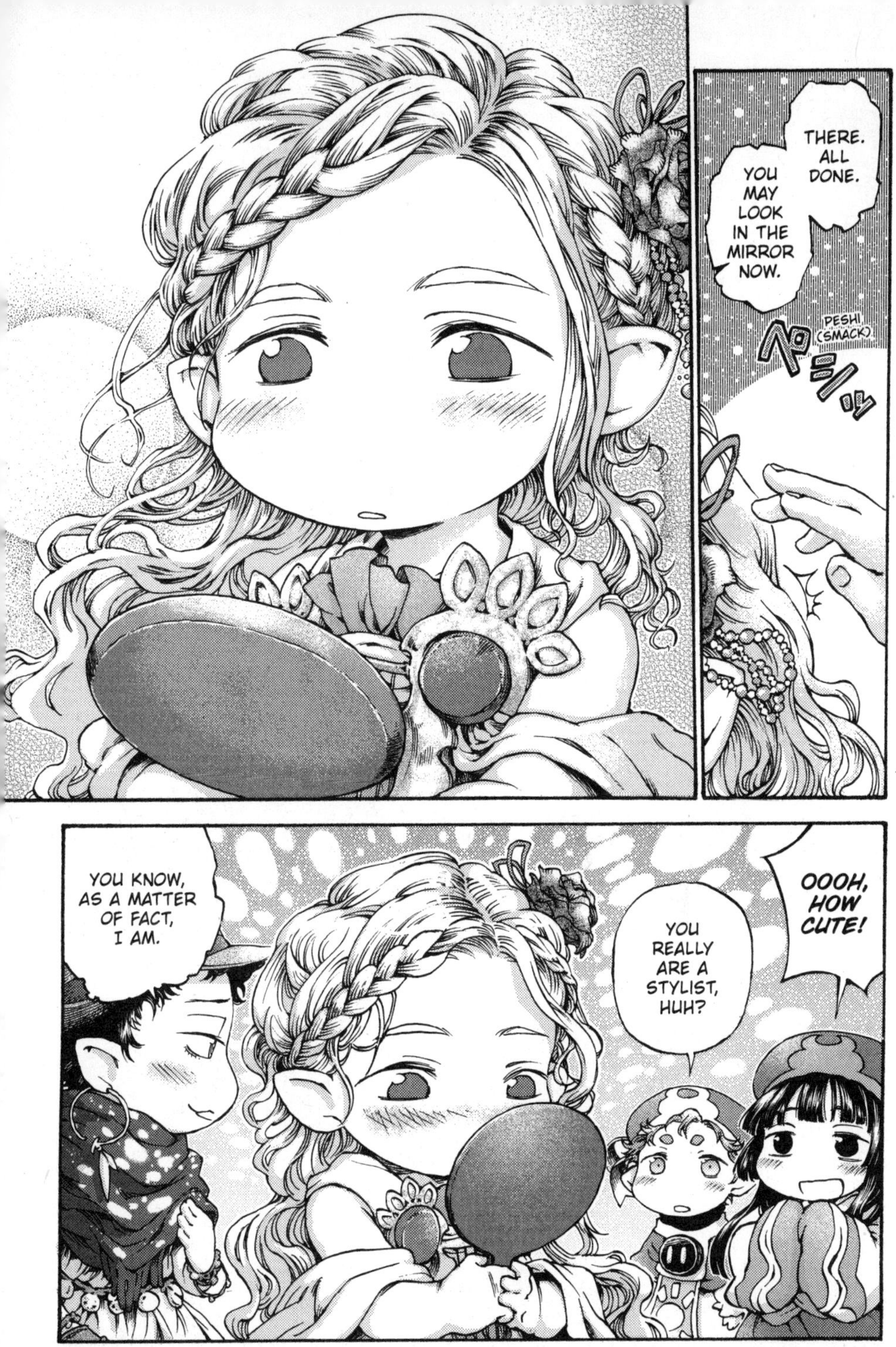
THERE. ALL DONE.
YOU MAY LOOK IN THE MIRROR NOW.
PESHI (SMACK)
OOOH, HOW CUTE!
YOU REALLY ARE A STYLIST, HUH?
YOU KNOW, AS A MATTER OF FACT, I AM.

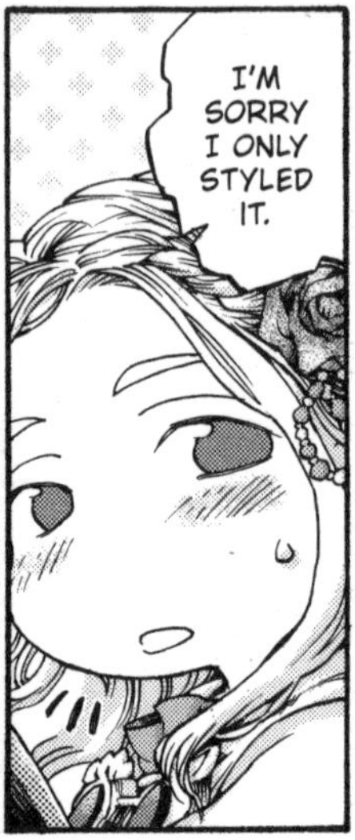
I'M SORRY I ONLY STYLED IT.

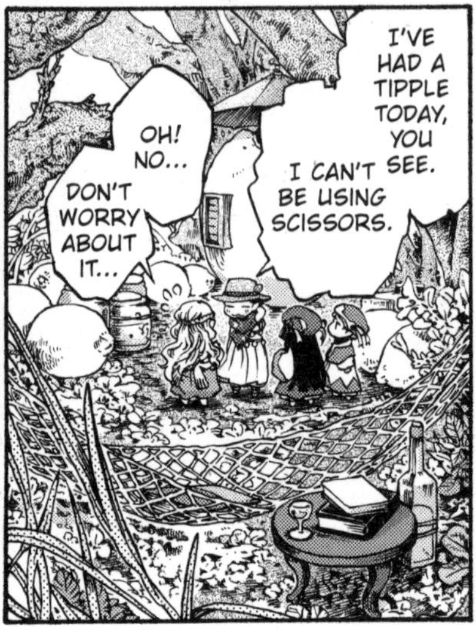
I'VE HAD A TIPPLE TODAY, YOU SEE.
I CAN'T BE USING SCISSORS.
OH! NO...
DON'T WORRY ABOUT IT...

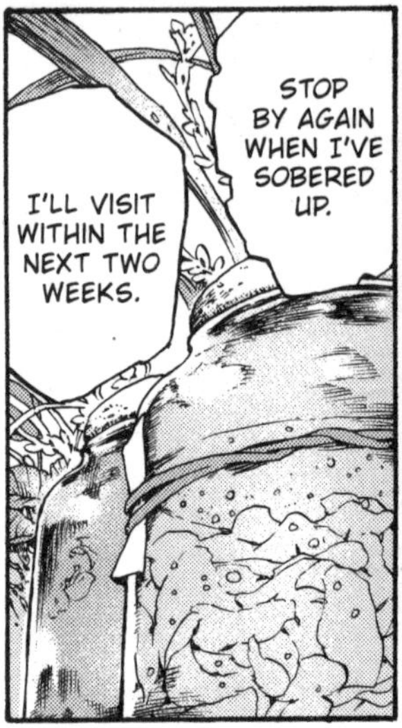
STOP BY AGAIN WHEN I'VE SOBERED UP.
I'LL VISIT WITHIN THE NEXT TWO WEEKS.

LATER

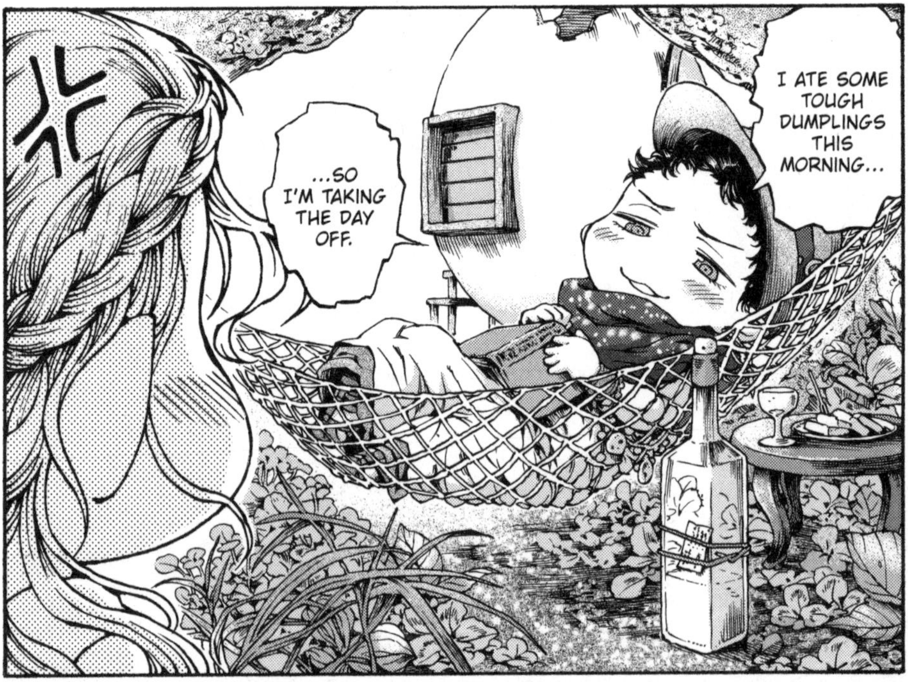
I ATE SOME TOUGH DUMPLINGS THIS MORNING...
...SO I'M TAKING THE DAY OFF.

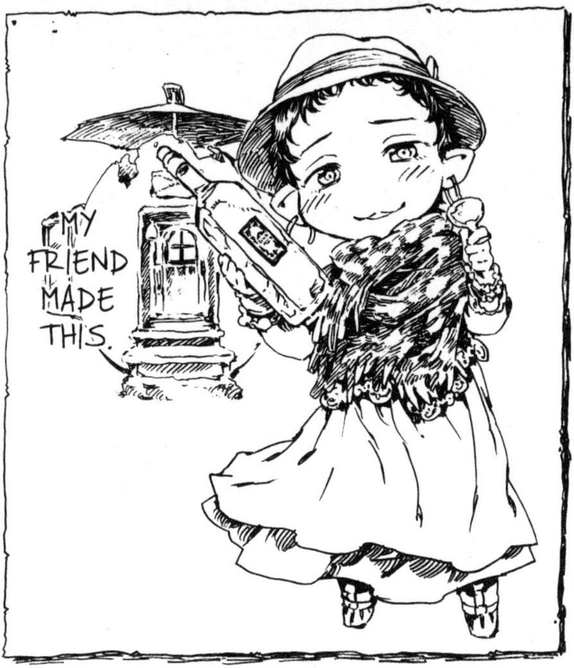
MY FRIEND MADE THIS.

The limoncello found at a salon called Jade Egg has secretly been the hottest topic among Makinata's liquor aficionados. This superb libation is made with an abundance of half-wild lemons, and although simple, its generous fragrance and faint, lingering bitterness are magnificent. Not only that, but—astonishingly—it's available very nearly free of charge. While you're there, you can have fun talking with the gloriously eccentric shopkeeper.

Apparently, once the limoncello is gone, it's gone for good, so stop by soon if you're interested.

–Excerpt from *Makinata Daily*'s Beauty Salon Spotlight

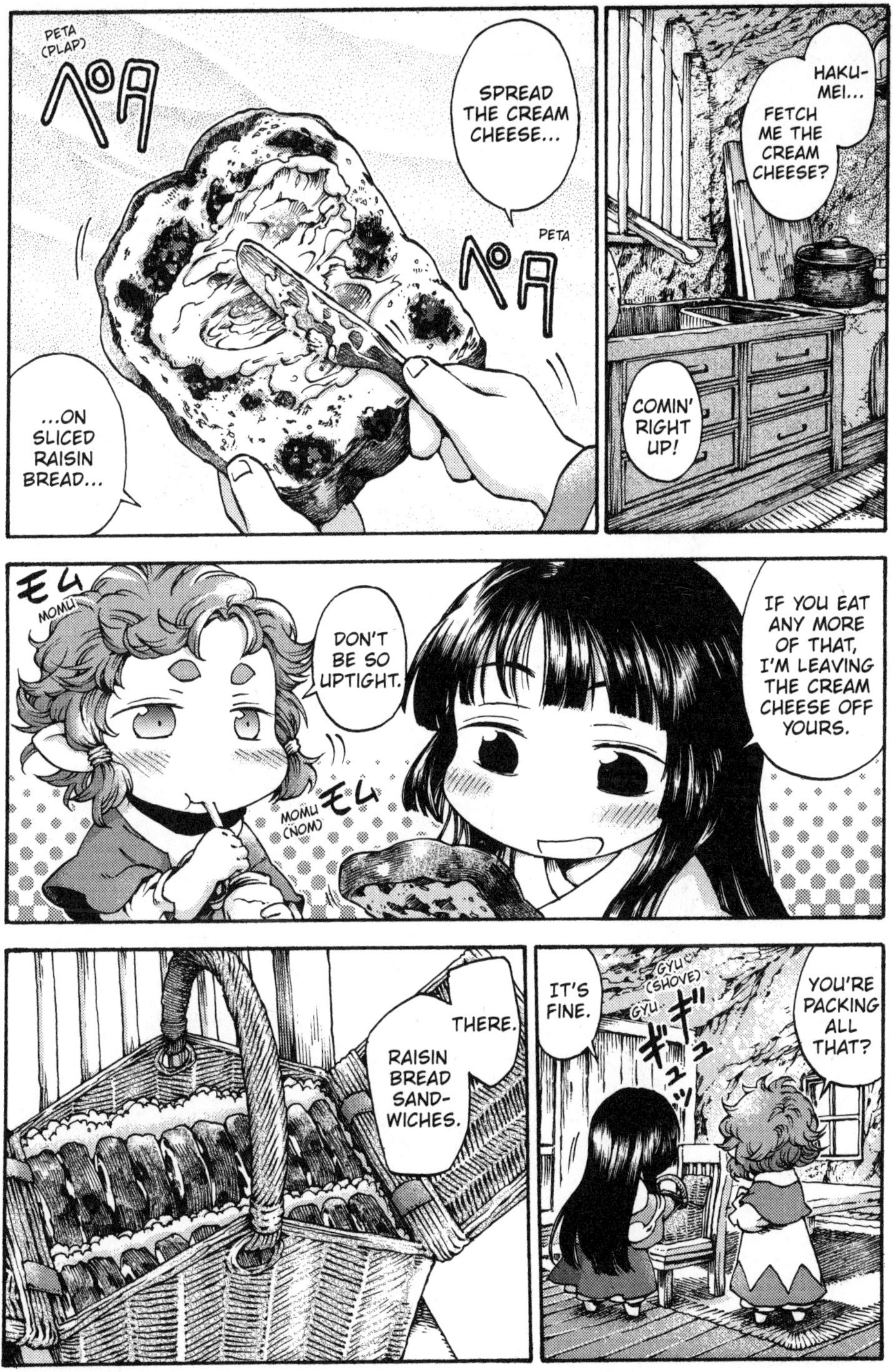
HAKU-MEI... FETCH ME THE CREAM CHEESE?
COMIN' RIGHT UP!
PETA (PLAP)
ペタ
SPREAD THE CREAM CHEESE...
PETA
ペタ
...ON SLICED RAISIN BREAD...
IF YOU EAT ANY MORE OF THAT, I'M LEAVING THE CREAM CHEESE OFF YOURS.
DON'T BE SO UPTIGHT.
モム
MOMU
MOMU (NOM)
モム
YOU'RE PACKING ALL THAT?
GYU (SHOVE)
ギュ
GYU
ギュッ
IT'S FINE.
THERE.
RAISIN BREAD SANDWICHES.

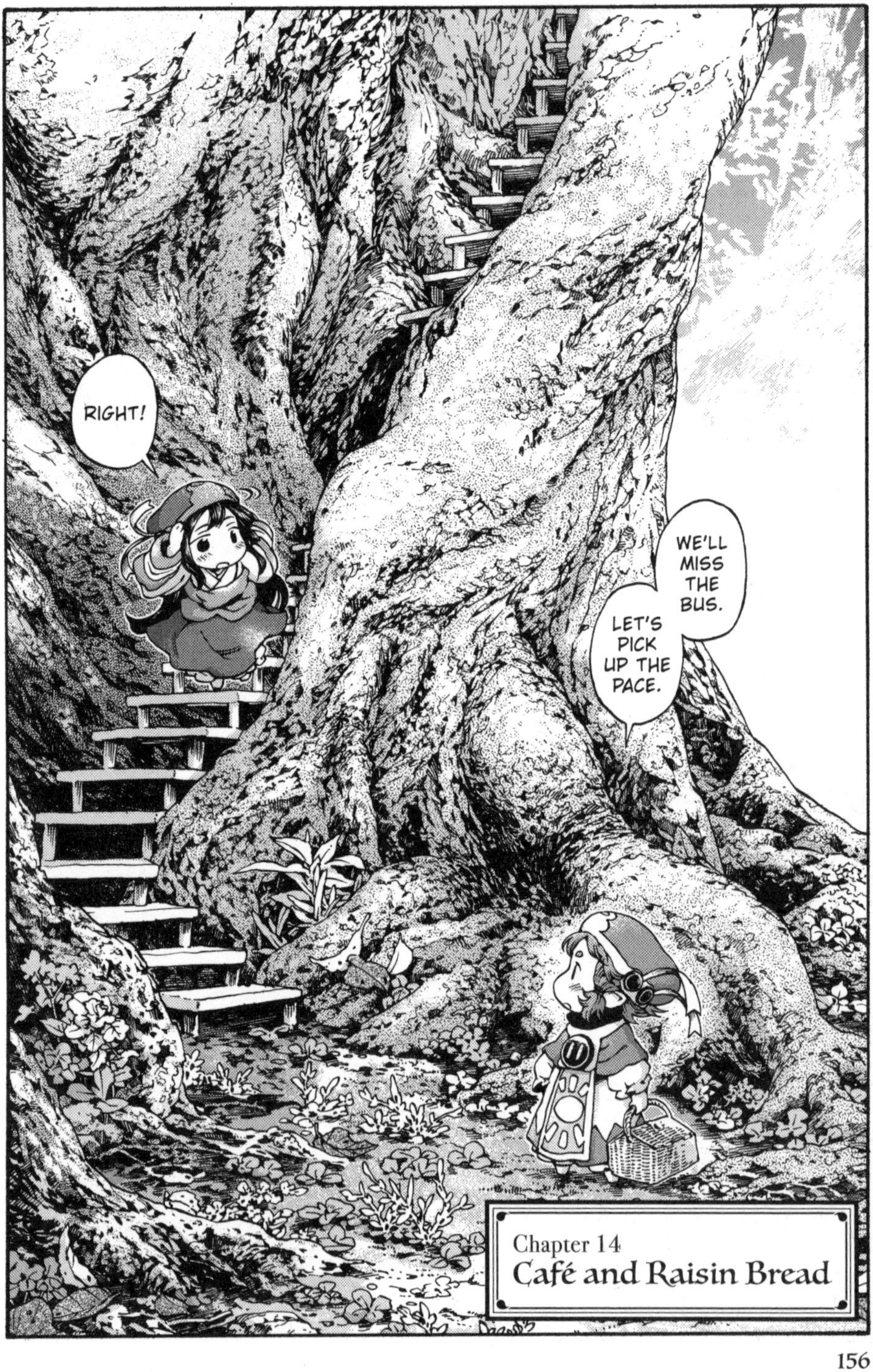
WE'LL MISS THE BUS.
LET'S PICK UP THE PACE.
RIGHT!

Chapter 14
Café and Raisin Bread

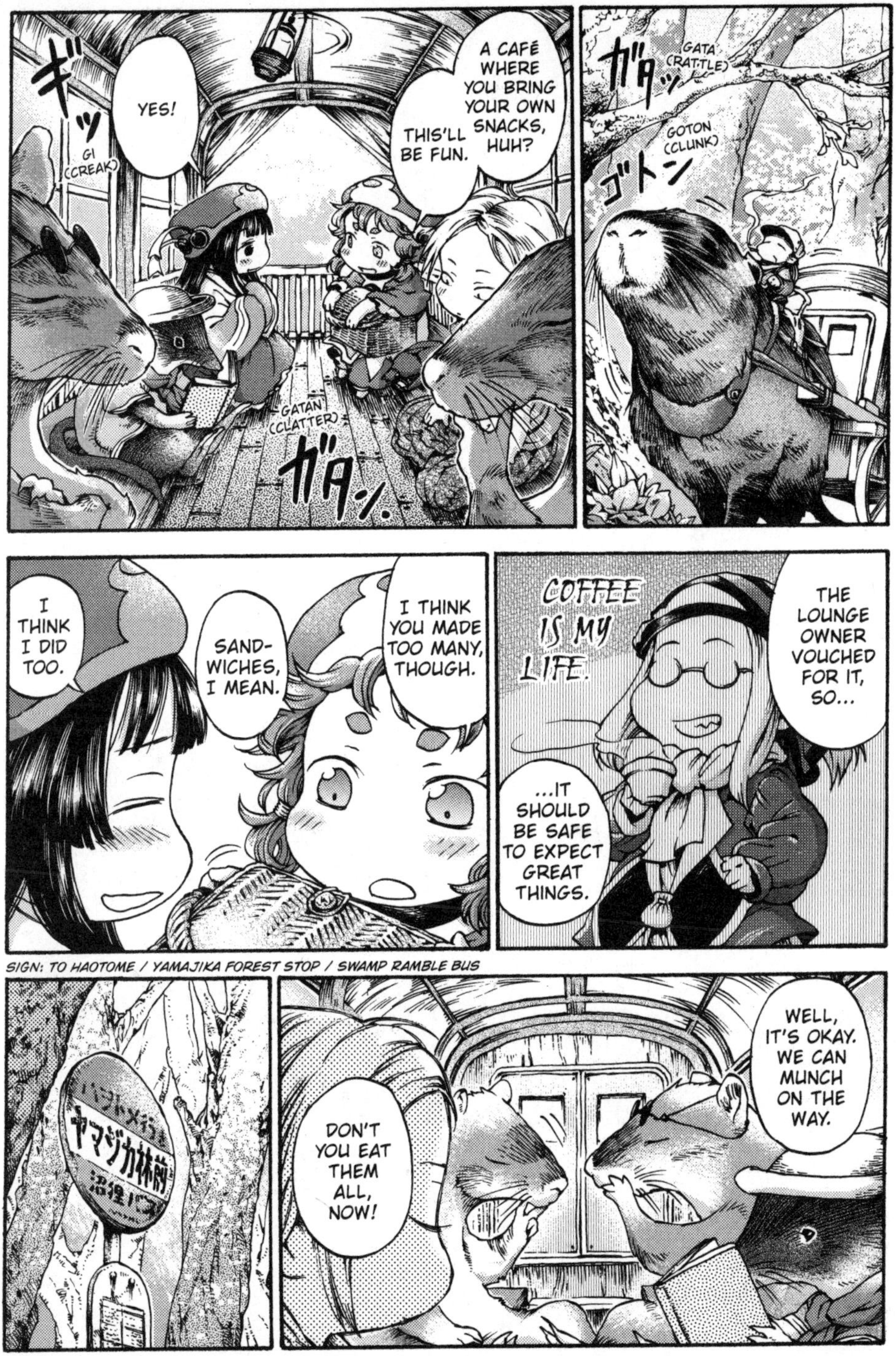
ガタッ
GATA (RATTLE)
ゴトン
GOTON (CLUNK)
A CAFÉ WHERE YOU BRING YOUR OWN SNACKS, HUH?
THIS'LL BE FUN.
YES!
ギッ
GI (CREAK)
GATAN (CLATTER)
ガタン
THE LOUNGE OWNER VOUCHED FOR IT, SO...
COFFEE IS MY LIFE.
...IT SHOULD BE SAFE TO EXPECT GREAT THINGS.
I THINK YOU MADE TOO MANY, THOUGH.
SAND-WICHES, I MEAN.
I THINK I DID TOO.
SIGN: TO HAOTOME / YAMAJIKA FOREST STOP / SWAMP RAMBLE BUS
WELL, IT'S OKAY. WE CAN MUNCH ON THE WAY.
DON'T YOU EAT THEM ALL, NOW!

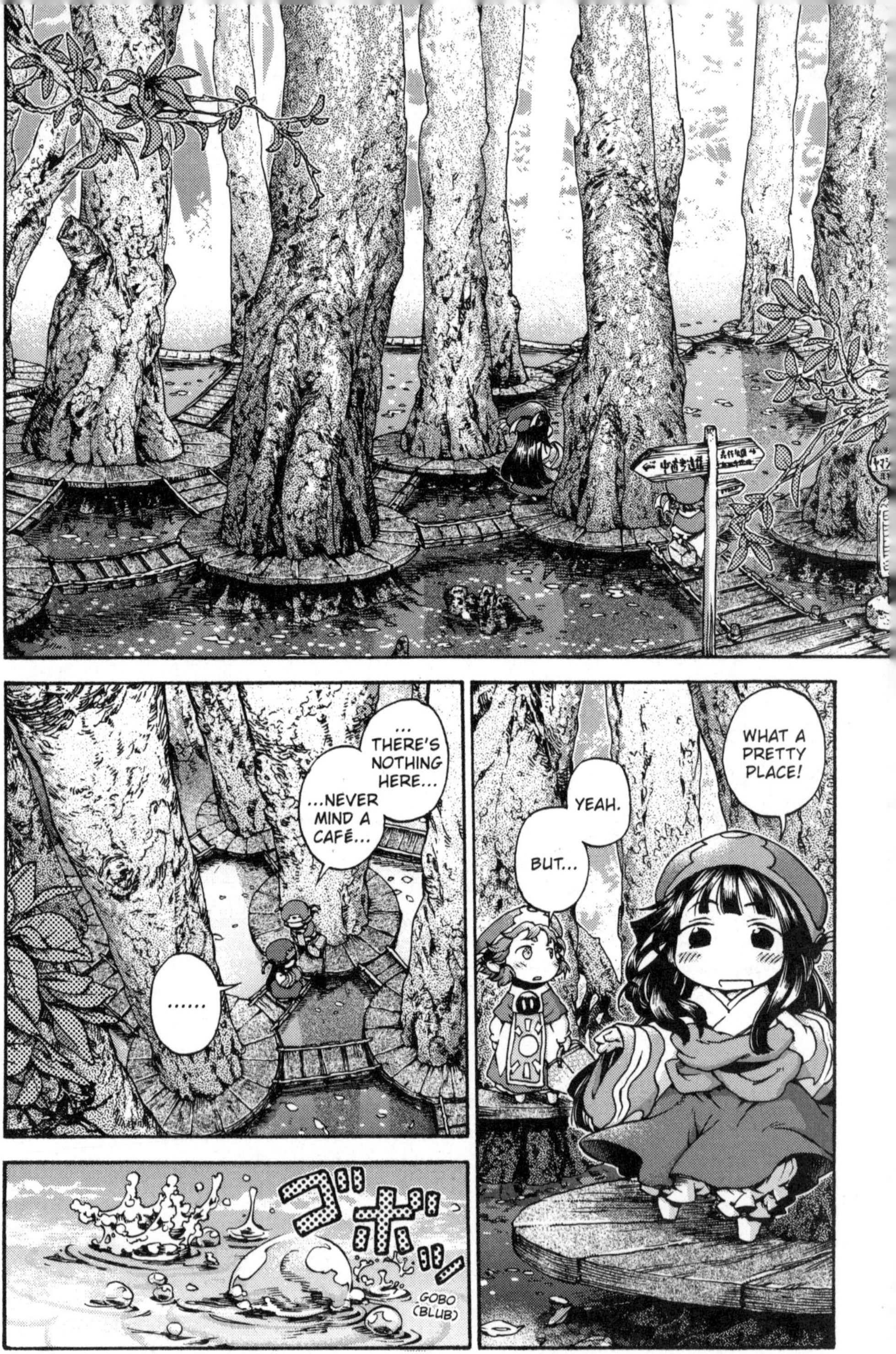
WHAT A PRETTY PLACE!
YEAH.
BUT...
... THERE'S NOTHING HERE...
...NEVER MIND A CAFÉ...
......
ゴボッ
GOBO (BLUB)

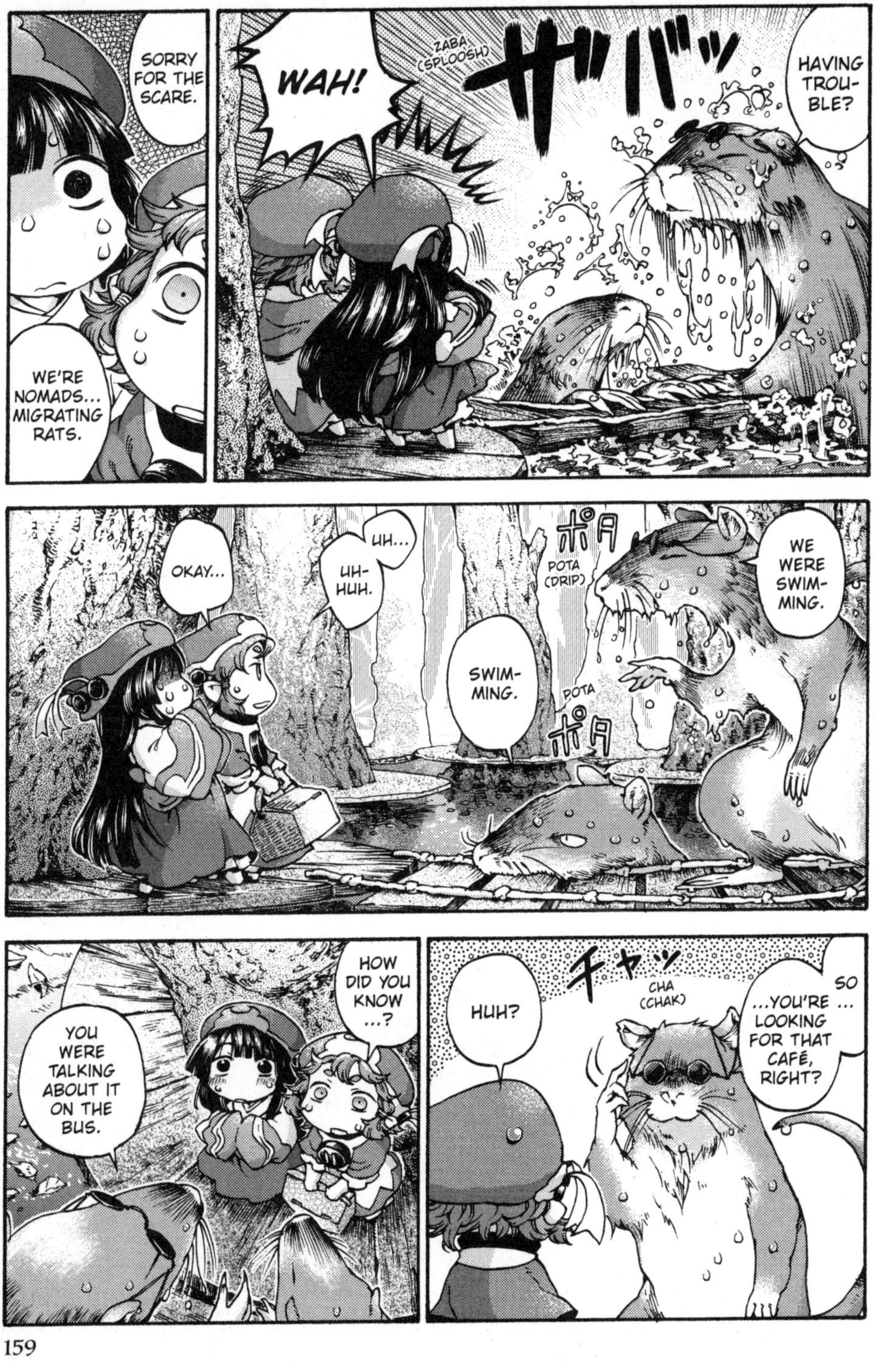
HAVING TROUBLE?
ザバッ
ZABA (SPLOOSH)
WAH!
SORRY FOR THE SCARE.
WE'RE NOMADS... MIGRATING RATS.
WE WERE SWIMMING.
ポタ
POTA (DRIP)
UH... UH-HUH.
OKAY...
SWIMMING.
POTA
ポタ
SO ...YOU'RE ... LOOKING FOR THAT CAFÉ, RIGHT?
チャッ
CHA (CHAK)
HUH?
HOW DID YOU KNOW ...?
YOU WERE TALKING ABOUT IT ON THE BUS.

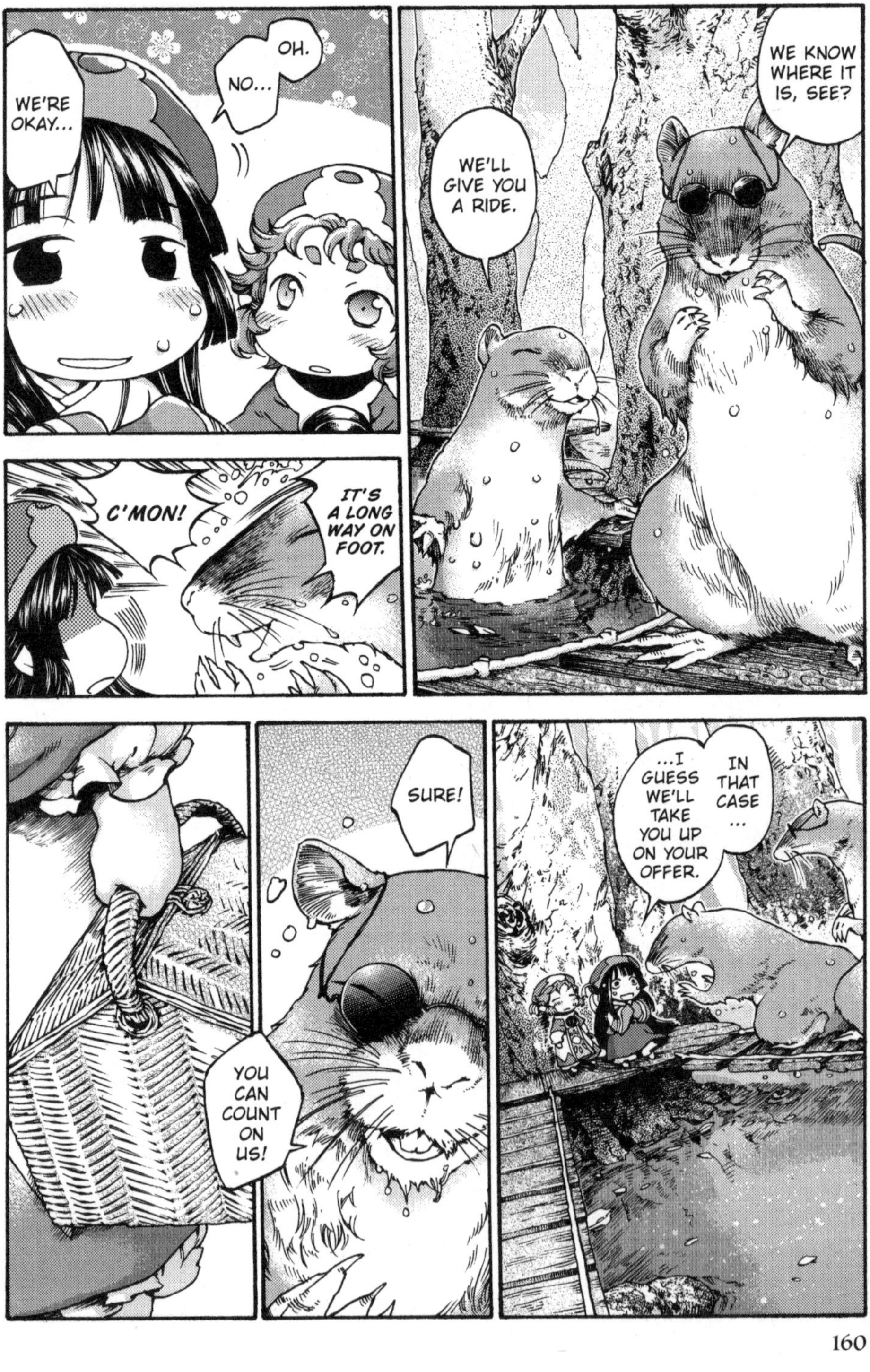

WE KNOW WHERE IT IS, SEE?
WE'LL GIVE YOU A RIDE.
OH. NO...
WE'RE OKAY...
IT'S A LONG WAY ON FOOT.
C'MON!
IN THAT CASE ...
...I GUESS WE'LL TAKE YOU UP ON YOUR OFFER.
SURE!
YOU CAN COUNT ON US!

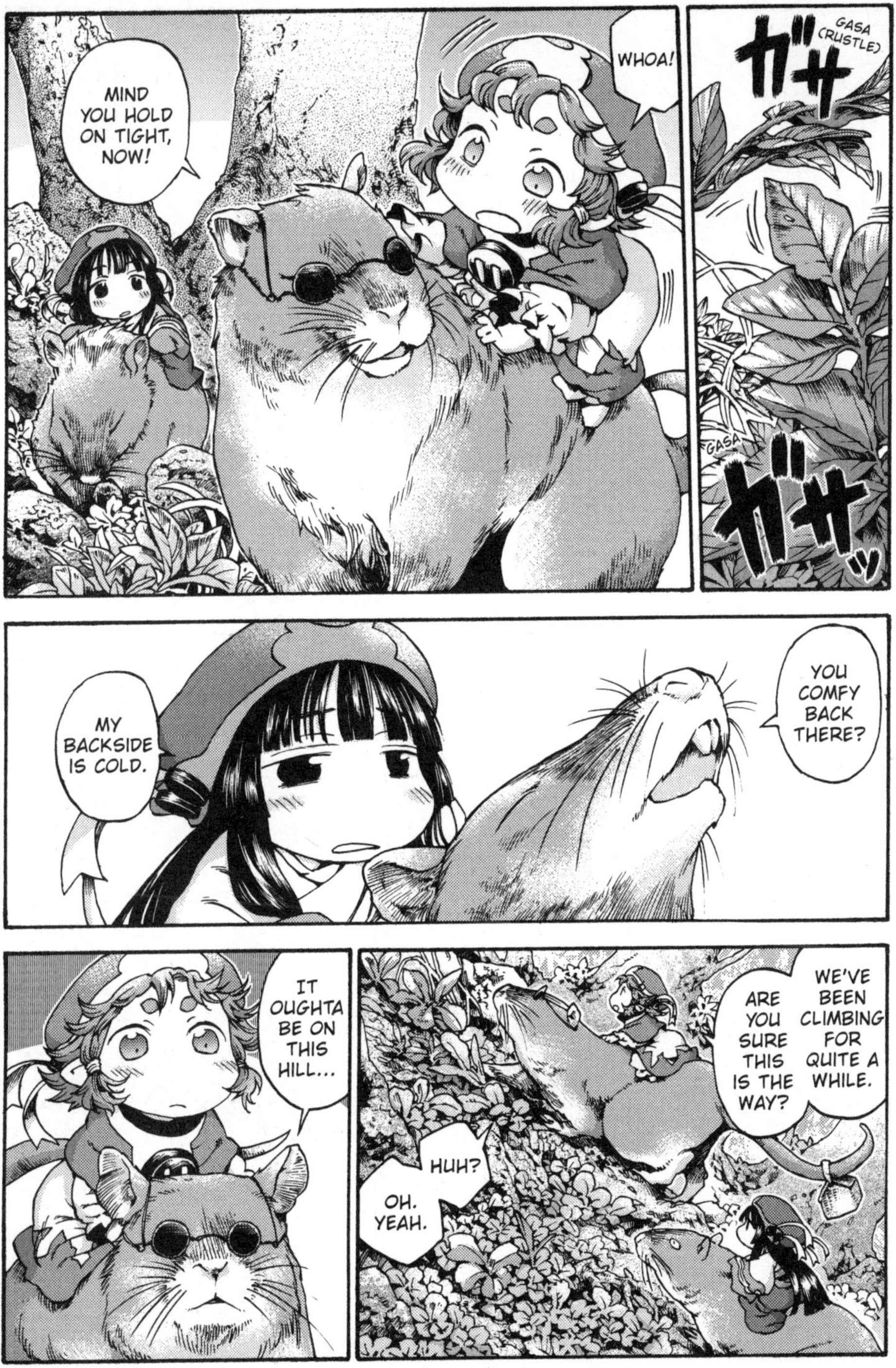
ガサ
GASA (RUSTLE)
ガサッ
GASA
WHOA!
MIND YOU HOLD ON TIGHT, NOW!
YOU COMFY BACK THERE?
MY BACKSIDE IS COLD.
WE'VE BEEN CLIMBING FOR QUITE A WHILE.
ARE YOU SURE THIS IS THE WAY?
HUH?
OH. YEAH.
IT OUGHTA BE ON THIS HILL...

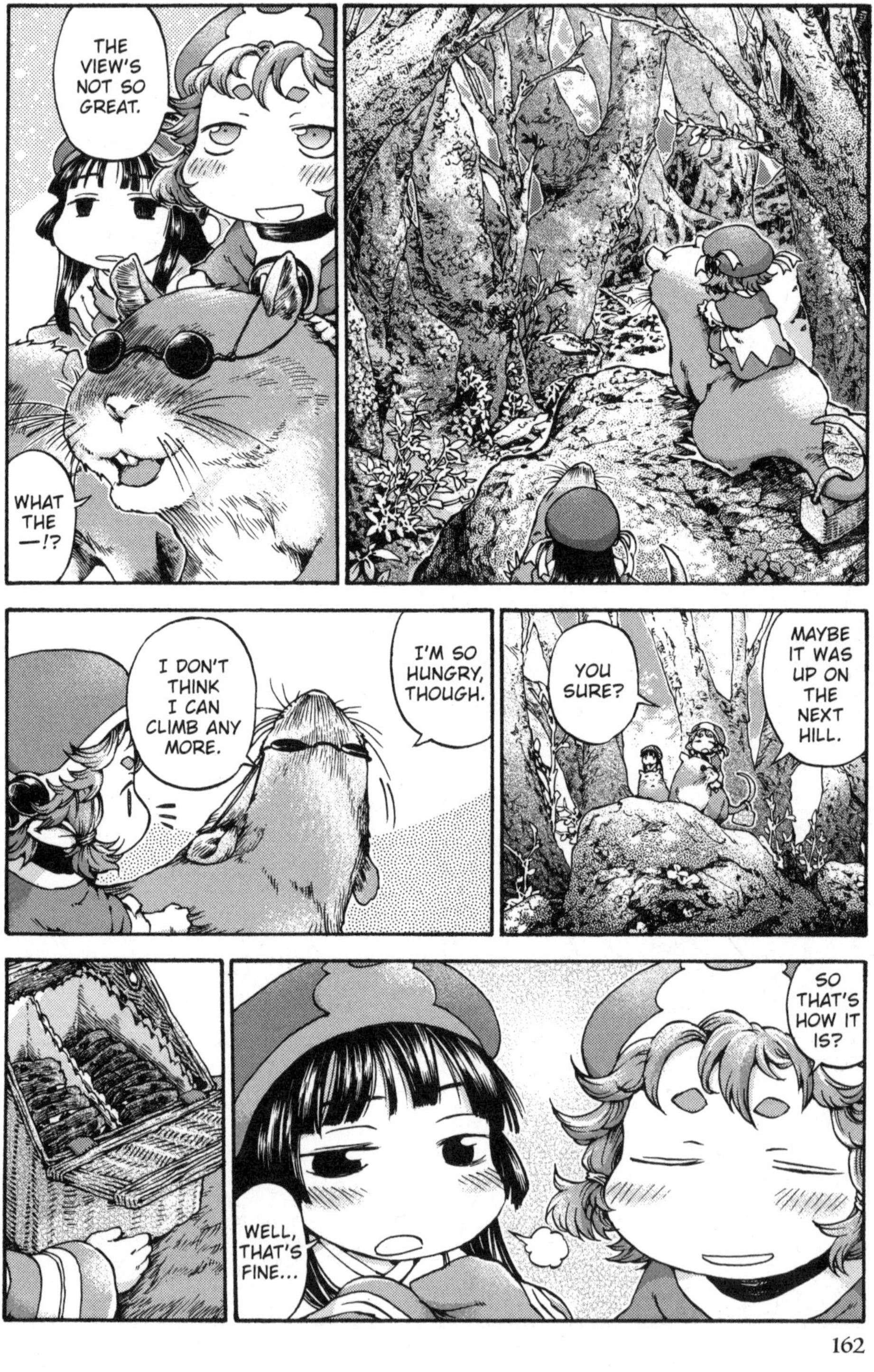
THE VIEW'S NOT SO GREAT.
WHAT THE—!?
MAYBE IT WAS UP ON THE NEXT HILL.
YOU SURE?
I'M SO HUNGRY, THOUGH.
I DON'T THINK I CAN CLIMB ANY MORE.
SO THAT'S HOW IT IS?
WELL, THAT'S FINE...

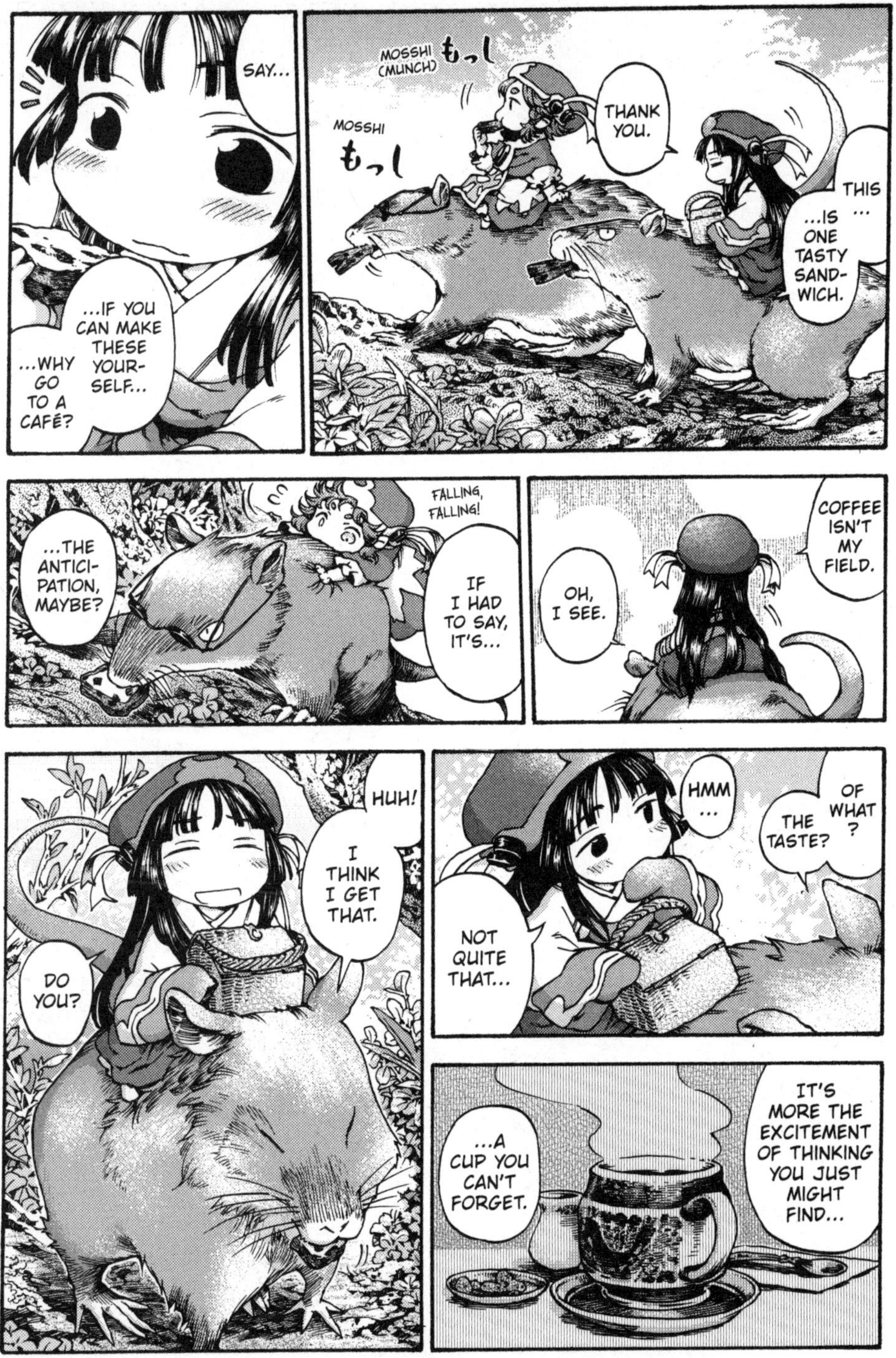
THIS... ...IS ONE TASTY SANDWICH.
THANK YOU.
MOSSHI (MUNCH) もっし
MOSSHI もっし
SAY...
...IF YOU CAN MAKE THESE YOURSELF...
...WHY GO TO A CAFÉ?
COFFEE ISN'T MY FIELD.
OH, I SEE.
FALLING, FALLING!
IF I HAD TO SAY, IT'S...
...THE ANTICIPATION, MAYBE?
OF WHAT?
THE TASTE?
HMM...
NOT QUITE THAT...
IT'S MORE THE EXCITEMENT OF THINKING YOU JUST MIGHT FIND...
...A CUP YOU CAN'T FORGET.
HUH!
I THINK I GET THAT.
DO YOU?

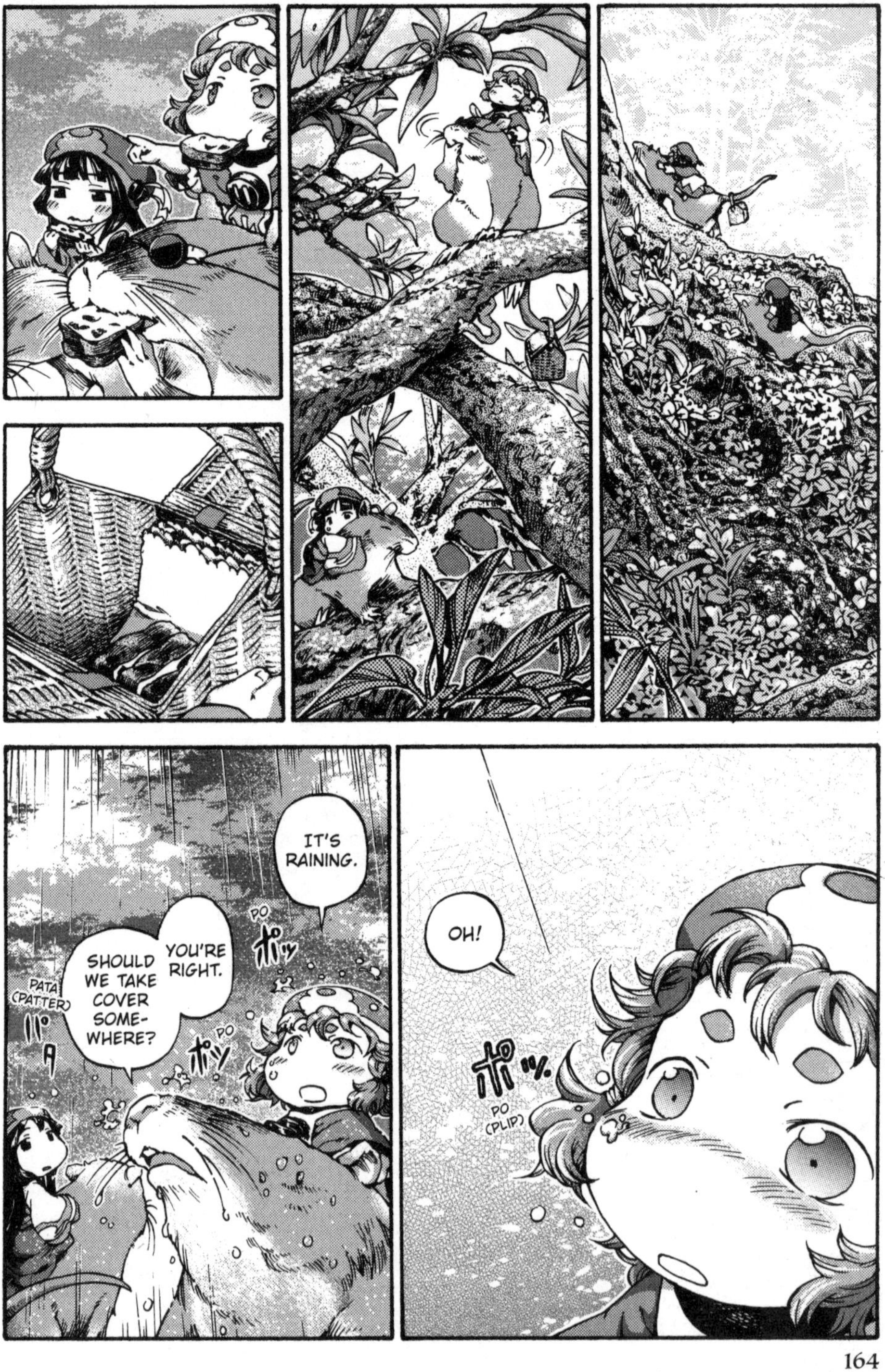
OH!
ポッ
PO (PLIP)
IT'S RAINING.
PO
ポッ
YOU'RE RIGHT.
SHOULD WE TAKE COVER SOME-WHERE?
PATA (PATTER)
パタ
PO
ポッ

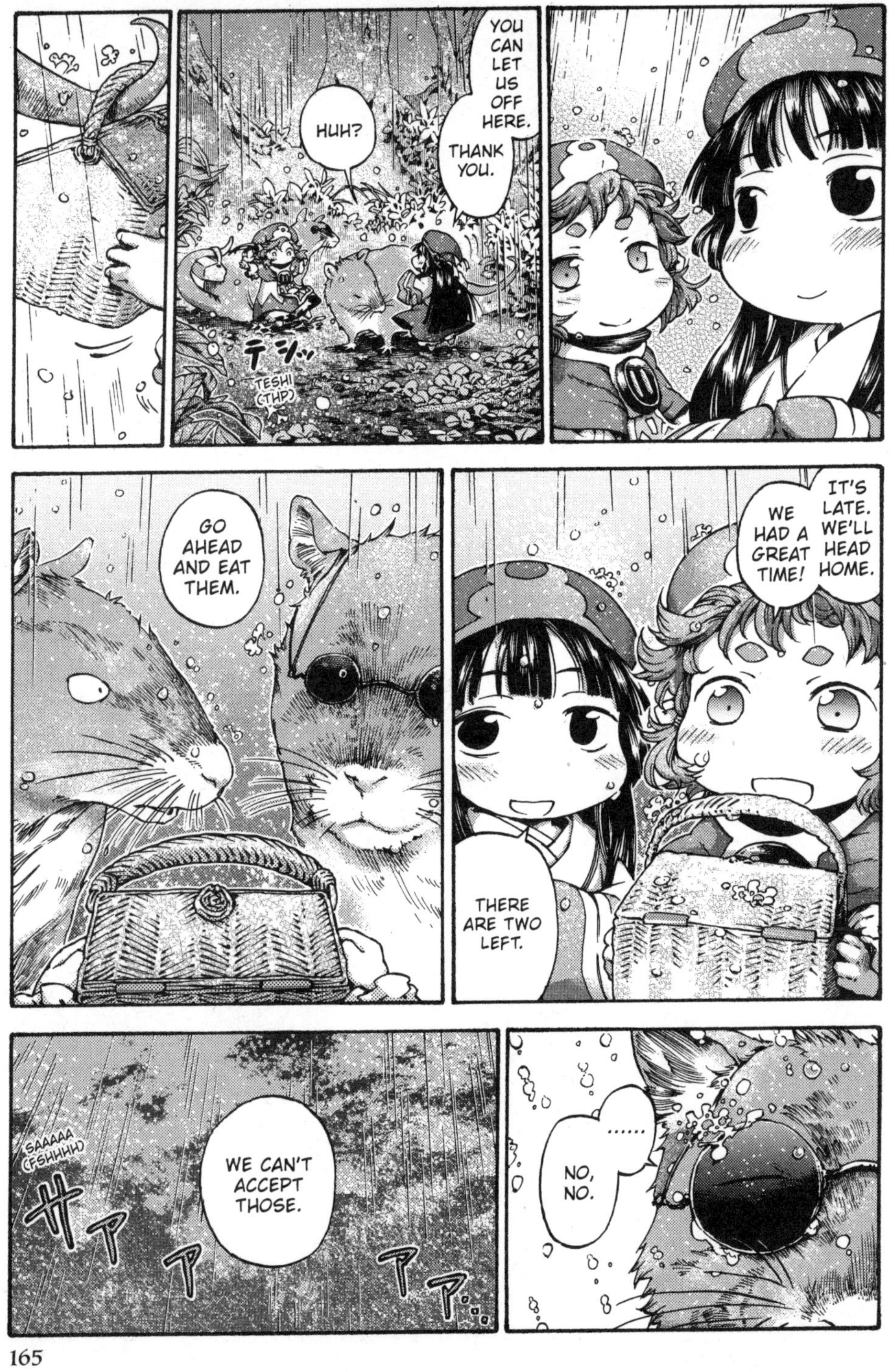
YOU CAN LET US OFF HERE.
THANK YOU.
HUH?
テシッ
TESHI (THP)
IT'S LATE. WE'LL HEAD HOME.
WE HAD A GREAT TIME!
THERE ARE TWO LEFT.
GO AHEAD AND EAT THEM.
......
NO, NO.
WE CAN'T ACCEPT THOSE.
サァァァ
SAAAAA (FSHHHH)

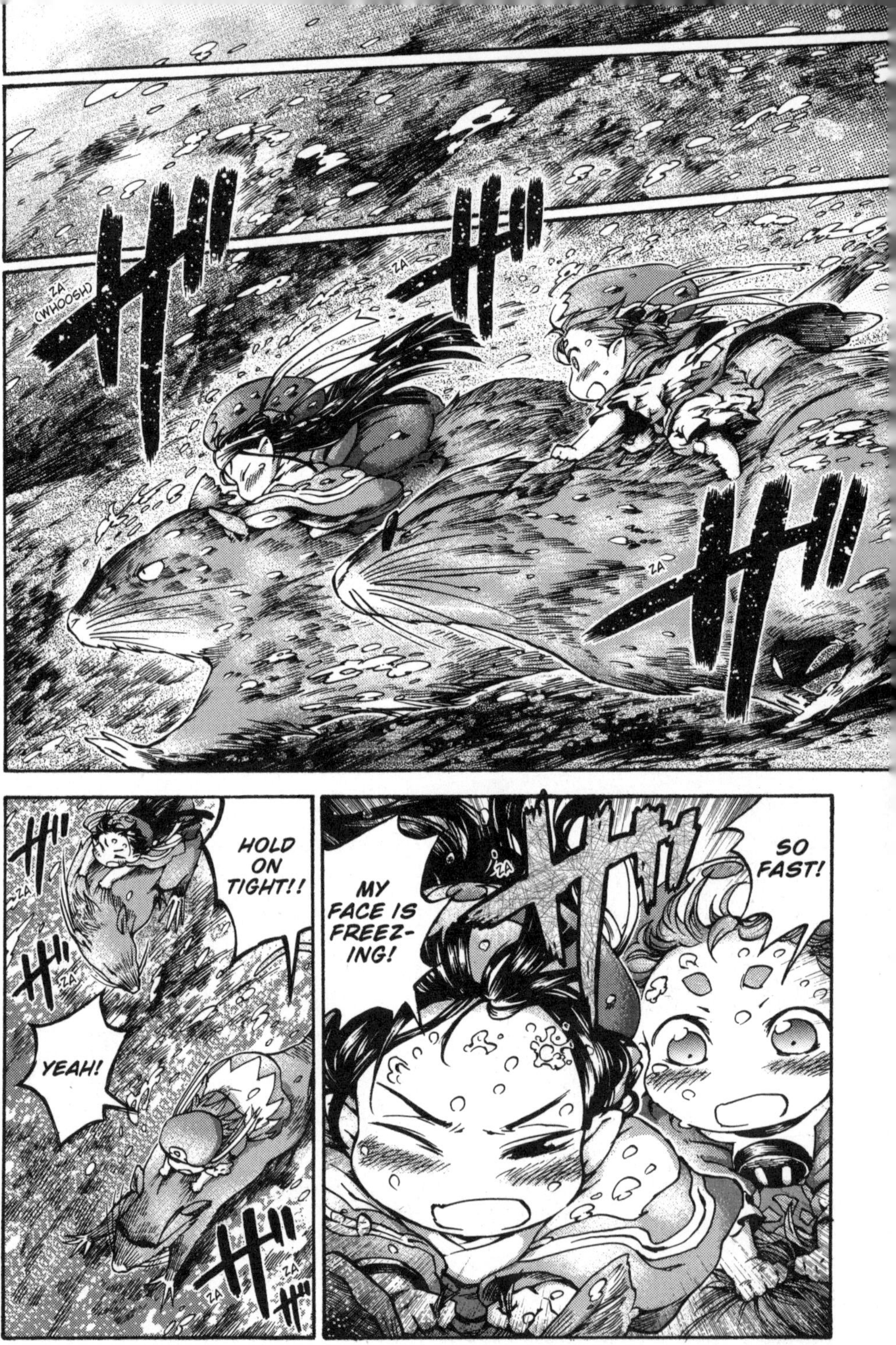
ZA (WHOOSH)
ZA
ZA
SO FAST!
MY FACE IS FREEZ-ING!
ZA
HOLD ON TIGHT!!
YEAH!
ZA
ZA
ZA
ZA

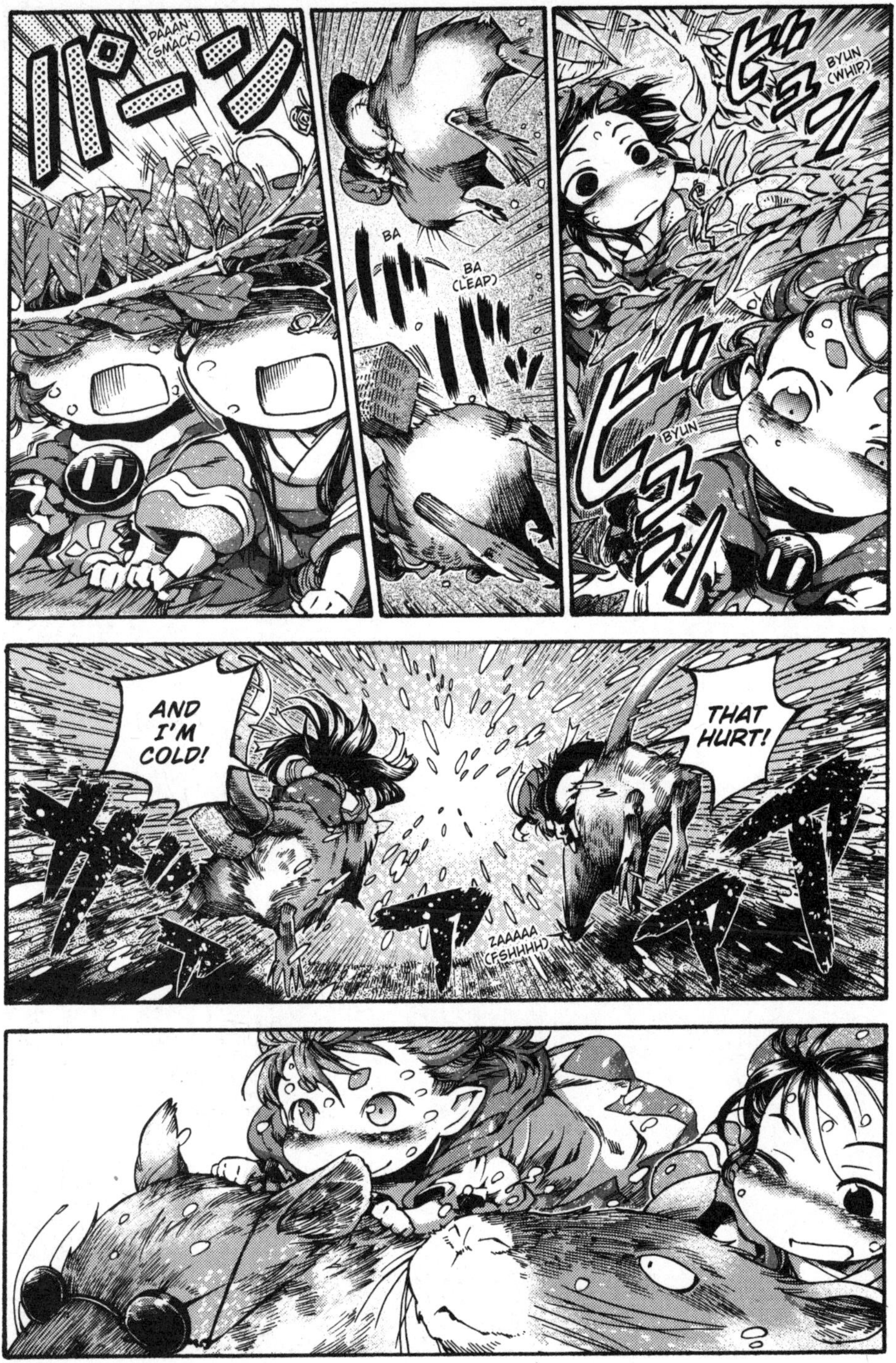
BYUN (WHIP)
BYUN
BA
BA (LEAP)
PAAAN (SMACK)
THAT HURT!
AND I'M COLD!
ZAAAAA (FSHHHH)

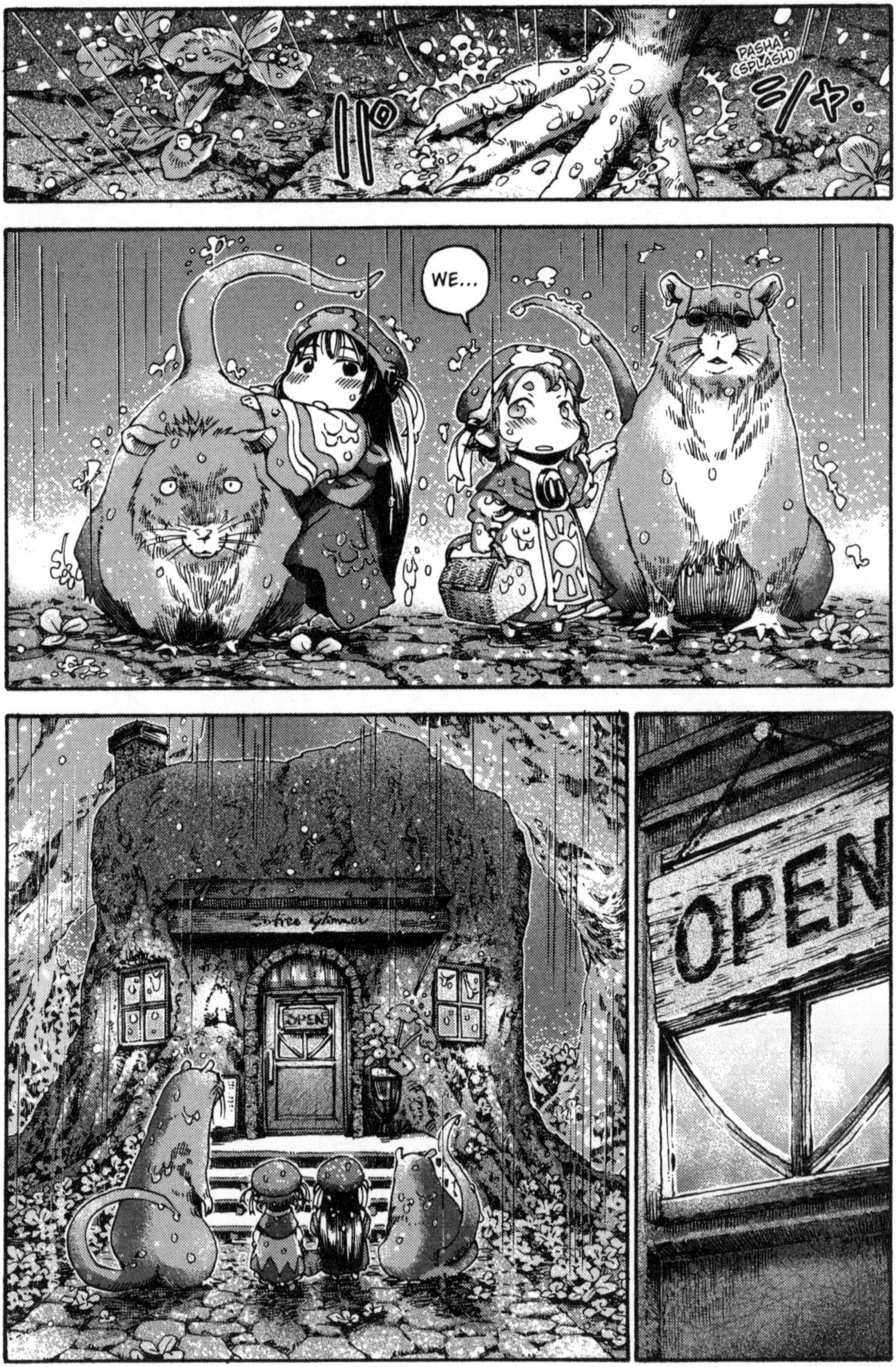
PASHA (SPLASH)
WE...
OPEN
OPEN

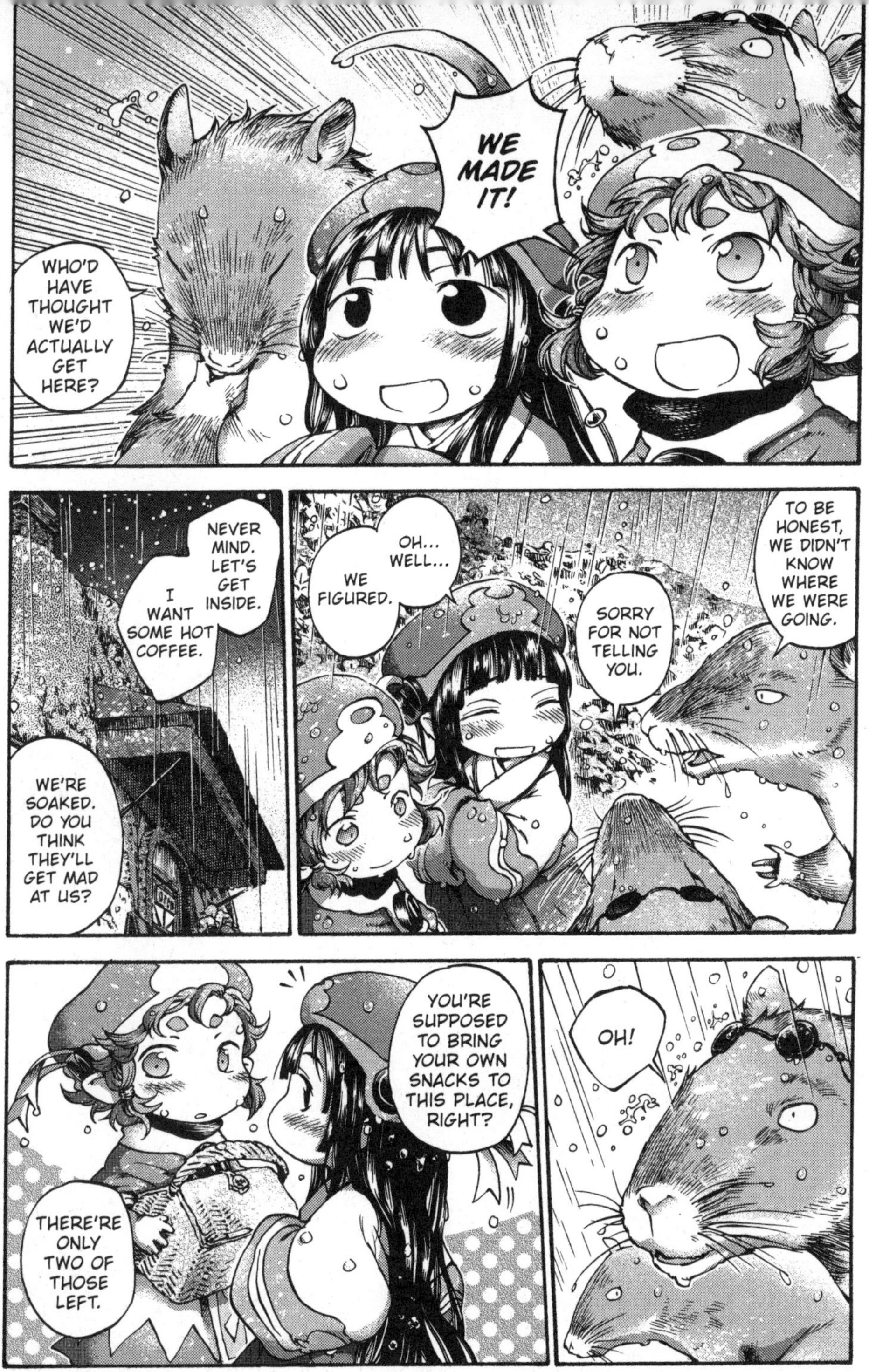
WE MADE IT!
WHO'D HAVE THOUGHT WE'D ACTUALLY GET HERE?
TO BE HONEST, WE DIDN'T KNOW WHERE WE WERE GOING.
SORRY FOR NOT TELLING YOU.
OH... WELL... WE FIGURED.
NEVER MIND. LET'S GET INSIDE.
I WANT SOME HOT COFFEE.
WE'RE SOAKED. DO YOU THINK THEY'LL GET MAD AT US?
OH!
YOU'RE SUPPOSED TO BRING YOUR OWN SNACKS TO THIS PLACE, RIGHT?
THERE'RE ONLY TWO OF THOSE LEFT.

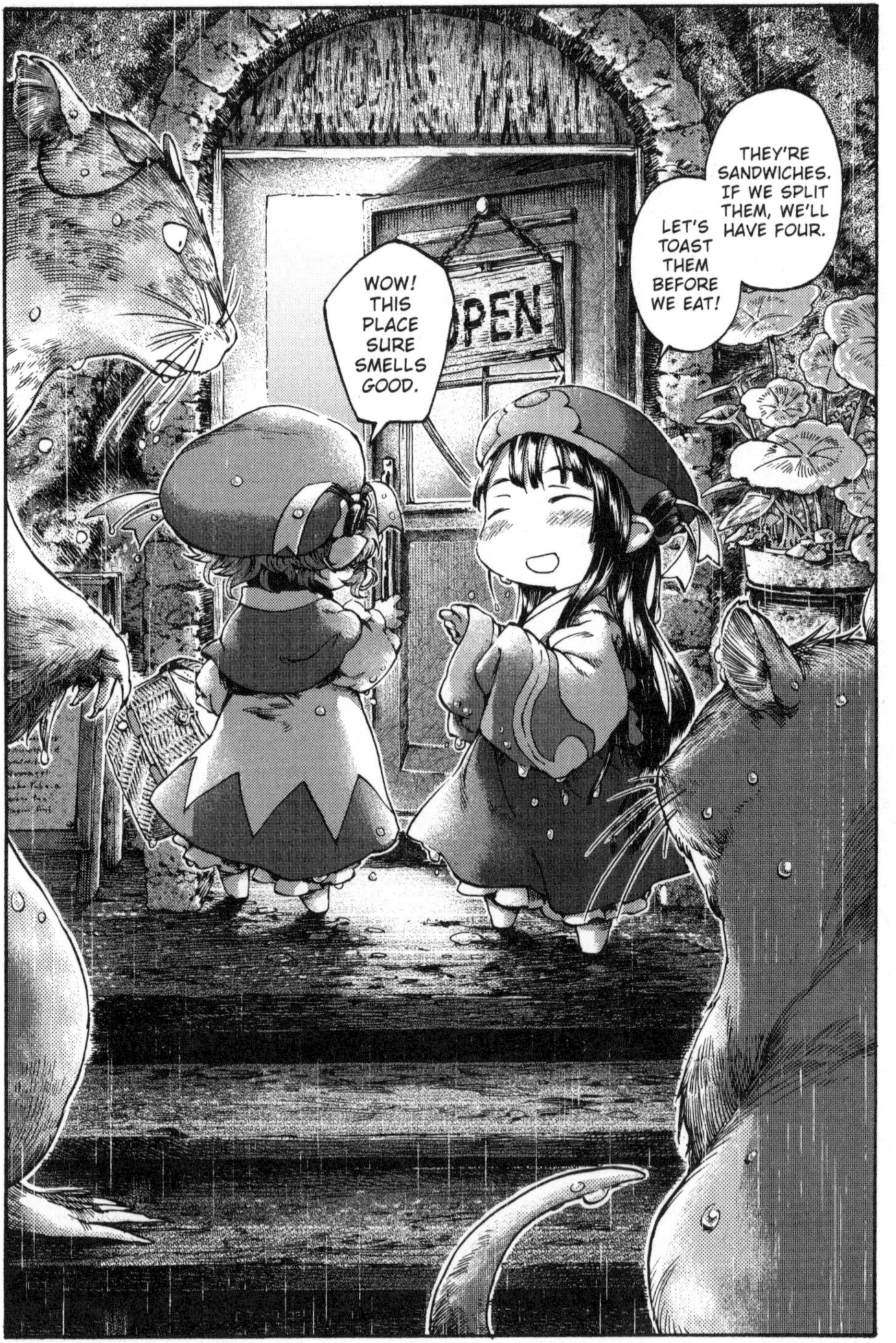
THEY'RE SANDWICHES. IF WE SPLIT THEM, WE'LL HAVE FOUR.
LET'S TOAST THEM BEFORE WE EAT!
OPEN
WOW! THIS PLACE SURE SMELLS GOOD.

Chapter 14 • End

Glimmer is—
"A café that's just for you."
When you visit us, please bring your own snacks.

You can spend a quiet hour here on your own or enjoy
the time as part of a large and lively group.

Here in the shop, as we roast carefully selected beans,
as we pour hot water through cloth filters,
as we light the siphon brewers' alcohol lamps,
as we choose records to put on our phonograph,
we await your visit.

*

"Is this a high roast, do you think? It's a little bitter."
"Hey, I like it."

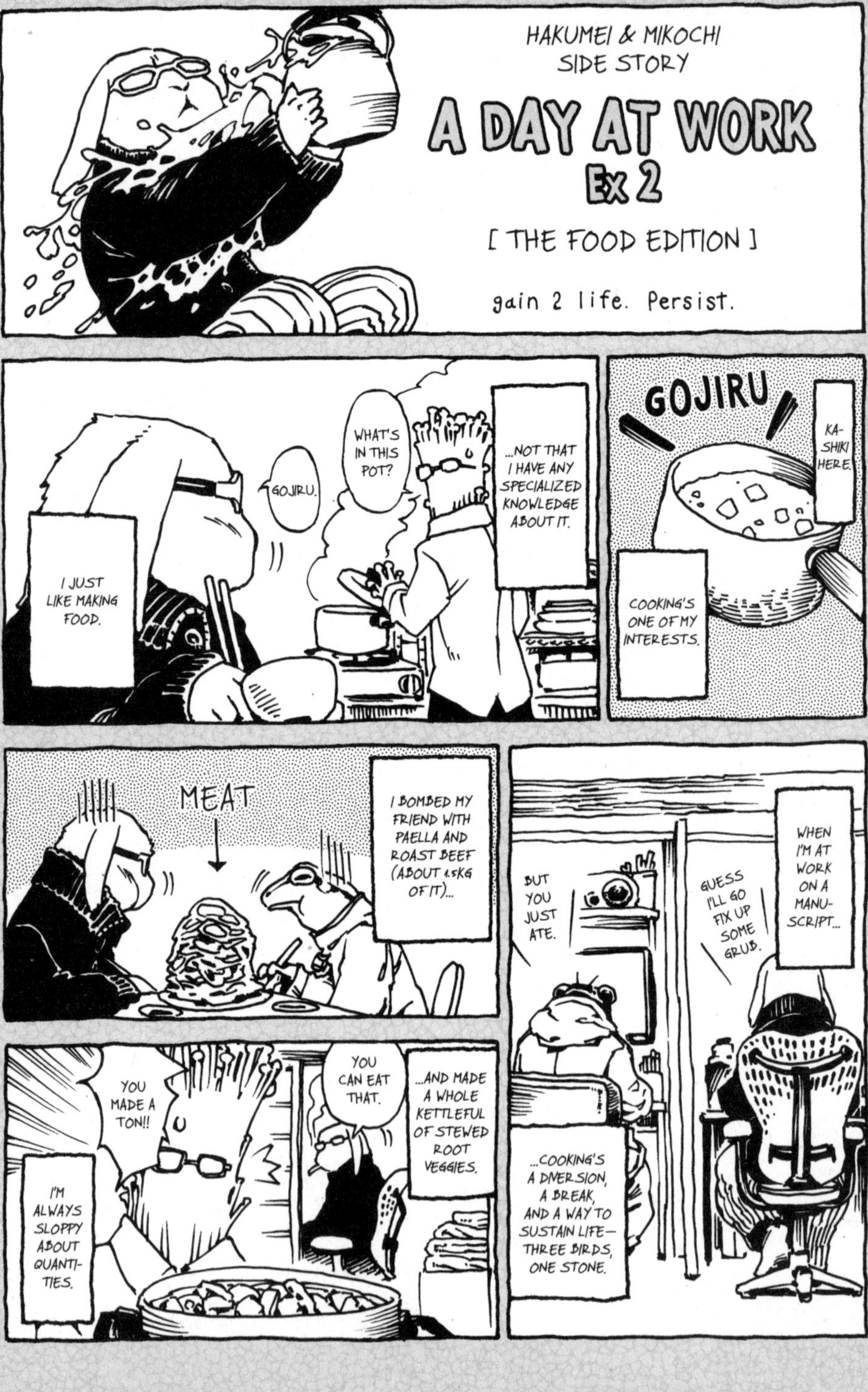
HAKUMEI & MIKOCHI SIDE STORY
A DAY AT WORK Ex 2
[THE FOOD EDITION]
gain 2 life. Persist.
GOJIRU
KA-SHIKI HERE.
COOKING'S ONE OF MY INTERESTS.
...NOT THAT I HAVE ANY SPECIALIZED KNOWLEDGE ABOUT IT.
WHAT'S IN THIS POT?
GOJIRU.
I JUST LIKE MAKING FOOD.
WHEN I'M AT WORK ON A MANU-SCRIPT...
GUESS I'LL GO FIX UP SOME GRUB.
BUT YOU JUST ATE.
...COOKING'S A DIVERSION, A BREAK, AND A WAY TO SUSTAIN LIFE—THREE BIRDS, ONE STONE.
I BOMBED MY FRIEND WITH PAELLA AND ROAST BEEF (ABOUT 1.5KG OF IT)...
MEAT
...AND MADE A WHOLE KETTLEFUL OF STEWED ROOT VEGGIES.
YOU CAN EAT THAT.
YOU MADE A TON!!
I'M ALWAYS SLOPPY ABOUT QUANTI-TIES.

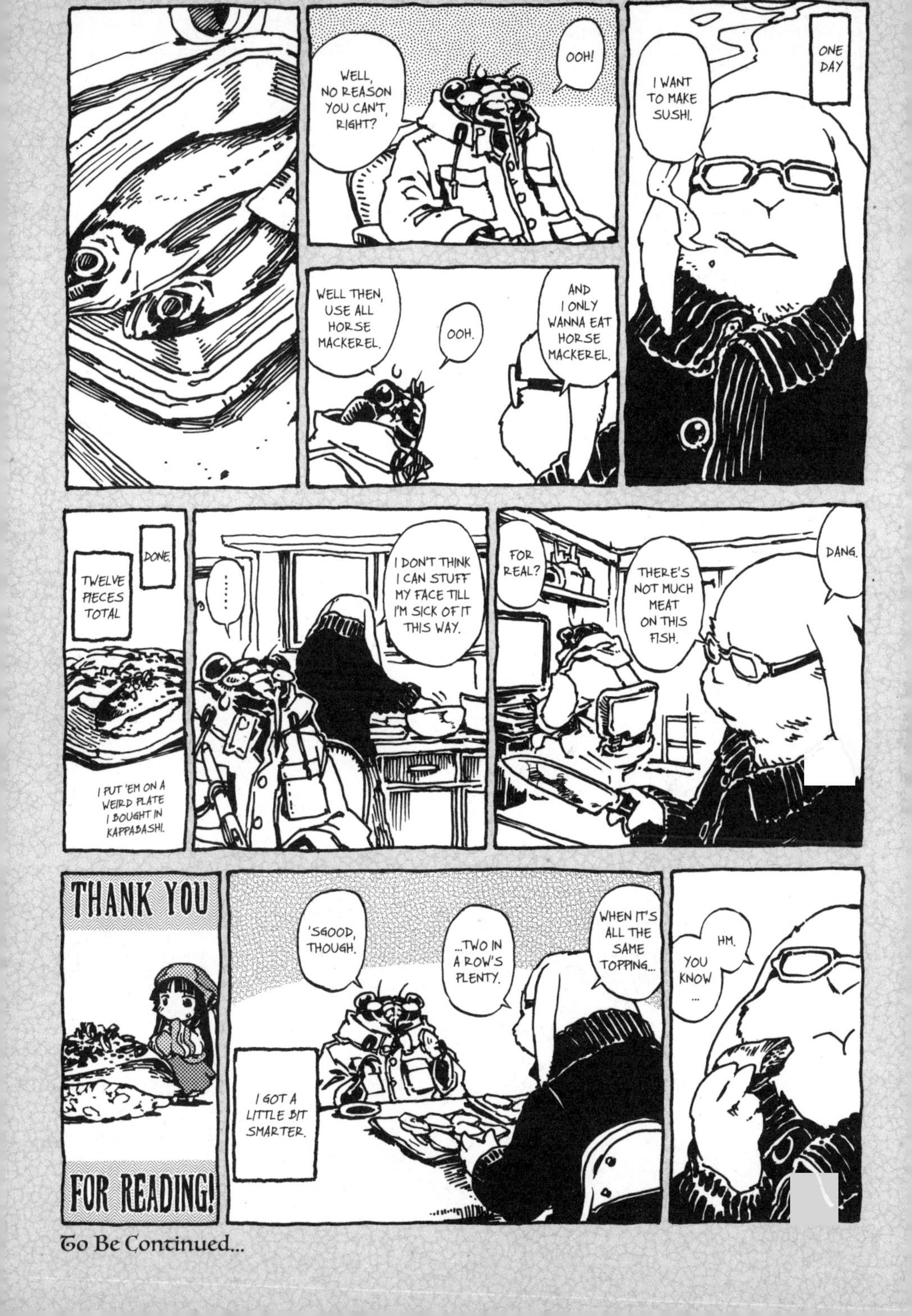
ONE DAY
I WANT TO MAKE SUSHI.
OOH!
WELL, NO REASON YOU CAN'T, RIGHT?
AND I ONLY WANNA EAT HORSE MACKEREL.
OOH.
WELL THEN, USE ALL HORSE MACKEREL.
DANG.
THERE'S NOT MUCH MEAT ON THIS FISH.
FOR REAL?
I DON'T THINK I CAN STUFF MY FACE TILL I'M SICK OF IT THIS WAY.
......
DONE.
TWELVE PIECES TOTAL
I PUT 'EM ON A WEIRD PLATE I BOUGHT IN KAPPABASHI.
HM.
YOU KNOW...
WHEN IT'S ALL THE SAME TOPPING...
...TWO IN A ROW'S PLENTY.
'SGOOD, THOUGH.
I GOT A LITTLE BIT SMARTER.
THANK YOU
FOR READING!

To Be Continued...

Translation Notes

Common Honorifics
no honorific: Indicates familiarity or closeness; if used without permission or reason, addressing someone in this manner would constitute an insult.
-san: The Japanese equivalent of Mr./Mrs./Miss. If a situation calls for politeness, this is the fail-safe honorific.
-chan: An affectionate honorific indicating familiarity used mostly in reference to girls; also used in reference to cute persons or animals of any gender.

Currency conversion: Although exchange rates fluctuate daily, a good general estimate is ¥100 to 1USD.

Page 6: **Savory** is an herb that comes in two varieties—summer and winter. The annual summer variety is more commonly used in cooking because it's sweeter and more delicate, whereas the perennial winter kind is more bitter.

Page 7: Hakumei is right to be worried, for **great horned owls** like Oroshi are terrifying indeed! They are famous for eating pretty much anything they can catch and can kill prey as large as rabbits and ducks. While the original Japanese edition never genders Oroshi, the task of defending territory is usually left to the males of the species.

Page 21: **Parched beans**, or *irimame*, are made by soaking dried soybeans in water, then simply heating the beans in a frying pan until the skins dry and pop off. The result is a light, crunchy snack.

Page 21: **Giant butterbur** (*fuki*) **buds** and **angelica tree shoots** (*taranome*) are early spring delicacies in Japan.

Page 28: **Oroshi's expression** is probably a smile because one way to say someone is smiling in Japanese is to describe them as "narrowing their eyes."

Page 36: Many parts of the **betel palm** (leaves, bark, seeds) can be used to create a variety of shades of brown dye.

Page 38: **Sawtooth oak** acorn cups can be boiled to make a brown or black dye, while **alder** bark yields a brown dye.

Page 41: A **mordant** is a fixative substance that helps bind dyes to fabric. The kind of mordant one chooses can also affect the final color of the textiles being dyed.

Page 84: In Japan, when **stone blocks** were quarried to make castle walls and such, they were cut to be roughly the same size, to make it easier both to transport them and to piece them together at the work site.

Page 96: ***Haori*** are short, traditional coats that are generally worn over kimonos.

Page 101: The honorific ***-neesan*** usually means "sister," but it can also be used to address an unrelated woman of higher social standing (in this case, President Narai's wife). It indicates a close, casual, but also respectful relationship.

Page 143: In Japan, **many shops are closed on one set day per week**, but the day is arbitrary and depends on the establishment. Shops will generally post which day of the week they're closed alongside their business hours.

Page 145: ***After the Apples*** is the title of a 2011 solo minialbum by Kazuya Yoshii, lead vocalist of Japanese rock band The Yellow Monkey.

Page 146: **Limoncello** hails from southern Italy, where it is often drunk as a digestif.

Page 171: A **siphon brewer**, or vacuum coffee maker, would probably look more at home in Sen's lab than in a café. As shown in the illustration at the top of the page, it's a two-chambered device that allows for a more precise brew. When an alcohol lamp is placed under the bottom chamber, which is filled with water, the pressure from the created vapor forces the liquid into the upper chamber, where the water meets the coffee grounds.

Page 171: A **high roast** is a type of coffee roast that falls somewhere between medium and medium-dark roasts. Its flavor is well-balanced in terms of bitterness and acidity.

Page 172: **Gain 2 life. Persist.** is a reference to the *Magic: The Gathering* card "Kitchen Finks."

Page 172: ***Gojiru*** is miso soup with a paste of mashed soybeans added in.

Page 173: **Kappabashi-doori** is a street in Tokyo that runs between Ueno and Asakusa. It has lots of restaurant supply stores that sell nearly everything used in the trade, including (famously) those plastic food samples that are displayed in restaurant windows.

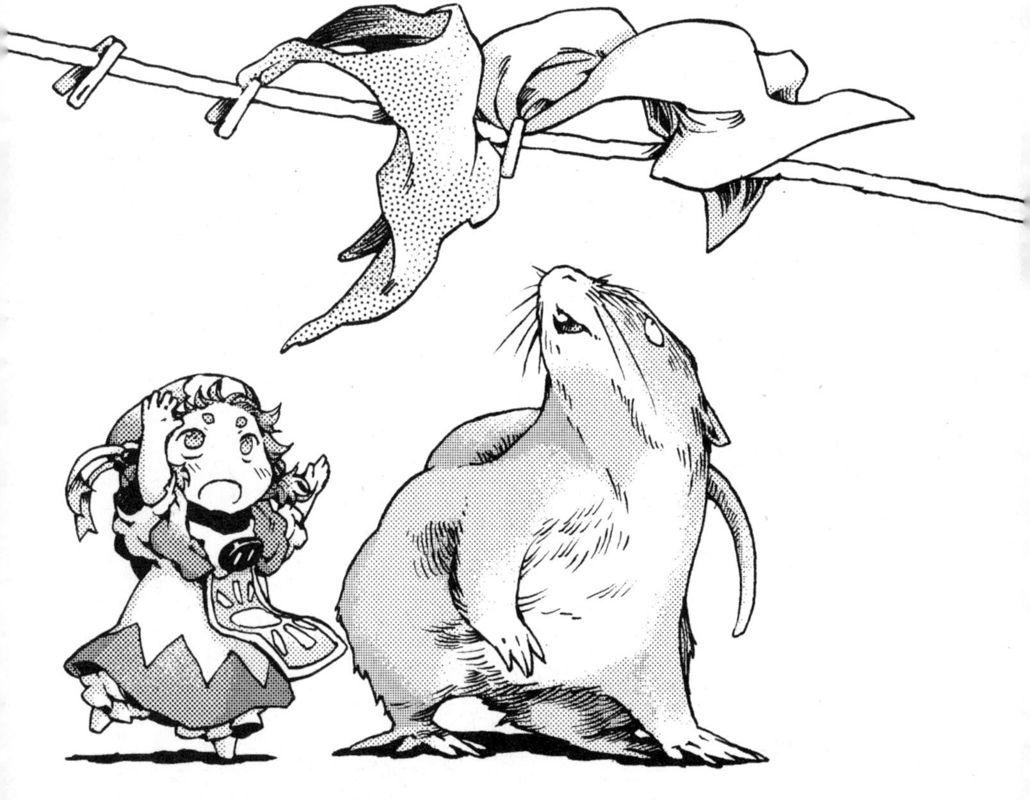

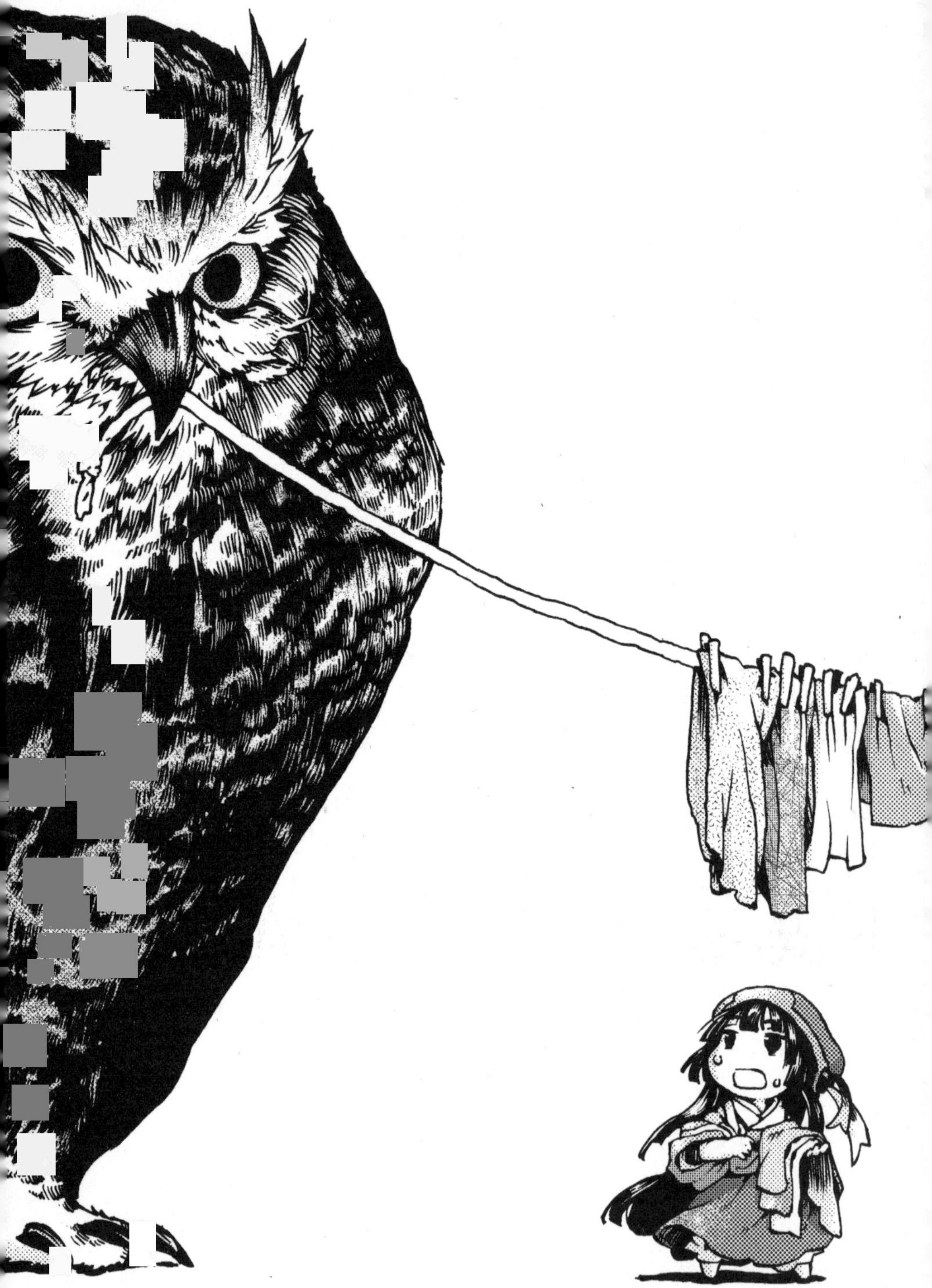

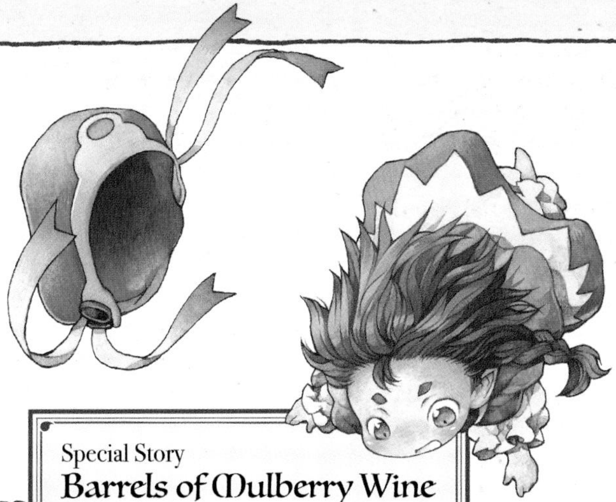

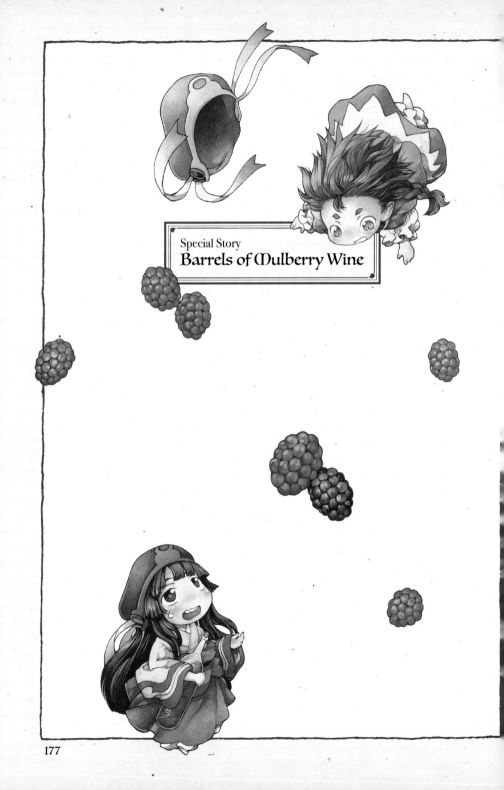

Special Story
Barrels of Mulberry Wine

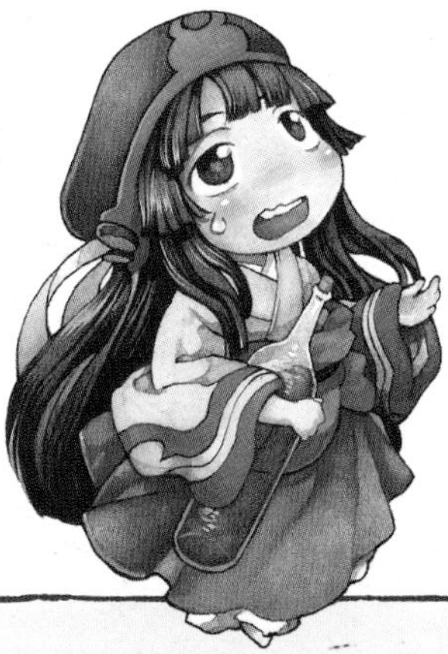

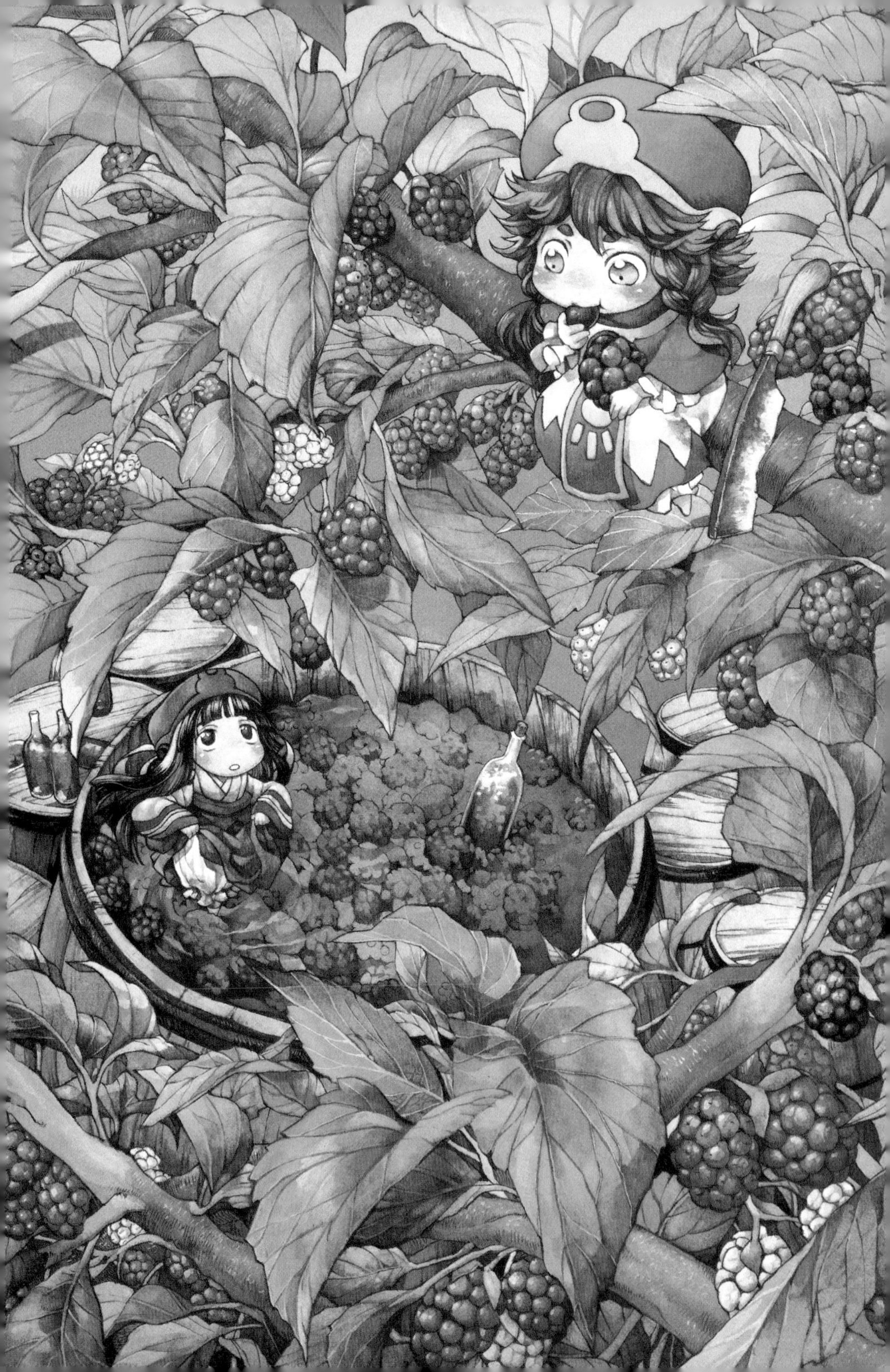

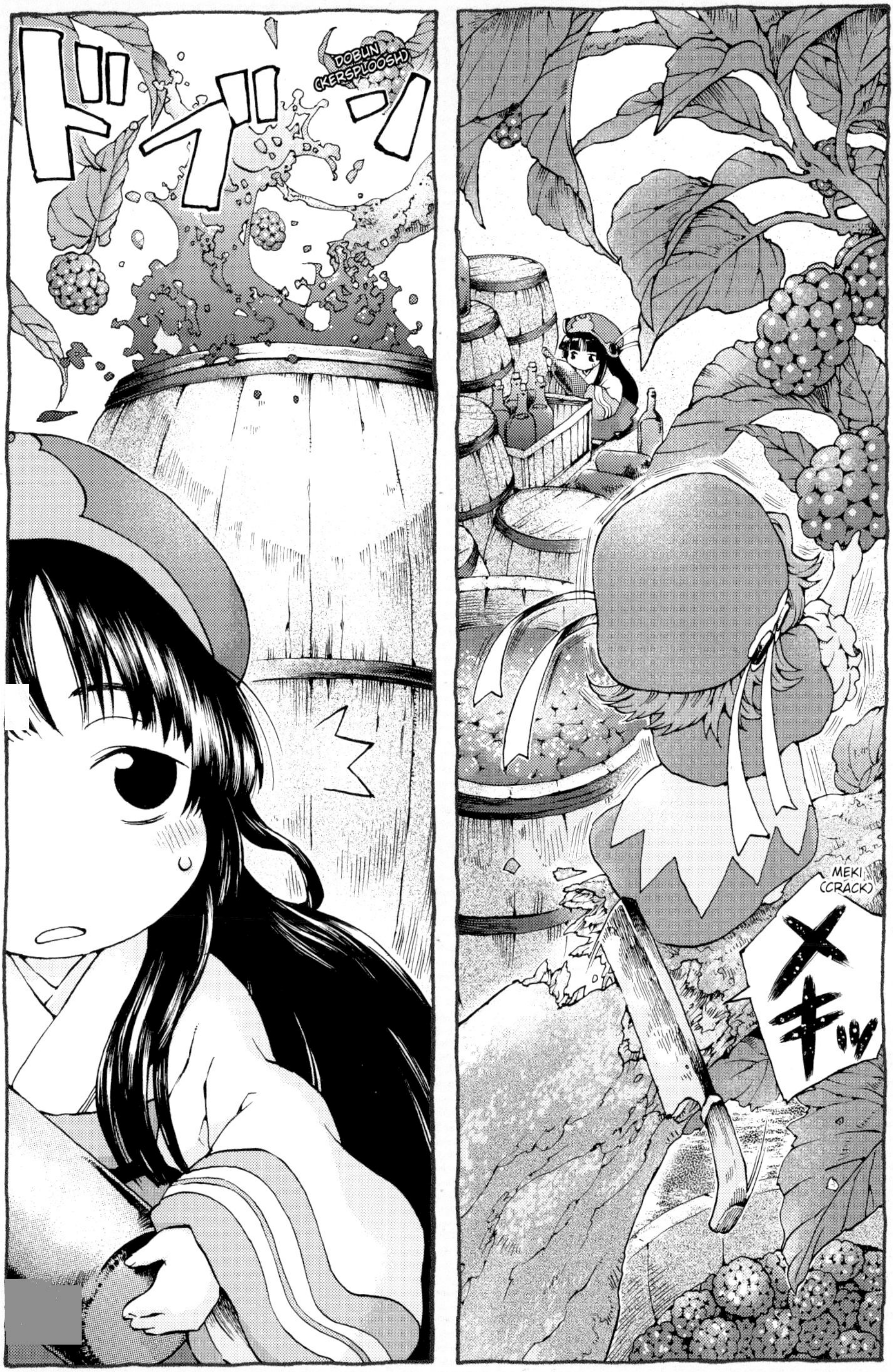
MEKI (CRACK)
メキッ
DOBUN (KERSPLOOSH)
ドブーン

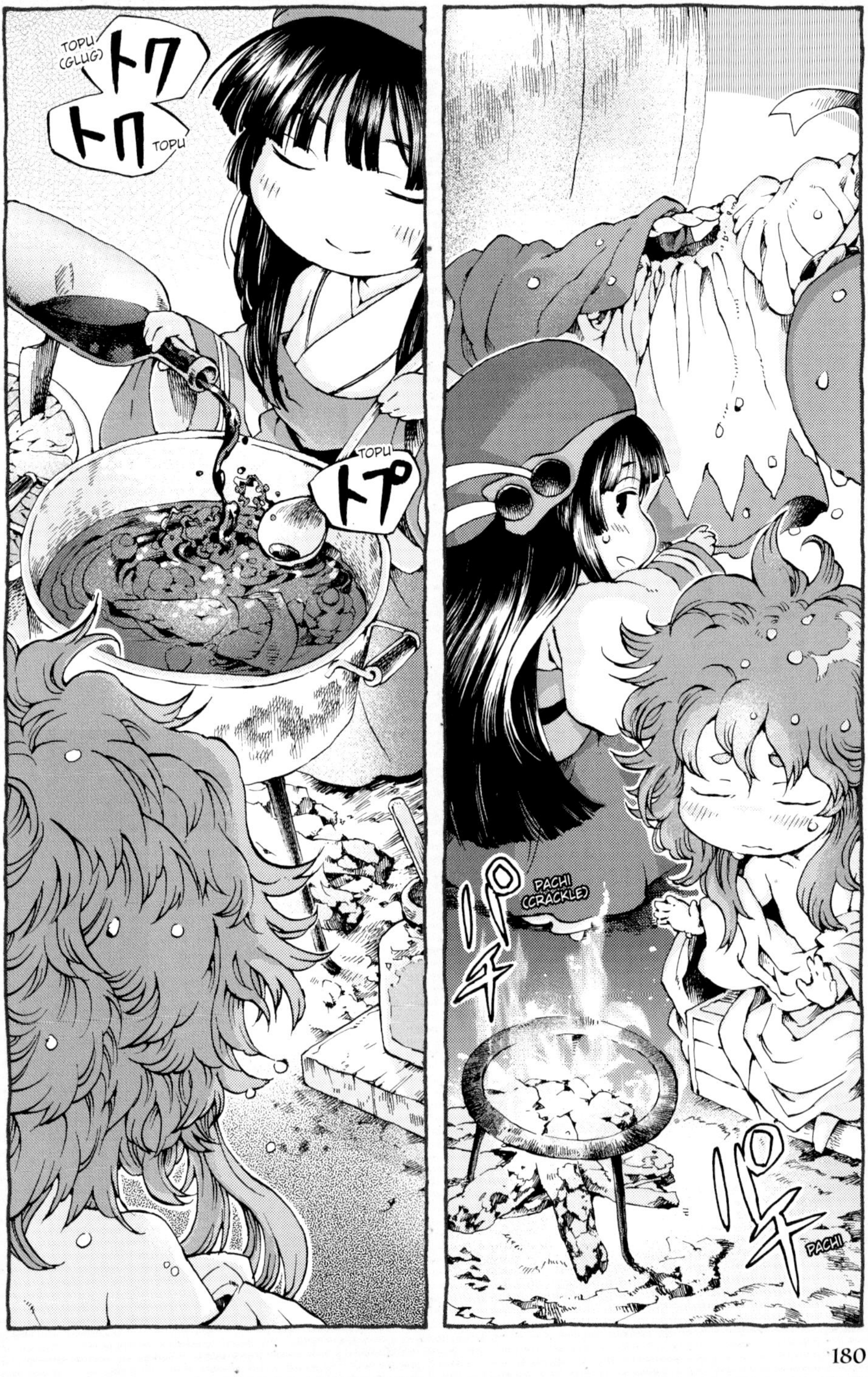
パチ
PACHI (CRACKLE)
パチ
PACHI
トク
TOPU (GLUG)
トク
TOPU
トプ
TOPU

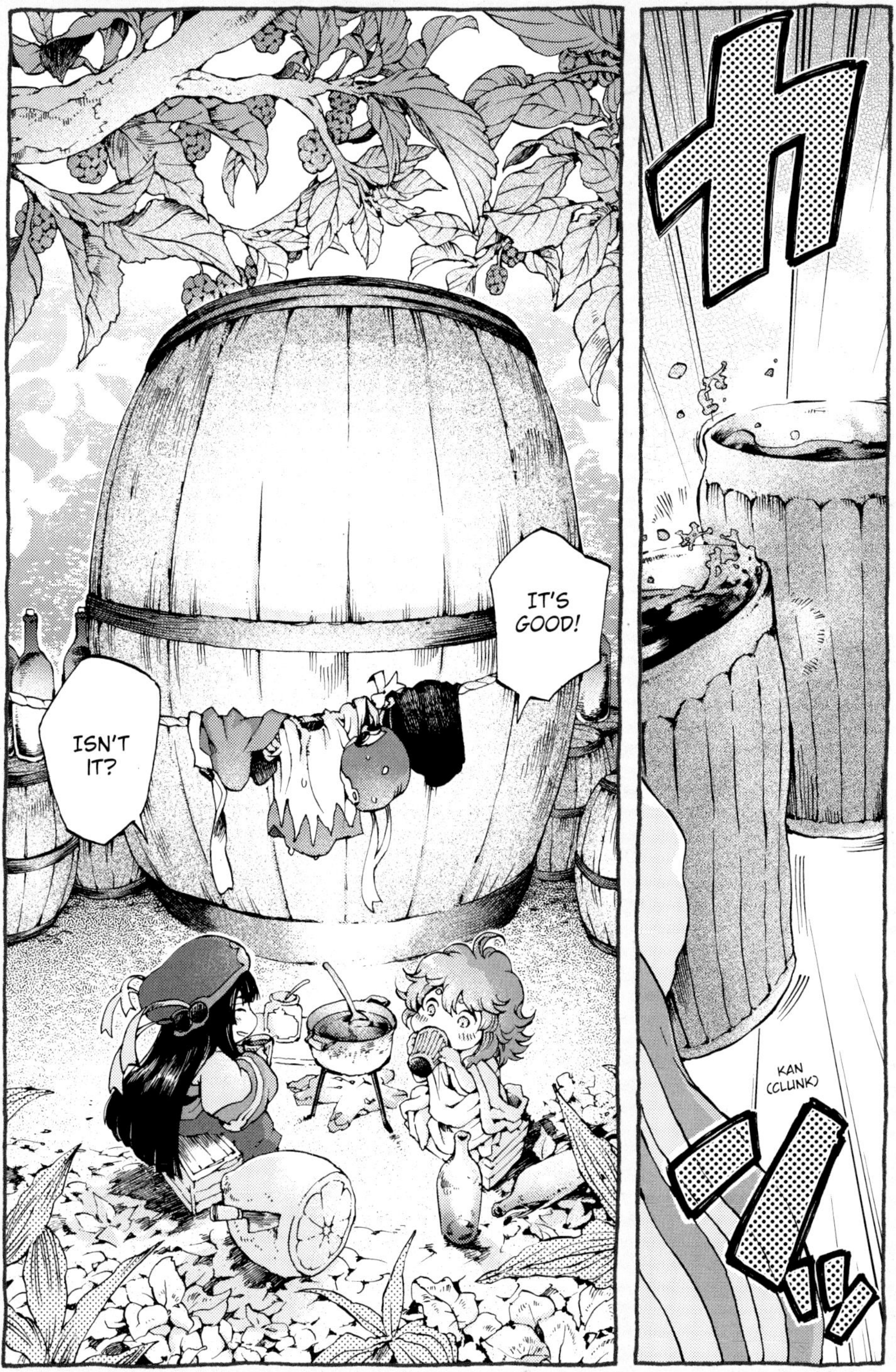
KAN
(CLUNK)
IT'S
GOOD!
ISN'T
IT?

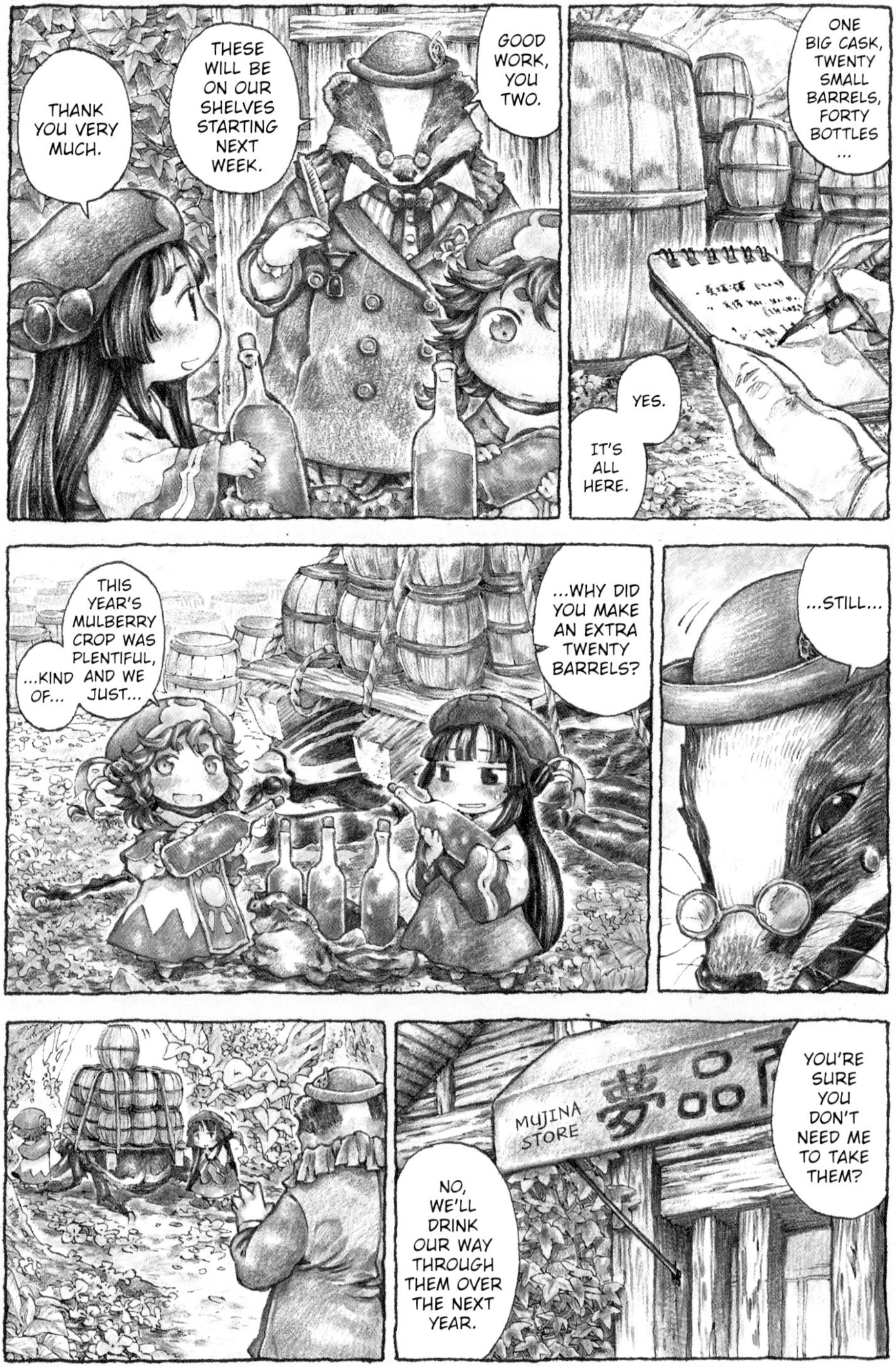
ONE BIG CASK, TWENTY SMALL BARRELS, FORTY BOTTLES ...
YES.
IT'S ALL HERE.
GOOD WORK, YOU TWO.
THESE WILL BE ON OUR SHELVES STARTING NEXT WEEK.
THANK YOU VERY MUCH.
...STILL...
...WHY DID YOU MAKE AN EXTRA TWENTY BARRELS?
THIS YEAR'S MULBERRY CROP WAS PLENTIFUL, AND WE JUST...
...KIND OF...
YOU'RE SURE YOU DON'T NEED ME TO TAKE THEM?
MUJINA STORE
NO, WE'LL DRINK OUR WAY THROUGH THEM OVER THE NEXT YEAR.

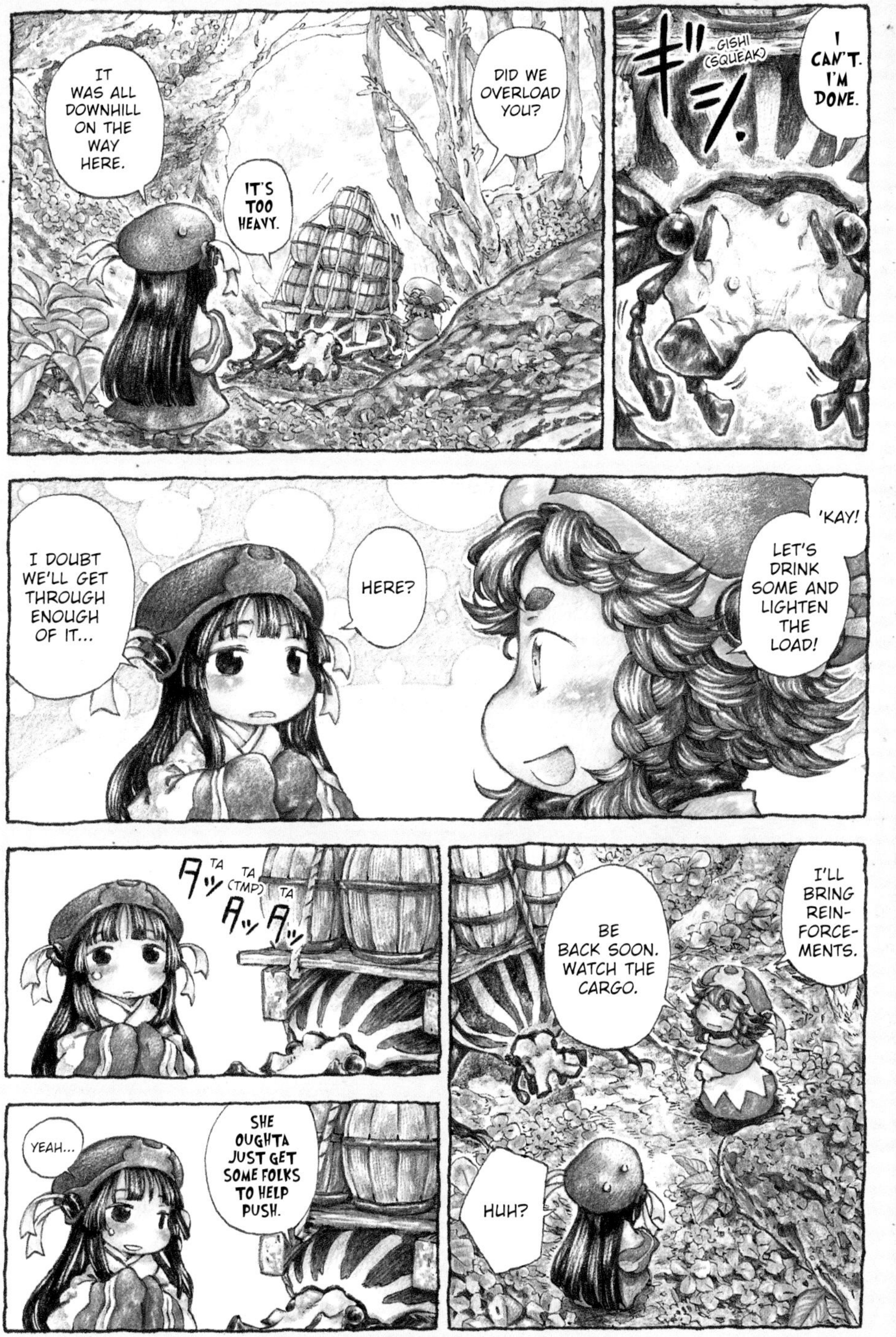
ギシ
GISHI (SQUEAK)
I CAN'T. I'M DONE.
DID WE OVERLOAD YOU?
IT WAS ALL DOWNHILL ON THE WAY HERE.
IT'S TOO HEAVY.
'KAY!
LET'S DRINK SOME AND LIGHTEN THE LOAD!
HERE?
I DOUBT WE'LL GET THROUGH ENOUGH OF IT...
I'LL BRING REIN-FORCE-MENTS.
BE BACK SOON. WATCH THE CARGO.
HUH?
TA TA (TMP) TA
SHE OUGHTA JUST GET SOME FOLKS TO HELP PUSH.
YEAH...

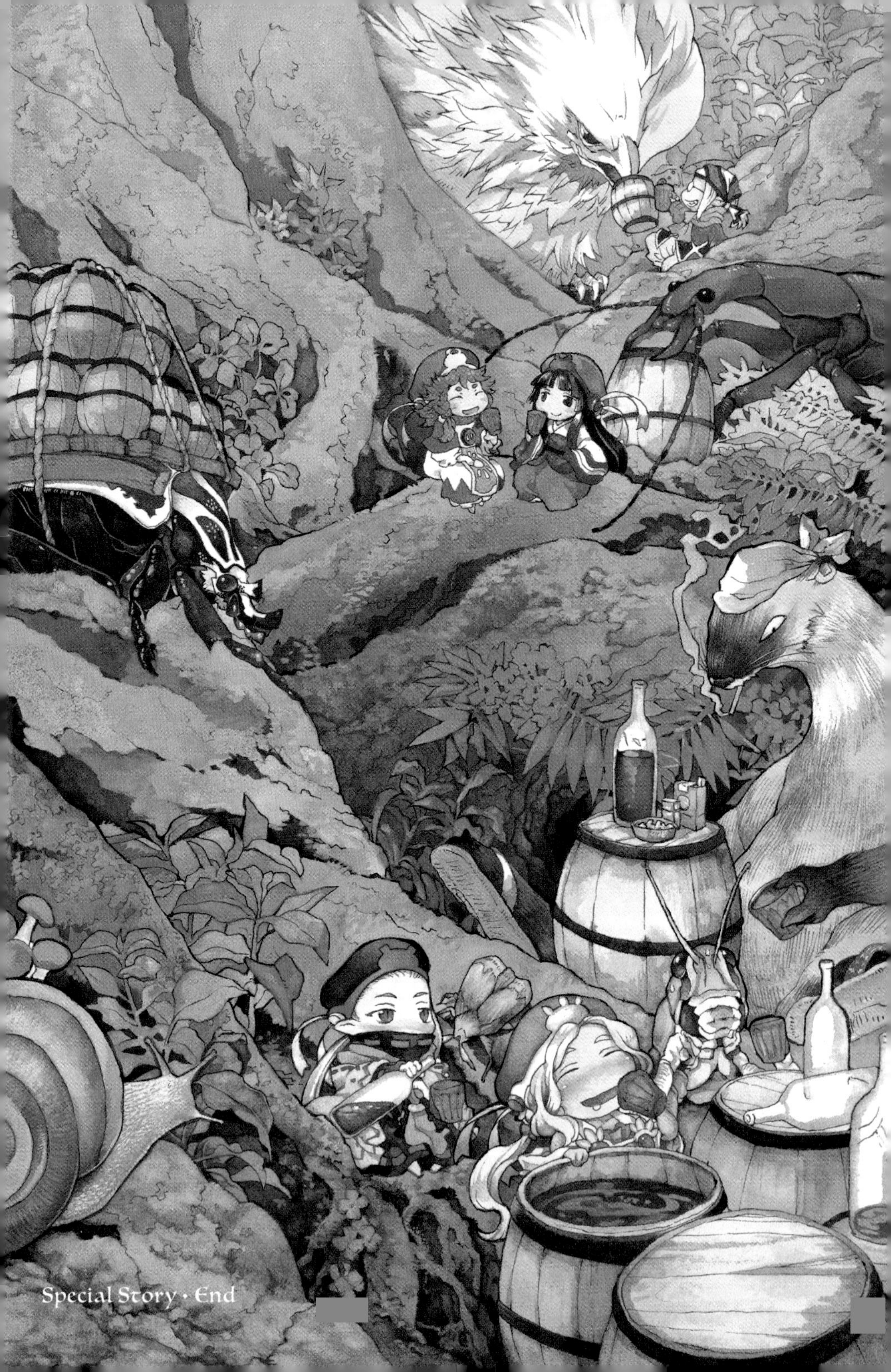
Special Story • End

Hakumei & Mikochi 2
Tiny Little Life in the Woods

❧ Takuto Kashiki ❧

Translation: **TAYLOR ENGEL**   ♣   *Lettering:* **ABIGAIL BLACKMAN**

HAKUMEI TO MIKOCHI Volume 2
© Takuto Kashiki 2014
First published in Japan in 2014 by KADOKAWA CORPORATION, Tokyo.
English translation rights arranged with KADOKAWA CORPORATION, Tokyo through TUTTLE-MORI AGENCY, Inc., Tokyo.

English translation © 2018 by Yen Press, LLC

Yen Press
1290 Avenue of the Americas
New York, NY 10104

Visit us at yenpress.com
facebook.com/yenpress
twitter.com/yenpress
yenpress.tumblr.com
instagram.com/yenpress

First Yen Press Edition: October 2018

Yen Press is an imprint of Yen Press, LLC.
The Yen Press name and logo are trademarks of Yen Press, LLC.

The publisher is not responsible for websites (or their content) that are not owned by the publisher.

Library of Congress Control Number: 2018941284

ISBN: 978-1-9753-0290-0

10 9 8 7 6 5 4 3 2 1

WOR

Printed in the United States of America